Ethnolinguistic Diver
and Education

In recent decades, the linguistic and cultural diversity of school populations in the United States and other industrialized countries has rapidly increased along with globalization processes. At the same time, schooling as it is currently constituted continues to be ineffective for large numbers of students. Exploring crucial issues that emerge at the intersection of linguistic diversity and education, this volume:

- Provides an up-to-date review of sociolinguistic research and practice aimed at improving education for students who speak vernacular varieties of U.S. English, English-based Creole languages, and non-English languages
- Explores the impact of dialect differences and community languages on ethnolinguistically diverse students' academic achievement
- Challenges the dominant monolingual standard language ideology
- Presents sociolinguistically based approaches to language and literacy education that acknowledge and build on the linguistic and cultural resources students bring into the school

Throughout, the authors argue for the application of research-based knowledge to the dire situation (as measured by school failure and drop-out rates) of many ethnolinguistic populations in U.S. schools. The overall aim of the volume is to heighten acknowledgement and recognition of the linguistic and cultural resources students bring into the schools and to explore ways in which these resources can be used to extend the sociolinguistic repertoires, including academic English, of all students.

Marcia Farr is Professor of Education and English at the Ohio State University and Professor Emerita of English and Linguistics at the University of Illinois at Chicago.

Lisya Seloni is Assistant Professor of English in the Composition and TESOL graduate program at Indiana University of Pennsylvania.

Juyoung Song is Assistant Professor in the department of English and Philosophy at Murray State University.

Ethnolinguistic Diversity and Education

Language, Literacy, and Culture

Edited by Marcia Farr, Lisya Seloni, and Juyoung Song

Routledge
Taylor & Francis Group

NEW YORK AND LONDON

First published 2010
by Routledge
711 Third Avenue, New York, NY 10017

Simultaneously published in the UK
by Routledge
2 Park Square, Milton Park, Abingdon, Oxon OX14 4RN

Routledge is an imprint of the Taylor & Francis Group, an informa business

© 2010 Taylor & Francis

Typeset in Minion by
RefineCatch Limited, Bungay, Suffolk

The authors and publisher wish to thank those who have generously given permission to reprint borrowed material:

Chapter 2 – This chapter has been revised and fully updated from Wiley, 2005 (Chapter 2, "Common Myths and Stereotypes about Literacy and Language Diversity in the United States") with permission from the Center for Applied Linguistics. See Crawford (1999) and Krashen (1981) for a discussion of the limitations of historical and contemporary approaches.

See, for example, Edelsky (2006); Krashen and Biber (1988); Merino and Lyons (1990); Quezada, Wiley, and Ramírez, (2002). Ramírez (1992); and Troike (1978) for research related to children; and Burtoff (1985); Meléndez (1990); Robson (1982); Spener (1994); and Wiley (2005) for studies on adults.

The role of age in language and literacy acquisition is complex. See Singleton (1989) for a survey and critique of the major theoretical views and research on the age factor.

Chapter 3 – This chapter contains a revised version of chapters three and four from Farr (2006), the book that reports on the larger study on which this chapter is based. Adapted from Farr, M., *Rancheros in Chicagoacán: Language and Identity in a Transnational Community.* Copyright © 2006. University of Texas Press. Adapted with permission from the publishers.

The term *ranchero/ranchera* refers minimally to people who come from rural Mexican *ranchos* (small settlements, often in the mountains and relatively isolated from urban centers). Farr (2006) explores the multiple meanings of this term as a marker of identity for rural Mexicans who identify as non-indigenous and emphasize the Spanish side of their *mestizo* heritage.

Chapter 7 – Adapted from H. Samy Alim, "Creating 'an empire within an empire:' Critical Hip Hop Language Pedagogies and the Role of Sociolinguistics," in H. Samy Alim, Awad Ibrahim, & Alastair Pennycook, (Eds). (2008), *Global Linguistic Flows: Hip Hop Cultures, Youth Identities, and the Politics of Language.* Adapted with permission from the publishers.

Library of Congress Cataloging in Publication Data
Ethnolinguistic diversity and education : language, literacy, and culture / edited by Marcia Farr,
Lisya Seloni and Juyoung Song.
p. cm.
1. Anthropological linguistics. 2. Language and languages—Variation. 3. Multicultural education.
4. Language and education. 5. Language and culture. I. Farr, Marcia. II. Seloni, Lisya. III. Song,
Juyoung.
P35.E8698 2010
306.44—dc22   2009045167

ISBN 10: 0–415–80278–4 (hbk)
ISBN 10: 0–415–80279–2 (pbk)
ISBN 10: 0–203–86344–5 (ebk)

ISBN 13: 978–0–415–80278–9 (hbk)
ISBN 13: 978–0–415–80279–6 (pbk)
ISBN 13: 978–0–203–86344–2 (ebk)

Contents

Preface

This book explores crucial issues that emerge at the intersection of linguistic diversity and education. In recent decades, the linguistic and cultural diversity of school populations in the United States and other industrialized countries has rapidly increased along with globalization processes. At the same time, schooling as it is currently constituted continues to be ineffective for large numbers of students, especially those who speak vernacular dialects, Creoles, and non-English languages. The recent increase in diversity, however, only exacerbates a long-standing problem.

Since its inception as an academic field in the 1960s and 1970s, the field of Sociolinguistics has included studies intended to improve schooling for such students. Much of this research has been directed at changing negative public opinion, and therefore teacher attitudes, toward language diversity and variation, since teacher expectations clearly influence student achievement. This negative public opinion is based not on research, which shows the linguistic and cognitive adequacy of all varieties of language, but on ideologies about language without scientific merit but with significant social and economic import. In addition to research aimed at changing public opinion, fewer studies have proposed pedagogical strategies and approaches based on the linguistic and cultural resources of particular student populations. Here we provide an up-to-date overview of such research and practice aimed at improving education for students who speak vernacular varieties of (U.S.) English, English-based Creole languages, and non-English languages. Throughout the book, all contributors argue for the application of research-based knowledge to the dire situation (as measured by school failure and drop-out rates) of many ethnolinguistic populations in U.S. schools.

The book is organized in two parts. Part I is comprised of four chapters that contribute to our understanding of ethnolinguistic diversity in the United States. The Introduction provides a conceptual foundation for understanding the common frameworks of the book's chapters, as well as a more detailed overview of chapters. Wiley and de Klerk (Chapter 2) discuss the language myths underlying public attitudes toward language, and how these myths, or ideologies, have been shown to be false by much linguistic research. Farr (Chapter 3) provides an ethnographic description of oral language abilities, educational attitudes and levels, and literacy practices within Mexican transnational families, as representative of the largest Spanish-speaking population in the United States. McCarty and her colleagues (Chapter 4) explore complex and sometimes conflicting language ideologies in the midst of language use and change among Native American youth. Finally, Hirvela (Chapter 5) reviews a wide range of research on literacy practices among a variety of Asian language populations.

Part II is comprised of six chapters that explore how the results of sociolinguistic research can be integrated into the school curriculum to improve the language and literacy education of linguistic minority students. Wolfram (Chapter 6) proposes pedagogical approaches that promote dialect awareness as something positive for communities and schools. Alim and Baugh (Chapter 7) also do this, but with a specific focus on integrating hip hop language into language arts curricula. Charity Hudley (Chapter 8) thoroughly investigates standardized assessment procedures that are implicitly and explicitly biased against speakers of African American English and proposes some solutions to this problem. García (Chapter 9) proposes new approaches to literacy education based on actual and dynamic, not imagined and static, language practices among bilingual Latinos. Nero (Chapter 10) describes a pilot study that analyzes the language and literacy practices of Caribbean Creole English-speaking adolescents in New York City public schools while simultaneously educating their English teachers about the language, literacy, and culture of these students. Finally, the last chapter by Rickford and Rickford (Chapter 11) discusses how to utilize sociolinguistic research in developing more effective pedagogies for speakers of English-based Creoles and African American Vernacular English.

This volume's overall aim, then, is to heighten acknowledgement and recognition of the linguistic and cultural resources students bring into the schools and to explore ways in which these resources can be used to extend the sociolinguistic repertoires, including academic English, of all students. For this to happen, of course, the material in this book will have to be read and used by many people. We thus hope the book will appeal to a wide range of readers, undergraduate and graduate students, practicing teachers and other educators, professors, and independent researchers, as well as the college-educated public. Chapters are written so as to be accessible across disciplines, fields, and specializations, and we hope that the book will be used in classes that focus on language and ethnicity, bilingualism, teaching and learning, literacy, folklore, rhetoric and communication, and urban studies, among others.

This volume originated in the creation of two panels on Ethnolinguistic Diversity and Education for the 36th annual Sociolinguistics conference, New Ways of Analyzing Variation (NWAV 35), that was sponsored by the Linguistic Department at Ohio State University, November 9–12, 2006. It also originated as a way to honor Gladys Foster Anderson's contributions as a professor of Education at Ohio State University during the 1950s. We are grateful for the support of these panels provided by the endowment in her name from her son, Richard Foster, to the School of Teaching and Learning, and we dedicate this volume to her.

At the time of the conference, both Lisya Seloni and Juyoung Song were advanced Ph.D. candidates in the School of Teaching and Learning who have since become faculty colleagues at other universities. Lisya's dissertation on the socialization of speakers of English-as-a-second-language into academic discourses in U.S. graduate programs and Juyoung's dissertation on language socialization and identity among young Korean-English bilinguals appropriately fit the focus of the panels and extended my own background in dialect variation, literacy, and bilingualism. The three of us thus formed a team in organizing these panels and developing the material that is published in this volume.

After the original conference panels, this project evolved in various ways. Most of the chapters in this volume were contributed by original participants in the panels, but as the volume took shape, we recognized the need to expand in specific directions: Anne Charity Hudley's chapter added important material on assessment, Alan Hirvela's chapter provided information on literacy among Asian language populations, Shondel Nero's chapter expanded our coverage of Creole language speakers, and my own chapter supplied more description of language and literacy among Spanish-speaking populations. Finally, Mariko Haneda, who served as Chair of one of the panels, agreed to write an Afterword to synthesize and comment upon the various contributions.

It is difficult to separate the trajectory of this book from my own personal research trajectory. Having begun my career in Sociolinguistics with an exploration of Dialect Influence in Writing ([Farr] Whiteman, 1981), my interest turned toward ethnographies of communication in linguistic minority communities. This interest culminated, in part, in two edited volumes that serve as precursors to this one: *Ethnolinguistic Chicago: Language and Literacy in the City's Neighborhoods* (Farr, 2004) and *Latino Language and Literacy in Ethnolinguistic Chicago* (Farr, 2005). These two volumes contain chapters from former graduate students and other colleagues that explore an archetypal U.S. city known for its "ethnic" populations and therefore for its linguistic (and literacy) diversity (see also Farr, 2007). This third volume in the "series" moves beyond an exploration of such diversity for its own sake into considerations for educational practice in an attempt to bring research-based knowledge to bear on an important social problem.

Acknowledgements

We thank Richard Foster for the endowment in his mother's name, the Gladys Foster Anderson fund, which supported the original panels at NWAV 35 and allowed contributors to present and then to prepare their manuscripts for publication. We also thank Dr. Rebecca Kantor-Martin, Director of the School of Teaching and Learning in the College of Education and Human Ecology at Ohio State University, for her administrative and intellectual support of this work. We are grateful as well to Maria Alejandra Leon Garcia, my Graduate Research Assistant at Ohio State University, for preparing the manuscript for publication and for locating elusive references.

Finally, we thank Naomi Silverman, formerly of Lawrence Erlbaum Associates and now with Routledge / Taylor & Francis, for her considerable editorial support, which included specific requested advice as well as more general understanding and support, in the development of this volume.

Marcia Farr
May 6, 2009

References

Farr, M. (Ed.). (2004). *Ethnolinguistic Chicago: Language and literacy in the city's neighborhoods*. Mahwah, NJ: Erlbaum.

—— (Ed.). (2005). *Latino language and literacy in ethnolinguistic Chicago*. Mahwah, NJ: Erlbaum.

—— (2007). Literacies and ethnolinguistic diversity: Chicago. In B. Street (Ed.), Volume on literacy, Nancy Hornberger (Ed.), *Encyclopedia of language and education*. Heidelberg, Germany: Springer-Verlag.

Whiteman, M.F. (1981). Dialect influence in writing. In M.F. Whiteman (Ed.), *Variation in writing: Functional and linguistic-cultural differences*. Hillsdale, NJ: Lawrence Erlbaum Associates.

List of Contributors

H. Samy Alim	Stanford University
John Baugh	Washington University in St. Louis
Anne H. Charity Hudley	The College of William and Mary
Marcia Farr	The Ohio State University
Ofelia García	Graduate Center, City University of New York
Mari Haneda	The Ohio State University
Alan Hirvela	The Ohio State University
Gerda de Klerk	Arizona State University
Teresa L. McCarty	Arizona State University
Shondel Nero	New York University
Angela E. Rickford	San Jose State University
John R. Rickford	Stanford University
Mary Eunice Romero-Little	Arizona State University
Lisya Seloni	Indiana University of Pennsylvania
Juyoung Song	Murray State University
Larisa Warhol	Arizona State University
Terrence G. Wiley	Arizona State University
Walt Wolfram	North Carolina State University
Ofelia Zepeda	University of Arizona

1 Introduction

Ethnolinguistic Diversity in Language and Literacy Education

Marcia Farr, Lisya Seloni, and Juyoung Song

Introduction: Defining Terms

In an increasingly globalized world, different peoples, languages, ideas, cultural practices, and material goods can be found far from their traditional homes. In fact, many places in the world now have relatively low percentages of indigenous populations. Although some scholars trace globalization processes back many centuries (Frank, 1996), the ethnolinguistic diversity we focus on in this book can be traced to the European colonization of the Americas and, more recently, to migration during the twentieth century. In the United States, this multiplicity of peoples and languages has spread from large cities, which have been diverse since their very beginnings (see, for example, Farr, 2007), to small towns and rural counties throughout the country.

The term ethnolinguistic minimally refers to all the speech codes, or the languages and dialects, spoken by the various groups of people who either are indigenous to, or have migrated to (from colonial times on), the contemporary United States. Current ethnolinguistic diversity in the U.S. includes many, if not all, of the languages of the world, various varieties (or dialects) of those languages, and Creole languages formed from mixing two or more languages. English, for example, now has many international varieties, as well as dialects within those varieties (Crystal, 2003). Moreover, English-based Creoles emerged (as new languages) when English came into contact with indigenous languages, combining an English lexicon with the indigenous grammar (Nichols, 2004). Such Creoles in the U.S. include Gullah (in South Carolina), Hawaiian Creole, and, more recently, other varieties such as Jamaican Creole, Nigerian Pidgin English, and Sierra Leone Krio. English-based Creoles are similar to global "nativized" varieties of English like Indian English in that all of these "new Englishes" emerged through the colonial spread of English and its contact with other languages (Mufwene, 2000; Winford, 1997, 1998). Even some vernacular dialects, such as African American Vernacular English, are theorized (by some but not all scholars) to have evolved from former Creoles, such as Gullah (Green, 2002), and thus from the spread of English from England to the American continent in contact with the West African languages which the African slaves spoke (Green, 2002; Rickford & Rickford, 2000).

Creole languages, like all languages, also have their own variations, from basolects (the varieties that are most vernacular and "of the people") to mesolects (middle-range varieties) to acrolects (varieties that are closest to the standard language). For example, Jamaican Creole is not one uniform language, but a range of variations relatively distant from or close to Jamaican Standard English. Thus variation is everywhere: all languages have dialects and even so-called Standard languages exist more at the level of abstraction than reality. Standard U.S. English, for example, is perhaps defined most easily by the absence of socially marked vernacular features (such as multiple negatives, the use of *ain't*), than by what features characterize it, since it too varies across speakers, contexts, and modes (speech, print, electronic media). Out of this wide range of variation, we focus in this book on vernacular varieties of English; varieties of Spanish; Chinese, Korean, and Japanese; and Caribbean Creole English.

Linguistic codes, however, do not exist in a vacuum; rather, they are always used in, and draw meaning from, particular cultural contexts. One cannot communicate simply by knowing the grammar and lexicon of a language; one must also understand the cultural context in order to communicate meaning. Consequently, we use the phrase ethnolinguistic diversity to refer not only to the linguistic codes used by various populations, but also to the cultural meanings embedded in those codes. Cultural meanings are inevitably embedded not only in linguistic codes, of course, but also in social structure, and social structure implicates such aspects of identity as race/ethnicity, gender, and social class. Since these terms are rife with conflict and debate, we briefly discuss here how they can be understood in this book.

First, we draw from the term ethnicity rather than race for the term ethnolinguistic, since language diversity has nothing to do with race (and everything to do with society and culture). Children learn the languages, and particular varieties of those languages, within the families and communities in which they are socialized, not according to the so-called "racial" group to which they belong. Race itself, of course, is a social, not a biological, construct; there is more genetic variation within one "racial" group, for example, than across such groups (see http://www.aaanet.org/resources/A-Public-Education-Program.cfm for clarification about what "race" is and is not). Thus the capacity for language is shared across the human race, but particular varieties of language emerge in different places among different groups of speakers according to local social and cultural constraints. Key to this understanding of language variation is the notion of identity: using a particular variety of a language indicates, and even constructs on-the-spot, specific identities, and people may choose (consciously or unconsciously) between varieties and/or languages to construct varying identities depending on the context. For example, a child may learn to use a vernacular English (or Spanish, Chinese, etc.) at home, but a more standard English (or Spanish, Chinese, etc.) at school or church. For bilingual populations, a particular variety of a heritage language (e.g., Mexican rural Spanish) may be used at home within the family, and a more formal variety of a second language (e.g., "standard" U.S. English) may be used at school (and vernacular varieties of the second language also are often learned and used in yet other contexts).

Vernacular, of course, refers to a local variety of a language in a particular region (as opposed to varieties that are considered more "cultured," literary, or formal, i.e., the "normal spoken form of a language" (http://www.merriam-webster.com/dictionary/vernacular). Thus vernacular refers to language (or another aspect of society) that is local, or "of the folk." This term is now preferred over the traditional term dialect, since the latter has accumulated some low-status connotations (Adger, Wolfram & Christian, 2007). The term vernacular brings up another aspect of linguistic diversity treated in this book: that of socioeconomic status or class. Vernacular speech varieties are most often associated with working-class speakers, although many non-working-class speakers also use a vernacular variety, as well as other, more formal varieties, as already noted (see, for example, Rickford & Rickford, 2000). Although the notion of socioeconomic class is treated in traditional sociolinguistic studies as a stable aspect of a person's identity (based on occupation, income, education, and other measurable variables), some recent research has treated this notion more critically. Rickford (1986) critiques the use of such static class labels, arguing that they might not even be relevant local categories for some communities, and that this is a matter to be determined ethnographically. Eckert (2000) builds on this critique by arguing that vernacular varieties can be viewed instead as resources people use to express a local identity in opposition to other identities. Thus someone may choose to express a (valued) working-class identity in particular contexts for particular reasons.

Gender is a third aspect of identity that intersects in complex ways with other aspects such as ethnicity, class, and age. Here we use the notion of gender as distinct from biological sex, as "the meanings that a particular society gives to the physical or biological traits that differentiate males and females. These meanings provide members of a society with ideas about how to act, what to believe, and how to make sense of their experiences" (Mascia-Lees & Johnson Black, 2000, p. 1).

Moreover, there are multiple "femininities" and "masculinities" in different communities and cultures (Stern, 1995), in spite of the fact that many (although not all) societies insist on only two categories, male and female. In reality, however, as already noted for social class, people use gendered linguistic features as resources to express varying identities in particular contexts for particular reasons (Eckert & McConnell-Ginet, 2003). In addition, as with the discussion of social class, gender is an aspect of identity that cannot be applied as a static label; instead, the particular meanings of gender must be determined ethnographically for different communities, and even for different parts of the same community.

Thus far we have defined important terms as aspects of identity tied to ethnolinguistic diversity. Although such diversity is evident in many settings, a particularly salient one is the public school. In the next section we consider ethnolinguistic diversity in the U.S. generally and in U.S. schools, focusing on important issues that emerge at the intersection of such diversity with language and literacy education.

Ethnolinguistic Diversity and Schooling

A basic premise of this book is that research-based understandings of the ethnolinguistic diversity among students are crucial to effective language and literacy education. Although English is clearly the dominant language in the U.S., the presence of other languages is notable: over 55 million people (20 percent of those aged 5 and older) speak a language other than English in the U.S., which is one out of every five people (U.S. Census Bureau, 2007). This figure has increased by almost 2 percent since 2000 and by 6 percent since 1990 (for more statistics, see Wiley & de Klerk in this volume). Among these other languages, Spanish (including Spanish creoles) is the most common language—it is spoken by 34,547,077 people (62 percent of all speakers of other languages and 12 percent of the U.S. population over 5 years of age). Spanish is followed by Chinese (2,464,572 or 4 percent), Tagalog (1,480,429 or 3 percent), French, (1,355,805 or 2 percent), and Vietnamese (1,207,004 or 2 percent). Figure 1.1 shows the ten most widely spoken languages other than English in the U.S.

As can be seen in Figure 1.1, Spanish is by far the most widely spoken language (other than English) in the U.S., and the number of Spanish speakers has increased since 1990. Speakers of Asian and Pacific languages such as Chinese, Tagalog, Vietnamese, and Korean also increased, totaling 3 percent of the U.S. population 5 and older in 2007. In contrast, speakers of European languages such as Italian, German, and French, decreased since 1990, yet in 2007 still were spoken by 4 percent of the U.S. population 5 and older.

Geographically, speakers of languages other than English are spread throughout the nation, although they are most concentrated in particular regions and in

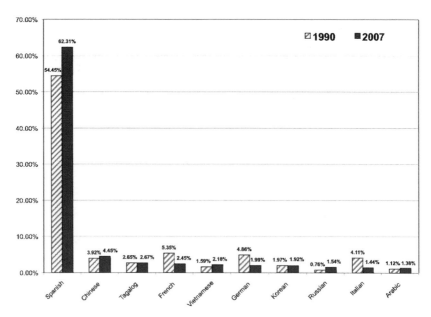

Figure 1.1 Percentage of Ten Most Widely Spoken Languages other than English in 2007 and Their Changes between 2007 and 1990.

Sources: U.S. Census Bureau (1990) and U.S. Census Bureau (2007).

metropolitan areas. The map in Figure 1.2 shows the state-level percentages of people over 5 speaking a language other than English at home in 2007.

As can be seen in Figure 1.2, states in the South and West regions of the U.S. generally have higher percentages than those in the East or Midwest regions. Particular states in the East and Midwest, however, also show high percentages. The state of California has the highest percentage (43%), indicating that almost one out of two people speak a language other than English. Other states with more than 20 percent who speak another language include (in descending order) New Mexico (36%), New York (29%), Arizona (29%), New Jersey (28%), Nevada (27%), Florida (26%), Hawaii (26%), Illinois (22%), Rhode Island (21%), and Massachusetts (20%).

It is important to point out, however, that in 2007, more than half of the people (56 percent) who reported speaking another language also reported that they speak English "very well," and an additional 20 percent that they speak English "well." This means that over two thirds (76 percent) of those who speak a non-English language are bilingual and have good English skills. This figure is even higher among younger age groups: 92 percent of 5–17-year-olds who speak a non-English language also speak English either very well or well. Only 8 percent of these children and adolescents answered that they do not have good English skills or have no English skills at all. Out of the total number of 5–17-year-olds in the U.S. (53,237,254), however, only 8 percent (10,918,344) are bilingual; the rest speak only English. The number of older bilinguals is larger: 20 percent of those 18–64 (39,237,930) speak a language other than English, and 73 percent of these bilingual adults speak English well or very well. We can infer from the discrepancy between the percentage of child and adolescent bilinguals vs. adult bilinguals that English continues to be the dominant U.S. language and that many younger speakers are likely to become English-dominant, even if they retain some ability in a non-English language. The most striking conclusion from all these figures,

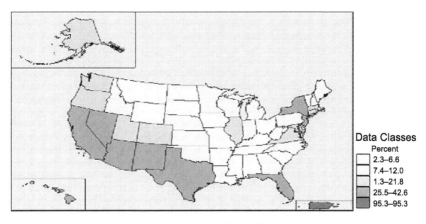

Figure 1.2 Percentage of People (5 Years and Over) Who Speak a Language other than English at Home in 2007.

Source: U.S. Census Bureau (2007).

however, is that English is not even close to being challenged as the dominant and primary language of the U.S., in spite of public fears to the contrary (see Wiley & de Klerk's chapter for more discussion of such fears).

Given the unchallenged status of English in the U.S., what is underdiscussed yet critical for education is how to assist the children and adolescents in K–12 schools who speak heritage languages and have little or no facility in English. In addition, it is important to address the needs of bilingual populations in school (those who speak both a heritage language and English)—currently one out of a dozen children nationally—in terms of how to accommodate their cultural and linguistic characteristics in supporting the development of both languages (and literacies). Meeting these students' needs begins with research-based understandings of their heritage cultures and the roles of their native languages (and varieties of those languages) in their academic and personal lives. Such an understanding is urgent as schooling only in academic English can lead to identity conflicts and even to leaving school. In fact, those students who speak vernacular varieties of English or languages other than English drop out of school at disproportionately high rates, indicating a relationship between students' language backgrounds, performance scores in school, and dropout rates (see McCarty et al.'s chapter for Native American students and Charity Hudley's for African American students). Statistics from the National Center for Education Statistics (NCES, 2008) show that for 2005–2006 high school dropout rates are highest for American Indians/ Alaska Natives (6.9% of the total students in this ethnic group), followed by African Americans (6.3%), Hispanics (5.8%), Whites (2.6%), and Asian/Pacific Islanders (2.4%). The discrepancies in these figures illustrate the importance of ensuring that children who speak devalued dialects and languages are assessed fairly and at the same time have access to learning opportunities through necessary and relevant support.

Language and Literacy Ideologies

The problematic situation for linguistic minorities in U.S. school systems clearly goes beyond language-related issues (e.g., a policy that bases school funding on local taxes, which results in a dramatically unequal allocation of resources for schools). Language differences, and particularly *language ideologies* about such differences, nevertheless play a crucial role in the differential achievement of various populations. We argue that a large part of this problem is that educational policies are formed on the basis of "conventional wisdom" informed by language and literacy ideologies, rather than by research-based knowledge. We use the term *language [and literacy] ideology* to mean widely-shared beliefs about language and literacy that organize social relations. These ideologies are particularly damaging because they seem to be "commonsense" notions about, for example, what is good, bad, elegant, or impoverished language, simultaneously placing the speakers of such labeled language into hierarchical social relations (Woolard, 1998). Speakers whose language is deemed prestigious are placed higher in social status than those whose language is deemed inadequate or full of "error." Thus although all dialects of English have been shown scientifically to be fully formed, systematic, and adequate, even elegant, linguistic systems, dominant language ideology in the U.S., expressed in "conventional wisdom," devalues vernacular dialects (of all languages) by considering them sloppy or badly-formed. We explore three such ideologies here: the ideology of language standardization, the ideology of language purism, and the ideology of monolingualism, showing how each of these ideologies contradicts research results regarding actual linguistic realities.

First, what is referred to as "standard" English exists more as an abstract concept than as an actual (spoken) variety of English. As already noted, it is defined more easily by what it lacks (e.g., socially stigmatized phonological or syntactic features) than by the presence of particular features. Moreover, the concept of a standard is viable only when applied to written, not spoken, language (Milroy & Milroy, 2003). The standardization of (written) English occurred over several centuries in England, beginning with the advent of print in the fifteenth century, becoming the established official language by about 1700, and continuing to adopt fine points of usage (e.g., <u>different from</u> rather than <u>different than</u>) as defined by the lexicographer Samuel Johnson and various published grammarians. All these eighteenth-century efforts at codification, however, impacted only the written language: although the notion of a standard was adhered to in writing, people continued to use various dialects for daily speech (as they still do). A significant outcome of the eighteenth-century codification efforts, however, was an *ideology of standardization*, that is, a belief in a superior uniform standard language that was accepted by virtually all speakers (Milroy and Milroy, 2003; Agha, 2003). This language ideology continues today, in both the U.S. and England, in spite of the documented reality of many "Englishes," both global and local.

A second ideology, language purism, is closely related to the ideology of standardization. Not only is there a widespread belief in the existence of a uniform standard, but this standard is believed to be superior to all other varieties, both cognitively and linguistically. This belief persists despite the fact that numerous linguistic studies have shown clearly that all varieties in use are complex and regularly patterned linguistic systems, and that none of them are superior or inferior to any other. The nub of the problem is that many of these varieties are *believed to be* inferior and their speakers are treated likewise. In other words, people are discriminated against on the basis of their *language*, not on the basis of their ethnic, class, or other identities. This is a subtle but dangerous shift in discriminatory practice. Children who come to school speaking vernacular varieties are then treated as though they have linguistic and cognitive deficits, rather than simply language differences (Adger, Wolfram & Christian, 2007; González, 2001). Instead of building on their strengths, teachers and administrators misclassify them and teach them to be ashamed of the way their families speak (Rickford & Rickford, 2000; Zentella, 2005). This most often results in a lack of self-esteem, a rejection of "school" language and activities, and high drop-out (or "push-out") rates.

A third ideology, of monolingualism, holds that knowing only one language is best, that one language is needed to unify the nation, and, moreover, that two (or more) languages are "confusing" for children. This ideology is widespread in the U.S., even though it is strikingly contradicted by the actual multilingualism both of the contemporary U.S. and throughout its history (Farr, in press; Kloss, 1998 [1977]; Macias, 2000; Wiley, 2005). Multilingualism, in fact, is more common than monolingualism across the world (Tucker, 1999). The belief in the U.S. that one language unifies a nation can be traced to the link between language and nation that emerged in Western Europe in the eighteenth and nineteenth centuries (Anderson, 1983). Citizenship may be enhanced with a common language for communication (although the U.S. colonial government translated for the 200,000 German speakers in Pennsylvania), yet a common language does not require monolingualism. An entire nation's population could be bilingual, as long as one language functioned as the common language (as is the case in much of China). Moreover, bi/multilingualism has many advantages, both for individuals and for societies. Research has shown cognitive advantages to bilingualism for individuals, including children (Hakuta, 1987; King & Mackey, 2007), and multilingual societies have advantages in 1) international relations and diplomacy, 2) competitiveness in global markets, and 3) cross-cultural communication and understanding among ethnic groups (Crystal, 2003).

In spite of all this research-based evidence, however, students generally are taught to replace the languages and dialects in which they were nurtured with "standard" or academic English. Our argument in this book is not that students should not be taught academic English; it is, rather, that the policy be one of additive, not subtractive, bilingualism (and bidialectalism). Academic English should be added to students' linguistic repertoires, but not at the expense (emotional, psychological, and ultimately material) of the loss of their first languages. Unfortunately, educational policy seems to be based not on research-based evidence, but on dominant and persisting language and literacy ideologies cloaked in "conventional wisdom." A good example of this is provided by the city of Chicago, which is known for its ethnolinguistic diversity (Farr, 2004, 2005). Although the city government promotes its cultural diversity to promote tourism, linguistic diversity is not featured as part of this multiculturalism. Similarly, the Chicago Public Schools Policy Manual affirms the importance of multicultural education, yet mentions only once the role of language in cultural identity. Moreover, the manual assumes English to be the first language of children, "with second language proficiency being a desirable goal and a reflection of a precious cultural heritage" (Chicago Public Schools Policy Manual, Section 102.2: Multicultural Education and Diversity). Thus, while multiculturalism is affirmed, at least in policy, bilingualism is only "a desirable goal," as a "second" language after English, and variation within English is not even mentioned.

As we discuss the implications of multiculturalism in U.S. classrooms, we also need to reflect on our understanding of literacy, a concept that is central to schooling. In today's linguistically and culturally diverse classrooms, students not only draw on their oral language abilities in various dialects and languages, but, if they are literate, they also draw on literacy practices in their first language and culture. The repertoire of literacy practices that they draw on is either hindered or promoted by the academic literacy practices they are asked to do in school. As

McCarty et al. (this volume) note, some of these "literacy resources are often misunderstood or 'invisibilized' in school." In order to adequately address the literacy needs of ethnolinguistically diverse students, then, it is crucial to problematize monolingual approaches to literacy education and acknowledge the wide range of literacies that students are bringing into the classroom. Fortunately, recent research on literacy has focused on such diversity, as we discuss in the next section.

Literacy as a Social Practice

Research on literacy, especially as it impacts schooling, has evolved as migration to the U.S. has increased and diversified since the 1960s. Much of this evolution was stimulated by the urgency to address an increasingly diverse student population's needs and expectations. Given the multiplicity of linguistic and sociocultural backgrounds that students now bring to school, in the U.S. and elsewhere, scholarship moved from an understanding of literacy as a set of isolated skills independent of social context to a more ideological model of literacy that portrays literacy as a set of culturally and politically involved practices (Street, 1993). In this volume, we draw from this socially-embedded view of literacy, which, as Brandt and Clinton (2002) note, is "orthodoxy in literacy research today" (p. 337). In this view, literacy activities of ethnolinguistically diverse students are seen within the contexts in which they occur. These contexts include sites and communities based not only in school but outside of it (e.g., churches, homes, playgrounds, workplaces, etc.). In this ideological model, literacy is perceived as "inextricably linked to cultural and power structures in society" and recognizes "the variety of cultural practices associated with reading and writing in different contexts" (Street, 1993, p. 7). Adopting an ethnolinguistic perspective to literacy education, the chapters in this book thus move beyond looking at diverse individual students' knowledge of reading and writing to include their "behavior and conceptualizations related to the use of reading and writing" (p. 12).

Challenging earlier work (e.g., Goody & Watt, 1963; Olson, 1977) that proposed what is now referred to as the Great Divide theory, and opening up literacy theories to focus more broadly on the social consequences of "being literate," various scholars provided evidence of literacy as intertwined with the various social contexts in which people use written language for a variety of social and cultural purposes (Scribner & Cole, 1981; Street, 1984, 1993; Heath, 1983; Graff, 1981; Collins & Blot, 2003). Heath's well-known study (1983), for example, investigated oral and literate traditions at home and at school in two working-class communities (one African American and one white Appalachian) and a middle-class community (both African American and white) in the southern U.S. Heath's definition of literacy captures the multiple and situated nature of literacy from which we are drawing in this edited volume: "the concept of literacy covers a multiplicity of meanings, and definitions of literacy carry implicit but generally unrecognized views of its functions (what literacy can do for individuals) and its uses (what individuals can do with literacy)" (Heath, 1983, p. 3). Such a pragmatic definition situates literacy in broader social processes and as part of everyday life (Barton, Hamilton, & Ivanic, 2000). More specifically, literacies of everyday life are "positioned in relation to the social institutions and power relations which sustain them" (Barton et al., 2000, p. 1). Barton's ecological view of literacy underscores the strong connection between individuals and their social environments and emphasizes "the social and mental embeddedness of human activities in a way which allows change" (Barton, 1994, p. 32). Barton (1994) also urges researchers to adopt an ecological view of literacy so that,

> Instead of studying the separate skills which underlie reading and writing . . . [we] . . . shift to studying *literacy*, a set of social practices associated with particular symbol systems and their related technologies. To be literate is to be active; it is to be confident within these practices. (Barton, 1994, p. x)

Thus literacy is more accurately referred to in its plural form, or as Szwed noted some time ago, as a "plurality of literacies" best studied ethnographically (Szwed, 1981, p. 16). Szwed suggests five elements for such study: text, context, function, participants, and motivation, and he organizes these elements under two basic research questions: What is it that people read and write? Why and under what circumstances is reading and writing done?

Recently the term literacy has been extended to refer to a wide range of knowledge and competencies, e.g., computer literacy, visual literacy, design literacy, scientific literacy, information literacy, health literacy, etc. These broader uses of the term "literate" seem to mean "competent and knowledgeable in specialized areas" (Barton, 1994, p. 19) and do not always involve written language, i.e., reading and writing. Many of these uses, however, do involve a symbol, or semiotic, system, albeit not one based on language (the quintessential symbol system). For example, visual literacy in the arts includes the "reading" of art works, and design literacy includes, in architecture, the "reading" of columns and other parts of buildings. Other metaphorical uses of the term do not require the use of a symbol system and may only involve domain-specific knowledge and competence; for example, scientific literacy implies knowledge of and competence in the scientific method and scientific processes, i.e., understanding science and thinking scientifically (with or without reading and writing). Although the dominant use of the term literacy still implies some use of written language, historical and archeological research indicate that the origins of writing in both the Middle East and Mesoamerica were not based on language (Schmandt-Besserat, 1996; Boone & Mignolo, 1994). Moreover, the history of literacy in the West shows a wide range of practices entwined with both oral language and various social institutions (e.g., the church and the state), as well as particular histories (Graff, 2007). All of this work cautions us not to be too narrow or prescriptive in defining literacy. Thus, we take in this volume a broad and socially-embedded view of literacy that allows an individual to acquire and navigate in more than one type of literacy. Such a view, and the research that follows from it, has important educational implications for policy-makers, teachers and practitioners.

Scholars who have focused on a socially embedded concept of literacy also rely on notions of identity as expressed in habitus (Bourdieu, 1977): "socially and historically constituted, durable, embodied dispositions to act in certain ways" (Holland et al., 1998, p. 52 as cited in Street & Lefstein, 2006, p. 153). Street and Lefstein link the concept of habitus to Holland et al.'s notion of figured worlds: "socially and culturally constructed realm[s] of interpretation in which particular characters and actors are recognized, significance is assigned to certain acts, and particular outcomes are valued over others" (1988, p. 52). An individual's figured world is composed of various artifacts and "practices of self" which are reinforced in the course of social interaction. Unfortunately, most linguistic minority students' figured worlds, the worlds in which they can be who they are through their native cultures and languages, are neither reinforced in social interactions in school nor used in a meaningful way. Instead of being used as bridges to academic literacy, these figured worlds and their identities in these worlds are often rejected. Applying the concept of figured worlds to literacy practices, for example, Bartlett and Holland (2002) suggest that the figured world of literacy may include "functional illiterates," "good readers," and "illiterates," and any of these categories may be invoked, enacted, or challenged by participation in literacy practices. Adopting this concept to school literacy, Dagenais, Day, and Toohey (2006) and Bartlett (2007) show how bilingual children's literacy practices, identities, and future educational trajectories are shaped positively by the notions of "literate child" and "good student," respectively, in the figured world of literacy. Thus, it is important for school literacy practices to evoke and utilize minority students' positive identities in their figured worlds, acknowledging their different roles in these worlds.

Bourdieu's notion of habitus and Holland et al.'s figured worlds remind us of the close connection between language and identity and the importance of mediated action that can position students for failure or success. As the chapters in this volume illustrate, the main problem is that schools adhere to an autonomous and narrow model of literacy, and of "standard" or academic English, while denigrating vernacular varieties of English (including Creoles) and bilingualism with non-English languages. This standardized, purist, and monolingual educational practice, inasmuch as it rejects and devalues students' languages and cultures, frequently leads to their alienation from school and consequently to low levels of achievement in language, literacy, and other curricular areas, failure in standardized testing, and eventually higher school drop-out rates.

Overview of Chapters

This volume consists of two parts. Part I focuses on ethnolinguistic diversity in the United States and four chapters in this section explore this diversity, arguing for the need to become aware of and then build on students' linguistic resources in language and literacy education. Each chapter addresses a different population, including speakers of (different varieties of) English, heritage languages, American Native languages, Spanish, Asian languages, and English language learners.

In the first chapter, Terrence Wiley and Gerda de Klerk provide an overview of

U.S. ethnolinguistic diversity and critique common myths or misconceptions about such diversity—the myth that understates ethnolinguistic diversity in the U.S, the myth that views English as a language in danger vis-à-vis other languages in the U.S., the myth that blames recent immigrants and language minority groups for illiteracy rates, and the myth that views English-only immersion as the best way to teach minority children English literacy. Providing historical evidence as well as contemporary data on ethnolinguistic diversity, bilingualism, and minority groups in the U.S, Wiley and de Klerk argue that these myths are based on a dominant "monolingual" ideology rather than on research-based evidence, and, unfortunately, that such myths underlie current educational policy and practices. They point out that current national surveys do not consider literacy skills in non-English languages (another reflection of the dominant ideology of English monolingualism), which leads to a misevaluation of respondents' overall literacy skills.

Farr's chapter takes up the discussion of language ideology and ethnolinguistic diversity in the archetypal U.S. city of Chicago. Based on her transnational ethnography of Mexicans in both Chicago and Michoacán, a state in western Mexico, Farr describes language, education, and literacy practices within a social network of Mexican families. She first describes the families' transnational lives, then their creative and skillful uses of oral language. She particularly shows how *franqueza* (a frank and direct speech style) is complemented by playful speech and various poetic genres such as sayings, jokes, and riddles in their everyday life. She points out that, despite such verbal creativity and skill, their language use is denigrated by the (U.S. and Mexican) school-taught language ideology of purism. This ideology applies both to their rural Mexican Spanish dialect and to their Chicago vernacular English, and it particularly impacts students with schooling both in Chicago and in Mexico. Similarly, although these families use literacy functionally in their daily activities (especially in Spanish), widely-believed literacy ideologies label them "illiterate." Farr concludes her chapter with a call for research that documents the "invisible" practices and abilities of various groups of people, and urges policy-makers and educators to use such research-based knowledge to undermine ideology-based myths and to educate children in school.

In the following chapter, Teresa McCarty, Mary Eunice Romero-Little, Larisa Warhol, and Ofelia Zepeda focus on Native American youth's language practices and language shift (to English) in the Southwest. Nearly 90 percent of all (175) indigenous U.S. languages have no children learning them as first languages, and 30 percent of these languages face imminent extinction. This chapter examines Native American children's language use patterns across a range of school-community settings, discussing the urgent situation of these students' speaking increasingly only a nativized variety of English, rather than their indigenous heritage languages. The authors note that English-only schooling was cited by community members as a leading cause of language shift. While these students are losing their native languages in English-only schooling, they are still largely classified as "limited English proficient," and their test scores in reading and language arts fall well below state and national norms. The authors contend that, while many children seem to lack proficiency in the Native language as well as in academic English, there is strong evidence that these children are acquiring receptive and sometimes spoken and written proficiency in the Native language even as they are acquiring multiple varieties of English and for some, Spanish, both inside and outside of school. The authors criticize standardized tests for their inability to take these varieties into account and to elucidate the competencies that children actually possess.

The authors also relate youth attitudes and language ideologies to the current language shift to English. On the one hand, the participants in their study viewed English as universal, utilitarian, and necessary, yet at the same time as a colonizing language—a threat to Indigenous identities. On the other hand, the participants referenced sentimental attachments to their heritage languages, emphasizing their centrality as markers of Indigenous identity, but also described feelings of Native-language embarrassment and shame. McCarty et al. suggest using discourses of both pride and shame as resources for supporting the simultaneous development of heritage languages and academic English. The authors conclude with some broader implications of their research for literacy education in multilingual and multiethnic settings, including expanding heritage language programs in and out of school, raising awareness among children by conducting research on their language use, and optimizing coordinated school-community efforts.

In Chapter 5, Alan Hirvela explores the reading and writing practices of Asian language populations by synthesizing the extant research literature on different groups within these populations. As already noted, the number of speakers of Asian languages has grown rapidly in the U.S. As a result, Asian students' language and literacy practices are divergent from one group to another and even within a group. Hirvela's chapter explores these diverse practices among various subgroups within the populations, including 1.5 generation students, heritage language learners, and English language learners. He notes that these populations, being bilingual, biliterate, and bicultural to one degree or another, experience literacy learning differently than do mainstream students in U.S. classrooms. Their constellation of "bi-ness" characteristics, he argues, affords them unique access to literacy resources, but also presents them, as well as their teachers and families, with unique challenges with respect to their literacy (and biliteracy) development. Thus a broad review of research in this chapter provides a critical reflection on the "model minority" view of Asian populations that stereotypes these children's academic achievement. Additionally, through a review of research in diverse school and community-based settings, this chapter shows that out-of-school literacy practices, whether they are literacy practices in community-based institutions (e.g., Sunday school or church-affiliated school) or "voluntary out-of-school" literacy in students' first (heritage) or second language, play a significant role in the development of academic English literacy skills in school. Hirvela's chapter continuously discusses how language ideologies and identity in a bi- or multilingual setting shape students' learning practices both in and out of school. In addition to identifying and discussing key findings from research in this area, Hirvela examines the research methodologies employed in these studies.

The six chapters in Part II of this book apply the ethnolinguistic diversity discussed in Part I to the context of language and literacy teaching and learning in school. These chapters discuss pedagogies that use ethnolinguistic diversity as a resource in the classroom and explore standards and assessment issues related to the misevaluation of language and literacy among speakers of non-standard dialects and minority languages.

Walt Wolfram's chapter presents a Dialect Awareness program that addresses the disparity between research-based sociolinguistic knowledge and popular beliefs about language diversity. He points out that, whereas the standards for teacher training such as those of NCATE (National Council for Accreditation of Teacher Education) include specific objectives for language diversity, teacher-training programs rarely achieve "acceptable" and "target" standards in terms of these goals. Despite the prevalent ethnolinguistic diversity among students and across communities, curricula focusing explicitly on language diversity are virtually non-existent in formal public education programs. Moreover, most public discussions of English dialect differences are still based on the presumption of a right and wrong way to use the English language, with labels such as "correct," "proper," "right," and "grammatical." Wolfram argues that such "prescriptive" labels directly reflect the underlying language ideology that non-mainstream and minority varieties of English are simply unworthy approximations of the standard variety. Building on public curiosity about language differences, he shows how the North Carolina Language and Life Project uses a range of public education venues to effectively challenge standard language ideologies that denigrate vernacular speech. Providing specific pedagogical examples that utilize and promote language diversity in communities, Wolfram calls for researchers and educators to play an active role in developing and fostering research-based understandings about dialects in the public interest.

In Chapter 7, H. Samy Alim and John Baugh discuss Critical Hip Hop Language Pedagogies in the context of their ethnographic studies of two African American speech communities: African American adults working at a recreational facility at an inner-city public park in St. Louis and youth at a high school in Northern California. The authors also discuss how they used an Ethnography of Speaking approach with their students. In this research, the authors ask their students to act as ethnographers and do their own fieldwork on the linguistic variation in their lives. Calling for critical language pedagogies in classrooms through the use of ethnographic interviews and classroom research, Alim and Baugh emphasize that schools are key sites of "language ideological combat" in which standard language ideology is deeply imposed and rooted in everyday practices. More specifically, they point out that in today's schooling context, Critical Hip Hop language pedagogies (CHHLP) offer important insights aimed at "incorporating theory and practice, so that innovative approaches might begin to be implemented in classrooms." As Alim and Baugh carefully illustrate, CHHLPs could be utilized to "uncover both the official, articulated language ideologies of the school, as well as the unofficial, unarticulated language ideologies of teachers and students." These language pedagogies, which raise marginalized students' awareness of their own linguistic repertoires, help raise vital issues about "how language is used and, importantly, how language can be used against them." This chapter shares practical examples of how schooling can develop deeper sociolinguistic and cultural understandings of students' linguistic backgrounds.

Ann Charity Hudley's chapter carefully discusses the historical development and consequences of standardized assessment practices on African American children's academic achievement. Charity Hudley begins with a detailed analysis of the history of standardized testing in the U.S. education system. She argues that even today racial categorization is used to assess and evaluate the intelligence and academic performance of minority student populations. In addition, she further argues that although much sociolinguistic research has proven that African American Vernacular English (AAVE) is a systematic variety of English, the use of AAVE is still not taken into account in standardized testing, causing various unequal practices inside and outside the school. Focusing on various types of tests (norm referenced, criterion referenced and achievement referenced) Charity Hudley critiques their shortcomings in terms of reliability, validity and cultural sensitivity. She argues that it is the linguistic and cultural ignorance in schools that inhibit the achievement of many African American children on standardized tests. To decrease discriminatory practices in standardized testing and to better prepare African American children for the testing world, this chapter also includes specific suggestions for how linguists can help test designers create culturally sensitive test items and classroom teachers can better prepare students for standardized testing. She concludes her chapter by arguing for funding to help teachers and schools create culturally and linguistically sensitive methods and materials for testing. Charity Hudley provides a very informative chapter for the various actors who are directly and indirectly involved in such discriminatory testing practices.

In the following chapter, Ofelia García moves the focus to the Latino student population, the largest language minority group in the U.S. García illustrates the complex language and literacy practices of Latino student populations, noting the failure of mainstream schooling practices in meeting Latino students' academic needs and expectations. Building on the notion of "languaging" instead of "languages" of Latinos, she emphasizes the dynamism of bilingual language practices, arguing the importance of additive bilingualism in schooling contexts. Emphasizing the lack of understanding about what it actually means to be bilingual, she defines bilingualism "as recursive and moving back and forth as it blends its components, or as dynamic with both languages coming in and out and mixing." Throughout this chapter, García eloquently links Latino failures in the U.S. school system to the fact that bilingualism is seen as a static language practice, rather than a "complex languaging practice." To debunk this conventional understanding of bilingualism and move away from discriminatory assessment practices of Latino students in the U.S., she offers the notion of "pluriliteracy practices" (García, Bartlett & Kleifgen, 2007), which "includes literacy practices in sociocultural contexts, the hybridity of literacy practices afforded by new technologies, and the increasing interrelationship of semiotic systems." This understanding of language and literacy, according to García, could help the students utilize their linguistic backgrounds and create more meaningful educational practices in schools. Finally, García calls for more equitable assessment practices in which schools begin to implement "bilingual tap assessment" to provide Latino students opportunities to build on and activate their Spanish literacy knowledge.

Shondel Nero's chapter (10) moves our focus to students from the English-speaking Caribbean. Noting the paucity of research on this population, in spite of their growing presence in U.S. schools, she urges educators to deepen their understandings of the language and literacy issues of this group. This chapter adds to that understanding by exploring the language of the majority of recent immigrants from the English-speaking Caribbean, called Caribbean Creole English (CCE); the extent to which their language practices impact their literacy development in school; and the degree to which teacher training and professional development in sociolinguistics as well as the history, structure, and use of CCE might influence pedagogical approaches in order to enhance the literacy development of CCE speakers. Taking into account the language demands of the New York State middle and high school English Language Arts curriculum, Nero explores creative ways to harness the students' multidialectal linguistic repertoire while working within a narrowly prescribed curriculum that privileges essayist print literacy.

The final chapter of this book (Chapter 11) is devoted to improving both Creole and Vernacular-speaking students' academic success in schools. Calling for a more active sociolinguistic involvement in improving the reading and writing skills of Creole and Vernacular speaking students, in this chapter Angela Rickford and John Rickford draw on their experiences with various projects focused on AAVE and Creole speakers learning academic English in schools. Some of these projects include educating teachers and literacy coaches about strategies for teaching various writing forms to AAVE speakers, observing a bilingual class experiment in a Jamaican elementary school with a Creole/English bilingual program, and personal experiences with student teachers. Throughout the chapter, Rickford and Rickford emphasize the importance of sociolinguists' involvement in "raising the literacy level of vernacular and Creole speakers . . . [to] help them master academic or standard English." The authors also call for continued research in addressing the literacy issues of vernacular and Creole speaking students in the U.S. school system. They also provide practical pedagogical suggestions to "inside agitators" such as teachers, administrators, advisors, and school district staff in using sociolinguistic research as a resource, including educating teachers about specific grammatical rules of AAVE and Creole English.

Conclusion

The chapters in this book explore crucial issues that emerge at the intersection of linguistic diversity and education. More specifically, they provide an up-to-date overview of sociolinguistic research and practice on this topic, including not only work on vernacular varieties of (U.S.) English, but also English-based Creoles, bilingualism with non-English languages, and bidialectalism within and across languages. The issues involved in using research on such linguistic diversity to improve language and literacy education are similar across these areas, since boundaries between vernacular language varieties, Creole languages, and other non-English languages are not as discrete as might be assumed. All of these language varieties, as they co-exist with academic English in schools, are better viewed on a continuum (or multiple continua) than as distinct language codes with finite boundaries. At the same time, bilingualism with languages that are relatively distant from English does involve more issues, especially if the writing system of the non-English language is not based on the Roman alphabet, as is English. Although research on vernacular dialects and bilingualism usually has proceeded separately, research on Creole languages connects these two areas, and we argue here that considering them all together is more fruitful than focusing on them separately. Ultimately, we argue for the application of such research-based knowledge to the dire situation (as measured by school failure and drop-out rates) of many ethnolinguistic populations in U.S. schools.

The chapters in this book thus contribute to our understanding of contemporary ethnolinguistic diversity in schools and explore ways in which sociolinguistic knowledge of this diversity can be used to heighten acknowledgement and recognition of the linguistic and cultural resources students bring into the schools. The authors of these chapters represent various linguistic, cultural, and professional backgrounds and bring their unique perspectives and research to the issues surrounding sociolinguistic knowledge and language and literacy education. The significance of the chapters in this volume lies in the fact that each student's "home" language(s), whether they be a variety of English, a Creole language, a heritage language, or a mixture of any of these, is an asset through which they can connect to their families and communities, as well as recognize and express their various identities. Affirming children through the languages they bring to school empowers each of them as a "whole" person open to growth and learning. At the same time, teachers can use these ethnolinguistic resources to support the children's schooling and academic development, including the acquisition of academic English.

In order to value ethnolinguistic diversity as asset and resource, the chapters in this volume urge educators and policy-makers to question endemic common myths based on monolingual and purist language ideologies, and to open their eyes and minds to the evidence from sociolinguistic research as discussed in this volume. For their part, researchers are called on to rigorously document ethnolinguistic diversity in communicative practices in various schools and communities in order to engender academic discussion and public interest in this important area. Through such research, the multilingual and multicultural nature of the school context, and thus the existence of a plurality of languages and literacies in addition to academic English, can be acknowledged and accentuated. Most importantly, findings from such research will open a window into students' multiple language and literacy abilities, a critical move in understanding and supporting these children's performance in school. In spite of these efforts, however, if individual teachers maintain negative attitudes toward the languages that students use in their classrooms, a number of negative consequences will ensue: the maintenance and further development of these languages (including opportunities for biliteracy) will be constrained, as will the students' relationships with their home and community cultures, which in turn can have negative implications for their individual and academic growth. It is crucial, then, for researchers, policy-makers, and teacher educators to work collaboratively in ensuring that these children's needs and "language rights" are properly addressed. After all, our missions as educators, researchers, and policy-makers are common—to provide these children with as many and as fair opportunities as possible, so that they can excel in their academic and life careers.

References

Adger, C., Wolfram, W. & Christian, D. (2007). *Dialects in schools and communities*, second edition. Mahwah, NJ: Erlbaum Associates.

Agha, A. (2003). The social life of cultural value, in *Language and communication* 23: 231–273.

American Anthropological Association. (2009) Retrieved March 31, 2009, from http://www.aaanet.org/resources/A-Public-Education-Program.cfm

Anderson, B. (1983). *Imagined communities: Reflections on the origin and spread of nationalism*. London: Verso.

Boone, E.H., & Mignolo, W.D. (Eds.). (1994). *Writing without words: Alternative literacies in Mesoamerica and the Andes*. Durham, NC: Duke University Press.

Bartlett, L. (2007). Bilingual literacies, social identification, and educational trajectories. *Linguistics and Education, 18* (3–4), 215–231.

Bartlett, L., & Holland, D. (2002). Theorizing the space in literacy practices. *Ways of Knowing,* 2(1), 10–22.

Barton, D. (1994). *Literacy: An introduction to the ecology of written language.* Oxford: Blackwell.

Barton, D., Hamilton, M., & Ivanic, R. (Eds.) (2000). *Situated literacies. Reading and writing in context.* London: Routledge.

Bourdieu, P. (1977). *Outline of a theory of practice.* Cambridge and New York: Cambridge University Press.

Brandt, D., & Clinton, K. (2002). Limits of the local: expending perspectives on literacy as a social practice. *Journal of Literacy Research,* 34 (3), 337–356.

Collins, J. & Blot, R.K. (2003). *Literacy and literacies: Texts, power, and identity.* Cambridge: Cambridge University Press.

Crystal, D. (2003). *English as a global language,* second edition. Cambridge: Cambridge University Press.

Eckert, P. (2000). *Linguistic variation as social practice.* Oxford: Blackwell.

Eckert, P., & McConnell-Ginet, S. (2003). *Language and gender.* Cambridge, UK; New York: Cambridge University Press.

Dagenais, D., Day, E., & Toohey, K. (2006). A multilingual child's literacy practices and contrasting identities in the figured worlds of French immersion classrooms, *The International Journal of Bilingual Education and Bilingualism, 9* (2), 205–218.

Farr, M. (Ed.). (2004). *Ethnolinguistic Chicago: Language and literacy in the city's neighborhoods.* Mahwah, NJ: Erlbaum.

—— (Ed.). (2005). *Latino language and literacy in ethnolinguistic Chicago.* Mahwah, NJ: Erlbaum.

—— (2007). Literacies and ethnolinguistic diversity: Chicago. In B. Street (Ed.), Volume on literacy, Nancy Hornberger (Ed.), *Encyclopedia of language and education.* Heidelberg, Germany: Springer-Verlag.

—— (in press). Urban multilingualism: Language practices and language policy in

Chicago. In J. Jaspers & J. Verschueren (Eds.), Urban multilingualism and intercultural communication, special issue of *Pragmatics*.

Frank, A.G. (1996). *The world system: Five hundred years or five thousand?* Berkeley: University of California Press.

García, O., Bartlett, L., & Kleifgen, J.A. (2007). From biliteracy to pluriliteracies. In P. Auer & L. Wei (Eds.) *Handbook of applied linguistics*. Vol. 5: *Multilingualism* (pp. 207–228). Berlin: Mouton/de Gruyter.

González, N. (2001). *I am my language: Discourse of women and children in the borderlands*. Tucson: The University of Arizona Press.

Goody, J., & Watt, I. (1963). The consequences of literacy. *Comparative Studies in Society and History*, 5, 3, pp. 304–345; Cambridge; Cambridge University Press.

Graff, H.J. (1981). *Literacy and social development in the West: A reader*. Cambridge: Cambridge University Press.

—— (Ed.) (2007). *Literacy and historical development: a reader*. Carbondale: Southern Illinois University Press.

Green, L. (2002). *African American English: A linguistic introduction*. Cambridge: Cambridge University Press.

Hakuta, K. (1987). *Mirror of language: The debate on bilingualism*. New York: Basic Books.

Heath, S. (1983). *Ways with words. Language, life, and work in communities and classrooms*. Cambridge: Cambridge University Press.

Holland, D., Lachicotte, W., Skinner, D., & Cain, C. (1998). *Identity and agency in cultural worlds*. Cambridge, MA: Harvard University Press.

King, K., & Mackey, A. (2007). *The bilingual edge: Why, when, and how to teach your child a second language*. New York: HarperCollins.

Kloss, H. (1998 [1977]). *The American bilingual tradition*. Washington, DC and McHenry, IL: Center for Applied Linguistics and Delta Systems.

Macias, R. (2000). The flowering of America: Linguistic diversity in the United States. In S. McKay and S.C. Wong (Eds.), *New immigrants in the United States* (pp. 11–57). Cambridge: Cambridge University Press.

Mascia-Lees, F., & Johnson Black, N. (2000). *Gender and anthropology*. Illinois: Waveland Press.

Merriam-Webster Dictionary. Retrieved April 1, 2009 from http://www.merriam-webster.com/dictionary/vernacular.

Milroy, J., & Milroy, L. (2003). *Authority in language*, second edition. New York: Routledge.

Mufwene, S. (2000). Some sociohistorical inferences about the development of African American English. In S. Poplack (Ed.), *The English history of African American English*. Malden, MA: Blackwell.

National Center for Education Statistics. (2008). Table 6. Public school high school number of dropouts and event dropout rate, by race/ethnicity and state or jurisdiction: School year 2005–06. Retrieved February 27, 2009 from http://nces.ed.gov/ccd/tables/2008353_06.asp.

Nero, S.J. (Ed.). (2006). *Dialects, Englishes, Creoles, and education*. Mahwah, NJ: Erlbaum.

Nichols, P. (2004). Pidgins and Creoles. In S. McKay & N. Hornberger (Eds.), *Sociolinguistics and language teaching*. Cambridge: Cambridge University Press.

Olson, D. (1977) From utterance to text: The bias of language in speech and writing. *Harvard Educational Review*, 41: 257–281.

Rickford, J. (1986). The need for new approaches to social class analysis in sociolinguistics. *Journal of Communication* 6: 215–21.

Rickford, J.R., & Rickford, R.J. (2000). *Spoken soul: The story of Black English*, New York; Chichester: Wiley.

Schmandt-Besserat, D. (1996) *How writing came about.* Austin: University of Texas Press.

Scribner, S., & Cole, M. (1981). *The psychology of literacy.* Cambridge, MA: Harvard University Press.

Stern, S.J. (1995). *The secret history of gender: Women, men & power in late colonial Mexico.* Chapel Hill, NC: University of North Carolina Press.

Street, B. (1984). *Literacy in theory and practice.* Cambridge: Cambridge University Press.

Street, B. (Ed.) (1993). *Cross-cultural approaches to literacy.* Cambridge: Cambridge University Press.

Street, B., & Lefstein, A. (2006). *Literacy: An advanced resource book.* New York, NY: Routledge.

Szwed, J. (1981). *The ethnography of literacy.* In Writing: *Functional and linguistic-cultural variation,* edited by M. Farr Whiteman, pp. 13–23. Hillsdale, NJ: Erlbaum.

Tucker, G.R. (1999) *A global perspective on bilingualism and bilingual education.* Carnegie: Mellon University. Retrieved June 24, 2009 from http://www.cal.org/resources/Digest/digestglobal.html.

U.S. Census Bureau (1990). Detailed language spoken at home and ability to speak English for persons 5 years and over—50 languages with greatest number of speakers. Retrieved March 10, 2009, from http://www.census.gov/population/socdemo.

—— (2007). *American community survey 1-year estimates.* B16001. Language spoken at home by ability to speak English for the population 5 years and over. Retrieved March 5, 2009, from http://factfinder.census.gov/.

—— (2007). *American community survey 1-year estimates.* C16004. Age by language spoken at home by ability to speak English for the population 5 years and over. Retreved March 5, 2009, from http://factfinder.census.gov.

—— (2007). *American community survey 1-Year estimates.* GCT1601. Percent of people 5 years and over who speak a language other than English at home. Retrieved March 5, 2009, from http://factfinder.census.gov.

—— (2007). *American community survey 1-Year estimates.* M1601. Percent of people 5 years and over who speak a language other than English at home. Retrieved March 5, 2009, from http://factfinder.census.gov.

Wiley, T. (2005). *Literacy and language diversity in the United States,* second edition. Washington, DC: Center for Applied Linguistics.

Winford, D. (1997). On the origins of African American English—a creolist perspective. Part I: The sociohistorical background. *Diachronica* 14: 305–44.

—— (1998). On the origins of African American English—a creolist perspective. Part II: A linguistic perspective. *Diachronica* 15: 99–154.

Wolfram, W., & Schilling-Estes, N. (2006). *American English,* second edition. Oxford: Blackwell.

Woolard, K. (1998). Introduction: Language ideology as a field of inquiry. In B. Schieffelin, K. Woolard, & P. Kroskrity (Eds.), *Language ideologies: Practice and theory.* Oxford: Oxford University Press.

Zentella, A.C. (Ed.). (2005). *Building on strength: Language and literacy in Latino families and communities.* New York: Teachers College Press.

Part I

Ethnolinguistic Diversity in the United States

2 Common Myths and Stereotypes Regarding Literacy and Language Diversity in the Multilingual United States[1]

Terrence G. Wiley and Gerda de Klerk

It may seem rather indelicate . . . to stress . . . that biliteracy—the mastery of reading in particular and at times also writing, in two (or more) languages—is not at all a rare skill among that portion of mankind that has successfully won the battle for literacy.

(Fishman, 1980a, p. 49)

A number of popular myths surround discussions of literacy and language diversity in the United States. To adequately discuss literacy, it is necessary to look also at dominant attitudes and beliefs about language diversity. Taken as a whole, these attitudes and beliefs are part of the dominant ideology about language and literacy in the United States, which is characterized by English monolingualism. Ideology refers to beliefs and convictions that dictate, direct, or influence policy and behavior. English monolingualism reflects an ideology that languages other than English must be aberrant and bilingualism must be unnatural (Ovando & Wiley, 2007; Ricento & Wiley, 2002; Wiley, 2004, 2007a). These assumptions underlie much of the public discussion about literacy and language diversity and shed light on much of the education research, policy, and practice directed at language and literacy issues.

The first part of this chapter critiques six common myths or misconceptions about literacy and language diversity in the United States by drawing on both historical evidence and contemporary data. The latter part of the chapter looks at the impact of the ideology of English monolingualism on the way that scholarly issues and research are framed with respect to language, literacy, and diversity. The chapter concludes with implications for policy and practice.

Common Myths about Literacy and Language Diversity

Myth 1: The United States is most appropriately described as an English-speaking, monolingual nation. Over two decades ago, the late Senator Paul Simon (1988) lamented the cultural isolation and lack of interest by the English-speaking majority in foreign languages in the United States, noting that, "We should erect a sign at each point of entry into the United States [saying]: Welcome to the United States—we cannot speak your language" (p. 1). Although the "we" in this case refers to the majority of monolingual English speakers, at the time there were approximately 23.1 million speakers of languages other than English, and based on 2007 data there are 55.4 million (see Table 2.1).

Over the past three decades, the U.S. Census, Current Population Survey, and American Community Survey have been used to provide information about language diversity at the national level. As of this printing, the most recent language data are from the 2007 American Community Survey. Table 2.2 shows the numbers of speakers of languages other than English in 1990, 2000, and 2007 for the twenty largest languages. Looking at trends, it is clear that English is overwhelmingly the majority language; however, the current presence of over 55 million individuals who speak other languages indicates that the United States is more appropriately described as a multilingual nation in which English is the dominant language.

Among these 55 million people, the vast majority has some ability in English; in fact, it is important to note that among those who reported speaking a language other than English at home, most people speak English "well" or "very well." Unfortunately, the U.S. Census does not ask for relative speaking abilities in languages other than English (see Table 2.3).

English ability varies with the age of speakers and the language(s) in question. The older the respondents, the larger are the proportions who do not speak English at all. Spanish speakers have the largest proportion of non-English speakers, while Asian and Pacific Island languages have the smallest proportion. It is important to note the very small numbers as well as percentages of respondents (from all languages) of school-going age who do not speak English. This suggests that across all language groups, in the aggregate, school-age children from families where a language other than English is spoken are bilingual to some extent, usually with strong English fluency.

Myth 2: The predominance of English and English literacy is threatened. English has been the dominant language of the United States since its founding, and there is no reason to assume that it is in any danger of being eclipsed in the near or foreseeable future. Nevertheless, it is equally true that the country has always been linguistically diverse.

Although the dominance of English was established at the time of the first census in 1790, estimates of the ethnic origins of the population can be taken as

Table 2.1 Estimates of People (Aged 5+) Who Speak a Language Other than English at Home

	1980	*1990*	*2000*
United States Census	23.1 million (11%)	31.8 million (13.8%)	46.9 million (17.9%)
American Community Survey	*2007* 55.4 million (19.7 %)		

Sources: McArthur, 1993, p. 43 and 2000 United States Census 2000, Summary File 3, Table DP-2. U.S. Bureau of the Census American Community Survey 2007, 1-year estimates.

Table 2.2 Twenty Languages Most Frequently Spoken at Home for the Population, Age 5 and Older: 1990, 2000, and 2007

Language spoken at home (ranked for 2006)	1990		2000		2007	
	Rank	Number of speakers	Rank	Number of speakers	Rank	Number of speakers
United States	X	230,445,777	X	262,375,152	X	280,950,438
English only	X	198,600,798	X	215,423,557	X	225,505,953
Total	X	31,844,979	X	46,961,595	X	55,444,485
non-English		13.8%		17.9%		19.7%
Spanish	1	17,339,172	1	28,101,052	1	34,547,077
Chinese	5	1,249,213	2	2,022,143	2	2,464,572
Tagalog	6	843,251	5	1,224,241	3	1,480,429
French	2	1,702,176	3	1,643,838	4	1,355,805
Vietnamese[1]	9	507,069	6	1,009,627	5	1,207,004
German	3	1,547,099	4	1,078,997	6	1,104,354
Korean	8	626,478	8	894,063	7	1,062,337
Russian	15	241,798	9	706,242	8	851,174
Italian[1]	4	1,308,648	7	1,008,370	9	798,801
Arabic	13	355,150	11	614,582	10	767,319
Portuguese[2]	10	429,860	12	564,630	11	687,126
Polish	7	723,483	10	667,414	12	638,059
French Creole	19	187,658	14	453,368	13	629,019
Hindi[3]	14	331,484	16	317,057	14	532,911
Japanese[2]	11	427,657	13	477,997	15	458,717
Persian[4]	18	201,865	17	312,085	16	349,686
Urdu[3][4]	NA	NA	18	262,900	17	344,942
Greek[4]	12	388,260	15	365,436	18	329,825
Gujarathi	(26)	102,418	19	235,988	19	287,367
Serbo-Croatian	(34)	70,964	20	233,865	20	276,550
Armenian	20	149,694	(21)	202,708	(21)	221,865

NA Not available
X Not applicable

Source 1990: U.S. Census Bureau, Census 1990 CPHL-133
Source 2000: U.S. Census Bureau, Census 2000 Summary File 3
Source 2007: U.S. Census Bureau, American Community Survey 2007, 1-year estimates

1 In 2000, the number of Vietnamese speakers and number of Italian speakers were not statistically different from one another.
2 In 1990, the number of Portuguese speakers and number of Japanese speakers were not statistically different from one another.
3 In 1990, Hindi included those who spoke Urdu.
4 In 2007, the number of Persian speakers and number of Urdu speakers were not statistically different from one another. Similarly the numbers of Urdu speakers were not statistically different from the number of Greek speakers.

Note: Data based on sample. The estimates in this table vary from actual values due to sampling errors. As a result, the numbers of some languages shown in this table may not be statistically different from the number of speakers of languages not shown in this table.

Table 2.3 Language Spoken at Home by Age and Ability to Speak English (Population 5 years and over)

	United States	
	Estimate	Margin of Error
Total:	280,950,438	+/−17,610
5 to 17 years:	53,237,254	+/−25,343
Speak only English	42,318,910	+/−46,666
Speak Spanish:	7,872,291	+/−34,011
Speak English "very well"	5,803,982	+/−36,843
"well"	1,361,914	+/−25,336
"not well"	579,208	+/−15,333
"not at all"	127,187	+/−8,096
Speak other Indo-European languages:	1,478,516	+/−22,745
Speak English "very well"	1,189,205	+/−20,993
"well"	202,362	+/−8,954
"not well"	76,296	+/−5,265
"not at all"	10,653	+/−2,129
Speak Asian and Pacific Island languages:	1,173,442	+/−17,303
Speak English "very well"	853,363	+/−17,610
"well"	229,298	+/−8,535
"not well"	84,476	+/−5,200
"not at all"	6,305	+/−1,282
Speak other languages:	394,095	+/−16,269
Speak English "very well"	323,386	+/−14,524
"well"	47,851	+/−4,303
"not well"	20,319	+/−3,481
"not at all"	2,539	+/−960
18 to 64 years:	189,872,626	+/−26,305
Speak only English	150,634,696	+/−85,397
Speak Spanish:	24,333,144	+/−59,411
Speak English "very well"	11,542,254	+/−60,502
"well"	4,528,292	+/−41,679
"not well"	5,233,225	+/−41,086
"not at all"	3,029,373	+/−43,469
Speak other Indo-European languages:	7,033,993	+/−53,749
Speak English "very well"	4,743,074	+/−41,535
"well"	1,453,753	+/−24,705
"not well"	693,965	+/−15,682
"not at all"	143,201	+/−9,639
Speak Asian and Pacific Island languages:	6,201,891	+/−36,396
Speak English "very well"	3,167,714	+/−27,254
"well"	1,734,363	+/−21,933
"not well"	1,045,567	+/−20,197
"not at all"	254,247	+/−10,107
Speak other languages:	1,668,902	+/−31,150
Speak English "very well"	1,161,172	+/−24,467
"well"	355,542	+/−13,051
"not well"	126,088	+/−8,019
"not at all"	26,100	+/−3,912

65 years and over:	37,840,558	+/−17,617
Speak only English	32,552,347	+/−31,473
Speak Spanish:	2,341,642	+/−12,989
Speak English "very well"	833,294	+/−15,009
"well"	431,964	+/−11,240
"not well"	531,677	+/−12,127
"not at all"	544,707	+/−12,698
Speak other Indo-European languages:	1,808,221	+/−19,638
Speak English "very well"	1,004,529	+/−14,196
"well"	362,033	+/−8,338
"not well"	301,764	+/−10,041
"not at all"	139,895	+/−6,976
Speak Asian and Pacific Island languages:	941,093	+/−9,916
Speak English "very well"	253,717	+/−8,238
"well"	212,519	+/−6,118
"not well"	282,221	+/−8,509
"not at all"	192,636	+/−8,702
Speak other languages:	197,255	+/−7,490
Speak English "very well"	99,784	+/−3,952
"well"	42,831	+/−2,817
"not well"	36,492	+/−3,705
"not at all"	18,148	+/−2,671

Source: U.S. Census Bureau, 2007 American Community Survey 1-Year Estimates

Data are based on a sample and are subject to sampling variability. The degree of uncertainty for an estimate arising from sampling variability is represented through the use of a margin of error. The value shown here is the 90 percent margin of error.

indirect indicators of language diversity. According to Pitt (1976), roughly 49 percent of the population was of English origin; nearly 19 percent was of African origin; 12 percent was Scotch or Scotch Irish; and Irish accounted for about 3 percent of the total. Dutch, French, and Spanish origin peoples represented an aggregate 14 percent. Lepore (2002) estimates that by 1790, about 75 percent—a lower rate than presently—of the United States population spoke English as their native tongue among a population of around four million that included 600,000 Europeans, 150,000 enslaved Africans, and 150,000 Indians. Thus, there was a diverse pool of native speakers of other languages. If we trace the history of major urban centers (see Farr's case study of Chicago in this volume), there is a persistent pattern of multilingualism, despite the dominance of English.

Through the mid-nineteenth century, a high percentage of immigrants were from predominantly English-speaking areas; however, by the end of the twentieth century, the majority of immigrants spoke languages other than English. Native language instruction and bilingual education were not uncommon in areas where language minority groups comprised a major portion of the local population until the early twentieth century, when legislation was passed mandating English as the official language of instruction (Kloss, 1998; Leibowitz, 1971). By 1909, the United States Immigration Commission reported that among the nation's 37 largest cities, 57.8 percent of children in the schools were of foreign-born parentage. In New York, 71.5 percent of the parents of schoolchildren were foreign born; in Chicago, 67.5 percent; and in San Francisco, 57.8 percent (Weiss, 1982, p. xiii). In 1910, there were 92 million people in the United States. Some 13 million people age ten or older were foreign born, and 23 percent of this group did not speak English (Luebke, 1980, p. 2). A national wave of xenophobia, largely focused on all things German during World War I, and an intense period of Americanization occurred from roughly 1915 to 1925. In 1917, as the United States entered the war, restrictions against the use of German and foreign languages more generally resulted in a rapid decline in both foreign and bilingual education. Although the more extreme restrictions on foreign languages were struck down by the Supreme Court in 1923 (*Meyer v. Nebraska*), German language instruction never fully recovered (see Wiley, 1998; 2007a).

Contemporary immigration restrictionists point with alarm to the fact that recent immigration has reached historic highs. Although this claim is true in terms of raw numbers, it presents a distorted view of the impact of recent immigration in comparison to that of prior decades. When the total numbers of foreign born per decade are presented as a percentage of the total population, it is apparent that the impact of immigration on the composition of the U.S. population has been much smaller in most of the twentieth century and the twenty-first century, than in the nineteenth century and early twentieth century (see Figure 2.1), with a high point of approximately 15 percent for 1910.

Despite these increases, recent statistics on immigration and language diversity in the United States (see Table 2.3 above, for example) indicate that English is in no danger of being eclipsed by other languages; however, contemporary fears that the dominance of English is in danger echo concerns that have been raised periodically for more than 200 years (see Crawford 1992a, 1992b; 1999, 2000; Macías, 1999; Simpson, 1986; Wiley, 2004; see also Hirvela in this volume).

Myth 3: English literacy is the only literacy worth noting. Just as there is a failure to acknowledge the extent of language diversity in the United States, there is also a general failure to acknowledge literacy in languages other than English. This omission adds to the confusion about literacy. Although millions of people are literate in languages other than English, their abilities are ignored. By ignoring literacy in other languages, literacy becomes confused with English literacy. This confusion is reflected in most surveys and measures of literacy, which fail to accurately describe literacy characteristics among language minority groups because they focus only on English (Macías, 1994; Vargas, 1986; Wiley 1991, 2005). According to Macías (1990), there are three patterns of literacy among language minority groups in the United States: (1) native language literacy, which is literacy in one's native language; (2) second language literacy (usually in English), which implies no native language literacy; and (3) biliteracy, literacy in two languages (typically in one's native language and in English) (p. 18). Nonliteracy (i.e., no literacy in any language) is also a possibility as is literacy in a second language by native speakers of English.

Although English is the dominant language of the United States, and it is important that speakers of other languages learn to speak, read, and write it, it is not the case that English literacy can or should fulfill all of the needs of language minority groups (Fishman, 1980a). When all literacy is reduced to English

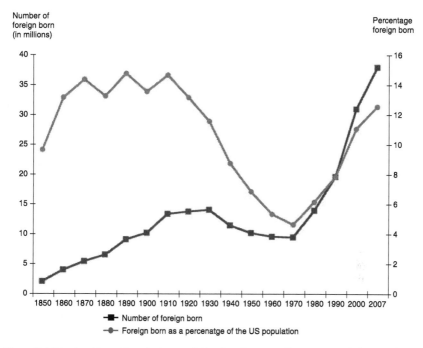

Figure 2.1 Foreign-Born Population and Foreign Born as Percentage of the Total U.S. Population, 1850 to 2007. (Copyright 2007 Migration Policy Institute.)

Source: Originally published on the Migration Policy Institute Data Hub (www.migrationpolicy.org), an independent, nonpartisan, nonprofit think tank dedicated to the study of movement of people worldwide.

Note: The term "foreign born" refers to people residing in the United States who were not U.S. citizens at birth. The foreign-born population includes naturalized citizens, lawful permanent residents (LPRs), certain legal nonimmigrants (e.g., persons on student or work visas), those admitted under refugee or asylum status, and persons illegally residing in the United States.

literacy, the myth that the United States is a monolingual nation is promoted (Wiley, 2004).

Limited English oral proficiency is commonly confused with illiteracy. Some language minority individuals read and write in English but may not speak the language well; conversely, some who are fluent orally in English are not English literate. The problems of becoming literate in a second language should be differentiated (1) from the challenges of learning to speak a second language and (2) from initial literacy in a first or second language (Vargas, 1986; Wiley, 2005).

Myth 4: English illiteracy is high because language minorities are not as eager to learn English and assimilate as prior generations were. A common criticism aimed at recent immigrants and language minority groups is that they are disinclined to learn English or acquire literacy in English because of their loyalty to their native languages and cultures. This myth is based partly on the assumption of the English-speaking majority that languages other than English should be surrendered as a kind of rite-of-passage (see Kloss, 1971). It is also based on the erroneous assumption that all non-English languages are "immigrant" languages (Macías, 1999; Wiley, 2004, 2007b). However, as indicated above, because approximately 40 percent (calculated from American Community Survey 2007 microdata) of the language minority population was born in the United States, these assumptions are specious. American Indian languages and languages such as Hawaiian are not foreign, but indigenous languages. Thus, it is inappropriate to view all language minorities as if they were immigrants—even if one could accept the assimilationist rite-of-passage point of view. Historically, indigenous languages antedate European and English colonization and the formation of the United States as an independent nation. English—in addition to being the dominant national language—is also accurately characterized as an "old colonial language" (as is Spanish; see Molesky, 1988; Wiley, 2007b).

It is also argued that recent non-English-speaking immigrants are different from those of a century ago who, it is believed, readily surrendered their languages and cultures. However, a study by Wyman (1993) of late nineteenth- and early twentieth-century European immigrants concludes that a high percentage of European immigrants returned to their homelands. As is the case now, millions of immigrants returned to their homelands while millions more remained. Then as now, the image of opportunistic, disloyal immigrants fostered resentment among restrictionists, who, in turn, created a past in which former immigrants were somehow more loyal and willing to be Americanized and Anglicized than those of the present.

During the period 1908–23, the USA experienced a net gain of immigrants, with the largest net number that of Jewish/Hebrew (906,608) persons, who had only a 5 percent return to Europe. Other groups were returning in often much larger proportions. The group with the largest proportion (66%) of immigrants returning was Romanian, leaving a net gain of 32,563 Romanian immigrants in the USA. Other groups with rates of return of more than 50 percent were south Italian (60%), Slovak (57%), Russian (52%), and Croat/Slovene (51%) nationals. Groups with return rates below 50 percent, but still above 30 percent, were Greek (46%), north Italian (37%), Polish (37%), and Portuguese (31%) nationals. Lower proportions of return to Europe were found among Irish (11%), Scottish (13%) and Welsh (13%) (Wyman, 1993, p. 11).

Are individuals who speak languages other than English really reluctant to learn English? Crawford (1992a) notes that in California on the day that Proposition 63 (a proposal to make English the official language of California) was passed, "more than 40,000 adults were on waiting lists for ESL [English as a second language] instruction in Los Angeles alone" (p. 17). Current estimates show that in 2006–7, 1,101,082 adults were enrolled in federally funded, state-administered ESL programs (CAL, 2008). Tucker (2006) surveyed 184 ESL providers in 16 states and found that adults have tremendous motivation to learn English; however, 57.4 percent of providers had a waiting list. Waiting times could range from a few weeks to three years. Many programs did not have waiting lists simply because students who could not be accommodated were turned away, or places were offered on a first come, first served basis.

Myth 5: Many language minority adults favor English Only policies. Ironically, while language minority populations are sometimes blamed for not wanting to learn English, supporters of "English Only" and official English initiatives boast of support for their positions among language minority groups. Opinion surveys citing support for learning English often focus *only* on English and fail either to ask for or report information regarding language minority persons' desire to maintain their native languages. To probe this issue, it is useful to consider data on attitudes within multilingual communities toward maintenance of languages other than English. Attitudes toward bilingualism and biliteracy are also of particular interest. The 1979 National Chicano Survey (see Wiley 2005, chapter 4) was one of the few national surveys that provided comprehensive data on such questions. The survey is particularly interesting because it provides data on one of the largest Spanish-speaking subpopulations in the United States. In one question on the survey, respondents were asked which language individuals of Mexican descent should speak in the United States. The results are indicated in Table 2.4.

From these data one could claim that 97 percent of Chicanos surveyed favored use of English. However, English Only advocates could hardly be encouraged that less than 4 percent indicated that English should be spoken exclusively. The great majority, about 93 percent, favored some degree of dual language use. These data illustrate the importance of framing language preference questions in such a way that the middle is not excluded (i.e., that dual language use is presented as an option). Subsequent surveys have likewise consistently found support for promoting bilingualism (see Table 2.5).

Similarly, in response to the question, "Should children of Mexican descent learn to read and write in both Spanish and English?" the results were solidly affirmative with nearly 96 percent agreeing that their children should learn both languages. Another question asked whether parents should discourage their children from speaking Spanish. Only one percent agreed. When asked whether children of Mexican descent should learn to speak Spanish, 99 percent agreed (Wiley, 1988). These data indicate that nearly all the Chicano parents surveyed supported the goals of bilingualism and biliteracy for their children.

More recently, the 2004 *Pew Hispanic Center/Kaiser Family Foundation National Survey of Latinos: Education* found that 92 percent of Latinos said that teaching English to the children of immigrant families is a "very" important goal and another 7 percent said it is a "somewhat" important goal. Almost nine in ten Latinos (88 percent)—over two-thirds (67 percent) of Latinos who said that it

Table 2.4 "Which Language Should Individuals of Mexican Descent Speak in the United States?"

Only English	3.6%
Mostly English	13.4%
Both English & Spanish	70.6%
Mostly Spanish	9.6%
Only Spanish	2.9%

Source: Wiley, 1988, p. 197.

Table 2.5 Support for Bilingual Education

<u>Torres 1988</u>: Support for "Home language as a teaching tool"

1. Parents on Bilingual School Advisory Committee (n=41)	Strongly agree or agree = 95.1%
2. Parents not on committee, but with children in bilingual education (n=106)	Strongly agree or agree = 99%
3. School principals (n=11)	Strongly agree or agree = 100%

<u>Youssef & Simpkins 1985</u>: Forty-four parents of children in an Arabic Bilingual Program

• "I am pleased my child is in a bilingual program." (question 1)	Strongly agree + agree = 97%
• "Bilingual education should not be part of the school curriculum" (question 19)	Strongly disagree + disagree = 55%
• "Do you want your child to attend bilingual classes?" (question 27)	Yes = 95%

<u>Attinasi 1985</u>: Sixty-five Latinos living in Northern Indiana

"Want children in bilingual education"	Yes = 89%

<u>Aguire 1985</u>: Six hundred parents of children in bilingual programs Sixty bilingual teachers

"Bilingual Education is acceptable in the school because it is the best means for meeting the educational needs of the LEP child." (question f)	Agree: Parents = 80% Agree: Teachers = 90%

<u>Hosch 1984</u>: Survey of 283 subjects, from random voter lists, El Paso County, Texas

"Last year, the state of Texas spent $31.00 per student enrolled in bilingual education programs. Do you think this should be eliminated/decreased . . . maintained/increased?"	Support for maintained or increased funding = 64.3%

<u>Shin & Kim *in press*</u>: Fifty-six Korean parents with children in elementary school

"Would you place your child in a bilingual classroom where both Korean and English are used as a medium of instruction?"	Yes = 70%

<u>Shin & Lee 1996</u>: Hmong parents with children in elementary school

"Would you place your child in a bilingual classroom where both Hmong and English are used as a medium of instruction?"	Yes = 60%

Source, with permission, Stephen D. Krashen (1996), *Under Attack: The Case for Bilingual Education*, pp. 44–45. Culver City, CA: Language Education Associates.

is "very" important and another 21 percent who said that it is "somewhat" important—said that it is important for public schools to help students from immigrant families maintain their native tongue.

Given the difficulties in acquiring two languages and becoming literate in both of them, it is reasonable to ask why there should have been such strong support for bilingualism and biliteracy among Chicanos. Responses to a related question help to explain. Respondents were asked whether there were advantages to being bilingual in the United States. Ninety-three percent felt there were (Wiley, 1988). There were ten response choices regarding the types of advantages bilingualism offered. Six related to perceived "personal benefits" of bilingualism (e.g., pride, self-esteem, and improved communication skills), and the other four concentrated on "practical benefits" (e.g., social communication, improved employment, and educational opportunities). Practical benefits were chosen more frequently than personal benefits as the respondents' first choice. "Improved employment opportunities" was ranked first, selected by 45 percent of the respondents. Improved personal communication was second; more than 26 percent selected this option. Improved social communication was third with more than 10 percent of the sample choosing it (see Table 2.6).

Other results from this study confirmed the practicality of these selections. Biliterates, for example, were slightly more likely to be employed. In multilingual communities, bilinguals and biliterates have valued skills as translators and as cultural brokers that monolinguals often lack. Thus, the fact that practical benefits were selected so frequently is significant because it is often argued that only English has practical relevance. Pomerantz (2002), for example, notes that learning Spanish as a heritage (or foreign) language is considered not only a marker of ethnic identity, but also a marketable commodity in a multilingual marketplace.

Myth 6: The best way to promote English literacy is to immerse language minority children and adults in English Only instruction. One of the more enduring misconceptions is that raising children bilingually confuses them and inhibits their cognitive development. This misconception was bolstered by several generations of biased and flawed research dating from the early twentieth century through the 1960s (see Hakuta, 1986). This old myth persists, however, and continues to underlie much of the opposition to bilingual education (Quezada, Wiley, & Ramírez, 2002). It has resulted in generations of language minority parents being admonished not to speak to children in their native language at home, even when parents have little facility in English. Hakuta (1986) concluded that this issue involves two key assumptions:

> [The first is] the effect of bilingualism—indeed, the human mind—can be reduced to a single dimension [ranging from "good" to "bad"], and that the treatment [bilingualism] moves the individual child's standing up or down the dimension. The second assumption is that choosing whether the child is to be raised bilingually or not is like choosing a brand of diaper, that it is relatively free of the social circumstances surrounding the choice. (pp. 43–44)

Table 2.6 "What Are the Advantages of Being Bilingual in the United States?"

Personal Benefits	
a. Improves self esteem, personal satisfaction	0.6%
b. Broadens cross-cultural understanding generally	2.9%
c. Increases communication skills	26.4%
d. Improves one's image	1.0%
e. Home/family advantages	0.5%
Practical Benefits	
f. Societal/community benefits	10.4%
g. Improves employment opportunities	45.1%
h. Improves education opportunities or success	5.8%
i. General approval, improves opportunities generally	6.6%

Source: Adapted from Wiley, 1988, pp. 199–200.

It is also often argued that the best way to promote literacy is to push people into English-only immersion (i.e., sink-or-swim) programs.[2] However, again, neither the historical record nor the research support this view. Contemporary debates regarding the efficacy of various methods for teaching language minorities often frame issues solely in terms of immigrants. The most extreme attempt to implement an English-only education, however, began after the Civil War when the U.S. government began to pursue an aggressive Indian deculturation and domestication program. According to Spring (1994), deculturation involves "replacing the use of native languages with English, destroying Indian customs, and teaching allegiance to the U.S. government" (p. 18). Education programs were seen as the principal means by which this could be accomplished. Central to this "educational policy was the boarding school, which was designed to remove children from their families at an early age and, thereby, isolate them from the language and customs of their parents and tribes" (p. 18). The main concern was to ensure that the Indian child became literate in English which would "habituate them to the customs and advantages of a civilized life . . . and at the same time cause them to look with feelings of repugnance on their native state" (Adams, 1995, p. 21).

The schools vigorously taught the Indian children to "despise every custom of their forefathers, including religion, language, song, dress, ideas, and methods of living" (p. 206). Among the tactics used "was an absolute prohibition on Native American children speaking their own languages, and those that did were humiliated, beaten, and had their mouths washed with lye soap" (Norgren & Nanda, 1988, p. 186). In spite of these practices, Weinberg (1995) notes that "Indian children were notoriously slow learners of the English language [not because English was difficult to learn, but because] they had been taught from earliest childhood to despise their conquerors, their language, dress, customs—in fact everything that pertained to them" (p. 206). Sometimes the methods of instruction were punishment enough: "Carlisle's instructions taught using a text called *First Lessons for the Deaf and Dumb.* . . . The instructor walked from desk to desk, stopping frequently to guide a student's hand as he or she painstakingly formed each letter" (Cooper, 1999, pp. 51–52). Ohiysa (renamed Charles Eastman) recalled an initial English literacy lesson, which lasted a whole week while

> we youthful warriors were held up and harassed with words of those letters. Like raspberry bushes in the path, they tore, bled, and sweated us—those little words like *rat, eat,* and so forth until not a semblance of our native dignity and self-respect was left. (cited in Cooper, 1999, pp. 52–54)

Such tactics were not particularly useful in promoting English literacy. According to Weinberg (1995), these lessons of deculturation were learned more readily than those related to instruction in reading (see also Child, 1998).

The impact of English-only policies on Cherokee literacy is particularly noteworthy. In 1822, the Cherokee had developed a syllabary to promote literacy in their own language. Sequoyah, the syllabary named after its inventor, had been enthusiastically embraced and widely used among the Cherokee (see Lepore, 2002). It provided the basis for a Cherokee financed and governed school system that allowed instruction through high school. Missionaries working with the Cherokee in 1833 estimated that "three-fifths of the Cherokee were literate in their own language and one-fifth in English" (Weinberg, 1995, p. 184). Cherokee educational progress, based largely on the development of native language literacy, was so dramatic that one observer noted in 1852, "the Cherokee Nation had a better common school system than either Arkansas or Missouri, the two neighboring states" (Weinberg, 1995, p. 185). The literacy rate may have reached over 90 percent during the 1850s (Crawford, 1999). By 1906, however, in the aftermath of deculturation policies carried out by the U.S. government, the Cherokee Nation, its reservations, and school system had been destroyed. According to Weinberg (1995):

> The loss of tribal [Cherokee language] schools spelled the end of the widespread bilingual literacy that had distinguished Cherokees in the nineteenth century. In the [English-only] public schools of northeastern Oklahoma the Cherokee children were served poorly. During the thirty-five years or so after 1932 the percentage of Cherokees who could read English well increased only from 38 to 58. The median school grade completed among Cherokees over eighteen years of age rose from third grade in 1933 to fifth grade in 1952 to the second half of the fifth grade in 1963. Should a Cherokee move to one of the cities in Oklahoma ... he [or she] would encounter a population whose median level of school completion was six or more years beyond his. (pp. 222–223)

The attack on Cherokee language and literacy was not motivated by a desire to promote their literacy or their educational achievement. Similarly, Crawford (1992a) maintains that the attack on languages other than English and on bilingual education today is motivated solely by agendas unrelated to effective literacy instruction.

Current research on the effectiveness of bilingual education indicates that it is generally more effective than the sink-or-swim approach if students are put into comparable programs with comparable resources. Federal and state-assisted bilingual education programs, however, reach a fraction of the students who meet the eligibility criteria for such programs. Thus, although it is often assumed that lower rates of academic performance can be blamed on bilingual programs, the burden appears to reside more with the English-only programs that do not provide for native language development.

Assumptions Underlying Scholarly Work

Scholars are not immune to framing issues in terms of the dominant ideology of English monolingualism. Even in academic discussions of literacy, a number of tenuous assumptions have been made about language diversity. In foundational work on this topic, Bhatia (1984) analyzed these and concluded that there are four dominant assumptions about societies that are predominantly monolingual:

> (1) in comparison to multilingual societies, linguistic diversity is negligible in ML [monolingual] societies; (2) the phenomenon of monolingualism has a feeding relationship with literacy, whereas multilingualism induces a bleeding relationship . . .; (3) communication problems are more severe and complex in multilingual than in ML societies . . ., and (4) the linguistic situation is too obvious to warrant any serious language planning in ML societies. (pp. 23–24)

These assumptions have important implications for literacy policy. An underlying theme is that language diversity is a problem rather than a resource (Ruíz, 1984). Most disturbing is the assumption that given the dominance of one language, such as English, the linguistic situation does not require any thoughtful language planning—other than perhaps simply transitioning language minorities into the dominant language. Bhatia (cf. Agnihotri 2007) noted that the linguistic situation in so-called monolingual societies is always more complex than is commonly assumed, because monolingualism in any speech community is a myth and because no speech community "is either linguistically homogeneous or free from variation" (Bhatia, 1984, p. 24; see also Fishman, 1967). The persistence of the myth of monolingualism reflects the dominant relationship of one language over others. It is also perpetuated by attitudes toward dialect and register (i.e., the appropriate level of discourse), whereby one variety of language, the school-taught standard, is seen as being inherently superior to other varieties. Thus, attitudes toward non-English literacy are often tied to negative predispositions toward nonstandard varieties of English.

The emphasis on English monolingualism influences the way in which research questions are formulated by scholars in other ways. For example, if researchers assume that an intergenerational shift from other languages to English is desirable and inevitable, they narrow the range of their research findings by excluding bilingualism. By so doing, they also narrow their research task to one of merely documenting the rate of shift from other languages to English. Veltman (1983, 1999), for example, has made a strong empirical case for the unidirectional shift from other languages toward English. Significantly, he contends that not only is there a general language shift toward English, but also that any movement away from English is so negligible that it is equal to zero. This argument is worth presenting in detail.

> There is almost no in-migration into language groups from the English language group. We are not here referring to the numbers of people from English language backgrounds who learn a minority language. Rather, when we speak of linguistic migration into a language group, we require that a person of English language origin adopt the minority language as his principal language of use. This is a rather stringent test. . . . What is important to understand, however, is that in terms of this definition, there is virtually

no linguistic in-migration into minority language groups. *A high degree of bilingualism in a minority language does not constitute linguistic immigration.* A linguistic immigrant to the Spanish group is someone who becomes Spanish-speaking in the full sense of the term. He is an active participant in the daily life of the Spanish language group, not someone who simply speaks Spanish, however well. (Veltman, 1983, pp. 12–13, emphasis added)

Veltman's definition of language shift is so intentionally "stringent" that the *bi* of bilingualism does not count; determining the extent of bilingualism in society is excluded. As a result, language shift is presented as an either/or phenomenon in which one is either an English-speaking person or a speaker of another language. By virtue of facility in English, one becomes a statistic in the world of English speakers, regardless of his or her facility in other languages. In other words, the research is designed in such a way that bilinguals are treated as if they were English-speaking monolinguals. In reality, however, some bilinguals, despite their facility in English, drift more toward the world of other languages when their spouses, friends, families, and co-workers use these languages more than English. Veltman's more recent work (1999) also follows these assumptions, making a strong case for language shift. Those who fear that English is about to be weakened by foreign language can be encouraged by his arguments, because they support the conclusion that English is in no danger.

Nevertheless, despite general shifts toward English from minority language speakers, language loyalty and maintenance persist (Fishman, 1966, 1980b; 2001). Many factors contribute to language loyalty and maintenance, including economic, political, and personal factors, such as a desire to use language as a means of maintaining one's cultural identity. A monolingual English ideology would seem to support the notion that one can change his or her linguistic membership for whatever reason (e.g., to improve one's economic and social position or to meet the expectations of the majority, dominant, or "host" [from an immigrant perspective] society).

To the extent that language is changeable, the issue becomes one of language choice. However, many factors affect language loyalty. Fishman has argued that "[e]thnic newspapers, radio programs, schools, organizations, and churches are not the chief nurturers of language maintenance in the United States; all these institutions may even decrease in number without greatly influencing American non-English-language maintenance . . ." (1980b, p. 634). More important are "certain central role relationships within the narrower circles (for example, parent-child, cleric-lay) [that] are preserved in the original . . . language alone. These may be (and usually are) the most intimate or emotional relationships" (1980b, p. 634; see also Fishman, 2001). Many factors also need to be considered to explain why languages are maintained, not the least of which are physiological factors related to advanced age[3] or to aphasia that cause some individuals to lose facility in English or cease identifying with and using the language (Wiley, 1986).

Some scholars (see Baker, 2006 for a well-informed review of major second language acquisition theories) have emphasized attitudes (along with other factors) of the language minority groups toward the dominant language as a major factor in language acquisition. What is frequently ignored, however, is the dynamic interaction between language minorities and members of the receiving or dominant society. It is not unusual, for example, for language minority individuals to encounter the irritation of some members of the monolingual English-speaking majority if they are perceived as imperfect speakers and writers of English. This is especially true for adults, because adults are not given the same license as children for deviation from the expected norm. Such encounters with the receiving/dominant society have been found to negatively affect the desire of adults to continue attempting to learn a new language (see Perdue, 1984; Wiley, 2005). This indicates that attitudinal studies on second language and literacy acquisition should concentrate on the interaction between language minorities and the dominant society rather than only on the attitudes of the language minorities, as is typically the case.

Beyond the issues related to the motivation to learn a new language or to maintain one's native language is the issue of language rights. To mandate that speakers of languages other than English should not use or maintain their native languages is in violation of what the United Nations views as a basic human right: that is, the right to use and maintain one's mother tongue. Thus, more is involved than merely whether one *can* change his or her language (Wiley, 2007a). Based on the evidence available, we can conclude that most language minority groups in the United States favor both learning English *and* retaining their ancestral languages. These attitudes tend to promote expanding the language resources of the United States.

Implications for Policy and Practice

To determine the full extent of literacy in the United States, it is necessary to make explicit which language or languages are being discussed (e.g., by referring to *English literacy* as opposed to *literacy*, if only English literacy is in question). Most national literacy estimates in the United States are based solely on English, and this tends to inflate the magnitude of the "literacy crisis." They also stigmatize those who are literate in languages other than English (Wiley, 1991, 2005). Biliteracy, literacy in two languages, likewise has been largely overlooked in most policy discussions despite a large body of scholarship on this topic (e.g., Greenberg, Macías, Rhodes, & Chan, 2001; Hornberger & Hardman, 1994; Kalmar, 1994; Macías 1994; Ramírez, 1992; Spener, 1994; and Wiley, 1991, 2005). The notion of biliteracy implies equal abilities in two (or more) languages; however, it is unlikely that most biliterates have perfectly "balanced" abilities, because, as Valdés (2001) has noted, "While absolutely equivalent abilities in two languages are theoretically possible, individuals seldom have access to two languages in exactly the same contexts." Valdés (2001; see also García, this volume) suggests conceptualizing bilingualism and biliteracy along a continuum of abilities based on the experiences and abilities of bilinguals and biliterates.

Again, even though literacy in languages other than English is rarely surveyed, it is not uncommon. Even in the absence of such surveys, extant data can be manipulated to shed light on literacy in these languages. De Klerk and Wiley

(2008) used the American Community Survey (ACS) 2006 micro data to examine bilingualism among Vietnamese immigrants who had come to the USA at age 12 or older. The ACS dataset contains information about level of oral English fluency, whether a language other than English was spoken at home, education level, age of respondents, and age of arrival in the U.S. Through these variables it was possible to calculate which respondents had received education in Vietnamese, and how many years of such education, before they came to the U.S. This smaller subset of Vietnamese immigrants, identified from the larger ACS, formed the sample for the analysis. Even though the ACS micro data provide no information about literacy in the first language, the subset analysis showed that 91.9 percent of the sample must have some Vietnamese literacy by virtue of having completed at least primary school through the medium of Vietnamese. The ACS and Census questionnaires ask respondents to rate their ability to speak English as: "Very well;" "Well;" "Not well," or "Not at all." Among those in the sample who indicated they did not speak English at all, and spoke Vietnamese at home, 66.8 percent were literate in Vietnamese. The way the Census question is asked foregrounds for the latter group their lack of English oral proficiency, and their oral use of Vietnamese at home. The fact that two-thirds of the "not at all" group have literacy skills remains invisible. Those in the sample who reported they speak only English, and answered "no" to the question, "Do you speak any language other than English at home?" would be considered English monolinguals when using only the existing variables in the survey. However, using the composite variables, it emerges that the vast majority (90.7 percent) of these so-called English monolinguals completed their primary schooling in Vietnamese, and thus must have literacy in Vietnamese, even though they do not speak the language at home. Assuming they have at least some English literacy, this ostensibly English monolingual group is biliterate to a certain degree, and if they used Vietnamese outside the home, could be regarded bilingual/biliterate.

Thus, claims made regarding the extent of "illiteracy" (meaning English non-literacy) among language minorities must be re-evaluated, and the assumption that English literacy is the only literacy that counts must be seen as reflective of the dominant ideology of English monolingualism. Whereas English may be the dominant language in the United States, it does not necessarily follow that English literacy can or does fulfill all the literacy needs of language minority groups (see Klassen & Burnaby, 1993). For the elderly, for recent immigrants, and for those who have lacked opportunities to study English, being able to use their native language provides their most immediate means for social participation. For indigenous peoples, native language literacy provides a means of preserving languages and cultures and reversing language shift (see Fishman, 2001).

The development of literacy in languages other than English also has positive benefits for the majority, monolingual English-speaking population. Over two decades ago, Senator Paul Simon (1988), for example, contended that the United States was at a disadvantage internationally in trade, diplomacy, and national security because it had not further developed its linguistic resources. The situation has not changed (Peyton, Carreira, Wang, & Wiley, 2008), nor will it until we acknowledge the multilingual and multi-literate resources in our midst.

References

Adams, D.W. (1995). *Education for extinction: American Indians and the boarding school experience, 1875–1928.* Lawrence, KS: University of Kansas Press.

Agnihotri, R. (2007). Towards a pedagogical paradigm rooted in multilinguality. *International Multilingual Research Journal* 1(2), 79–88.

Baker, C. (2006). *Foundations of education and bilingualism,* Third Edition. Clevedon, Multilingual Matters.

Bhatia, T.K. (1984). Literacy in monolingual societies. In R.B. Kaplan (Ed.) *Annual review of applied linguistics* (pp. 23–38). Rowley, MA: Newbury House.

Burtoff, M. (1985). *Haitian Creole literacy evaluation study.* Washington, DC: Center for Applied Linguistics.

Center for Applied Linguistics (CAL) (2008). *Education for Adult English Language Learners in the United States: Trends, research, and promising practices* [Electronic version]. Retrieved January 2, 2009, from http://www.cal.org/caelanetwork/pd_resources/AdultESLInstruction.html.

Child, B.J. (1998). *Boarding school seasons: American Indian families, 1900–1940.* Lincoln: University of Nebraska Press.

Cooper, M.L. (1999). *Indian school: Teaching the white man's way.* New York: Clarion Books.

Crawford, J. (1992a). *Hold your tongue: Bilingualism and the politics of "English Only."* Reading, MA: Addison-Wesley.

—— (Ed.). (1992b). *Language loyalties: A source book on the Official English controversy.* Chicago: University of Chicago Press.

—— (1999). *Bilingual education: History, politics, theory, and practice* (4th ed.). Los Angeles: Bilingual Education Services.

—— (2000). *At war with diversity: U.S. language policy in an age of anxiety.* Clevedon, UK: Multilingual Matters.

De Klerk, G., & Wiley, T.G. (2008). Using the American Community Language Survey to investigate bilingualism and biliteracy among immigrant communities. *Journal of Southeast Asian Education and Advancement, 3,* 68–78.

Edelsky, C. (2006). *With literacy and justice for all: Rethinking the social in language and education* (2nd ed.). Mahwah, NJ: Lawrence Erlbaum Associates.

Fishman, J.A. (1966). *Language loyalty in the United States: The maintenance and perpetuation of non-English mother tongues by American ethnic and religious groups.* Berlin: Mouton.

—— (1967). Bilingualism with and without diglossia: Diglossia with and without bilingualism. *Journal of Social Issues, 23*(2), 29–38.

—— (1980a). Ethnocultural dimensions in the acquisition and retention of biliteracy. *Basic Writing, 3*(1), 48–61.

—— (1980b). Language maintenance. In S.T. Thernstrom et al. (Eds.), *Harvard encyclopedia of American ethnic groups* (pp. 629–638). Cambridge: Cambridge University Press.

—— (2001). *Reversing language shift: Theoretical and empirical foundations of assistance to threatened languages.* Philadelphia, PA: Multilingual Matters.

Greenburg, E., Macías, R.F., Rhodes, D., & Chan, T. (2001). *English literacy and language minorities in the United States.* Washington, DC: Center for Educational Statistics, U.S. Department of Education.

Hakuta, K. (1986). *Mirror of language: The debate on bilingualism.* New York: Basic Books.

Hornberger, N.H., & Hardman, J. (1994). Literacy as cultural practice and cognitive skill:

Biliteracy in an ESL class and a GED program. In D. Spener (Ed.), *Adult biliteracy in the United States* (pp. 147–169). Washington, DC and McHenry, IL: Center for Applied Linguistics and Delta Systems.

Kalmar, T.M. (1994). ¿Guariyusei?: Adult biliteracy in its natural habitat. In D. Spener (Ed.), *Adult biliteracy in the United States* (pp. 123–146). Washington, DC and McHenry, IL: Center for Applied Linguistics and Delta Systems.

Klassen, C., & Burnaby, B. (1993). "Those who know:" Views on literacy among adult immigrants in Canada. *TESOL Quarterly, 27,* 377–397.

Kloss, H. (1971). Language rights of immigrant groups. *International Migration Review,* 5, 250–268.

—— (1998). *The American bilingual tradition.* Washington, DC & McHenry, IL: Center for Applied Linguistics & Delta Systems. Reprint. Kloss, H. (1977). *The American bilingual tradition.* Rowley, MA: Newbury House.

Krashen, S.D. (1981). Bilingual education and second language acquisition theory. In California State Department of Education, Office of Bilingual Education (Ed.), *Schooling and language minority students: A theoretical framework* (pp. 51–116). Los Angeles: California State University, Evaluation, Dissemination and Assessment Center.

—— (1996), *Under Attack: The Case for Bilingual Education.* Culver City, CA: Language Education Associates.

Krashen, S., & Biber, D. (1988). *On course: Bilingual education's success in California.* Sacramento, CA: California Association for Bilingual Education.

Leibowitz, A.H. (1971). *Educational policy and political acceptance: The imposition of English as the language of instruction in American schools.* Washington, DC: Center for Applied Linguistics, ERIC Clearinghouse for Linguistics. (ERIC Document Reproduction Service No. ED 047 321)

Lepore, J. (2002). *A is for American: Letters and other characters in the newly United States.* New York: Alfred Knopf.

Luebke, F.C. (1980). Legal restrictions on foreign languages in the Great Plains states, 1917–1923. In P. Schach (Ed.) *Languages in conflict: Linguistic acculturation on the Great Plains,* pp. 1–19. Lincoln, NE: University of Nebraska Press.

Macías, R.F. (1990). Definitions of literacy: A response. In R.L. Venezky, D.A. Wagner, & B.S. Ciliberti (Eds.), *Toward defining literacy* (pp. 17–23). Newark, DE: International Reading Association.

—— (1994). Inheriting sins while seeking absolution: Language diversity and national statistical data sets. In D. Spener (Ed.), *Adult biliteracy in the United States* (pp. 15–45). Washington, DC and McHenry, IL: Center for Applied Linguistics and Delta Systems.

—— (1999). The flowering of America. In S.L. McKay & S.C. Wong (Eds.), *New immigrants in the United States* (pp. 11–57). Cambridge: Cambridge University Press.

McArthur, E.K. (1993). *Language characteristics and schooling in the United States: A changing picture: 1979–1989.* Washington, DC: U.S. Department of Education, Office of Educational Research and Improvement, National Center for Educational Statistics. (NCES Report 93–699).

Meléndez, W.A. (1990). *Native language instruction: An approach to combat illiteracy among language minority communities.* Research report. Sacramento, CA: California Literacy Task Force.

Merino, B.J., & Lyons, J. (1990). The effectiveness of a model bilingual program: A longitudinal analysis. *CPS Brief, 2*(3), 1–5.

Molesky, J. (1988). Understanding the American linguistic mosaic: A historical overview of language maintenance and language shift. In S.L. McKay & S.C. Wong (Eds.), *Language diversity: Problem or resource* (pp. 29–68). Cambridge, MA: Newbury House.

Norgren, J., & Nanda, S. (1988). *American cultural pluralism and the law*. New York: Praeger.

Ovando, C.J., & Wiley, T.G. (2007). Language education in the conflicted United States. In R. Joshee & L. Johnson (Eds.). *Multicultural education policies in Canada and the United States: Symbol and substance* (pp. 107–119). Vancouver, BC: University of British Columbia Press. Reprint.

Perdue, C. (Ed.). (1984). *Second language acquisition by adult immigrants: A field manual*. Rowley, MA: Newbury House.

Pew Hispanic Center/Kaiser Family Foundation (2004). *National Survey of Latinos: Education*. Washington, DC: Pew Hispanic Center and The Henry J. Kaiser Family Foundation.

Peyton, J.K., Carreira, M., Wang, S., & Wiley, T.G. (2008). Heritage language education in the United States: A need to reconceptualize and restructure. In K.A. King, N. Schilling-Estes, L.W. Fogle, J.J. Lou, & B. Soukup (Eds.), *Sustaining linguistic diversity: Endangered and minority languages and language varieties*. Washington, DC: Georgetown University Press.

Pitt, L. (1976). *We Americans. Vol I. Colonial times to 1877*. Glenview, IL: Scott Foresman.

Pomerantz, A. (2002). Language ideologies and the production of identities: Spanish as a resource for participation in a multilingual marketplace. *Multilingua, 21*, 275–302.

Quezada, M.S., Wiley, T.G., & Ramírez, D. (2002). How the reform agenda shortchanges English learners. In E.W. Stevens & G.H. Wood (Eds.), *Justice, ideology, and education: An introduction to the social foundations of education*, pp. 104–109. 4th Edition. New York: McGraw-Hill. Reprint.

Ramírez, J.D. (1992). Executive summary. *Bilingual Research Journal, 16*(1–2), 1–62.

Ricento, T., & Wiley, T.G. (2002). Introduction: Language, identity, and education and the challenges of monoculturalism and globalization. *Journal of Language, Identity, and Education, 1*(1), 1–5.

Robson, B. (1982). Hmong literacy, formal education, and their effects on performance in an ESL class. In B.T. Downing & D.P. Olney (Eds.), *The Hmong in the West* (pp. 201–225). Minneapolis: University of Minnesota, Center for Urban and Regional Affairs.

Ruíz, R. (1984). Orientations in language planning. *NABE Journal 8*:2, 15–34.

Simon, P. (1988). *The tongue-tied American* (2nd ed.). New York: Continuum.

Simpson, D. (1986). *The politics of American English, 1776–1850*. New York: Oxford University Press.

Singleton, D. (1989). *Language acquisition: The age factor*. Philadelphia, PA: Multilingual Matters.

Spener, D. (Ed.). (1994). *Adult biliteracy in the United States*. Washington, DC and McHenry, IL: Center for Applied Linguistics and Delta Systems.

Spring, J. (1994). *Deculturalization and the struggle for equality: A brief history of the education of dominated cultures in the United States*. New York: McGraw-Hill.

Troike, R.C. (1978). Research evidence for the effectiveness of bilingual education. *NABE Journal, 3*(1), 13–24.

Tse, L. (2001). *"Why don't they learn English?" Separating fact from fallacy in the U.S. Language debate*. New York: Teachers College Press.

Tucker, J.T. (2006). Waiting Times for Adult ESL Classes and the Impact on English Learners. NALEO. Educational Fund.

Valdés, G. (2001). Heritage language students: Profiles and possibilities. In J.K. Peyton, D.A. Ranard, & S. McGinnis (Eds.), *Heritage languages in America: Preserving a National Resource*. Washington, DC: Center for Applied Linguistics.

Vargas, A. (1986). *Illiteracy in the Hispanic community*. Washington, DC: National Council of La Raza.

Veltman, C. (1983). *Language shift in the United States.* Berlin: Mouton.

—— (1999). The American linguistic mosaic. In McKay & Wong (Eds.), *New immigrants in the United States* (pp. 58–93). Cambridge: Cambridge University Press.

Weinberg, M. (1995). *A chance to learn: A history of race and education in the United States* (2nd ed.). Long Beach, CA: California State University Press.

Weiss, B.J. (Ed.). (1982). *Education and the European immigrant: 1840–1940.* Champaign/Urbana, IL: University of Illinois Press.

Wiley, T.G. (1986). The significance of language and cultural barriers for the Euro-American elderly. In C. Hayes, R.A. Kalish, & D. Guttman (Eds.), *The Euro-American elderly: A guide to practice* (pp. 35–50). New York: Springer.

—— (1988). *Literacy, biliteracy, and educational achievement among the Mexican-origin population in the United States.* Unpublished doctoral dissertation, University of Southern California, Los Angeles.

—— (1991). *Measuring the nation's literacy: Important considerations.* ERIC Digest. Washington, DC: National Clearinghouse on Literacy Education. (ERIC Document Reproduction Service No. ED 334 870)

—— (1998). The imposition of World War I era English-Only policies and the fate of German in North America. In T. Ricento & B. Burnaby (Eds.), *Language politics in the United States and Canada: Myths and realities* (pp. 211–241).

—— (2002). Biliteracy. In B. Guzzetti (Ed.), *Literacy in America: An encyclopedia: An encyclopedia of history, theory, and practice* (pp. 57–60). Santa Barbara: ABC-CLIO Publishers.

—— (2004). Language policy and English-only. In E. Finegan & J.R. Rickford (Eds.), *Language in the USA: Perspectives for the twenty-first century.* Cambridge: Cambridge University Press.

—— (2005). *Literacy and language diversity in the United States.* Washington, DC & McHenry, IL: Center for Applied Linguistics & Delta Systems.

—— (2007a). Accessing language rights in education: A brief history of the U.S. context. In O. Garcia & C. Baker (Eds.). *Bilingual education An introductory reader* (pp. 89–109). Clevedon, U.K.: Multilingual Matters.

—— (2007b). Immigrant minorities: USA. In M. Hellinger & A. Pauwels (Eds.), *Handbooks of applied linguistics, Vol. 9: Language and communication: Diversity and change* (53–85). Berlin: Mouton de Gruyter.

Wyman, M. (1993). *Round-trip to Europe: The immigrants return to Europe, 1880–1930.* Ithaca, NY: Cornell University Press.

3 Language, Education, and Literacy in a Mexican Transnational Community[1]

Marcia Farr

Chicago is often called an archetypal U.S. city, given its location in the Midwest and its history as a place to which multitudes of migrants headed for ambition and "self-making" (Spears, 2005, p. 8). This history is notable for its multilingualism (Farr, 2008a), even as *Checagou* when Native Americans used Ojibway as a trading language, before 1760 when Europeans and Africans began to arrive (and the Haitian Jean Baptiste Point du Sable, of both French and African origin, founded Chicago). The city grew as a trading center, and then with industrialization became a magnet both for domestic migrants and for very large numbers of Europeans during the latter half of the nineteenth and the early twentieth centuries. Over the course of the twentieth century, especially during its final decades, immigrants from Asia and Latin America, in fact from all over the world, came to Chicago to work. Today Chicago is a vibrant urban center of about three million people with extensive multilingualism (and multiliteracy). Although English is by far the most dominant language, adopted by ethnic communities over the generations, the living presence of other languages is notable in homes, churches, stores, and other workplaces, as well as on radio and television stations, in newspapers, and on neighborhood signs.

By far the largest contemporary ethnic community is that of Mexicans, who comprise about two-thirds of those of Latin American origin and who themselves comprise about one million people in the multi-county Chicago area according to the 2000 Census (Farr, 2006). This relative percentage of those of Mexican origin parallels that of the larger U.S., although Chicago is unusual in that it simultaneously is characterized by other groups of Spanish speakers of Puerto Rican, Cuban, Central and South American origins. Thus not only does English show variation across populations in Chicago (e.g., African Americans, Appalachians, and northern Euro-Americans), so does Spanish, although for demographic reasons Mexican Spanish is dominant. In spite of these linguistic realities, however, the language ideologies of purism and standardization (see Introduction to this volume) denigrate all varieties of these languages except "standard" English and Spanish, at least in school. Vernacular language, however, lives on at sports events ("Da Bulls") and elsewhere.

In this chapter I explore such language practices among a social network of Mexican families in Chicago with close ties to its village of origin in Michoacán, Mexico. I also provide an overview of their educational attitudes and achievement and discuss their literacy practices. Such research-based understandings can facilitate efforts to improve education for this population, especially since understanding a group can improve attitudes toward them. Ideally, recognizing the creative language abilities characteristic of particular populations enables teachers and other educators to build on the group's strengths and to adapt instruction appropriately to make it more effective (Zentella, 2005). Domínguez Barajas (2002), for example, argues that proverbs, an oral language tradition found in many cultural groups, can be used effectively to teach academic writing. Before describing the language, educational, and literacy practices of this group, however, I first provide a brief description of this transnational community, both in terms of the two places in which they live and in terms of the people themselves.

A Transnational Community

Radio announcers on a Spanish-speaking station in the Chicago area ask those who call in: "Where are you calling from?" If the caller responds with "Chicago" (or another town or suburb in the metropolitan Chicago area), the announcer then asks, "Where are you from in Mexico?" If the caller replies "Michoacán," as is frequently the case, the announcer gleefully shouts, "¡Bueno! Y en Chicago, Michoacán, ¿qual manda?" (OK! And in Chicago, Michoacán, what [station] rules?), to which the caller is expected to answer, "¡La Ley manda!" (The Law rules!). La Ley, the most expressively ranchero[2] Mexican FM station in the Chicago area, names itself playfully: "The Law" refers both to the top billing that the station claims for itself and to U.S. law enforcement, a troubling presence for migrants living in Chicago without legal papers. By appropriating this source of trouble as the very name of the station, the announcers, and by extension their listeners, enact a typically ranchero assertive stance by joking about potential danger. This stance, enacted by men but also women, is notably assertive and authoritative. Many well-worn phrases in Mexican Spanish personify "the law" and use the verb *mandar* to invoke authority, for example, that of parents (particularly fathers) within the home: "¿Quien manda aquí?" (Who rules around here?). Such hierarchical authority is characteristic of traditional Mexican society, which valorizes social order through a code of *respeto*, the verbal and non-verbal demonstration of respect for other persons and the roles they inhabit (Valdés, 1996). The radio routine thus echoes the authority evoked by *mandar*, and this is repeated many times each day, which entertains and then becomes ingrained in the minds of thousands of listeners.

What is taken for granted in this routine is the cohesiveness of Chicago and Michoacán. The announcer seamlessly blends two distant places, each one far from the national border that separates Mexico and the United States. Figure 3.1 illustrates the transnational circuit of the social network of Mexican families described in detail in Farr (2006) that provide the focus of this chapter. The discussion of language, education, and literacy within these families is based on a long-term transnational ethnography based in Chicago and in their village of origin (their rancho) in Michoacán, Mexico. A social network—a unit of analysis developed within anthropology and put to use in the study of naturally occurring

Figure 3.1 The Route from Chicago, Illinois, to San Juanico, Michoacán.

language (Milroy 1987)—is a group of individuals who are in close interaction on a frequent basis. Here it refers to a group of families organized around nine siblings (now grandparents) who began to migrate to Chicago in 1964 from their rancho in northwestern Michoacán, a state in western Mexico.

These families constitute part of what has been called a transnational community (Schiller, Basch, & Blanc-Szanton, 1992), which lives on both sides of a nation-state border and maintains social, economic, political, and emotional ties that extend across that border. I add another aspect to this definition, however: the discourse of people on both sides of the border is filled with references to people and places on the other side, a concrete verbal indication that this is indeed a transnational community. Daily talk, whether in Chicago or in the rancho, is peopled with those on the end of the migrant circuit; such talk reinforces the social bonds that include all those within the transnational community, whether they are in Chicago or in Mexico at the time. The radio routine's verbal blending of two locations thus accurately depicts the on-the-ground experiences of daily living in transnational social fields that characterize migrants' lives.

Description of Transnational Sites

Chicago is evident everywhere in the rancho: English print, with references to specific institutions (the Bulls basketball team, construction companies, television channels and radio stations, and restaurants), is omnipresent on clothing, ashtrays, dishes, and calendars. Many houses have a pickup truck parked in front, usually with Illinois plates; one truck in particular exhibited a decal in the rear window depicting a Chicago winter complete with falling snow—in jarring contrast to the dry sunny climate in which the pickup sat. Although ranchos are not planned towns but small settlements that grew around the fields residents cultivated, in the last two decades people in the rancho and in Chicago collaborated on urban planning. They built an official entrance to the rancho; they paved more of the main road (with *topes* or speed bumps to slow cars down); and, like many other transnational Mexican communities during the 1990s, they constructed a plaza, an icon of urbanity and modern (Mexican) life.

Houses lining the mostly unpaved roads of the rancho vary dramatically: a few are still small unpainted adobe huts with outhouses, but many others are brightly painted, with indoor bathrooms, screened-in kitchens, and extra bedrooms added. Yet other houses are in various stages of construction, as their owners labor in Chicago for money to complete the house. A few homes rival suburban U.S. houses in conveniences and attractive decor, with brightly tiled kitchens and elegant hardwood cabinets, china closets, and furniture filled with *artesanías* (Mexican crafts). Additionally, many houses in the rancho have *parabólicas* (satellite dishes) on their roofs that bring in national and international television programs. Virtually all these signs of prosperity have resulted from dollars earned in the U.S.

If Chicago is endemic in the rancho, the rancho is also endemic in Chicago. People fill the streets of Mexican neighborhoods in Chicago dressed as they would be in western Mexico: men with cowboy hats, embroidered belts, tight jeans, and mustaches; women with *rebozos* (large Mexican shawls with embroidered ends) tightly wrapped around themselves and the young children they carry in them, as protection from the early morning chill. In the Mexican neighborhood of Pilsen, children attend elementary school clad in Mexican-style school uniforms (navy blue skirts or pants and light blue shirts). Mexican music spills out on to sidewalks from nearby stores, and pedestrians cross themselves as they pass Catholic churches named for European saints that now have shrines to the Virgin of Guadalupe, Mexico's patron saint. Mexican street vendors sell *atole* (a corn-based drink) and *elote* (chili-sprinkled corn on the cob), just as they do in Mexico, as well as frozen popsicles (*paletas*), an industry built by ranchero settlements slightly to the west of the rancho in this study (Quinones, 2001). Mexican bakeries and grocery stores advertise Mexican foods, dry cleaners announce themselves as *tintorerías*, and bars (*cantinas*) sport Mexican names or have biliterate signs: *Tenemos vía Satellite* (We have satellite TV). Thus have transnational migrants transformed both western Mexico and Chicago, imprinting themselves and their practices on the built environments.

Description of Social Network

This dense and multiplex social network (Milroy, 1987) is based on multiple connections among families during the past three centuries in the micro-region in Michoacán in which the rancho is located. Interaction within the network, not so long ago within the context of a face-to-face agrarian society, is frequent; and people within the network tend to turn to each other for information, knowledge, and advice bearing on specific problems and situations. Examples of such resource sharing involve language and literacy (high school and college students in Chicago are called upon to deal with letters in English from U.S. institutions), financing (a number of people collaborate to lend home-buyers the money necessary for the purchase), and job-seeking (brothers from Mexico were sent for to fill jobs in railroad construction where original migrants worked).

Interconnections between individuals are based primarily on kinship, of both the genetic and ritual type (*compadrazgo*); people are aunts, uncles, nieces, nephews, and cousins, as well as *ahijado/as* (godsons/daughters) and *comadres* and *compadres* (literally co-mothers and co-fathers) to each other. *Comadres* and *compadres* are more important than godparents in non-Latino U.S. society, since *compadrazgo* emphasizes not only the relationship with the child for whom one has been chosen to be a godparent but also and especially the relationship with the child's parents, with whom one now has a special tie. Since these godparents are chosen for three to four ritual occasions over the life span—baptism, first communion, confirmation (sometimes now omitted), and marriage—there are multiple opportunities to celebrate and reinforce social ties within the network.

Beyond kinship and *compadrazgo* relations, network members relate as friends and as co-workers; the older generation especially, most of whom are now retired in Mexico, worked and socialized together, and age-equivalent cousins tend to be "best friends." Thus network members form much of the fabric of each other's lives. These multiple interconnections provide a safety net, which they prefer to rely on rather than public welfare, a practice that also was noted among early Mexican migrants in Chicago (Kerr, 1976).

Even though members of generations two and three increasingly interact with people outside the network at school and at work, they nevertheless continue to participate actively in the network, including attending family events, which they sometimes organize themselves. Moreover, they communicate with each other by e-mail and instant messaging, from Mexico or Chicago (those without computers in the rancho access the Internet in the nearby township center). This underscores the continuing importance of the extended family (*la familia*) even within a context of increasing participation in U.S. social practices over the generations.

Although work and school are the most likely places for interacting with those outside of the social network and, in Chicago, with non-Mexicans, this is not as common as might be expected. As Guerra (1998) has argued, rather than deeply experiencing "contact zones" (Pratt, 1991), members of this social network, especially the adults, are grounded in a "home front." This home front is due both to Chicago's segregated ethnic neighborhoods and to demographics that continually refresh Mexican cultural practices in Chicago (Kerr, 1984). Thus much interaction is with each other (or with other rancheros from western Mexico), rather than with out-group members such as African Americans or European Americans or even other Spanish-speakers such as Puerto Ricans. Most marriages, for example, are within the community, or with people from similar backgrounds (from western Mexico) encountered in Chicago. A few marriages, however, are with Chicago Latinos (e.g., a young man with Puerto Rican, Mexican, and Italian heritage), Italian Americans, and Polish Americans.

Work and Gender

Rancheros define work itself as hard, physical labor, preferably for oneself, not for a boss (Barragán, 1990). For most of the first generation, work in Chicago was a means to an end: supporting their families and accumulating enough money to live comfortably (and with self-sufficiency) in Mexico. They work hard at these jobs, but the characteristically independent spirit of rancheros often puts the jobs in second place after personal and familial desires and decisions—for example, to return to Mexico to live (without salaried labor). At both ends of the migrant circuit, all family members contribute to economic projects and goals, as was usual in their traditional economy of subsistence agriculture. With the transformation of the rancho's economy to commercial agriculture and the move to industrial jobs in Chicago, however, new work patterns emerged with significant implications for gender. Work-related gender patterns, in turn, have significant implications for education, as I discuss later in this chapter.

Masculinity continues to be largely constructed through work, although a strong work ethic, especially regarding physical labor, pervades a sense of personhood for ranchero men, women, and even children. Many first and some second generation women in the network work with each other in Chicago at poultry-processing plants, printing companies, glass-painting and other factories, and catalog warehouses. Young women with high school diplomas or GEDs (General Equivalency Diplomas) work as aides in schools and health clinics in the neighborhood or as clerks in nearby offices. Most first and some second generation men work (often with each other) on *el traque* (the track), either for railroad construction companies that build and repair tracks or for the city transit system; many others work for general construction (or demolition) companies; and a very few work in restaurants.

In agrarian Mexico masculinity is closely associated with going to *el labor* (literally "work" but meaning the fields) (Alonso, 1995). With the move to industrial employment, manliness is linked to the dignity and respect that men are accorded for the wage-earning jobs that support their families, especially if these jobs require "strength, courage, and endurance" (Vargas, 1993, p. 42). Men in this network are proud of doing demanding, even dangerous, jobs that can pose serious risks to their health and welfare. Part of a man's sense of self-worth depends on the ability to provide total familial support, so that wives do not leave the home to work. With some difficulty, however, husbands accepted their wives' working outside the home, at times out of necessity but at other times simply as part of the larger family goal of earning as much money as possible. Women often do not want to relinquish their own incomes, and in Chicago virtually everyone works for wages, even married women and teenaged (and older) sons and daughters, who manage jobs while attending school or university. Yet within the second generation in Chicago, some women stay home to raise the children, if finances allow it, reducing the tensions inherent in managing the family and household while working at often unsatisfying jobs outside the home.

In the rancho, most married women work only within their own households, cooking, cleaning, and washing clothes as well as tending smaller animals and gardens and even helping out in the avocado fields when necessary. Young single women, widows, and occasionally married women, however, now work in the packing plants that were established during the 1990s. This work pays well in the Mexican economy, and teenaged girls are eager to enter this labor force in order to have their own money. Although the hours are long and intense during peak packing seasons (and would be unacceptable to U.S. unions), many young women consider this work easier than helping out in the avocado *huertas* (orchards) that their families own. The difference, of course, is that this work earns them their own money, which has inevitable implications for gender relations (see Mummert, 1994), as women partially or fully fill the traditionally male role of providing economically for the family. Whereas women think that helping out in the household justifies their working outside the home, men often assume the women are working for their own personal betterment, not for the family. The individualist ethos of the rancho, however, concedes that even women have some right to money earned: *cada quien su dinero* (to each his/her money), as one man put it.

With this brief description of the social network and the two sites of their transnational lives, I now focus on a central aspect of their culture: the use of inventive and resourceful daily talk filled with a variety of oral genres. Following this discussion of oral language practices, I provide an overview of education within the network from a transnational perspective. I end the chapter with a brief discussion of the literacy practices embedded in their daily activities, focusing in particular on the practice of religious literacy.

Language: Rhetoric, Poetics, and Dialect

Families of this social network, like other Mexican-origin populations, enjoy and esteem language competence (Briggs, 1988; Limón, 1992, 1994). In particular, rhetorical abilities that include persuasiveness, expressiveness, grace, and wit are highly valued (Farr, 1993). Although a primary framework for speech (Goffman, 1974) involves being quite direct, playful uses of language also have an important place in their lives.

Serious or "regular" talk calls for *franqueza*, a style of speech that is frank, candid, and direct, expressed in frequent direct questions and directives (Farr, 2005a). During my fieldwork I was frequently surprised by direct questions addressed to me by men, women, and even children. Once in the rancho a young boy asked me in front of his family if I liked it better staying with them or where I had moved (I had to think quickly to answer tactfully); on another occasion a woman confronted me in front of her family, saying that she was sensitive about my having been in the rancho for several days without visiting her, while her husband interrogated me with "¡¿Por qué tú no has venido?!" (Why haven't you come?!).

Such unadorned and direct speech is complemented, however, by indirect playful speech. That is, in contrast to the primary framework of straightforward serious talk, much other talk is framed as "play." Being *un/a hablador/a* (a skilled speaker) sometimes connotes being "boastful," but it also invokes the entertainment value associated with good tellers of stories, jokes, and other genres. People routinely engage in wordplay, often through *doble sentido* (double meaning, one of which can be sexual). For example, Bernardo, a man in the rancho, used wordplay to tease someone coming into his home. Instead of saying the expected, "Pásale sin pena" (literally, Come in without embarrassment or Please do come in), he said, "Pásale sin vergüenza" (literally the same meaning, with *vergüenza* replacing *pena*). The humor here relies on ambiguity (revealed in intonation): his utterance could be heard not as the two-word adverbial phrase *sin vergüenza* (without shame) but as the one-word noun *sinvergüenza* (a person who is shameless). Another example of such wordplay occurred in Chicago, when Santiago recounted a conversation that took place in his amnesty class at the local community center: "El maestro de nosotros nos dijo que los frijoles engordan" (Our teacher told us that beans fatten). He continued: "Pues una señora allí dijo, 'No maestro, los frijoles no engordan,' dice, 'los que engordamos somos nosotros' " (Then a woman there said, "No, teacher, beans don't fatten," she says, "those who fatten are us").

Playing with language, in fact talking itself, is so important that one woman complained about her niece's home in Chicago, where they "didn't even talk anymore, but just watched television." The first generation of this network, of course, grew up without television in the rancho, where genre-filled talk passed leisure time pleasurably. Such talk fulfills important social functions, entertaining, sanctioning, and knitting people together through the shared valuing of such linguistic abilities.

Many oral genres are favored by these families: *dichos* (sayings), *refranes* (proverbs), *chistes* (jokes), *cuentos* (stories), *adivinanzas* (riddles), and especially *anécdotas* (personal anecdotes). All of these genres evidence an emphasis on poetics (Farr, 1994b). That is, as these men and women generate these genres in their daily talk, they foreground the aesthetic potential of language (Bauman, 1986; Hymes, 1981; Sherzer, 2002; Tannen, 1989; Tedlock, 1983). Jakobson (1960) noted that the fundamental principle underlying the poetic function is "equivalence," abundantly illustrated through the repetition and parallelism deployed in the oral genres that enliven daily speech within this network. An example of such poetic patterning is illustrated in a personal narrative told by a young woman in

Chicago. In this story, she justifies herself to her peers for allowing her mother to take her newborn child back to Mexico with her (where she and the young mother's father were retired). Her mother's concern was the welfare of the child while being taken care of by others when the young mother was at work. As the young woman uses reported speech to quote her mother's persuasive words, she structures them as a "constructed dialogue" (Tannen, 1989) replete with parallelism in intonation and syntax, measured by the repetition of the connective *y* (and) between lines:

[weepy, complaining tone]	[weepy, complaining tone]
"¿QUIÉN se la va a cuidar?"	"WHO is going to care for her?"
y	and
"¡NO me le van a dar de comer!"	"They are NOT going to feed her [for me]!"
y	and
"¡ME la van a hacer llorar!"	"They're going to make her cry!"
y	and
"¿QUÉ, MIRA, qué si me le pegan ahora?"	"LOOK, what if they hit her?"
[laughter]	[laughter]

In this excerpt from her longer story, the young woman repeats the same intonation pattern in each line, followed by a slight pause, and she structures her mother's alleged words into the same repeated syntactic pattern. (Cleverly, the mother is represented as using Spanish syntax to insert herself [*me* in the last three questions] into the repeated clauses, implicitly laying claim to the baby as hers as well as the young mother's.) The young mother builds to a climax in her story by repeating and strengthening the rhythmic pattern of each line: the words in capitals at the beginning of each line indicate their higher pitch and heavier stress relative to the rest of the words in each line. The final line lengthens this initial emphasized stress and pitch into two words rather than the one of the previous three lines, possibly signaling the end of this mini-story to her hearers, who time their laughter perfectly with the end of her story. Thus a story that could have been told quite prosaically is instead structured poetically, both to entertain and to garner sympathy and support from her immediate audience by detailing the considerable pressure on her that led to her decision to let her mother take her child to Mexico. Such poetic structuring within narratives is frequent within these families, although some individuals are better at such storytelling than others.

Other genres commonly used in daily speech, the *adivinanza* (riddle), the *refrán* (proverb), and the *dicho* (saying), are traditional oral texts also constructed with poetic patterning. For example, on a Sunday afternoon at one young family's home in Chicago the young husband, Gabriel, hustled back and forth, going about the carpentry, tiling, and plumbing tasks that were part of his plan to improve their house by adding on apartments for relatives to rent. The rest of us, including several visiting young families, sat in the living room chatting. Once, as the young husband passed through, a visiting young mother teased him with a *dicho: A todo le hace y a nada le pega* (Jack of all trades, master of none). As everyone laughed, his wife's cousin Beatriz defended him, "Sí, hizo una cosa muy buena! Nació Belén!" (Yes, he did one thing very well! Belen [his daughter] was born!). Even more, and more delighted, laughter followed this playful use of *doble sentido*.

Many other times, such as at breakfast in the rancho or during dinner preparations in Chicago, people initiated such speech play, sometimes at the arrival of a third person (in addition to me and one other woman). On these occasions, the very presence of a third person seemed to reframe the situation as an opportunity for playful language: the new arrival was immediately challenged with a riddle to solve, or was teased and responded with a joke, riddle, or proverb. One time the new arrival was teased about a *novio* (boyfriend), and she responded with "¡Pasión de minga!" (minga passion [*minga* is a vulgar word for penis, here meaning sexual arousal]). When I asked what *minga* meant, the teaser and teased together chanted rhythmically, "¿Por qué minga? [pause] ¡Porque no mata pero sí chinga!" (Why minga? Because it won't kill you, but it certainly screws you up!). The wordplay relied on the sound parallels of *mata* and *chinga* with *minga*: the first sound of *mata* combined with the *-inga* of *minga* rhymes with *chinga*. The sexual connotations of both *minga* and *chinga* (from the well-known Mexican verb *chingar*, literally to have intercourse, but metaphorically to screw) create a message that a relationship leading only to sexual arousal won't kill you but will leave you messed up. The entire speech play not only commingled words but was structured poetically, utilizing rhyme and a measured rhythm.

Equally frequently people weave proverbs and other sayings into more serious conversation, performing a variety of functions. Proverbs and other sayings always carry a poetic function, for they are structured according to poetic features, such as metrical rhythm, rhyme, and the "regular reiteration of equivalent units" (Jakobson, 1960, p. 358). In addition to a poetic function, however, particular instances serve other functions as well.

Domínguez Barajas (2002) explores four uses of proverbs in the daily speech of Mexican transmigrants: censuring, teaching, uniting, and entertaining. Within these families *refranes* and *dichos* also are used in these ways. For example, I was aroused from bed by a young woman late one morning in Mexico (and censured) with "¡La vida es más bonita cuando se levanta temprano! ¡No sea floja!" (Life is more beautiful when one rises early! Don't be lazy!). Her brother later that day intoned, "La vida enseña más que la escuela" (Life teaches more than school does), as moral commentary on the importance of practical knowledge (a proverb uttered frequently by different people in the network). Others in the network supported me in Chicago at times of personal difficulty with "Uno debe tener valor y fe para seguir adelante" (One must have courage and faith to continue moving forward) and "Mientras que tengas esperanza puedes lograr todo" (When you have hope you can achieve anything) or "Querer es poder" (Where there's a will, there's a way). Once during conversation after a meal in Mexico, a woman and her elderly mother commented that I was *muy católica* (very Catholic), presumably because I went to church with them and took communion. I demurred, saying, well, not very Catholic but more or less, to which they nodded and responded: "Ni mucho que queme al santo ni tanto que no le alumbre"

(Not so much that you burn the saint but enough to illuminate him or her, using the metaphor of lighting a candle in church). In other words, I was not overly religious, but I was religious enough.

A final example of proverb use followed the ill-considered, and regretted, purchase of a car by a woman in the rancho. With $1,000 sent by her son from Chicago, she bought the car in a nearby town. After men in the rancho pointed out that the car was a "gas guzzler" and that she should have bought a smaller, more economical car, she became very anxious. (She eventually returned the car for a promise of her returned money, but she never received the money.) She then turned to her brother for advice, and he used a *dicho* to reassure her and calm her nerves: *El dinero va y viene, la vida no* (Money comes and goes, life doesn't), followed with *Tenemos una vida* (We have one life, i.e., life is worth more than money).

This brief description of poetic genres in the daily speech of this network indicates the frequency with which they are used, the verbal creativity of those who weave these genres into their talk, and the high regard that network members have for those who excel in such verbal art. This propensity for, and valuing of, artistic and playful language stands in stark contrast to the school-taught language ideology of purism that denigrates the dialect of rural Mexican Spanish in which these genres are expressed.

The most socially marked features of ranchero dialect may be remnants of an archaic colonial Spanish "formed in the New World during the sixteenth century" (Santa Ana & Parodi, 1998, pp. 35–36) out of the leveling of several peninsular dialects brought from Spain (Parodi, 1995). Archaic usages such as *fui/fue > jui/ jue, naiden, asina/ansina*, and *haiga*, as well as archaic verb forms such as *ser > semos, traer > truje, trujiste, trujo, trujimos, trujeron*, and *ver > vía* (Cárdenas, 1967), are viewed pejoratively as rustic and uneducated, and socially marked by the larger Mexican society as ranchero. Although members of the younger generations do sometimes use such features in their speech, they also more frequently articulate a language ideology of purism, which they learned through formal schooling, either in Mexico or in the United States. Thus they believe that there is a "correct" way to talk (either Spanish or English), and any deviations from this are "incorrect" (see also Zentella, 1997).

People experience this dominant linguistic ideology both in Mexico and the U.S. For example, a Spanish teacher (born in Argentina) at a heavily Mexican public high school in Chicago denigrated a young (second generation) man's use of these linguistic features as *su español ranchereado* (your ranchero Spanish) and believed it his mission to "improve" his students' Spanish by insisting that they avoid these features in favor of their standard counterparts. An elderly woman in the rancho, however, commented to me on the topic of ranchero Spanish: "¡Dice que somos mochos, pero nos comunicamos!" (They say that we are "mochos" [don't speak properly and cut off our words], but we communicate with each other!). Yet her daughter and granddaughter (both of whom finished *preparatoria* or high school in Mexico) regularly corrected their relatively unschooled father and husband's use of *semos* for the standard *somos* (we are) and *venemos* for the standard *venimos* (we come).

Thus the abundantly creative and skillful uses of oral language that I have described in this chapter are overshadowed by a purist language ideology learned in school. Modern schooling, whether in Mexico or the U.S., teaches that language with such vernacular features (whether it is Spanish or English) is incorrect (not simply different). As much research has shown (e.g., Wolfram & Schilling-Estes, 2006), such vernacular dialects are fully-formed linguistic systems, yet their speakers are placed at a distinct disadvantage in school (Adger, Wolfram, & Christian, 2007). Unfortunately, the children of these transnational migrants face such obstacles in two languages, since both their Spanish and their English is vernacular. In the next section I discuss education more broadly among these families from a transnational perspective.

Education

Educación carries broader meanings than the English word "education" and is distinguished from the more focused term *enseñanza* (teaching). *Educación* includes raising children to behave well in terms of manners and morals (see Valdés, 1996, p. 125), whereas *enseñanza* refers to direct teaching and usually to formal schooling. People from the rancho, then, can be *bien educado* (well brought up) even when they have little or no schooling. Parents, and other relatives, teach children proper behavior with *consejos*, "spontaneous homilies designed to influence behaviors and attitudes" (Valdés, 1996, p. 125), proverbs, and traditional sayings. For example, one mother in Mexico supported her husband's restriction of their teenaged daughter's mobility at night with a proverb: "Más sabe el diablo por viejo que por diablo" (The devil knows more from being old than from being the devil), adding, "Tu papá tiene más años" (your father is older [and wiser]).

The rancho now has federal schools at the preschool (*pre-escolar*) and elementary (*primaria*) levels, the former for children over four years old and the latter for grades 1 to 6. A government *secundaria* (grades 7–9) is located on the outskirts of the nearby township center, a short bus ride from the rancho. Those who continue their schooling into *preparatoria* (grades 10–12) must take longer bus rides (thirty minutes or more) to nearby towns, unless they want to attend an agricultural high school about 15 minutes away by bus. In addition to government schools, there are private schools (*colegios*) in nearby towns which some children from the rancho, especially those with U.S. dollars, attend. Since schooling has only been available in the rancho since 1940, older members of the network have had limited exposure to it. People from the rancho began to petition the government for a teacher around 1937, and the first one arrived three years later. A succession of teachers taught out of their houses for five centavos a week (virtually pennies, even at that time). Yet even at this price, many could not afford to go to school, and others who had to help their families in the fields were unable to attend. Even when a public school was built in the 1950s (which at first had only one to two grade levels), some students only attended a few months a year, when they were not needed at home or in the fields. The current school was authorized by the Secretariat of Public Education (SEP) in 1973.

In spite of the lack of educational opportunity, most people in the rancho know how to read and write, at least minimally. In 1990 and again in 1997, only

5 percent in the rancho reported themselves as unable to read and write. Those who need to calculate numbers (*hacer cuentas*; e.g., to ascertain the amount of fertilizer to buy for their avocado orchards) know how to do so, whether they learned in school or *lírico* (see Farr, 1994b). Learning to do arithmetic—or to read and write—*lírico* (lyrically) refers to a learning process carried out informally and orally, being taught by another person who knows how to do whatever it is that one is learning. This way of learning is extremely important among rancheros and is linked to the assumption that one should go to a person with the appropriate knowledge for guidance in particular areas. Thus necessary skills—using the alphabet to encode or decode written Spanish or manipulating numbers in arithmetic processes—are learned in a decidedly social way, as knowledge is transmitted from one person to another. This process and the resultant literacy practices in which they use their reading and writing skills are discussed more fully in the final section of this chapter.

With the increase in the availability of schooling over the decades, years of attendance in school increased over the generations in this social network, whether in Mexico, in Chicago, or at both ends of the migrant circuit over the course of individual lives. Educational opportunities in Chicago, in fact, vastly increased the level of schooling for members of the second and third generations of this network. For the first generation that migrated to Chicago, formal schooling in Mexico generally did not exceed elementary school, ranging from two to six years in all. This level of schooling matches that of their generational counterparts who remained in the rancho rather than migrating to the United States, with the exception of those who were younger siblings in their families and thus able to continue their schooling at least through high school while their older siblings worked. Most members of the second generation in the rancho are more likely to have completed *primaria* and continued their schooling into *secundaria*; some have completed *secundaria*; and a few younger members of this generation have completed *preparatoria*. One young woman of the second generation even completed college in Mexico, commuting daily to nearby Zamora. A woman in the rancho commented on the increasing importance of education:

> Sí, actualmente la educación es muy necesaria. Antes con la primaria bastaba, pero ahora la primaria no significa ni siquiera el nivel básico. Actualmente, en los trabajos piden como mínimo que tengan la prepa.
>
> (Yes, nowadays education is very necessary. Before primary school was sufficient, but now primary school doesn't even mean a basic level. Nowadays workplaces ask as a minimum that one have completed *preparatoria*.)

Members of the second and third generations of the families that migrated to Chicago frequently completed even more schooling than their generational counterparts in the rancho. For some, this involved schooling in both Mexico and Chicago. A frequent pattern for second generation members in several families is primary school in Chicago and secondary school in Mexico (then work, rather than high school, in Chicago). For two other families who lived during various periods in Chicago, Mexico, then Chicago again, the pattern of binational school-ing is more mixed. Binational schooling experiences, of course, develop both bilingualism and biliteracy. For example, those in the second generation who attended elementary school in Chicago learned English sufficiently to develop it further when they later returned to Chicago as young adults. These individuals easily speak colloquial English that is difficult for others in the network, faced with learning English as adults, to attain. Yet there are some disadvantages to the pattern of dual schooling as well. The two school systems are quite different, as are the cultural contexts in which they are embedded. As a teacher in the rancho noted,

> Los [estudiantes] que vienen de allá son muy extrovertidos. Allá es otro el sistema de enseñar; los enseñan a participar más. Aquí uno está acostumb-rado [a] que el maestro es él que enseña, él que habla, y los niños sólo escuchan.

> (Those [students] that come from over there are very extroverted. The sys-tem of teaching is different over there; they teach them to participate more. Here one is accustomed to the teacher being the one who teaches, the one who speaks, and the children only listen.)

Thus children returning from the United States often are viewed critically for being "extroverted" for the way they behave in school. They also are criticized for their clothing styles (baggy, low-hanging pants and earrings among boys; short skirts and shorts among girls) and more open gender relations, both of which are perceived as disrespectful and possibly gang-related. *Secundaria* administrators noted what was considered inappropriate for boys within the school: *vestirse como cholos, fumar, estar en bandas o tener novia* (dress like *cholos* [Mexican American delinquents], smoke, be in a gang, or have a girlfriend). Academically as well, some returning children are considered by both parents and teachers to be deficient in several respects. First, for their lack of (schooled) Spanish:

> Aún los niños que van en Estados Unidos en escuelas bilingües, no saben bien el español, ni tampoco leer ni escribir bien . . .

> (Even those children who go to bilingual school in the United States don't know Spanish well, nor to read or write [it] well . . .)

Beyond a lack of Spanish, these children are perceived as having had inadequate academic preparation in other areas, as the teacher noted:

> Varios papás de aquí me han dicho que ellos ven que la educación en México es mejor que la de Estados Unidos, y yo como maestro he notado que los niños que estudian allá vienen muy deficientes—bueno, en matemáticas lle-gan muy bien preparados, como que allá le dan mucha atención a esa mate-ria; también en educación física y en actividades artísticas, porque allá hay un maestro para cada actividad y se tienen los recursos para apoyarlos . . . [pero]

hay otras materias donde llegan muy mal, deficientes, como español, geografía, historia, ciencias naturales . . . hay veces que llegan niños de quinto
o sexto grado y hay que bajarlos uno, porque no tienen el mismo nivel. Hay
maestros que no los quieren recibir en sus grupos, porque dicen que implica
mucho trabajo y no pueden retrasar a todo el grupo por un sólo niño.

(Various parents from here have told me that they see that the education in
Mexico is better than that in the United States, and I as a teacher have noted
that the children who study over there come back very deficient—well, in
mathematics they arrive very well prepared, since over there they give much
attention to this material; also in physical education and in artistic activities,
because there they have one teacher for each activity and they have resources
to support them . . . [but] there are other subjects in which they arrive very
badly [prepared], deficient, such as Spanish, geography, history, natural sciences. . . . There are times when fifth or sixth grade children arrive and you
have to put them back a year, because they don't have the same level [as
children here]. There are teachers who don't want them in their classes,
because they say that they require a lot of work, and they can't hold back
the entire class for one child.)

Many people also note that U.S. schools have an advantage in that they provide
computer instruction. Despite acknowledged advantages in specific subjects,
however, many teachers and parents still believe that children study more subjects
and are better schooled academically in Mexico, at least at the *secundaria* level
and beyond, if not at the local elementary school in the rancho.

Those members of the second and third generations who were schooled entirely
in Chicago generally go further in school and have fewer problems with language
and literacy, especially writing English compositions. A few students with schooling both in Chicago and in Mexico have experienced difficulties in this regard, no
doubt partly due to devalued dialect features in both their Spanish and English
(Farr [Whiteman], 1981). Nevertheless, a number of second-generation individuals completed college, and a few attended graduate school. Most of these
more advanced students are female, possibly because of social norms that link
masculinity to productive work. Such productive work traditionally meant
going to *el labor* (the fields), but it now means going to the United States. One
older man now retired in the rancho urged his nephew as he came of working
age: "¡Vete a la frontera!" (Get yourself to the border!), meaning get himself to
Chicago to work. Young men who do not attempt to cross the border can be
criticized for being "lazy," especially if they stay in school "too long."

Such views represent traditional ranchero attitudes toward work and school,
attitudes that once fit their agrarian society, but now these attitudes are changing,
as is their society. In fact, the wife of the man who urged their nephew to cross the
border once chastised her niece and another young girl for not liking school and
for doing their homework at the last minute. She warned them that if they did not
go to school they'd be *burros trabajando en el campo* ([stupid] mules working in
the fields) and then looked to me for affirmation: "¿Verdad, Marcia?" (Isn't that

right, Marcia?). The girls objected, saying that she herself hadn't gone to school much, to which she quickly replied, "That's because we didn't have the opportunity! You do!" Nevertheless, many young women in the rancho now want to leave school at fifteen in order to work in the packing plants, to have "their own money." Others continue their education beyond that which their parents were able to attain.

In Chicago both males and females in the second and third generations take advantage of the increased opportunities for schooling and go further in school than their parents did; but proportionately more females do this, as many of their male cousins and brothers go to work. Thus there are both gender and age differences regarding attitudes toward education and years of education attained, both of which are tied to changes in the social and material contexts of their lives, either in Chicago or in the rancho. Figure 3.2 shows actual levels of schooling (as of 2002) by date of birth for men and women. This figure includes only people born before 1981. Virtually all children in Chicago born in 1981 or after are fully schooled to their appropriate grade levels, as are many but not all of their age-mates in the rancho.

Figure 3.2 shows both age and gender patterns in the total years of schooling achieved (each circle or triangle represents one individual). A clear pattern is the rise in years of schooling over time, reflecting increased opportunities in both locations. Even more striking, however, is the contrast between males and females. Over time, females achieve higher levels of schooling in both locations but especially in Chicago. Clearly, being female and being in Chicago leads to more schooling in this network. This is especially notable because there is little difference in schooling levels between males and females with dates of birth before 1950 (the first generation of migrants). For females born after 1950, however, levels of schooling rise rapidly. Many females in Mexico born after 1950 achieve notably higher levels (note the white circles near the upper right corner of Figure 3.2: Women), but females in Chicago achieve even higher levels (note the cluster of black circles and triangles in the upper right corner of Figure 3.2: Women).

In contrast, many males born after 1950 do not achieve such higher levels of schooling. Several male "outliers" with higher levels of schooling (near the top in Figure 3.2: Men) either married into the network (two teachers, one in the rancho and one in Chicago, and a computer programmer with a Chicago B.S. degree) or were younger siblings in the first generation who went to college while older siblings worked. Generally, however, unlike their male counterparts, women began to complete twelve years of schooling in Mexico late in the first generation and into the second. Overall, more second-generation women than men attended college or university, either in Mexico or in Chicago, but particularly in Chicago.

One explanation for the lower levels of schooling for males, even those with increased opportunities, involves the link between masculinity and work. A number of second-generation males, for example, migrated to Chicago specifically to work, not to go to school. While some of their male cousins raised in Chicago continued in school, others dropped out because of pressures from gangs. In one case a young man dropped out of high school, moving to North Carolina to live with an older sister and work, to avoid the pressure to join a gang in Chicago. In

Years of Schooling

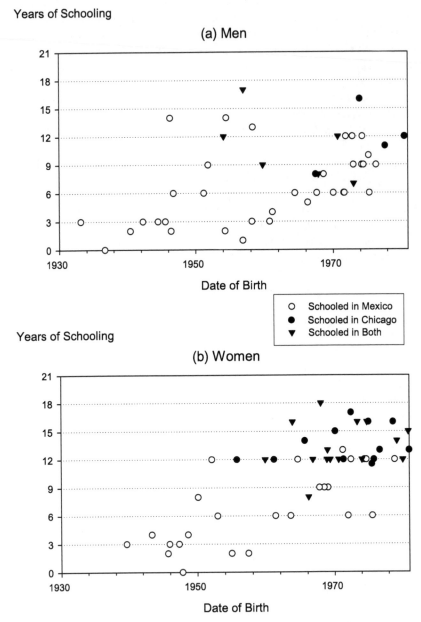

Figure 3.2 Years of Schooling by Date of Birth and Place of Schooling.

another case a young man did join a gang and began to do poorly in school, so his entire family quit their jobs and withdrew from school in order to move back to Mexico to get him away from the gang. In both of these gang-related cases, leaving school meant entering the workforce.

Despite the lower levels of schooling achieved by males, generally there is a dramatic increase in high school and college degrees across time, a trend that is continuing into the third generation. In addition, many have pursued other kinds of schooling in Chicago, obtaining GED certificates (represented in Figure 3.2 as twelve years of schooling) and becoming certified electricians, chefs, photographers, and cosmetologists (none of which are included in Figure 3.2). Thus the ranchero ideology of hard work and progress encourages many in these families to take advantage of increasingly available opportunities to prepare themselves and their children for a better future.

Literacy Learning and Use

Even with minimal exposure to formal schooling, the adults in this social network use literacy functionally in their daily activities (Farr, 1994a, 1994b). Moreover, some women use it extensively in the religious domain of their lives (Farr, 2005b; Guerra & Farr, 2002). In what follows I first more fully describe the already-mentioned process of learning literacy *lírico* (literally "lyrically" but meaning informally, outside of school). After this I provide a brief overview of the literacy practices in these families and how they are perceived in the context of dominant literacy ideologies.

Learning Literacy Lírico

One man explained the process of learning *lírico*, and he did so quite poetically:

> Lírico es . . . puro hablado . . . que no haya libros ni nada. Puede ser también con maestro, pero que no haya nada de libros. La voz, pues, nada mas pura voz. La voz y la palabra.

> (Lyrically is . . . pure speaking . . . there are no books or anything. It can also be with a teacher, but without any books at all. The voice, then, nothing but pure voice. The voice and the word.)

Another man emphasized that although you can learn things without books, you cannot do it without other people. This man recounted how he began to learn literacy in his rancho as a child, partly from his brief schooling experiences and partly from others who were able to go to school more than he.

His schooling was very limited, because he had to work at age eight ("Unfortunately, over there, when you are eight years old and can walk well, you have go look over the animals"). Moreover, his mother had died and his father usually was in the U.S. working (while his aunt looked after him). With help from others and by practicing on his own, he gradually learned to write and read. As he describes it, first he recognized then copied the letters from available print, e.g., on old cigarette cartons. Then, "the point came" when he knew all the letters, and could put them together to form words. Eventually he read magazines and comic book stories (*novelas*) left to him by older friends. After migrating to Chicago as a young adult, and motivated by the desire to communicate with people back home, he improved his literacy skills with the help of a good friend he met there. Although he could have hired a letter writer (see Kalman, 1998), he preferred to fulfill his "obligation" by writing his own letters, so that he knew exactly what was being written.

This man's experience as an autodidact (see Spufford, 1981 for a similar account from seventeenth-century rural England) reminds us, first of all, that writing must be taught, in contrast to speech, which is acquired. It also indicates that learning to read and write on one's own is difficult and requires much practice for gradual improvement, and, moreover, that learning to read is not the same process as learning to write. This man describes writing as "more difficult" and as following learning to read. Another man, however, who also learned literacy *lírico* from a friend after migrating to Chicago, and for the same reason (to write his own letters home), explains that he learned first to write, then read:

> Bueno, yo empecé a escribir cuando salía de mi tierra, cuando empecé a escribir para mi casa . . . Me acuerdo que la primer' carta que mandé me dure como dos días, bueno, después del trabajo . . . Y entonces yo escribía mal hechito como podía, y me llegaba la carta . . . pero no podía yo leerlas. Yo la daba a leer porque no podía. Hasta, después ya con el tiempo ya fui a, poco a poquito a poderlas ir leyendo.

> (Well, I began to write when I left my homeland, when I began to write home . . . I remember that the first letter I sent took me about two days to write, well, after work I would work on it . . . And so, I would write badly, any way I could, and then I would get a letter . . . but I could not read it. I gave it to someone to read because I couldn't. Not until later, with time, little by little was I able to read them.)

These men's accounts illustrate the difficulty of learning literacy on their own, but they also show that motivation springs from context and that *querer es poder* (where there is a will, there is a way). In spite of all this self-motivated hard work, however, and despite their functional literacy, both of these men nevertheless would be labeled "illiterate" by prevailing literacy ideologies in the United States. First of all, many tests of "literacy" are actually tests of English literacy, not literacy itself. Second, a widely accepted ideology of standardization (Milroy & Milroy, 2003) promotes the idea that there is a written standard for a language, and that only this standard is "correct." This ideology is similar to the ideology of language purism already discussed in this chapter. As noted, these ideologies are taught via formal schooling, where teachers generally insist on "correct" versions of standard languages. Such purism is accepted even by those whose language and literacy practices are thereby labeled "incorrect" and inadequate. Both of the men who learned literacy *lírico* note, for example, that their writing is not "like the writing in school;" nor is their reading (out loud) like that of more educated people:

Pero ya que yo escriba, yo sé que no las voy a escribir como debe de ser. Ahora, puntos, acentos, ¿Donde los lleva? Quien sabe, no tengo idea . . . eso de que punto, coma y eso, eso sí no sé nada. Nomas las letras.

(But once I begin writing, I know that I am not going to write as it should be. Now, periods, accents, where do they go? Who knows, I have no idea . . . about periods, commas and that, I know nothing. Only the letters.)

He does, however, defend himself, and others, for not knowing such details because of learning literacy on their own:

Porque los que aprendemos a leer y a escribir acá lírico, qué vamos a saber de ortografía, qué vamos a saber dónde va un acento, que vamos a saber que dónde está un punto se tiene uno que detener cuando está leyendo, ¿qué sabe uno de eso? Uno le sigue derecho. ¿Sí or no? Yo no me fijo en eso . . . Y la gente que está educada, que ha tenido su escuela, pos oye, ve un punto y se para. O ve unas rayitas allí que les dicen signos . . . le dan su sonido a la lectura. Yo no, yo, parejo. Nada de bajadas y subidas, no, no, no, no, ¿que es eso?

(Because those of us who learn to read and write over here *lírico,* what are we going to know about spelling, how are we going to know where an accent goes, that when there is a period you pause when you are reading, what does one know about that? One goes on straight ahead. Yes or no? I pay no attention to that . . . And the people who are educated, that have had school- ing, well, they see a period and they pause. Or they see a bunch of small lines there, and they are signs for them to give a special sound to their reading. Not me, no, I am even. None of those ups and downs, no, no, no, no, what is that?)

Literacy Practices

Even with unschooled literacy, however, the first generation men and women in these families manage a variety of literacy practices in their daily lives, some- times being helped by those in the network with more advanced literacy abilities (primarily second and third generation family members). These practices, inconspicuously embedded in daily activities, involve both Spanish and English as print on food wrappings, wall calendars, audiotapes and CDs, television, invi- tations to events, religious magazines, newspapers, letters, official documents, and both educational and religious books. I have organized these practices according to societal domains (Farr 1994a, 1994b); here I provide examples of those tied to religion, commerce, and government. The most important of these, because of the more extensive use of literacy, is religion, but before describing the religious literacy in this community, I provide brief examples of commercial and govern- mental literacy activities.

Commercial literacy occurs in four primary areas for these families: on the job, in entrepreneurial activities, while shopping, and when paying bills. Workplace demands for literacy vary widely, from short lists of work tasks, to reading catalogue orders and writing on the boxes in which those orders are filled, to writing quality control reports (the only activity said to be difficult). Entrepreneurial literacy involves maintaining records for rental apartments and for the sale (by some women) of Tupperware, Stanley home products, and Jafra cosmetics. Three second generation cousins even developed a business (in a storefront) selling baptism and other ceremonial religious clothing which family members bring from Mexico on frequent trips. Shopping and paying bills, as in entrepreneurial activities, involve both literacy and mathematics; individuals with limited skills in these areas are helped by other family members.

Governmental literacy demands involve written communications from and to agencies such as the Immigration and Naturalization Service (INS) and the Internal Revenue Service (IRS). Again, first generation adults generally understand these communications but often ask relatives with more knowledge of English literacy to read, interpret, and if necessary respond to, the correspondence for them.

Most literacy practices in these families, then, are embedded almost invisibly in daily activities at work, at home, while shopping, etc. These literacy practices involve both Spanish and English, and sometimes are collaboratively dealt with by more than one family member. In contrast the religious literacy practices carried out or led primarily by women are primarily in Spanish and do not involve the assistance of others. Most significantly, these practices involve the reading and writing of relatively extended texts. Materials that are read include books that promote Catholic values and ways of life, songs and prayers as part of religious ceremonies carried out in homes, and (bilingual) *doctrina* or catechism books for young children.

Religious activities cluster around holidays such as Christmas, and special events occur in people's homes, including processions that move through community streets and end up in someone's home. During the nine days before Christmas *Las Posadas* (the inns) enact Joseph and Mary's difficulty in finding an inn in which to birth Jesus in candlelit processions that end with a visit to a home each night (see http://www.nacnet.org/assunta/nacimnto.htm for a more detailed explanation). In an event referred to as *el acostamiento* a "baby Jesus" is laid down in the last home's nativity scene, and this "baby Jesus" is taken up and put away for another year in an event called *el levantamiento* during January. These occasions are not only religious events, but literacy events, since printed material, usually in Spanish, is an integral part of the celebration, and, in fact, is used to structure the event. People sing songs and recite prayers, either from memory (sometimes using the print as a reminder) or by reading these texts from booklets. On occasion the women leading these events expand upon the printed prayers with formulaic phrases of their own.

Doctrina class, held on Saturday mornings in a family's home and led by two teenaged women, also included the reading or reciting of prayers and the singing of songs. In addition, the approximately ten children in this class carried out school-like activities of reading and writing structured by the lessons in a large paperbound book, *Creciendo con Jesús* (Growing with Jesus), which was printed in both Spanish and English. These literacy activities, as noted by Baquedano-López (1997), provide a context for the children's construction of identity as Mexican-origin Catholics.

By far the most extensive use of reading and writing, however, is done by the women who take part in the Catholic Charismatic Renovation in Chicago. Because of its similarity to Protestant evangelical movements, priests in Mexico, and some in the U.S., do not approve of this group. Some of the women in these families, however, participate in a Charismatic group that meets in the basement of a Catholic Church. This movement encourages individuals to read and study the Bible themselves and to communicate directly with God (in traditional Catholicism priests interpreted the Bible for parishioners and saints interceded with God in response to prayers from parishioners). One woman in particular regularly reads books and writes letters to God as part of her Charismatic activities (Farr, 2005b; Guerra & Farr, 2002). Her reading is so involving that, she says, there are times "que me meto en un libro y no quiero dejarlo" (that I get into a book and don't want to leave it), and she distinguishes between books that are *bien narrado* (well written and crafted for the reader) and those that are simply experience written down. These and other comments she makes about her reading indicate that it is quite extensive; it clearly has developed considerably the literacy abilities she learned in only three years of schooling in Mexico. These abilities now include the use of text for critical (political) thinking and an awareness of the historical context of the text. Moreover, such spiritualism is linked to power within the Charismatic movement, and she exercises this power to challenge traditional gender roles by asserting herself at church and within the family on religious occasions (Farr, 2005b).

Again, in spite of the reality of such literacy practices, this woman, like the men who learned literacy *lírico*, would be counted as "illiterate" due to her limited schooling and knowledge of English. Dominant ideologies of language purism and literacy standardization label her language and literacy practices "incorrect" and inadequate, in spite of their fluency and even eloquence. Both her speech and her writing, as in the letters to God she writes as part of her weekly prayer circle (Guerra & Farr, 2002), show frequent rural Mexican features. Yet she writes and reads extensively, using text in some ways similar to academic literacy (Farr, 2005b).

This paradox raises some serious questions: How is literacy being defined, and how are literacy abilities being measured? Clearly tests and other instruments that claim to measure literacy, but count only English literacy (or measure literacy by years of schooling), are not validly capturing the actual abilities of people like those described here. In particular, the complex language abilities of such people are not taken into account by standardized tests and surveys (Menken, 2008); these abilities range from vernacular to standard Spanish, and from vernacular to standard English, including code-switching among these varieties (see García, this volume). Moreover, the religious literacy practiced by this woman may generate critical thinking in ways not captured on standardized tests, even if they were in Spanish. Ethnographic research, of course, because it focuses on actual social practices and emphasizes the perspectives of those studied, is ideally suited to document the "invisible" practices and abilities of various groups of people. Such research-based knowledge can then be used to critique the "conventional wisdom" that is informed by ideologies rather than evidence and that has such serious material consequences in people's lives (Farr, 2008b).

References

Adger, C., Wolfram, W., & Christian, D. (2007). *Dialects in schools and communities*, second edition. Mahwah, NJ: Erlbaum Associates.

Alonso, A.M. (1995). *Thread of blood: Colonialism, revolution and gender on Mexico's northern frontier.* Tucson: University of Arizona Press.

Baquedano-López, P. (1997). Creating social identities through Doctrina narratives. *Issues in Applied Linguistics 8*(1), 27–45. [Reprinted in A. Duranti (Ed.). (2001). *Linguistic anthropology: A reader.* (pp. 343–358). Malden, MA: Blackwell.]

Barragán, E. (1990). *Más allá de los Caminos: Los Rancheros del Potrero de Herrera.* Zamora, Michoacán, Mexico: El Colegio de Michoacán.

Bauman, R. (1986). *Story, performance, and event: Contextual studies of oral narrative.* Cambridge: Cambridge University Press.

Briggs, C. (1988). *Competence in performance: The creativity of tradition in Mexicano verbal art.* Philadelphia: University of Pennsylvania Press.

Cárdenas, N.D. (1967). El español de Jalisco: Contribución a la geografía lingüística hispanoamericana. *Revista de Filología Española*, Supplement 85.

Domínguez Barajas, E. (2002). *Reconciling cognitive universals and cultural particulars: A Mexican social network's use of proverbs.* Ph.D. dissertation, University of Illinois at Chicago.

Farr, M. (1993). Essayist Literacy and Other Verbal Performances. *Written Communication* 10 (1): 4–38.

—— (1994a). Biliteracy in the Home: Practices among Mexicano Families in Chicago. In D. Spener (Ed.), *Adult biliteracy in the United States.* McHenry, IL: The Center for Applied Linguistics and Delta Systems.

—— (1994b). En los dos Idiomas: Literacy Practices among Chicago Mexicanos. In B. Moss (Ed.) *Literacy across communities.* Cresskill, NJ: Hampton Press.

—— (2005a). *A Mi No Me Manda Nadie!* Individualism and Identity in Mexican Ranchero Speech. In M. Farr (Ed.), *Latino language and literacy in ethnolinguistic Chicago.* Hillsdale, NJ: Erlbaum.

—— (2005b). Literacy and Religion: Reading, Writing, and Gender among Mexican Women in Chicago. In M. Farr (Ed.), *Latino language and literacy in ethnolinguistic Chicago.* Hillsdale, NJ: Erlbaum.

—— (2006). *Rancheros in Chicagoacán. Language and identity in a transnational community.* Austin: University of Texas Press.

—— (2008a). Urban multilingualism: Language practices and language policy in Chicago. Paper presented at University of Antwerp Workshop on Urban Multilingualism and Intercultural Communication.

—— (2008b). Literacy ideologies: Local practices and cultural definitions. Paper presented at Latin American Literacy Studies Seminar, CREFAL, Pátzcuaro, Mexico.

—— [Whiteman] (Ed.) (1981). Dialect Influence in Writing. In M. Farr Whiteman (Ed.), *Variation in writing: Functional and linguistic-cultural variation* (pp. 13–23). Hillsdale, NJ: Erlbaum.

Goffman, E. (1974). *Frame analysis: An essay on the organization of experience.* New York: Harper and Row.

Guerra, J. (1998). *Close to home: Oral and literate practices in a transnational Mexicano community,* New York: Teachers College Press.

Guerra, J., and Farr, M. (2002). Writing on the margins: Spiritual and autobiographical discourse among Mexicanas in Chicago. In G. Hull and K. Schultz (Eds.), *School's out!: Literacy at work and in the community* (pp. 96–123). New York: Teachers College Press.

Hymes, D. (1981). "In vain I tried to tell you:" *Essays in Native American ethnopoetics.* Philadelphia: University of Pennsylvania Press.

Jakobson, R. (1960). Closing statement: Linguistics and poetics. In T. Seboek (Ed.), *Style in language* (pp. 350–434). New York: John Wiley.

Kalman, J. (1998). *Writing on the Plaza: Mediated literacy practice among scribes and clients in Mexico City.* Cresskill, NJ: Hampton Press.

Kerr, L.A.N. (1976). *The Chicano experience in Chicago: 1920 to 1970.* Ph.D. dissertation. Department of History, University of Illinois at Chicago.

—— (1984). Mexican Chicago: Chicano assimilation aborted, 1939–54. In M. Holli and P. d'A. Jones (Eds.), *Ethnic Chicago* (pp. 270–298). Grand Rapids, MI: Eerdmans.

Limón, J. (1992). *Mexican ballads, Chicano poems: History and influence in Mexican-American social poetry.* Berkeley: University of California Press.

—— (1994). *Dancing with the devil: Society and cultural poetics in Mexican-American South Texas.* Madison: University of Wisconsin Press.

Menken, K. (2008). *English learners left behind: Standardized testing as language policy.* Clevedon, England: Multilingual Matters.

Milroy, L. (1987). *Language and social networks.* 2nd edn. Oxford: Blackwell.

Milroy, J., & Milroy, L. (2003). *Authority in language,* 2nd edn. New York: Routledge.

Mummert, G. (1994). From Metate to Despate: Rural Mexican women's salaried labor and the redefinition of gendered spaces and roles. In H. Fowler-Salamini and M.K. Vaughan (Eds.), *Women of the Mexican countryside, 1950–1990* (pp. 192–209). Tucson: University of Arizona Press.

Parodi, C. (1995) *Orígenes del español Americano, I: Reconstrucción de la pronunciación.* Mexico City: Universidad Nacional Autónoma de México.

Pratt, M.L. (1991). Arts of the contact zone. *Profession 91*: 33–40.

Quinones, S. (2001) *True tales from another Mexico: The Lynch Mob, the Popsicle Kings, Chalino, and the Bronx.* Albuquerque: University of New Mexico Press.

Santa Ana, O., & Parodi, C. (1998). Modeling the speech community: Configuration and variable types in the Mexican Spanish setting. *Language in Society* 27 (1): 23–51.

Sherzer, J. (2002). *Speech play and verbal art.* Austin: University of Texas Press.

Schiller, N.G., Basch, L., & Blanc-Szanton, C. (1992). *Transnationalism: A new analytic framework for understanding migration.* New York: New York Academy of Sciences.

Spears, T.B. (2005). *Chicago dreaming: Midwesterners and the city, 1871–1919.* Chicago: University of Chicago Press.

Spufford, M. (1981). First steps in literacy: The reading and writing experiences of the humblest spiritual autobiographers. In H. Graff (Ed.), *Literacy and social development in the West: A reader.* New York: Cambridge University Press.

Stern, S. (1995). *The secret history of gender: Women, men, and power in late colonial Mexico.* Chapel Hill: University of North Carolina Press.

Tannen, D. (1989). *Talking voices: Repetition, dialogue, and imagery in conversational discourse.* New York: Cambridge University Press.

Tedlock, D. (1983). *The spoken word and the work of interpretation.* Philadelphia: University of Pennsylvania Press.

Valdés, G. (1996). *Con respeto: Bridging the distances between culturally diverse families and schools: An ethnographic portrait.* New York: Teachers College Press.

Vargas, Z. (1993). *Proletarians of the North: A history of Mexican industrial workers in Detroit and the Midwest, 1917–1933.* Berkeley: University of California Press.

Wolfram, W., and Schilling-Estes, N. (1998). *American English: Dialects and Variation,* second edition. Oxford: Blackwell.

Woolard, K.A. 1998. Introduction: Language Ideology as a Field of Inquiry. In *Language Ideologies: Practice and Theory,* edited by B.B. Schieffelin, K.A. Woolard, and P. Kroskrity, pp. 3–47. Oxford: Oxford University Press.

Zentella, A.C. (1997). *Growing up bilingual: Puerto Rican children in New York.* Oxford: Blackwell.

—— (Ed.). (2005). *Building on Strength: Language and Literacy in Latino Families and Communities.* New York: Teachers College Press.

4 "I'm Speaking English Instead of My Culture"

Portraits of Language Use and Change among Native American Youth[1]

Teresa L. McCarty, Mary Eunice Romero-Little, Larisa Warhol, and Ofelia Zepeda

> I try to talk to them in Navajo but they don't respond back in Navajo, they respond in English . . . They say that they know what I am saying but they can't speak it.
>
> (Navajo educator, interview, March 28, 2003)

> If adults were to know the kids on a personal level, . . . they would see that these kids, . . . they know how to speak Navajo, but many times they might be ashamed. . . . That has been pumped into them; it is not something natural.
>
> (Navajo high school student, interview, May 6, 2004)

The statements above, by a bilingual teacher and a bilingual youth, highlight the complex sociolinguistic and ideological forces underpinning language practices in communities in which a minoritized language is losing ground to a dominating one—in this case, Navajo to English. Language shift is occurring at an escalating pace in American Indian and Alaska Native communities, and indeed, is cause for grave concern worldwide. Yet even as more Native students enter school speaking English as a primary or only language, they often speak a variety influenced by the structure and use patterns of the Native language, leading them to be stigmatized as "limited English proficient" (LEP) and placed in remedial tracks. Native American students are 237 percent more likely to drop out of school than their White peers—an astounding and deeply troubling statistic (National Caucus of Native American State Legislators, 2008, p. 5). Thus, the shift from the Native language to English does not in itself guarantee that students will acquire academic English or fare better in school, or that educational inequities will be redressed.

The conditions that give rise to language shift have been well studied (e.g., Crawford, 2000; Crystal, 2000; Dorian, 1981; Fishman, 1991, 2001; Kulick, 1992; Nettle & Romaine, 2000). For Native Americans, those conditions include a history of genocide, physical and social dislocation, and federal education policies explicitly designed to eradicate Native languages and lifeways. What is less well understood is how language shift is experienced by young people and influences their learning in school.[2] This lack of information contributes significantly to the dismal education statistics cited above.

In this chapter, we offer a grounded view of language shift as experienced by Native American youth across a range of school-community settings. Drawing on data from a large-scale, comparative study of Indigenous language shift and revitalization in the U.S. Southwest, we show that the linguistic ecologies in which Native American children are being socialized (Haugen, 1972; Hornberger, 2003; Mühlhäusler, 1996)—the environments in which language choices and practices play out—are much more complicated than the notion of "shift," with its uni-directional connotations, might lead us to believe. Before we can implement policies and practices intended to improve language and literacy education for Native American students in U.S. schools, we must first understand the socio-linguistic and sociocultural resources present in their communities, and that is where our study begins.

We preface our analysis with an overview of Native American demographics and the status of Native American languages. We then provide background on our research goals, methods, and participants. We focus our analysis on four key areas: (1) the context-specific sociohistorical underpinnings of language shift, (2) contemporary language practices, (3) youth sociolinguistic competencies, and (4) language attitudes and ideologies. Like King in her examination of Quichua language shift and revitalization in Ecuador (2000, 2001), we find it useful to distinguish between language *attitudes* and *ideologies*. Attitudes refer to positive or negative orientations toward languages and their speakers (see, e.g., Baugh, 2000; Fasold, 1984; Lambert et al., 1960). Ideologies are sets of beliefs about language(s) that link language, identity, and power relations (see King, 2000, p. 168; Silverstein, 1979). As Woolard (1998) explains, language ideologies "underpin not only linguistic form and use but also the very notion of the person and the social group" (p. 3). As will be seen, ideologies about language prevalent among the youth in our study are multilayered and often conflicting. Altogether, these data reveal portraits of language use across a continuum of early- to late-shift settings. We conclude by drawing out the implications of our findings for language education policy and practice for Native American learners.

Native American Languages and Speech Communities

At the turn of the twenty-first century, 4.1 million people in the U.S. (1.4 percent of the total population) identified as American Indian and Alaska Native, including 2.5 million who reported only American Indian and Alaska Native heritage (U.S. Census Bureau, 2002). An additional 874,000 people identified as Native Hawaiian and "other Pacific Islander" (U.S. Census Bureau, 2001). Native Americans reside in every state of the union and its territories, comprising more than 560 federally recognized tribes and 619 reservations and Alaska Native villages.

More than one-third of the Native American population are youth under age 18—a demographic that in itself calls attention to the need for better understanding of Indigenous youth language practices. Native students attend public, federal, parochial, and private schools. Although many of these schools are located in rural reservation areas and have a majority American Indian/Alaska Native enrollment, more than 90 percent of Native students attend public schools with less than 25 percent Native enrollment (Stancavage et al., 2006). These students' language and literacy resources are often misunderstood or "invisibilized" in school, in part because of low numbers of *both* Native students and teachers (less than 1 percent of teachers in schools serving Native students are Native American), but also because Native students increasingly enter school speaking English rather than an Indigenous language.

Of 175 Indigenous languages still spoken in the United States, only 20 are still being acquired as first languages by children (Krauss, 1998). The linguist Michael Krauss classifies the present status of Native North American languages as follows:

- Class A, the 20 languages still spoken by all generations;
- Class B, the 30 languages spoken by the parent generation and older;
- Class C, the 70 languages spoken by the grandparent generation and older; and
- Class D, the 55 languages spoken only by the very elderly, usually less than a dozen people.

(Krauss, 1998, p. 12)

As this classification reveals, nearly 90 percent of all Native American languages have no child speakers; more than 30 percent face imminent extinction. Native American language endangerment is verified by census data: In 2000, 72 percent of Native Americans 5 years of age or older reported speaking only English at home (U.S. Census Bureau, 2006, p. 7). This leaves roughly 28 percent who reported speaking a language other than English (i.e., a Native American language) along with English "very well" (18 percent) or "less than very well" (10 percent) (U.S. Census Bureau, 2006, p. 7).

Compounding the diversity of spoken languages is the variety of written forms and uses. Some Native American languages, such as Yup'ik, Navajo, Cherokee, and Cree, have been written for a century or more. (Both alphabetic and syllabic orthographies have been used.) Other Native languages have been committed to writing much more recently, often through federally funded bilingual education programs. For all Native communities, spoken language has traditionally taken precedence over written language: "It must not be forgotten," says Acoma educator and scholar Christine Sims, "that the primary function of these tribal languages has always been their use as the foundation of essentially oral tribal societies. That is where the validation of these languages resides" (2005, p. 105).

The Native Language Shift and Retention Study[3]

Understanding the factors influencing Native American children's language learning in communities undergoing rapid language shift was the goal of a recent

(2001–6) large-scale, federally funded study in the U.S. Southwest. The project responded to a 1998 executive order calling for research to "evaluate the role of native language and culture in the development of educational strategies" for Native American students (Executive Order 13096, 1998, Section 2, [f][3]), and to growing tribal concerns about the loss of community languages. The overarching focus of the study concerned the role of the Native language in the personal, family, community, and school lives of Native American youth. Here, we concentrate on one set of sub-questions:

What is the nature of language shift and retention among pre-K–12 Native American students in diverse cultural and linguistic settings?

a.   When, where, and for what purposes do students use the Native/heritage language and English?

b.   What oral and written language proficiencies in the Native/heritage language and English do students at selected research sites possess?

c.   What attitudes and ideologies do these students and their teachers and parents hold toward the Native/heritage language and English?

Research Design and Methodology

The study draws on disciplinary knowledge and methods from the fields of social-cultural anthropology, applied linguistics, and American Indian/Indigenous studies. These multidisciplinary perspectives are unified within a design emphasizing situated, long-term, first-hand ethnographic fieldwork.

From its inception, the study was guided by principles of participatory action research. According to Guba (1999), action research recognizes that "generalized, one-size-fits-all solutions do not work" (p. xii). Action research instead situates inquiry within local contexts, positioning community stakeholders as agents in the research. In keeping with this emphasis, we worked closely with teams of Indigenous community research collaborators (CRCs) at each site. The CRCs facilitated entrée and access, helped validate research protocols, assisted with interviews and the administration of questionnaires, and attended university classes on sociolinguistic and educational research methods and language planning and teaching. These educators represent the critical change agents who are now applying the research findings to language education programs in their own communities.

Research Sites and Participants

Study sites were identified on the basis of our long-term work with Native American educators, communities, and schools throughout the Southwest. The sites reflect a cross-section of demographic, linguistic, cultural, geographic, and school characteristics, including five Native languages; federal, public, and public charter school systems; and a total pre-K–12 Native American student enrollment of 2,039. Table 4.1 outlines the characteristics of participating sites. They include:

1. **Ak Wijid Community School** (AWCS),[4] a federally funded pre-K–8 school serving approximately 400 Akimel O'odham and Pee Posh students. Akimel O'odham (also called Pima) is a Uto-Aztecan language; Pee Posh (also called Maricopa) is a Yuman language. Ak Wijid is a community of about 1,116 people—266 families—located on the periphery of a major metropolitan area and representing 7 percent of the tribal population.
2. **Bahidaj High School** (BHS), an Indigenous-serving public charter school in a large metropolitan area. Ninety-five percent of BHS students are Tohono O'odham, a tribe of about 24,000 whose reservation stretches along the Arizona–Sonora border. Tohono O'odham and Akimel O'odham are mutually intelligible dialects of the Upper Piman branch of Uto-Aztecan languages.
3. **Beautiful Mountain Community School** (BMCS), a pre-K–12, federally funded community school on the Navajo Nation. Navajo is an Athabaskan language in the Western Apachean family. Situated in the Four Corners region of the Southwest, the Navajo Nation is the largest reservation in the U.S., with a land base the size of the state of West Virginia and a population of 298,000. Navajo also has the largest number of speakers of any Native American language—about 178,000 (Benally & Viri, 2005, p. 88). Beautiful Mountain is a community of about 1,300 people—113 households and 89 families. Approximately 600 students, 99 percent of whom are Navajo, attend BMCS.
4. **Black Foothills Unified School District** (BFUSD), among the largest public school districts in the U.S. with a highly diverse student body. Forty-five different languages are spoken by BFUSD students, with the "majority minority" language being Spanish. Within this district, three schools were selected because they serve a large Native American student population: Rainbow Primary School (pre-K–2), Desert Intermediate School (grades 3–5), and Cactus High School (grades 9–12). In addition to English and a Native American language, Spanish is also spoken in many of these children's homes.[5]
5. **U:s K:ek Community School** (UKCS), a pre-K–4 federally funded community school serving Akimel O'odham students. Situated adjacent to a sprawling metropolitan area, U:s K:ek was the smallest community in our study—about 500 people.

Census data illuminate stark economic and educational disparities between these communities and the U.S. population as a whole. Per capita income ranges from $5,921 to $8,674—27 to 40 percent of the national median per capita income. Median household income ranges from $18,599 to $33,599—in some cases, less than *half* the national median and *below even median per capita income* for the U.S. as a whole. As many as 52 percent of families in these communities are living in poverty—four times the national average (U.S. Census Bureau, 2007). The high school completion rate ranges from 32.7 to 51 percent—41 to 63 percent of the national average and lower than the American Indian/Alaska Native population as a whole (U.S. Census Bureau, 2006, 2007). These disparities

Table 4.1 Characteristics of Participating Sites

Site	Language(s) other than English	Native Language Vitality	Setting	School Type	No. of Native Students*
Ak Wijid Community School	Akimel O'odham (Pima) and Pee Posh (Maricopa)	Akimel O'odham spoken by parent/ grandparent generation; Pee Posh spoken by a few elders	Reservation near large metropolitan area	Federally funded pre-K–8 community school	428
Bahidaj High	Primarily Tohono O'odham	Spoken by all generations, but few youth speakers at the school	Large urban metropolitan area	Indigenous-serving charter high school	145
Beautiful Mountain Community School	Navajo	Spoken by all generations	Small, rural reservation community	Federally funded pre-K–12 community school	600
Black Foothills Unified School District: Rainbow Primary, Desert Intermediate, Cactus High	Native American language** and Spanish	Native language spoken by parent/ grandparent generation; Spanish spoken by all generations	Large urban metropolitan area	K–12 public school district	566 (all 3 school sites)
U:s K:ek Community School	Akimel O'odham (Pima)	Spoken by parent generation and older	Reservation near large metropolitan area	Federally funded pre-K–4 community school	300
7 school sites	**5 Indigenous languages (3 language families) + Spanish + English**	**Unstable bilingualism→ extreme language endangerment**	**Rural→ urban and urban periphery**	**Federal, public, charter, community/tribal**	**2,039 Native students enrolled**

* Because fieldwork at most sites was conducted over multiple years, some student enrollment figures represent averages for those years.
** The Native language in this case is not identified at the request of the tribe.

are major factors in children's everyday lives and have profound implications for their school achievement. They also influence the language issues of concern to this study, as later sections of this chapter show.

Multiple Methods of Data Collection

We employed a multiple case study approach and the anthropological method of controlled comparison, in which all variables are held as constant as possible except the "independent" variables under study. Between 2001 and 2006, our research team (three co-investigators and several research assistants) undertook

80 site visits for the purposes of data collection, CRC member checking and debriefing, and reporting back to participants on project progress and findings. Most site visits lasted a full day; visits to the most distant site (Beautiful Mountain, our Navajo site) were two to three days in length. In general, these visits included multiple members of the research team and multiple data collection activities. Data collection included:

1. demographic data on each site;
2. in-depth, recorded interviews with 168 adults and 62 youth in grades 3–12 (230 total interviewees);
3. 600 educational/sociolinguistic questionnaires administered to school staff, community members, and students (of which 529 were complete and usable for analysis);
4. long-term participant observation of language teaching and use at each school site (22 classroom observations and hundreds of hours of informal observation);
5. documents and archival materials (lesson plans, other curricula, school mission statements, school newsletters, etc.); and
6. achievement data maintained by the school district, state education agency, and the federal Office of Indian Education Programs (data sources depended on school type).

The bulk of the data is qualitative, and produced 3,326 single-spaced pages of text. Of these data, ethnographic interviews constitute the largest corpus. In structuring interviews, we adapted Seidman's (2006) three-interview sequence, condensing his tripartite format into single 60- to 90-minute interviews that included:

1. a focused life history, concentrating on schooling and language learning experiences;
2. details and observations of language use at home, in the school, and in the local community; and
3. normative assessments of the role of families, community members, tribal governments, and the school in language education planning.

Sociolinguistic questionnaires also were developed and administered to school administrators, teachers, students, parents, and grandparents. The questionnaires included 14 to 17 closed-answer questions (the number varied depending on the respondent group), with space for additional comments. The questions were designed to elicit participants' oral and written language proficiencies, assessments of language practices in and out of school, and language attitudes and ideologies.

Data Analysis Procedures

Qualitative data were analyzed using NVivo 7, a software tool for organizing, coding, and retrieving text data. In this part of the analysis, we generated codes inductively based on our research questions. These processes yielded a first-level, working set of codes (Miles & Huberman, 1994, p. 69). During several whole-day data analysis workshops, we elaborated codes according to features unique to each site and regularities across sites. NVivo 7 was then used to search, retrieve, and display data in a condensed, organized framework (see, e.g., Weitzman, 2000, pp. 805–806). Second-level or pattern coding involved grouping coded data into smaller sets of recurrent themes (Miles & Huberman, 1994). Quantitative analysis involved correlation analyses to determine relations between language proficiency and school performance; these data were then cross-referenced with qualitative data and archival materials. We conducted both within-case and cross-case analyses of these themes (McCarty et al., 2007).

Context-Specific Sociohistorical Factors Underlying Language Shift

Together, these data revealed a host of sociohistorical factors that contributed to language shift at each school-community site. All sites had experienced major social disruptions as a result of the invasion of their lands by outsiders, genocide, and the diffuse consequences of multiple cycles of colonization by Spaniards, Mexicans, and Anglo-Americans. At Ak Wijid and U:s K:ek, desert communities with deeply rooted agricultural traditions, critical water resources were confiscated by Whites during the nineteenth and early twentieth centuries, halting subsistence agriculture, scattering families, and disrupting traditional village structures and ways of life. This, and proximity to a large and growing metropolitan area, led the Akimel O'odham and Pee Posh languages and lifestyle to "fall by the wayside," in one elder's words (elder interview, 12/7/05). Study participants gave the number of Pee Posh speakers today as fewer than ten (all elderly), and, while there are many more Akimel O'odham speakers, they are primarily middle-aged and older (Krauss's [1998] class B and C).

For Native children at project sites in BFUSD, language shift occurred in the context of a late nineteenth-century/early twentieth-century diaspora; Spanish, then English became part of families' communicative repertoires. This Indigenous nation has become increasingly integrated into the regional and national economy and sociopolitical system. These developments, and the recent elimination of bilingual education within BFUSD, fueled a shift away from *both* the Native language and Spanish. Project and census data indicate about 100 Native-language speakers within BFUSD students' home community, almost all in the parent generation and older (Krauss's [1998] class B and C).

The Tohono O'odham and Navajo peoples stand in contrast to these experiences, as both remained relatively isolated, geographically and socially, on vast reservations well into the second half of the twentieth century. In the past 30 years, road and other transportation improvements, mass media, schooling, and myriad other assimilative forces triggered a tip toward English—factors that have also influenced language shift among other project sites. However, both Tohono O'odham and Navajo still have speakers of all ages, and can thus be placed in Krauss's (1998) class A and B.

Across all project sites, coercive, English-only schooling was cited as a leading cause of language shift. For years, physical and psychological abuse for speaking the Native language was standard practice in federal and mission schools for Indian pupils. For many school survivors, the response was extraordinary courage and resistance: "I am happy to say that these [punishments] did not stop me from speaking my language," one Akimel O'odham teacher stated, recalling how she had been locked in a dark school closet for hours for speaking her mother tongue (McCarty & Romero, 2005, p. 15). But the natural inclination for many graduates was to shield their own children from the perceived liabilities of speaking the mother tongue. Our database is replete with references to the impact of punitive English-only schooling on generations to come:

> My mother grew up and saw the bad things that were done . . . at the [mission] school, punishing them for speaking their own language, trying to convert them. . . . She didn't want us to go through that. . . . She spoke to us in English. (parent interview, 8/9/06)

> [My great-grandmother], she didn't teach [her children and grandchildren]. She was fluent but she didn't teach them because she [attended] . . . the boarding schools and she was whipped for knowing her language . . . so she didn't want her kids to grow up like that, so she didn't teach them at all. (youth interview, 4/19/06)

> When I was a young kid . . . I got teased [for speaking Navajo] when I went into kindergarten. . . . I felt really uncomfortable and embarrassed. . . . that's when I went to English. (school staff interview, 10/17/02)

The legacy of these experiences, as subsequent sections show, was ambivalent language attitudes and the socialization of children in a foreign language—English.

Domains for Native-Language Use

Within the study sites, where are Native children likely to hear the Native language spoken? Census data indicate that between 29 to 77 percent of students come from homes in which a language other than English is spoken (McCarty et al., 2007). The highest percentage is for Navajo students at Beautiful Mountain (76.8 percent); the lowest is for O'odham and Pee Posh students (29.3 percent) (McCarty et al., 2007).

These data are supported by project questionnaires and interviews. Figure 4.1 shows educators' assessments (n=102) of the percentage of their students who hear the Native language spoken at home. At Ak Wijid and U:s K:ek, most educators reported that 20 to 40 percent of their students hear O'odham spoken at home; because there are so few Pee Posh speakers (≤10), only a few students have grandparents who speak Pee Posh at home. At Bahidaj and the three school sites in BFUSD, educators reported that up to 60 percent of their students come

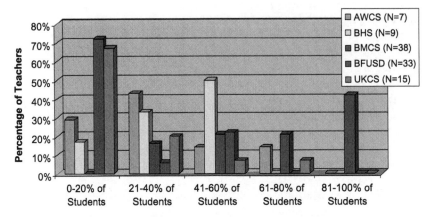

Figure 4.1 Educators' Assessments of the Percentage of Their Students Who Hear the Native Language Spoken at Home.

Source: Native Language Shift and Retention Project Teacher Questionnaires.

from homes in which the Native language is spoken. And at Beautiful Mountain, many educators agreed that 60 to 100 percent of their students hear Navajo spoken at home.

Figures 4.2, 4.3, and 4.4 show students' responses (n=393) to questionnaire items asking them to identify who speaks the Native language, where they hear it spoken in their homes and community, and where they hear it at school. By far the largest number of students who reported hearing the Native language spoken "all the time," speaking it themselves, and being spoken *to* by Native-speaking parents and grandparents were Navajo youth at BMCS. Tohono O'odham, Akimel O'odham, Pee Posh, and BFUSD students also indicated that their parents and grandparents speak the Native language, but not necessarily *to them.*

As shown in Figure 4.3, the most frequent places in which students are likely to hear the Native language are at home (47 percent to 90 percent of students), at community cultural events (50 to 66 percent), and at tribal events (60 percent to 81 percent). For Navajo students, the local store is another place where Navajo is likely to be spoken; Navajo children are also likely to hear Navajo spoken at the chapter house (the local branch of government), in healing ceremonies, and on regional radio stations that broadcast in Navajo. For BFUSD students, church and community-wide religious activities are strong domains for Native-language use.

Figure 4.4 shows students' reports of where they hear the Native language at school. The greatest degree of school-based Native language use is at BHS and BMCS, where 55 to 58 percent of students, respectively, reported hearing Tohono O'odham (BHS) and Navajo (BMCS) spoken in class. Twenty-two percent of BHS students and 55 percent of BMCS students reported hearing the Native language used informally in the hallways; these and BFUSD students also reported hearing the language in the school cafeteria. In contrast, no AWCS students reported hearing Akimel O'odham or Pee Posh spoken outside the classroom designated for this purpose.

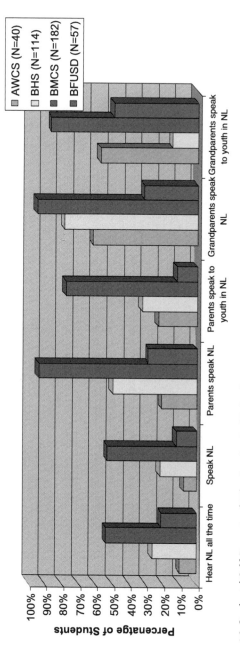

Figure 4.2 Students' Self-Reports of Who Speaks the Native Language.

Source: Native Language and Retention Project Student Questionnaires.

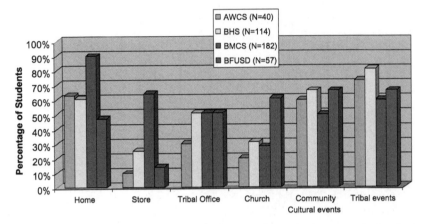

Figure 4.3 Students' Self-Reports of Where They Hear the Native Language Spoken in the Community.

Source: Native Language and Retention Project Student Questionnaires.

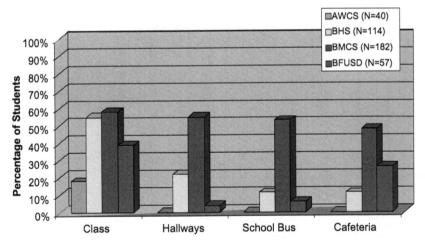

Figure 4.4 Students' Self-Reports of Where They Hear the Native Language Spoken at School.

Source: Native Language and Retention Project Student Questionnaires.

These questionnaire data are amplified by interviews. At Ak Wijid, where all participants agreed that very few students (≤5) spoke O'odham as a primary language, a bilingual educator noted that two students who were experiencing difficulty at testing time had parents and grandparents who "speak O'odham all the time." The teacher correctly surmised that these students "must speak O'odham" but were "just not speaking [it in school]" (educator interview, 11/3/05). A 12-year-old middle schooler revealed that he had learned both Pee Posh and O'odham from his grandmother as a young child; his grandmother still speaks to him in Pee Posh, he said, and both Pee Posh and O'odham are spoken among family members at home (youth interview, 6/2/04). A 13-year-old AWCS student related that her friend speaks O'odham at home: "[H]er mom talks it to her and she can understand," this student affirmed (youth interview, 6/1/04).

At the intermediate and high school sites in BFUSD, students' linguistic environments include the Native language, English, Spanish, and varieties of all three. Asked what language his parents and grandparents speak at home, one student reported, "Sometimes [the Native language], sometimes Spanish, and then English" (youth interview, 4/2/04). BFUSD students also reported using different languages with different siblings, depending upon sibling order: "To my brothers I use Spanish," one student stated, "[except with the youngest because] he doesn't understand Spanish that well" (youth interview, 5/11/04). Students also described parents using different languages in different domains: "My dad speaks English when he is working . . . and my mom speaks both . . . English and [the Native language]. But if they were to go outside [the reservation], they would speak English" (youth interview, 5/11/04). Similarly, students reported that different languages are used with family members of different generations, as reflected in one student's account that her father "talks [the Native language] when he is talking to the elders" but uses Spanish or English with younger generations. A trilingual BFUSD educator summed up these language practices this way: The elders speak Spanish, the Native language, "and maybe a little English;" the "next generation speaks English, Spanish and [the Native language]" and is literate in all three; while the "generation that is coming up . . . is English only. . . . So we have a trilingual family but each generation is slightly different than the one before it" (educator interview, 3/30/04).

At Beautiful Mountain, educators noted that their Navajo-dominant students tend to come from more rural parts of the reservation—"the ones that live kind of way out" and "still live without electricity and running water" (educator interview, 4/28/03; staff interview, 10/17/02). While adults at BMCS were not in agreement on the numbers of their students who were fluent Navajo speakers (see discussion in the following section), Navajo students insisted in interviews that "everyone speaks Navajo out here" (youth interview, 5/5/04). These responses are borne out in the questionnaire data, as Figures 4.3 and 4.4 show.

Highly Complex Sociolinguistic Environments

These data indicate that across all sites, Native children are growing up in highly complex social-linguistic environments. In their homes and communities, children are likely to hear varieties of the Native language spoken by parents and grandparents along with varieties of English and in some cases Spanish. Reflecting the classification of Native-language vitality described by Krauss (1998), there is a gradient of Native-language use in these children's homes and communities, with the greatest and most variegated use at Beautiful Mountain (Navajo) and the least at Ak Wijid and U:s K:ek (Akimel O'odham and Pee Posh).

Within each of these speech communities, however, there is an intricate interweaving of different languages and language varieties for distinct purposes. Our data indicate that Native language use is likely to be influenced by the following:

1. Sibling order: Both adults and youth reported greater frequencies of Native language use by and with older siblings.
2. Relative age and generational relationships: Parents tend to speak the Native language with their age-mates and those in the grandparent generation; grandparents and elders speak the Native language among themselves and to their children; and, with the exception of Navajo and to a lesser degree, Tohono O'odham, both generations use the Native language with children and grandchildren rarely, if at all.
3. Social status: Younger speakers use the Native language with elders, revered members of these communities.
4. Purpose and domain: The Native language is still used in domains associated with ritual activities (e.g., community cultural events, tribal events, cultural activities such as healing ceremonies). But with the exception of Navajo and Tohono O'odham, the Native language is little used at home.

Across all project sites, English is the language used most frequently in both school and community settings. English language use is equally complex, however, as different varieties are used for different purposes in distinct domains. The school is a primary domain for academic English—a variety that may have little currency in the home and community. As the next section indicates, this is of consequence in school labeling practices and students' performance on English standardized tests.

Youth Language Competencies

Native Language Proficiencies

At the time of the study, only BMCS was using a formal Native-language proficiency assessment. No similar assessments exist for the other language groups sampled. Hence, the primary data for assessing Native language proficiency are from questionnaires and interviews. The use of such instruments to assess Native language proficiency has a well-established history in educational and sociolinguistic research with Native populations lacking written Native language assessments, including Spolsky's (1975) evaluation of the language abilities of Navajo six-year-olds; Platero's (2001) examination of the language abilities of Navajo preschoolers; and Holm's (1995) assessment of the Navajo language proficiencies of more than 3,500 kindergartners (Holm & Holm, 1995).

Educators tended to assess students' Native-language proficiency as limited, although there was a gradient from Navajo (greatest proficiency) to Pee Posh (least proficiency). As Figure 4.5 indicates, between 38 and 100 percent of educators surveyed (n=102) reported that less than 20 percent of their students were fluent speakers of the Native language.

Interview data shed further light on these data. At Ak Wijid, educators agreed

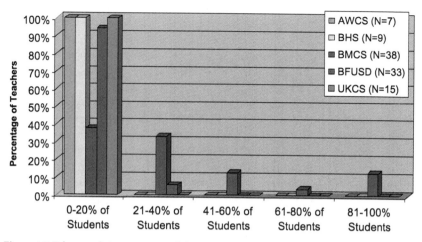

Figure 4.5 Educators' Assessments of the Percentage of Students Who Speak the Native Language Fluently, All Sites.

Source: Native Language and Retention Project Student Questionnaires.

that although "there's probably a few [students] that know [Akimel O'odham], . . . to be able to speak fluently . . . I doubt if we have any" (educator interview, 5/14/03). At U:s K:ek, teachers and parents agreed that the number of child speakers of Akimel O'odham was extremely low; in more than 25 years in the community, one teacher reported knowing "only one student that was completely fluent in O'odham—just one" (educator interview, 2/27/04). "It's a small, small percentage for first language," a BHS educator stated, referring to her Tohono O'odham students (educator interview, 2/27/04). "I feel that most [students] speak English and the next is probably Spanish, and I have never heard any of the [Native] students speak [the Native language]," a BFUSD high school teacher stated (educator interview, 5/10/04).

Educators at Beautiful Mountain expressed more divergent views of their students' Navajo proficiency. Some insisted that *none* of their students were fluent Navajo speakers; others judged the number of students who are fluent in Navajo to be as high as 70 to 90 percent. "I would say that most of them [students] have the ability to speak it," one educator stated, reflecting a view expressed by many other teachers at the school (educator interview, 10/17/02). One Beautiful Mountain educator summed up Navajo students' language proficiencies this way:

> I'd say one-third have a hard time understanding English. Then, one-third . . . will understand [Navajo] and speak some, and one-third [are] fluent. So they're all divided. . . . Most of the students I get from [this community] are . . . pretty fluent in Navajo; they can speak it and read some of it very well . . . (educator interview, 1/24/03)

According to educators, students who lack oral proficiency in the Native language are nonetheless likely to have receptive abilities acquired through formal instruction and hearing the language spoken in their homes and communities. At U:s K:ek, Ak Wijid, Bahidaj High, and BFUSD, educators judged as many as 40 to 60 percent of their students to have some receptive abilities in the Native language. At Beautiful Mountain, educators agreed that all of their students have some receptive ability in Navajo.

Overall, educators rated their students' Native language fluency as limited. This was poignantly illustrated in the metaphors they used to describe the Native language: "There is this *afterglow* of a language," one school administrator said (educator interview, 5/11/04; emphasis added). "[T]here are only *remnants* of an active Native language," another administrator maintained (field notes, 10/28/05; emphasis added). The Native language is *"withering away,"* a teacher said (educator interview, 5/11/04; emphasis added).

With some exceptions, students' self-reported Native language proficiencies confirmed those of teachers and administrators. Figure 4.6 shows students' self-assessments of their spoken language proficiencies as reported on project questionnaires. At Ak Wijid, only three students (8 percent of those surveyed) listed O'odham alongside English as a language spoken fluently (this parallels the reports of bilingual teachers in interviews). At Bahidaj, 24 students (21 percent of those surveyed) listed English and Tohono O'odham as languages in which they were orally proficient (virtually identical with BHS educators' reports). At the intermediate and high schools in Black Foothills, seven students (12 percent) said they spoke the Native language fluently along with English and/or Spanish. The percentage of students who claimed to be fluent speakers of the Native language was highest at Beautiful Mountain, where 90 students (49 percent) reported speaking both English and Navajo fluently, and seven (4 percent) claimed Navajo as their primary language (represented by the bar cluster "speak NL fluently"). The total number of BMCS students who reported being proficient Navajo speakers was 97, or 53 percent of those surveyed. In interviews, BMCS students consistently rated the number of their peers who are fluent Navajo speakers as between 75 to 80 percent.

A tiny percentage of students sampled reported being able to read and write the Native language. The highest percentages were at BHS and BMCS, where regular Native language classes were in place.

English Language Proficiencies

Data on students' English language proficiencies are derived from criterion-referenced and standardized tests, questionnaires, and interviews. On questionnaires, educators at AWCS, BHS, and UKCS identified virtually all their Native American students as fluent speakers of English. At BFUSD, the exceptions were Native students whose primary language is Spanish; at BMCS, the exceptions were Navajo students whose primary language is Navajo.

At the same time, a significant number of students at two school sites were identified as LEP. At Ak Wijid, the percentage of LEP students was the highest (63 percent); 58 percent of Beautiful Mountain students were identified as LEP

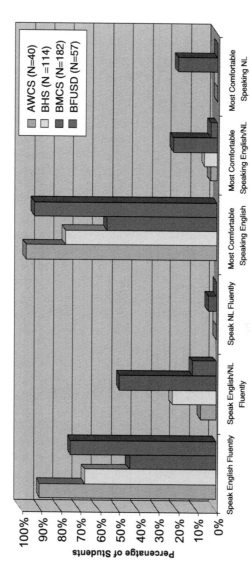

Figure 4.6 Students' Self-Assessment of Their Oral Proficiency in the Native Language and English, All Sites.

Source: Native Language Shift and Retention Project Student Questionnaires.

on the basis of standardized tests. The numbers of LEP students at other study sites ranged from 0 percent (BHS and UKCS) to 18 percent (BFUSD).

Children's Multi-Competencies in Multiple Language Varieties and Genres

Our data indicate a range of proficiencies in the Native language, English, and in some cases, Spanish. Very few (<10) Akimel O'odham and BFUSD students come to school speaking the Native language as a primary language. The number of BHS students who speak Tohono O'doham as a primary language is about 25 percent. The highest degree of Native language proficiency is among Navajo students at Beautiful Mountain, where approximately 50 percent of students reported being fluent speakers of Navajo. Project data also indicate that a majority of Native students at all sites have some receptive ability in the Native language, and that a small percentage of Tohono O'odham and Navajo students are able to read and write the Native language as a consequence of their Native-language classes at school. Census reports, questionnaires, and interview data indicate that Spanish is also spoken in some students' households, and that it is a first language for some students.

Across all project sites, English is the primary language for most youth and the language they report feeling "most comfortable" speaking (see Figure 4.6). Yet a sizable proportion of these students are identified as LEP, and their test scores in reading and language arts fall well below state and national norms. This suggests that these students possess *conversational* proficiency in English, but lack the *academic* proficiency necessary to perform well on English standardized tests and other context-reduced, cognitively demanding school tasks (cf. Cummins, 1989, ch. 3; 2000, chs. 3, 4). As Baker (2006) points out, "To cope in the curriculum, conversational language competence may not be enough" (p. 13).

Overall, project data reveal a complex array of language proficiencies across gradients of Native language vitality and spoken and written genres, as these interact with varieties of English and, in some cases, varieties of Spanish as well. Many children in our sample lack proficiency in the Native language as well as academic English. *This is not to suggest that these children are "semi-lingual" or lack competence in any language.* To the contrary, these children are acquiring receptive and sometimes spoken and written proficiency in the Native language even as they are acquiring multiple varieties of English and for some, Spanish, both inside and outside of school. As many researchers have noted, the notion of semilingualism is based on a flawed, deficit view of bi-/multilinguals on a narrow range of language abilities derived from standardized tests (see, e.g., Baker, 2006; Martin-Jones & Romaine, 1986; MacSwan, 2000; Skutnabb-Kangas, 2000; Wiley, 2005, pp. 75–76, 80–82). The notion of semi-lingualism ignores the social-historical and contextual factors that influence language use (such as those discussed previously in this chapter), as well as the great range of language competencies within given social-linguistic environments. Further, standardized tests of language proficiency "fail to measure the discourse patterns that children from different cultures use with considerable competence" (Baker, 2006, p. 11). Because they reflect dominant literacy practices, these tests are biased against speakers of non-standard varieties (Wiley, 2005). Consequently, the tests fail to elucidate the nature of those varieties and the competencies that children do, in fact, possess.

In contrast to notions of semi-lingualism, the present research highlights the fact that there are many types of bi-/multilingualism and "mono"-lingualism, especially among speech communities undergoing rapid language shift. To illustrate this, we apply a modified version of Arviso and Holm's (1990) typology of eight language proficiencies, developed for Navajo students, to the student sample in our study. In this typology, "AP" refers to academic proficiency—language proficiencies emphasized and tested in school. "CP" refers to conversational proficiencies needed for everyday social interaction (Arviso & Holm, 1990; cf. Cummins, 1989, 2000).[6]

1. **(AP)**Native Language/**(AP)**English: Children who enter school with, or who have the potential to develop academic proficiency in the Native language and English;
2. **(AP)**Native language/**(CP)**English: Children who possess academic proficiency in the Native language and conversational proficiency in English;
3. **(CP)**Native language/**(AP)**English: Children who control academic English and have conversational proficiency in the Native language;
4. **(CP)**Native language/**(CP)**English: Children who have conversational (but not academic) proficiency in the Native language and English;
5. **(AP)**Native language: Children who possess only or primarily academic proficiency in the Native language;
6. **(AP)**English: Children who possess only or primarily academic proficiency in English;
7. **(CP)**Native language: Children who possess only or primarily conversational proficiency in the Native language; and
8. **(CP)**English: Children who possess only or primarily conversational proficiency in English.

For some sites in the present study, to each of these eight categories can be added multi-competencies in Spanish, which expands the typology exponentially. Table 4.2 illustrates the range of competencies in the Indigenous language and English among children at project sites.

Table 4.2 Typology of Students' Linguistic Competencies in the Indigenous Language (IL) and English (E) (adapted from Arviso & Holm, 1990, 2001)

Bilingual Competencies	$_{(AP)}IL/_{(AP)}E$	$_{(AP)}IL/_{(CP)}E$	$_{(CP)}IL/_{(AP)}E$	$_{(CP)}IL/_{(CP)}E$
Monolingual Competencies	$_{(AP)}IL$	$_{(AP)}E$	$_{(CP)}IL$	$_{(CP)}E$

KEY: AP = academic proficiency; CP = conversational proficiency.

Language Attitudes and Ideologies

Youth in our study expressed both positive and negative attitudes toward English and the Native language. On the one hand, English was viewed as universal, utilitarian, and necessary; on the other hand, it was viewed as a colonizing language—a threat to Indigenous identities and lifeways. Participants referenced strong ethnolinguistic attachments to their heritage languages, emphasizing their centrality as markers of Indigenous identities, but also described feelings of Native language embarrassment and shame. These conflicting language attitudes and ideologies are analyzed in detail below.

English as Universal and Necessary/English as a Colonizing Language

Both youth and adults placed a utilitarian value on English, describing it as a "business language" and a "language of survival." As one school administrator pointedly stated, "[T]he bottom line is, this is the twenty-first century . . . they [students] have to compete in the dominant society, which means you have to compete in English" (educator interview, 12/13/05). English was also viewed as universal and therefore necessary. Asked whether knowing English was important to them and why, these were typical youth responses:

> Because that is something most people know how to speak. (youth interview, 6/1/04)

> Yeah, because mostly everyone around speaks some English. (youth interview, 6/1/04)

> If I go to college, I have to talk to professors and things . . . in English instead of my O'odham. (youth interview, 4/19/06)

> Because in the outside world we need [English] because . . . there are hardly any Navajo out there and that is where the English comes in. (youth interview, 5/5/05)

English was also viewed as a marker of social class and prestige. Reflecting on her grandchildren's language preferences, an elder mused, "And I think as they get older . . . they think they are more civilized if they can just speak English [only]" (elder interview, 8/9/06). The corollary to this was a high value on "standard" (schooled) English: "I remember people [making fun of Native language speakers] because they had that broken English accent," a Native-speaking teacher said, "[s]o in my mind, I remember this distinctly, that I wasn't going to have that accent. I was going to learn to speak [standard] English" (educator interview, 5/14/03).

But participants also viewed English as an alien, intrusive language—a tool for assimilation and colonization. These language ideologies were repeatedly expressed in the context of Anglo-American schooling as a primary cause of language loss: "Some [parents and grandparents] had really bad experiences in school," one educator said, "and they said, 'Forget it,' so they said ... 'English, English, English' " (educator interview, 5/10/04). Others, including youth, observed that English had literally been used to kill their forbears with words: "[A] long time ago they [Whites] killed Navajos with their White tongue even though we don't know what they said," a Beautiful Mountain high school student stated (youth interview, 5/5/04).

Native Language as a Source of Pride and Identity/Native Language as an Emblem of Shame

Participants regularly referenced deeply held attachments to the Native language, binding it iconically to Indigenous identities. "Without the language, the culture, I wouldn't know who [I am] as a Navajo," one educator declared (educator interview, 12/13/02). "I think it identifies [us] as an O'odham person ... that's who we are," a teacher at Ak Wijid reflected (educator interview, 11/3/05). Even if they were not fluent speakers of the Indigenous language, youth shared these sentiments, referring to the Native language as "my cultural language" and even "my blood language:"

> For me it's important because it's *my* language and ... when I speak the language, I think it makes me more Pima." (youth interview, 6/1/04)

> [O]'odham is] our blood language ... (youth interview, 6/1/04)

> I would like to know my cultural language ... (student questionnaire)

> [Knowing Navajo] helps me not to lose the identity of who I am, of where I come from ... (youth interview, 5/6/04)

The ties between language and identity are also evident in the contrasts participants drew between English and the Native language. "I really am speaking English instead of my culture," an O'odham youth stated.

Importantly, both youth and adults also placed a utilitarian value on the Native language and bi-/multilingualism. "I get the best of both worlds," a bilingual high school senior stated. "I want to become a doctor and to do that I have to know how to communicate with patients in Navajo and ... English" (youth interview, 5/5/04). Knowing Navajo "gives you a chance to communicate with elders," another high school student said, "and it gives you a chance to listen to what they have to say, and learn stuff from them in Navajo" (youth interview, 5/6/04).

In these discourses, youth also verbalized their concerns about the uncertain future of their heritage languages and the importance of maintaining them, calling into question the role of families, the community, and the school in language revitalization. Maintaining Navajo is important, one young man said, "because the language is dying out. . . . Navajo is supposed to be spoken at all times in the house ... and these parents, they should not be treating their Navajo like this" (youth interview, 5/5/04). "[R]ight now, we're losing it," a Tohono O'odham youth maintained, ". . . so it's very important for me to learn about it and to speak it" (youth interview, 4/19/06).

Adults acknowledged that their language behaviors often run counter to these sentiments. Maintaining the Native language "is extremely important," one teacher said, "[but] in my household, it's all English" (educator interview, 4/29/04). "I always hear people say, 'Oh you need to treasure the language,' " another teacher pointed out, "[b]ut when it comes down to their own homes, they don't do it. They speak English all the time" (educator interview, 4/29/04).

Further, not all youth shared sentiments of Native language pride and allegiance. "Jamie," for example, was a Navajo high school senior when we interviewed him in 2004. Having grown up in a reservation border town, his primary language was English. He suggested that Navajo language and culture were "just the past" (youth interview, 5/5/04). Discourses such as this reveal contradictory ideological currents that run throughout our interviews. A teacher aide reported that a few of her students had insisted, "I'm not going to learn [the Indigenous language] . . . I hate it" (educator interview, 12/12/03). Another teacher described the Native language as "dead" to many of her students; "it makes no sense" to them to learn it, the teacher added, paraphrasing students' reasoning as, "We live in an English-speaking society. Why should we learn this? . . . What are the benefits?" (educator interview, 5/14/05).

To explain these negative attitudes, youth and their teachers returned to the legacy of colonial schooling. "Parents said they did not speak to their children in Navajo because of shame and guilt," a school administrator explained (educator interview, 3/27/03). "It's being told that [the Indigenous language] is stupid . . . to speak Indian is the way of the devil," a 16-year-old declared, adding: "You know, you forsake who you are, you give up having to learn [the Indigenous language] . . . in order to accommodate the mainstream life" (youth interview, 5/6/04).

According to participants, the residue of linguistic shame and guilt and associations of Native languages with "backwardness" and poverty lead many youth to "hide" their Native language proficiencies. Youth "are judged by other people that speak English more clear than they do," a Navajo high school senior observed, "and they just kind of feel dirty about the whole thing, and that's why they put on a fake front and try to make people believe they speak more English than Navajo" (youth interview, 5/5/04). Tohono O'odham-speaking students "won't speak it," a BHS teacher noted, "because a lot of the kids don't, and they might be made fun of" (educator interview, 5/27/05). When children who speak Akimel O'odham "are around others who do not . . . they are made fun of and . . . are too ashamed to keep carrying on the conversation in their language," an elder from Ak Wijid concurred (elder interview, 8/9/06).

These feelings of language shame may be compounded by students' insecurities about their Native language abilities. "They're afraid they're going to make mistakes," a Navajo educator explained, "and if they do, they think that students will start laughing about them" (educator interview, 5/27/03). "If they continue to make mistakes . . . other students start making fun of them and the student becomes reluctant and will not speak in front of [her/his peers] again" (educator interview, 12/12/03).

Ambivalent and Conflicting Language Ideologies

Youth and adult discourses implicate a complex array of ideological forces that underpin Native-language shift and retention among younger generations. On the one hand, both youth and adults expressed pride in their heritage language, fusing it solidly to their sense of self. For these youth, the language is a tool for negotiating multiple cultural worlds, a badge of identity with utilitarian as well as sentimental value. Further, youth recognize, as their parents and grandparents do, that "the language is [declining] very vigorously now" (youth interview, 5/5/04). On the other hand, some youth have internalized the message—conveyed and legitimated by racialized societal discourses and colonial schooling—that speaking the Native language is an emblem of shame that must be renounced. For these youth, the Native language is linked with "backwardness," while English is associated with modernity, universality, and prestige; youth feel they must make an either–or choice. Even for those who place a high value on maintaining the Native language, there is acknowledgement that in "their own homes . . . [t]hey speak English all the time" (educator interview, 4/29/04).

Similar ideological cross-currents have been noted for other endangered-language communities. Writing of "language shame" among Garifuna children in Belize, Bonner (2001) notes that the cause is not language per se, but rather the marginalization of Garifuna and "the association of Garifuna ethnic identity with poverty and low social status" (p. 86). Reese and Goldenberg (2006) describe similar processes for Spanish speakers in southern California. In a collection of life histories representing the multiple "face[t]s" of heritage language loss, Kouritzin (1999) shows the further complicity of racism and linguicism. "I grew up feeling ashamed to be Chinese, and of course, to speak Cantonese," a young woman of Canadian-born Cantonese parents recalls, remembering the taunts of her classmates of "Chinky, Chinky Chinamen" (Kouritzin, 1999, p. 43). "You shame people away from their language," a Cree artist and writer told Kouritzin, ". . . you deal with it by speaking English . . . It's better because now you're white, right?" (Kouritzin, 1999, pp. 66–67).

Preliminary Conclusions and Implications for Language Education Planning

The portraits of language use and change presented here show these processes to be much more complicated than the simple replacement of one language by another. Even in communities with few Native speakers, children are likely to hear one or more Native languages spoken at home and in the community. Moreover, within these speech communities there are diverse Native-language varieties that mark speakers' locale, age, and social status. And, while Native languages find their greatest currency in their spoken form and oral traditions (Sims, 2005), many students also are acquiring Native-language literacy through their classes at school.

Children's linguistic environments also include Nativized varieties of English and, in some cases, Spanish, as well as academic or "schooled" English. While English is increasingly the language of choice, different varieties are used for distinct purposes. The school is the primary domain for academic English—a variety that children may have little exposure to at home. As a consequence, children may be stigmatized as LEP, or, as several educators in our study described it, as "language delayed."

Our data reveal much richer sociolinguistic repertoires among Native students, however, and multifaceted sociolinguistic strengths. As we have indicated above, youth in these rapidly changing linguistic ecologies possess *multiple* types of bi-/multilingualism and "mono"-lingualism. While the diversity of youth language proficiencies is evidence of language shift, it nonetheless represents a potential resource to counter the shift. Too often, though, these resources go unrecognized and unappreciated, or are treated as deficits in school.

This is further complicated by divergent language attitudes and ideologies. Although the overwhelming majority of adults and youth in our study placed a high value on the Native language, they also acknowledged feelings of shame, guilt, and embarrassment associated with speaking the Native language, and a disparity between the expressed ideals of language maintenance and actual language practices. These conflicting ideologies bear the imprint of assimilationist education policies; as Dauenhauer and Dauenhauer (1998) note, "The enduring message of the government and public schools has been that Native American students are of the wrong color, the wrong religion, the wrong language, and the wrong culture" (p. 65). Similar to the Dauenhauers' report for southeastern Alaska, our data show that many Native parents "have come to agree, believing that learning [the Native language] will hurt the students' development in English" (Dauenhauer & Dauenhauer, 1998, pp. 65–66). Shame, guilt, and fear profoundly influence language choices both inside and outside of school.

In her study of Navajo teenagers' language attitudes and choices, Navajo scholar Tiffany Lee interprets language shame and embarrassment "as more to do with their fear of judgment" and peer pressure "than with shame or indifference about their language" (Lee, 2007, pp. 28–29). "The students actually greatly respect their language," Lee maintains, "but the sociological influences surrounding their use of the language in school impede their efforts to speak it" (2007, p. 30). Our study also suggests that an unproductive adult–youth dynamic can ensue from these ideological forces. For example, a bilingual adult who believes the child to whom she or he is speaking has little knowledge of or is uninterested in the Native language is likely to address the child in English. For their part, youth may possess greater Native-language proficiency than they show, "hiding" it out of shame or embarrassment. The effect is to curtail opportunities for rich, natural, child–adult interaction in the heritage language. As one youth explained: "[A] lot of students . . . put a façade on, and . . . try to make teachers believe that they speak primarily [English] and weren't exposed to [the Native language]" (youth interview, 5/5/04).

Educators can counter these dynamics by providing authentic and varied opportunities for children to learn and use the Native language inside and outside of school. There is growing evidence that heritage language instruction can do much to strengthen children's acquisition of the Native/heritage language while also enhancing their English language and literacy development. In the largest longitudinal study of language-minority student achievement, involving 700,000 students representing 15 languages, Thomas and Collier (1997) found that "the most powerful predictor of academic success" was schooling for four to seven years in the Native language, even for children, like those in our study, who were dominant in English and "losing their heritage language" (p. 15). Longitudinal studies of Navajo and Hawaiian immersion show that students in these programs not only develop age-appropriate fluency and literacy in the Native/heritage language, they outperform their peers on standardized tests of English reading, writing, and mathematics (Arviso & Holm, 2001; Johnson & Legatz, 2006; Romero-Little & McCarty, 2006; Wilson & Kamanā, 2001; Wilson, Kamanā, & Rawlins, 2006).

Constructing heritage language programs to achieve the dual goals of Indigenous language revitalization and academic achievement requires some creative rethinking of language pedagogy. As Lee (2007) points out, an important resource is the influence of peers, which can be strategically repositioned from a negative pressure to a positive one by providing opportunities for students to use their heritage language to address contemporary issues of relevance in their everyday lives. "If [the Indigenous language] is to attain status equal to English in school contexts," Lee contends, "it needs to be related to the world of today's teenagers" (2007, p. 29). She mentions community-based service learning projects as one method of achieving this.

We believe that much can be accomplished by engaging youth directly in language-related research and planning. In the present study, the interview and dissemination processes themselves stimulated critical reflection and "ideological clarification" among participants about issues of language endangerment and revitalization—a foundational step in designing revitalization programs (Fishman, 1991; see also Dauenhauer & Dauenhauer, 1998; King, 2000, 2001). As one Navajo student emphasized, "This research you are doing is really a good thing . . . finding a way to bring the [Native] language back to the Native people . . . and hopefully what you are doing will bring a lot back" (youth interview, 5/5/04).

Finally, our research indicates that these endeavors are optimized through coordinated school-community efforts. In the present study, the CRCs both represented and facilitated those efforts. For instance, at one school with a limited (one-half-hour per week) Native language program, the CRCs mounted a reservation-wide language planning initiative that included teacher training in Native language immersion, curriculum development, a trilingual preschool, and Saturday Native language classes for families. These initiatives have begun to work their way back into the schools via those who have participated in the classes and training sessions, and through a newly created tribal language and culture office led by one of the CRCs. At another school, the CRCs are working with a core group of parents to offer voluntary Native language immersion classes at the elementary school.

In these types of school- and community-based language revitalization initiatives, Native youth can play an essential role. "I want to share my language with little kids," a Navajo high school senior told us, because "[t]heir family probably don't talk [Navajo] to them, and it would be best for them to know how to speak it" (youth interview, 5/5/04). "I think that there is definitely an awareness that [the Indigenous language] is important to their [youth's] identity," a teacher observed, "and I could see a lot of the kids stressing it to their own kids" (educator interview, 4/17/03). Our study suggests that these possibilities can best be realized by actively involving youth and young parents, not only as language learners, but also as language planners, researchers, and educators in their own right.

Notes

1 This chapter is adapted from McCarty (forthcoming) and McCarty et al. (in press). We wish to express our deep appreciation to the participating study sites referenced in this article, our graduate research assistants, and the Indigenous Community Research Collaborators (CRCs) with whom we worked closely over a five-year period. Without their dedicated efforts and expertise, none of the work reported here would have been possible.

2 As this chapter went to press, an encouraging profusion of new research on Indigenous youth language practices had recently been published or was forthcoming, including Lee's (2007, in press) surveys and interviews with Navajo and Pueblo youth, Messing's (in press) work with Nahuatl young adults, Nicholas's (2005, in press) study of Hopi youth, Wyman's (in press a, in press b) research on Yup'ik peer culture and language shift, and our own work on Native American youth language ideologies (McCarty et al., 2006a, 2006b). For a broad treatment of these cases and their place in the growing literature on youth language practices, see McCarty and Wyman (in press).

3 At the request of the Internal Review Board that sanctioned the Native Language Shift and Retention Study from 2005 to 2007, we include this disclaimer: All data, statements, opinions, and conclusions or implications in this discussion of the study solely reflect the view of the authors and research participants, and do not necessarily reflect the views of the funding agency, tribes or their tribal councils, the Arizona Board of Regents or Arizona State University, under whose auspices the project operated. This information is presented in the pursuit of academic research and is published in this volume solely for educational and research purposes.

4 All names are pseudonyms.

5 At the tribe's request and to protect its privacy, we do not name the tribe or the language group here.

6 We recognize that these language competencies are neither unitary nor mutually exclusive, and are problematic when interpreted as such (Edelsky, 2006; MacSwan, 2000). We nevertheless find the model helpful in illustrating the presence of *multiple* linguistic and sociolinguistic abilities across different populations and domains.

References

Arviso, M., & Holm, W. (1990). Native American language immersion programs: Can there be bilingual education when the language is going (or gone) as a child language? *Journal of Navajo Education, 8* (1), 39–47.

—— (2001). Tséhootsooídi Ólta'gi Diné bizaad bihoo'aah: A Navajo immersion program at Fort Defiance, Arizona. In L. Hinton & K. Hale (Eds.), *The green book of language revitalization in practice* (pp. 203–215). San Diego, CA: Academic Press.

Baker, C. (2006). *Foundations of bilingual education and bilingualism* (4th ed.). Clevedon, UK: Multilingual Matters.

Baugh, J. (2000). *Beyond Ebonics: Linguistic pride and racial prejudice.* Oxford, UK: Oxford University Press.

Benally, A., & Viri, D. (2005). Diné bizaad (Navajo language) at a crossroads: Extinction or renewal? *Bilingual Research Journal, 29* (1), 85–108.

Bonner, D. (2001). Garifuna children's language shame: Ethnic stereotypes, national affiliation, and transnational immigration as factors in language choice in southern Belize. *Language in Society, 30* (2), 81–96.

Crawford, J. (2000). Seven hypotheses on language loss. In J. Crawford, *At war with diversity: U.S. language policy in an age of anxiety* (pp. 66–83). Clevedon, UK: Multilingual Matters.

Crystal, D. (2000). *Language death.* Cambridge: Cambridge University Press.

Cummins, J. (1989). *Empowering minority students.* Sacramento: California Association for Bilingual Education.

—— (2000). *Language, power and pedagogy: Bilingual children in the crossfire.* Clevedon, UK: Multilingual Matters.

Dauenhauer, N.M., & Dauenhauer, R. (1998). Technical, emotional, and ideological issues in reversing language shift: Examples from southeast Alaska. In L.A. Grenoble & L.J. Whaley (Eds.), *Endangered languages: Language loss and community response* (pp. 57–98). Cambridge: Cambridge University Press.

Dorian, N.C. (1981). *Language death: The life cycle of a Scottish Gaelic dialect.* Philadelphia: University of Pennsylvania Press.

Edelsky, C. (2006). *With literacy and justice for all: Rethinking the social in language and education* (3rd ed.). New York: Routledge.

Executive Order 13096 of August 6, 1998 (1998). American Indian and Alaska Native education. *Federal Register, 63* (154), 42681–42684. Retrieved July 3, 2009 from http://www.eric.ed.gov/ERICDocs/data/ericdocs2sql/content_storage_01/0000019b/80/15/c4/f7.pdf.

Fasold, R.W. (1984). *Sociolinguistics of society.* Oxford: Basil Blackwell.

Fishman, J.A. (1991). *Reversing language shift: Theoretical and empirical foundations of assistance to threatened languages.* Clevedon, UK: Multilingual Matters.

—— (Ed.) (2001). *Can threatened languages be saved? Reversing language shift, revisited: A 21st century perspective.* Clevedon, UK: Multilingual Matters.

Guba, E. (1999) Foreword. In E. Stringer, *Action research* (2nd ed.) (pp. xi–xv). Thousand Oaks, CA: Sage.

Haugen, E. (1972). *The ecology of language.* Stanford, CA: Stanford University Press.

Holm, A., & Holm, W. (1995). Navajo language education: Retrospect and prospects. *The Bilingual Research Journal, 19* (1), 141–167.

Hornberger, N.H. (2003). Multilingual language policies and the continua of biliteracy: An ecological approach. In N.H. Hornberger (Ed.), *Continua of biliteracy: An ecological framework for educational policy, research, and practice in multilingual settings* (pp. 315–339). Clevedon, UK: Multilingual Matters.

Johnson, F.T., & Legatz, J. (2006). Tséhootsooí Diné Bi'ólta'. *Journal of Navajo Education, 45* (2), 26–33.

King, K.A. (2000). Language ideologies and heritage language education. *International Journal of Bilingual Education and Bilingualism, 3* (3), 167–184.

—— (2001). *Language revitalization processes and prospects: Quichua in the Ecuadorian Andes.* Clevedon, UK: Multilingual Matters.

Kouritzin, S.G. (1999). *Face[t]s of first language loss.* Mahwah, NJ: Lawrence Erlbaum.

Krauss, M. (1998). The condition of Native North American languages: The need for realistic assessment and action. *International Journal of the Sociology of Language*, *132*, 9–31.

Kulick, D. (1992). *Language shift and cultural reproduction: Socialization, self, and syncretism in a Papua New Guinean village.* Cambridge: Cambridge University Press.

Lambert, W.E., Hodgson, R.C., Gardner, R.C., & Fillenbaum, S. (1960). Evaluational reactions to spoken language. *Journal of Abnormal and Social Psychology*, *60*, 44–51.

Lee, T.S. (2007). "If they want Navajo to be learned, then they should require it in all schools": Navajo teenagers' experiences, choices, and demands regarding Navajo language. *Wicazo Sa Review*, Spring, 7–33.

—— (in press). Language, identity, and power: Navajo and Pueblo young adults' perspectives and experiences with competing language ideologies. *Journal of Language, Identity, and Education*, *8* (4).

MacSwan, J. (2000). The threshold hypothesis, semilingualism, and other contributions to a deficit view of linguistic minorities. *Hispanic Journal of Behavioral Sciences*, *22* (1), 3–45.

Martin-Jones, M., & Romaine, S. (1986). Semilingualism: A half baked theory of communicative competence. *Applied Linguistics*, *7* (1), 26–38.

McCarty, T.L. (2003). Revitalising Indigenous languages in homogenising times. *Comparative Education*, *39* (2), 147–163.

—— (forthcoming). *Language planning and policy in Native America—History, theory, praxis.* Clevedon, UK: Multilingual Matters.

McCarty, T.L., & Romero, M.E. (2005). What does it mean to lose a language? Investigating heritage language loss and revitalization among American Indians. *Show and Tell*, Fall, 14–17. Tempe: Arizona State University College of Education.

McCarty, T.L, Romero, M.E., & Zepeda, O. (2006a). Reclaiming the gift: Indigenous youth counter-narratives on Native language loss and revitalization. *American Indian Quarterly*, *30* (1 & 2), 28–48.

—— (2006b). Native American youth discourses on language shift and retention: Ideological cross-currents and their implications for language planning. *International Journal of Bilingual Education and Bilingualism*, *9* (5), 659–677.

McCarty, T.L., Romero-Little, M.E., Zepeda, O., & Warhol, L. (2007). *The impact of Native language shift and retention on American Indian students' English language learning and school achievement.* Final report on the Native Language Shift and Retention Study, Grant No. R305T030007. Report submitted to the U.S. Department of Education Institute of Education Sciences, Washington, DC.

McCarty, T.L., Romero-Little, M.E., Warhol, L., & Zepeda, O. (in press). Indigenous youth as language policymakers. *Journal of Language, Identity, and Education*, *8* (4).

McCarty, T.L. & Wyman, L. (Guest Eds.) (in press). *Indigenous youth and bilingualism.* Special issue, *Journal of Language, Identity, and Education*, *8* (4).

Messing, J. (in press). "I didn't know you knew Mexicano!": Shifting ideologies, identities, and ambivalence among youth in Tlaxcala. *Journal of Language, Identity, and Education*, *8* (4).

Miles, M.B., & Huberman, A.M. (1994). *Qualitative data analysis* (2nd ed.). Thousand Oaks, CA: Sage.

Mühlhäusler, P. (1996). *Linguistic ecology: Language change and linguistic imperialism in the Pacific region.* London: Routledge.

National Caucus of Native American State Legislators (2008). *Striving to achieve: Helping Native American students succeed.* Denver, CO: National Conference of State Legislatures.

Nettle, D., & Romaine, S. (2000). *Vanishing voices: The extinction of the world's languages.* Oxford: Oxford University Press.

Nicholas, S. (2005). Negotiating for the Hopi way of life through literacy and schooling. In T.L. McCarty (Ed.), *Language, literacy, and power in schooling* (pp. 29–46). Mahwah, NJ: Lawrence Erlbaum.

—— (in press). "I live Hopi, I just don't speak it:" The critical intersection of language, culture, and identity for contemporary Hopi youth. *Journal of Language, Identity, and Education, 8* (4).

Platero, P. (2001). The Navajo Head Start language study. In L. Hinton & K. Hale (Eds.), *The green book of language revitalization in practice* (pp. 87–97). San Diego, CA: Academic Press.

Reese, L., & Goldenberg, C. (2006). Community contexts for literacy development of Latina/o children: Contrasting case studies. *Anthropology and Education Quarterly, 37* (1), 42–61.

Romero-Little, M.E., & McCarty, T.L. (2006). *Language planning challenges and prospects in Native American communities and schools.* Tempe: Arizona State University Education Policy Studies Laboratory. Retrieved July 3, 2009, from http://www.language-policy.org/content/features/EPSL-0602-105-LPRU.pdf.

Seidman, I. (2006). *Interviewing as qualitative research: A guide for researchers in education and the social sciences* (3rd ed.). New York: Teachers College Press.

Silverstein, M. (1979). Language structure and linguistic ideology. In R. Clyne, W. Hanks, & C. Hofbauer (Eds.), *The elements: A parasession on linguistic units and levels* (pp. 219–259). Chicago: Chicago Linguistic Society.

Sims, C.P. (2005). Tribal languages and the challenges of revitalization. *Anthropology and Education Quarterly, 36* (1), 104–106.

Skutnabb-Kangas, T. (2000). *Linguistic genocide in education—Or worldwide diversity and human rights?* Mahwah, NJ: Lawrence Erlbaum.

Spolsky, B. (1975). Linguistics in practice: The Navajo Reading Study. *Theory into Practice, 14* (5), 347–352.

Stancavage, F.B., Mitchell, J.H., Bandeira de Mello, V., Gaertner, F.E., Spain, A.K., & Rahal, M.L. (2006). *National Indian Education Study: Part II: The educational experiences of fourth- and eighth-grade American Indian and Alaska Native students.* Washington, DC: Institute for Education Sciences, U.S. Department of Education.

Thomas, W.P., & Collier, V. (1997). *School effectiveness for language minority students.* Washington, DC: National Clearinghouse for Bilingual Education.

U.S. Census Bureau (2001). *The Native Hawaiian and other Pacific Islander population: 2000.* Census 2000 Brief. Washington, DC: U.S. Department of Commerce Economics and Statistics Administration.

—— (2002). *The American Indian and Alaska Native population: 2000.* Census 2000 Brief. Washington, DC: U.S. Department of Commerce Economics and Statistics Administration.

—— (2006). *We the people: American Indians and Alaska Natives in the United States.* Census 2000 Special Reports. Washington, DC: U.S. Department of Commerce Economics and Statistics Administration.

—— (2007). State and county QuickFacts. Washington, DC: U.S. Census Bureau. Retrieved August 17, 2007 from http://quickfacts.census.gov/qfd/.

Weitzman, E.B. (2000). Software and qualitative research. In N.K. Denzin & Y.S. Lincoln (Eds.), *Handbook of qualitative research* (2nd ed.) (pp. 803–820). Thousand Oaks, CA: Sage.

Wiley, T.G. (2005). *Literacy and language diversity in the United States* (2nd ed.). Washington, DC: Center for Applied Linguistics.

Wilson, W.H., & Kamanā, K. (2001). "*Mai loko mai o ka 'i'ini*: Proceeding from a dream."

The 'Aha Pūnana Leo connection in Hawaiian language revitalization. In L. Hinton & K. Hale (Eds.), *The green book of language revitalization in practice* (pp. 147–176). San Diego, CA: Academic Press.

Wilson, W.H., Kamanā, K., & Rawlins, N. (2006). Nāwahī Hawaiian Laboratory School. *Journal of American Indian Education, 45* (2), 42–44.

Woolard, K.A. (1998). Introduction: Language ideology as a field of inquiry. In B.B. Schieffelin, K.A. Woolard, & P.V. Kroskrity (Eds.), *Language ideologies: Practice and theory* (pp. 3–47). New York: Oxford University Press.

Wyman, L. (in press a) Youth, linguistic ecologies and bilingual practices: A Yup'ik example. *Journal of Language, Identity, and Education, 8* (4).

—— (in press b) *Language shift, youth culture, and ideology: A Yup'ik example.* Clevedon, UK: Multilingual Matters.

5 Diverse Literacy Practices among Asian Populations

Implications for Theory and Pedagogy

Alan Hirvela

Introduction

Stephen Kucer (2005) has observed that "Regardless of where one teaches, bilingual learners are sitting in our classrooms" (p. 13). In the North American context that is the focus of this chapter, many of those learners are Asian, especially Chinese and Korean students. Being bilingual, biliterate, and bicultural to one degree or another, they experience literacy learning differently than the mainstream students in North American classrooms. Their constellation of "bi-ness" characteristics affords them unique access to literacy resources, but also presents them, and their teachers and families, with unique challenges with respect to their literacy (and biliteracy) development. As Li (2006a) explains,

> For second language learners, who work in two cultural worlds, the process of acquiring a language(s) may involve the intersection of multiple/different cultural values and beliefs and multiple contexts of socialization. For such learners, language practices do not exist in isolation from each other, just as cultures and communities do not exist as discrete entities, but rather interact with each other in various degrees of complementarity or conflict. (p. 358)

In this chapter I explore a select sampling of recent literacy-based research on Asian populations in North America in an effort to draw attention to what we now know and are theorizing about the world of literacy as it is experienced by these populations and what this knowledge signifies with respect to future directions for theory, pedagogy, and research about them. In operational terms, I treat literacy more conventionally as reading and writing, with a particular focus on writing, but not strictly in the context of school-based literacy acquisition. What happens to these learners outside school is as important as what takes place in school with respect to literacy development.

Following a short review of key perspectives that tend to guide the research discussed in this chapter, I move to an examination of Heritage Language Learners (HLLs) and learning in various contexts and then shift to English Language Learners (ELLs). My primary focus in both cases is within the K–12 age range, but there is some exploration at the college level as well. The chapter concludes with a summary of conclusions and perspectives arising from the literature I review.

Key Perspectives

Researching the kinds of learners discussed in this chapter, as well as writing about such research, is not an easy matter for reasons discussed in two recent commentaries by Gutierrez and Orellana (2006) and Orellana and Gutierrez (2006). In Gutierrez and Orellana, for example, they note that the portrait of ELLs derived from research about them "is often flawed, incomplete, or one-dimensional, making it harder to challenge static, problematic, and racialized views of the practices and promise of English Learners" (p. 504). A similar point can be made about HLL research. In the same article they discuss the attempts of the (nearly always qualitative) research to "denote normativity or regularity in English Learners" by focusing "on a narrow range of what constitutes the students' literacy toolkit and repertoires" (p. 504) in what they call "slice of life" studies that fail to account for the full complexity and depth of these students' engagement with literacy. They add that there is a tendency in these studies to "selectively exemplify" these learners and thus reinforce stereotypes, whether in the context of emphasizing problems they encounter (reinforcing a deficit model that characterizes them negatively) or presenting them from what they call "romantic perspectives" that add weight to the well-known and problematic "model minority" view of Asian students as exemplars of learning and academic achievement.

In their follow-up article (Orellana and Gutierrez, 2006) they address (as they did in their earlier paper) what they refer to as the "difference framework" that relies on comparisons between ELLs and other (i.e., mainstream) students in ways which unfairly position the ELLs (p. 120). They argue for research designs that capture the "repertoires rather than the isolated practices" (p. 120) of these learners by exploring their literacy practices across multiple contexts of literacy activity. In this review I have tried to be sensitive to concerns they express while attempting to capture the essence of what has been learned about HLLs and ELLs during the past 20 years or so of research about them. I focus especially on more recent studies, i.e., those appearing within approximately the past ten years, since these studies capture the most current theories and findings about their literacy acquisition.

As noted briefly earlier, nearly all research involving these populations is qualitative in nature, with case studies dominating. These generally adopt a socio-cultural or New Literacies Studies theoretical framework. The sociocultural framework, drawing on the work of Vygotsky (among others), moves beyond the cognitive focus on the individual operating in isolation and embraces, instead, the notion of learning mediated through interaction with others, including more experienced mentors or peers, with language playing a central role in the learning process. As Guzetti and Gamboa (2004) explain, "Sociocultural perspectives perceive literacy as more than the technical skills of reading and writing. Learning and practicing are shaped by the social and cultural beliefs students hold about the value and purposes of literacy" (p. 413).

The New Literacies Studies (NLS) framework focuses on "multiple literacies" rather than simply one literacy, the predominant school-based literacy, and works from the belief that literacy activity occurs within larger social and cultural practices situated in various contexts of use (Gee, 1996; Street, 1993), thus necessitating a pluralization of the root term literacy. In this framework, says Schultz (2002), "the concept of literacy has been broadened beyond traditional school writing to include practices that are more often found in home and community settings" (p. 360). The sociocultural and NLS frameworks are particularly appealing for research involving bilingual, bicultural, and biliterate individuals, for whom literacy learning takes place across multiple settings and must be examined within them.

Another key framing device in many of these studies is the notion of "language socialization," which overlaps to some extent with sociocultural theory (Schiefflin & Ochs, 1986). Language socialization explores intersections between language and culture. As Lam (2004) explains, "language socialization looks at how language learning is part of a process of socialization through which the learner acquires particular status and relationships in the social environment where the learning takes place" (p. 45). The Asian populations discussed in this chapter are apparently continuously engaged in this process of socialization as they move between the native and second language cultures they exist within and seek to find comfortable alignments within them in their literacy (and other) practices, thus making language socialization an important theoretical framework for research in this area.

The notion of "language shift" likewise plays a role in such research. Language shift refers to the changing linguistic affiliation of learners who have grown up speaking a heritage (i.e., non-English) language at home and then, as they move through an English-dominated school (and perhaps social) environment, increasingly adopt English as their primary language of use, thus enacting a shift from the former emphasis on the HL (Fishman, 1991; Tse, 2001; Veltman, 1983). This shift is not a neutral process; it has outcomes that may carry profound consequences, particularly in the loss of the native language. Wong Fillmore (1991), for example, observes that "losing a first language has a negative effect on the social, emotional, cognitive, and educational development of language minority students, as well as the integrity of their families and the society they live in" (p. 342). As the number of immigrant and HL learners steadily increases in North America, the nature and extent of language shift has drawn growing attention among literacy researchers.

Also to be noted is the concept of "acculturation," introduced powerfully in the work of Schuman (1978) and expanded on since then. Acculturation, says Chinen (2005), "emphasizes identification with a community as a primary requirement of second language acquisition" (p. 32). Schuman (1978) describes this as "the social and psychological integration of the learner with the target language group" (p. 29). As in the related situation of language shift, acculturation as a theoretical framework informs literacy research that looks at how learners such as HLLs and ELLs generate their preferred identification with a particular language and cultural group.

Because these learners are engaged in bilingual contexts of learning, conceptualizations of bilingualism and biliteracy also play a major role in such research. Hornberger (1989), for example, has proposed an influential theoretical framework called a "continua of biliteracy" which identifies nine particular dichotomous forms of continua that impact on the development of biliteracy skills, such as relationships between speaking and writing and the native language (L1) and target language (L2). Hornberger discusses ways in which positive transfer can occur as learners move through these continua. She calls for educational settings and opportunities in which learners can draw on as many of these continua as possible. In her view, full biliteracy development will take place when learners experience learning situations in which they experience all of the continua. Hornberger and Skilton-Sylvester (2000) have extended Hornberger's original continua of biliteracy model by exploring in greater depth the content of biliteracy through an exploration of biliteracy development in two communities—Cambodian and Puerto Rican—in Philadelphia.

Working in a similar vein, Valdes and Figueroa (1994) make a distinction between what they call "elective bilinguals" and "circumstantial bilinguals." Elective bilinguals choose a path of bilingualism that involves engaging in meaningful and generally formal or structured opportunities for language learning, particularly in academic settings, while circumstantial bilinguals are those whose bilingual development occurs through participation in informal learning opportunities or environments. This distinction provides a helpful lens through which to examine the literacy experiences of HLLs and ELLs, in particular.

Using the theoretical frameworks just described as a backdrop, in the remainder of this chapter I discuss what a number of influential studies have revealed about the literacy development of both heritage and English language learners.

Heritage Language Learners

In this section I discuss heritage language learning and learners in two primary contexts: (1) learning that takes among K–12th grade students in the home environment and heritage language schools, and (2) voluntary or out-of-school literacy activity where the heritage language is the dominant one. I also look briefly at heritage language learning in college-level foreign language programs.

For my purposes, heritage language learners will be defined broadly to include a number of variations. By way of a general definition of heritage learners, they are characterized as students living in families where a language other than English is used at home and where the students are bilingual to some extent (Chevalier, 2004; Valdes, 2001). In practice, though, the term is used in a variety of ways. There are, for example, those learners who are born in the same country where they later study in school, such as American-born Koreans or Canadian-born Chinese. There are also "1.5 generation" learners, or immigrants, who were born overseas in a non-English-speaking country and who have taken up permanent residence in the country to which they have immigrated. Another group is known as "sojourners" or "parachute kids," that is, learners who reside temporarily in an English dominant country. Sojourners are those who accompany their parents, e.g., graduate students, to such a country, and who will eventually return to their native country with their parents. By contrast, "parachute kids" are those sent by their families to a country like the United States or Canada for educational purposes, with the intention of them returning to the native country upon completion of a high school education overseas.

The heritage language—that is, the dominant non-English language of the home—has been researched in three primary contexts. One is the *informal* learning guided by parents and influenced by the home literacy environment. Another is the *formal* learning that takes place in heritage language schools and is characterized by what Zhou and Kim (2006) refer to as an "ethnic system of supplementary education." These may be weekend schools funded and operated by local ethnic organizations or weekday after-school operations to which students go for tutoring or language study following completion of their school day in the mainstream school. These, too, exist as a result of efforts made by local ethnic communities. Chinese (buxiban) and Korean (hagwon) schools are the most dominant of these learning environments, while Japanese heritage schools (hoshuko) also exist in certain communities. The Chinese schools, which began appearing in the late 1880s, are mostly community run, while the large majority (around 75 percent) of Korean schools are affiliated with churches; these began to appear in the early 1970s (Zhou & Kim, 2006). Japanese schools, like the Chinese schools, are usually community-based. Finally, as some research has shown, there is also *voluntary out-of-school* heritage language literacy activity that is initiated by the students themselves as opposed to that facilitated by parents. All three types will be discussed in this section of the chapter.

Informal Heritage Language Learning

In this section I look at heritage language learning that takes place within the home environment and among peers, that is, in settings not governed by a school-type structure. This is a relatively recent line of research that dates only to around the mid-1990s, with case studies the primary source of data. These studies generally examine the nature of the heritage language literacy activities taking place in the home environment and the effects of parental involvement on such learning. A key term guiding these studies is the aforementioned *language shift*, which captures the dynamic nature of students' dominant language affiliation as they grow up, particularly as they enter and continue through mainstream schooling, where English is the medium of instruction and, increasingly as the students pass through school, their chosen language for communication at home and for social purposes. Informal parental efforts are intended to shift children back to the learning of the heritage language, or at least enable them to maintain fluency in it. Here we encounter another, and closely related, key term: *language maintenance*, that is, sustaining the heritage language ability that students have acquired, particularly in their early years. Tse (2001) observes that "we know far less about the conditions that support maintenance and development of the heritage language, especially in terms of literacy" (p. 677), than about language shift, while Li (2006a) notes the "paucity of research" concerning immigrant parents' "responsibility to maintain and develop the heritage language" (p. 356).

Kimi Kondo (1998) conducted one of the first major studies that looked at heritage language shift and maintenance. She examined six students of Japanese heritage in Hawaii; in each case, the mother was an immigrant from Japan, while the students had been born and raised in Hawaii. Kondo found that those students who had successfully maintained the heritage language benefited from efforts by the mothers to ensure a strong presence for Japanese in their lives, including speaking the language to them at home and finding ways for them to use the language outside the home. In those situations where strong parental involvement (particularly maternal) was not evident, language shift had occurred, resulting in increased loss of heritage language ability as the students grew older. Kondo's study is especially important because it draws attention to the role of parents in heritage language learning, which has been a key topic of similar research since then.

Another notable study of this kind is Guofang Li's (2006a) investigation of three Chinese elementary school (first/second grade) children in Canada. Li examined the nature, extent, and influence of home literacy practices and parental attitudes on the children's biliteracy development. As with similar studies of Chinese parents' attitude toward language maintenance (Li, 2002; Li, 2004; Luo & Wiseman, 2005), Li's study draws attention to how important those attitudes are. However, Li's study is especially noteworthy because it reveals the complexity extant in the home environment as a source of biliteracy development and especially heritage language growth and maintenance.

One of Li's participants, Anthony, born in Canada, was reluctant to speak Chinese at home (though he understood it) and tended to read (but not write) in English, though he attended a Chinese school on Saturdays. His resistance to Chinese and the apparent inevitably of the domination of English in his life were reluctantly accepted by his parents, who tried to align their home literacy practices with those expected of Anthony in school. This was consistent with their apparent open-minded attitude toward living in Canada. Another participant, Kevin (born in Canada), also resisted Chinese heritage learning and, like Anthony, spoke English at home while his family spoke Chinese. His home literacy activities revolved around English, though he, too, attended a Chinese language school where he received instruction in Chinese literacy. What was interesting in Kevin's case was his father's fear of discrimination in Canada against Chinese people. It was for this reason that he and his wife deferred to Kevin's preference for English use and English literacy; they saw this as necessary to his survival and success in Canada.

A third participant in this study, Alana, an immigrant from China, experienced a different set of reactions and influences from her parents, who were uncertain as to whether they would reside permanently in Canada. Because of the possibility that they would return to China, they insisted on Chinese language use at home. Alana was expected to speak Chinese, and her parents played a proactive role in teaching her to read and write Chinese, though not at the expense of her English language development. Unlike Anthony and Kevin, Alana did not attend a Chinese heritage language school. Interestingly, she was much more comfortable than they were with learning Chinese and, despite the lack of formal Chinese schooling, enjoyed and took pride in her Chinese literacy ability. Noting the importance of the home environment in biliteracy (and especially HLL) development, Li concluded that "It is necessary for parents to examine their own beliefs and practices at home and become aware of the importance of their role in supporting literacy development. They need not only to promote heritage language use but also to employ a variety of strategies to ensure the children's continued development in reading and writing their first language at home" (2006a, p. 378).

Hyungmi Joo's (2009) study of four middle school Korean immigrant students in the United States also reveals the importance and positive effects of the home environment and parental support for both heritage language and biliteracy development. In this study, the HL (Korean) "functioned as a primary language for communication with parents and community members in the students' everyday lives" and "played an intricate role in personal, cultural, and societal aspects of the participants' lives" (p. 82). Three of the four participants were especially active readers of Korean texts, while all four read English texts to some extent. Writing (in either language) was much less prominent, but it, like reading, appeared to play a key role in what Joo saw as "ethnic and cultural identity formation" (p. 93). That is, the participants were eager to maintain strong ties with their heritage language roots and so made a point of using Korean on a daily basis, but at the same time placed emphasis on English, the language they needed for success in school. To them it was important to be seen as the bilingual and biliterate individuals that they were.

Working along similar lines while investigating the influence of an informal environment outside the home setting, Lucy Tse (2001) conducted an important qualitative study on language shift and maintenance that included three Asian students among a research cohort of ten: Helen (Chinese), and Julie and Meg (Japanese), all of whom were early adults at the time of the study. Helen was born in Hong Kong and immigrated to the United States at the age of four; Julie and Meg were both born and raised in the United States. Tse identified two key categories of heritage language maintenance arising from her study: (1) language vitality, that is, the degree to which use of the heritage language is valued, especially outside the home; (2) literacy environment and experiences. With respect to language vitality, she found that, like Kondo (1998) cited earlier, parental contributions and those of other literate adults were a significant factor in HL maintenance in terms of using the HL in meaningful day-to-day activities and providing resources such as literacy materials. Of particular note in this category was Tse's finding that "peer influence is central to the development of positive attitudes toward and interest in the heritage language" (Tse, 2001, pp. 698–699). As Tse explained, all of her participants had developed strong relationships with HL peers, especially in school, and "peers not only helped the participants develop positive opinions about becoming highly literate in the heritage language, they also introduced literacy-related activities that many of the participants credited for their advanced heritage language development" (p. 683). Institutional support, such as opportunities to use the HL in local community organizations or churches, was also an important factor related to language vitality. Another noteworthy result related to the domain of literacy environment and experiences. Here Tse found considerable resentment among her Asian participants toward their heritage language school experiences, particularly the nature of that school-ing. From the participants' point of view, the approach to literacy instruction was in fact "an additional obstacle to building HL literacy" (p. 702), though Tse noted that such instruction may have been more beneficial than the participants recognized.

The newest line of research investigating Asian students' informal maintenance and development of the heritage language focuses on their literacy practices in online settings. These function as what Canagarajah (1997) has called important "safe houses" for communication in non-threatening circumstances. Warschauer (2000) insightfully predicted that the rise of the internet and computer-mediated forms of communication would encourage and nourish learners' use of a target language or a heritage language in need of further development. The handful of studies that have explored communication in this context have affirmed Warschauer's prediction.

In the context of heritage language maintenance, one noteworthy study is Jin Sook Lee's (2006) examination of the online experiences of two Korean-American sisters, Jendy and Lizzy, who participated actively in a Korean language social networking site. The sisters' relationship with Korean, their heritage language, was complex. They used it extensively within the family setting, where there was strong parental emphasis on its importance, including the provision of ample materials for reading in Korean (which the parents brought home after visits to Korea). However, between spending considerable time growing up in Saipan (after being born in Seattle) and then in small towns in California, they had encountered limited opportunities for interaction with Korean-speaking peers. Not surpris-ingly in these circumstances, they developed strong skills in English and felt especi-ally comfortable speaking, reading, and writing that language. However, reflecting findings reported in other studies cited earlier, there were strong positive effects arising from the importance the parents had attached to heritage language use. In particular, both sisters became deeply engaged in writing in Korean on a popular Korean language networking site called Cyworld. A key feature of writing in this environment is that, like other electronic forms of writing (such as text mes-saging), participants can choose, or alternate, between standard and deviant forms of the language in use in an atmosphere of linguistic freedom and creativ-ity. Lee found that both sisters used Cyworld as a place to "experiment" with their use of written Korean and thus expand their heritage language literacy skills. This was also an opportunity to connect "with popular Korean culture, including popular expressions, current fashion trends, as well as links to popular movies, television shows, celebrity news, and popular music" (p. 101). Indeed, "the pro-cess of using electronic literacy to interact with a social network of Korean speakers nurtured and sustained the feeling of being connected to a wider com-munity of Koreans" (p. 110). Thus, online experiences served both heritage language maintenance and personal as well as cultural identity building purposes.

In a series of recently published articles, Youngjoo Yi (2005, 2007, 2008a, 2008b, 2009) has reported similar findings with respect to Korean 1.5 generation high school students living in the United States. In each of these qualitative studies, her findings have shown that her participants were active readers and writers outside school, particularly in Korean but also in English to some degree. Here, too, participation in Cyworld played a key role in maintaining or developing heritage language skills and cultivating ties with Korean culture and peers in a process of identity construction. As in Lee's just cited (2006) study, online composing in the heritage language took place in a "safe house" environment that promoted heritage language literacy development. By communicating online with peers experiencing similar linguistic, cultural, and personal issues, both Yi's and Lee's participants felt empowered to "play" with the heritage language and thus enhance their literacy skills while forging stronger connections with their heritage culture. Of particular interest in one of Yi's studies (2008a) was her participants' engagement in a locally produced website called "Welcome to Buckeye City." Relying primarily on Korean, they used the site for a variety of related purposes, including the composing of "relay novels" in which they all contributed chapters. According to Yi (2008a), in this and their other composing on this website, "One significant aspect of these adolescents' out-of-school literacy practices is that they engaged in forming a 'diasporic' network while performing Korean 'language and cultural maintenance' as they actively engaged in online literacy practices" (p. 679).

It will be interesting to see, in future research, the extent to which this kind of internet-based, social networking involvement in heritage language literacy takes place among other Asian populations and what effect(s) this has on their development of heritage language literacy skills. At present, the research on informal heritage language learning provides a consistent picture with respect to the importance of encouragement in the home environment (especially parents) for heritage language use to prevent language shift if not to promote further development of the heritage language.

Formal Heritage Language Learning

As Zhou and Kim (2006) have shown, Asian students who were born in North America or immigrated there commonly engage in formal learning of their heritage language in addition to the informal learning available in the home environment or via their own voluntary efforts. This formal learning mainly takes place through participation in heritage language schools that operate after school hours during the week or, more commonly, on weekends, and sometimes through private tutoring. Zhou and Kim (2006) also describe the considerable importance placed on such learning and on the schools that provide it within various Asian communities.

Chinen and Tucker (2005) conducted one of the most frequently cited studies of heritage language schools. They examined the attitudes and experiences of 31 Japanese-American students who attended a Japanese school that held classes on Saturdays. These adolescent students expressed a positive overall view regarding the school and likewise reported positive beliefs with respect to its effect on the development of their Japanese language (and literacy) proficiency and the growth of their ethnic Japanese identity, with the older students expressing a stronger sense of such identity than the younger students.

Haneda and Monobe (2009) have also investigated the effects of participation in a Saturday Japanese school. However, their study looked at the experiences of four "sojourner" students (two boys and two girls), that is, students born and raised in Japan and residing temporarily overseas (in this case, the United States), with the full intention of returning to Japan. For these middle school age students, maintenance of their heritage language was crucial since they would be living in Japan again. However, as students studying in the American setting, development of their English language ability was crucial to ensure successful participation at school. In addition, the parents attached importance to the children's development of English proficiency, knowing that it would be beneficial to their futures in Japan as well as necessary for their school experience in America. Thus, while the children could continue speaking Japanese at home and maintain their oral skills, there could potentially be deleterious effects on their Japanese literacy skills in the quest to acquire proficiency in English. To combat this possibility, all four students attended the local Saturday Japanese school. What Haneda and Monobe found was that what they called the students' "envisioned future" in which Japanese proficiency would be so important motivated the students to invest considerable time and effort in their participation in the Japanese school. For the two boys, this meant placing priority on maintenance and development of their Japanese ability, while the two girls were inclined toward being bilingual and biliterate in the belief that English would likewise be beneficial in Japan. However, like the boys, they placed great emphasis on their heritage language school studies because they believed that Japanese "was core to who they were" (p. 25).

Maguire and Curdt-Christiansen (2007) have also explored the world of heritage language schools, in this case a Saturday Chinese language school in Montreal. Working from the belief that "children construe their language ideologies by appropriating from the language and cultural communities in which they participate" (p. 23), they examined the written Chinese texts of 48 children in grades 3 and 4. Nearly half (27) were born in China; the rest were born in Canada or elsewhere. Like the other studies reviewed here, in this one the parents had a strong belief in the importance of maintaining or developing the children's heritage language ability. While noting that some of the children disliked attending the Chinese school, they found that "most of them considered learning Chinese a necessary part of growing up, aligned themselves with Chinese culture, and expressed their allegiance to China and being Chinese. Many see learning Chinese as an ideological obligation towards their families and an important part of their identity" (p. 32).

The findings reported thus far, which cast the heritage language schools in a generally positive light, are especially interesting when juxtaposed against Li's (2006a) and Tse's (2001) studies cited earlier with respect to their participants' negative perceptions toward such schools. This apparent contradiction raises questions, though not necessarily doubts, about the value of these schools. They also draw attention to a more recent study by Jia (2009), who explored the literacy instruction practices at a Chinese heritage language school in the United States. Jia analyzed two contrasting models of literacy instruction: the student-centered, discussion-oriented approach adopted by two of the teachers and the teacher-centered approach favored by the third teacher in the study. All three teachers were born, raised, and thus educated in China. Those advocating the student-centered approach (Ms. Meng and Mr. Guo) linked literacy teaching to the acquisition of values via attempts to link assigned texts with real-life events and concerns in the students' lives. By contrast, the teacher-centered instructor (Ms. Young) employed a traditional memorization and drill approach to learning Chinese characters and followed the long-held Chinese belief that good handwriting is essential as a reflection of the character behind the writer. Jia also analyzed the responses and the home literacy practices of the parents, who were also from China and mostly highly educated after studying for advanced degrees in the United States. Jia found considerable acceptance among the students of the student-centered classes and resistance to the teacher-centered class. By contrast, many of the parents initially opposed this student-centered methodology, while preferring the traditional approach of Ms. Young. They saw a strong connection between literacy instruction and the inculcation of traditional Chinese values in children and believed the traditional mode of instruction better served this goal. Interestingly, they generally did not provide much literacy instruction at home; nor did they hold high expectations for the HL school. Still, "the parents regarded going to the Chinese school not as a matter of choice, but as a must" (p. 70). Eventually, as the students resisted the more traditional language socialization pedagogy of Ms. Young, the parents, while embracing the kind of socialization attempted by Ms. Meng and Mr. Guo, generally adjusted their attitudes toward acceptance of the student-centered approach. Jia concludes that this kind of spirit of negotiation between parents and teachers over HL literacy instruction is an important component in successful HL school literacy education.

Xiao Lan Curdt-Christiansen (2006) has likewise looked at the instructional practices in a Chinese HL school setting. She explored the discourse patterns in seven classrooms and found that the majority of the class time (60 percent) was what she called "teacher centered" or "teacher controlled" in the traditional power and authority mode that dominates Chinese education. The school itself had as its mission "transmitting and carrying forward the Chinese culture and traditions abroad" (p. 192) and utilized textbooks that promoted "Chinese moral and cultural values" (p. 192). Most of the teachers had been trained and had taught in China in the traditional mode of instruction. What was noteworthy in her study, particularly in contrast to Jia's previously cited article, was the finding that some of the teachers were able to utilize and adapt this conventional pedagogy in ways that allowed for some meaningful student participation that "facilitated students' learning" (p. 197) despite the reliance on recitation, memorization, and limited student responses to prompts from the teachers. Thus, while the traditional form of pedagogy "tends to be rigid and non-motivating for students" (p. 204), HL learning took place, leading the author to call for further exploration of a teaching practice that is generally criticized in contemporary foreign language teaching theory.

Formal HL learning is also examined at the college level, and here a very different picture emerges. One striking difference is the reliance on quantitative research methods, as opposed to the heavy reliance on qualitative methods in the studies cited earlier. In addition, at the college level, HL students are mixed with non-HL students, unlike in the HL schools. Thus, the thrust of much of the research in this area is to compare how HL and non-HL students learn the language being taught and to look at the influence of the resources the HL students bring to such a learning environment. Generally possessing at least some fluency in the speaking of the heritage language as well as some experience in the HL school environment, these students are seemingly at an advantage compared to their non-HL peers. However, the research has generally found that in the case of literacy skills, particularly the academic literacy skills emphasized in college foreign language programs, the HL students do not outperform the non-HL students. The findings from studies of students of Chinese (e.g., Ke, 1998; Shen, 2003; Weger-Guntharp, 2006; Wen, 1997; Xiao, 2006), Japanese (e.g., Kondo, 1999; Kondo-Brown, 2003, 2005; Matsunaga, 2003), and Korean (e.g., Jensen, 2007; Kim, 2007; Yu, 2007) raise important questions about how foreign language courses at this level should be taught so as to best accommodate and make use of the linguistic and cultural resources HL learners possess. Some researchers in this area, e.g., Kondo-Brown and Fukuda (2007), have recently called for the creation of separate language courses or tracks for HL and non-HL students to address what they see as the differing needs of these two groups of students.

On the whole, the research on formal heritage language learning presents a mixed picture, particularly with respect to the pedagogical practices employed in them. How much actual learning takes place with them, and what parents and teachers can and should do to make full and effective use of them, must be further explored.

English Language Learners

English language learners (ELLs) are defined in this review as non-native English-speaking students who intend to reside permanently in North America and are thus learning English for a variety of purposes: academic, social, vocational, etc. In this way they are distinguished from overseas or international students studying in Anglophone universities and requiring English more strictly for academic purposes, that is, ESL (English as a Second Language) students. In this chapter I restrict my focus to those students generally placed in the ELL category.

Research on Asian ELLs has been, like HLL research, primarily qualitative in nature, with a strong sociocultural framework driving data gathering and analysis. Much of the research focuses on learning in school settings, and this often brings into play a critical lens not seen nearly as much in the HLL research. This may not be surprising given the high stakes involved in ELLs' performance in school, particularly in the case of literacy skills. In this section of the chapter I look at ELL research in four contexts: studies comparing home and school-based learning, studies looking strictly at school-based learning, research emphasizing literacy activity outside school, and research which explores ELLs' transition from high school to college.

Home–School Comparative Studies

This line of research, which compares learners' literacy learning experiences in the home as well as school environments, arises from the fact that many ELLs live in circumstances where the home environment is bilingual in nature and in which parents place an emphasis on literacy acquisition at home as well as school. Guofang Li (2004, 2006b) has published two well-known studies that draw comparisons between home-based and school-based literacy practices and activities, with a particular interest in the kinds of alignment that take place in these environments and parental attitudes toward literacy development. The 2004 study explores the experiences of two Chinese primary school students, Billy and Jake. Each boy struggled to acquire literacy skills in English. Both were born in Canada but lived in a predominantly Chinese-speaking community. Each preferred to speak Cantonese at home and even at school whenever possible (perhaps not surprising given that nearly two-thirds of the students in their school were ethnic Chinese). Where they differed was in the nature of the home environment. In Billy's home, there was a strong parental emphasis on literacy and an equally strong support system. By contrast, Jake experienced little of such support; what he did receive was in the form of a non-Chinese tutor (to help with his English) hired by his mother well after the study began.

What Li found striking was what she called "discontinuities" in the home–school alignment. These took several forms. For instance, the parents believed in a bottom-up, word-by-word decoding approach to reading, while the school stressed the importance of meaning within a top-down orientation. There were also differences between the parents' and teachers' expectations for how much homework should be assigned and what its nature should be. They differed, too, in the interpretation of what was causing Billy and Jake's struggles with literacy. Finally, there was a lack of communication between the teachers and the parents. In this study Li identified a crucial aspect of the learning dynamics experienced by ELLs like Billy and Jake as they encounter literacy: "They not only had to learn to acquire their first-language literacy at home while learning second-language literacy at school, but they also had to constantly negotiate between school and home literacy practices that were embedded in different cultural values" (p. 60).

Interestingly, the "discontinuities" that resonated so strongly in Li's 2004 study do not appear with nearly as much strength in the 2006b study, which examined, via a survey, the attitudes toward literacy learning, homework, and school–home communication of 26 middle-class Chinese immigrant parents in the United States. Here Li found evidence of more common ground between parents and teachers, though differences did arise in some cases. On the other hand, what she found in this study echoed what was reported in her 2004 study with respect to the parents' attitudes toward how reading should be taught and learned. She found, too, that they believed strongly in the importance of learning to read and in the value of reading beyond school as well as the opportunity for reading to be experienced in a variety of ways. They also stressed the importance of writing outside school. In general, she found that "the parents still hold very strong traditional Chinese cultural values on how literacy should be learned and transmitted," but they place less stress on homework than had been seen in previous research and are making more efforts to adjust to the expectations and practices associated with literacy instruction in the American educational system (p. 43). Drawing from the results of this study and others like it, Li asserts the following: "There is a pressing need for schools to provide instruction that is meaningful and affirming to the cultural identities of students of diverse cultural backgrounds. However, what literacy is, how it is learned, and what is practiced depends upon many sociocultural factors of which schools are often not aware" (p. 28).

With respect to the literacy environment in the home setting, what Li found was also seen in an earlier study by Xu (1999), who examined the home literacy practices of six Chinese children in the United States and their schoolteachers' reactions to them. Xu, like Li, found that the parents actively encouraged and supported literacy learning in both Chinese and English, and in the case of Chinese often modeled reading and writing for their children. Xu also found, as in Li's studies, that the parents both supervised the children's learning and provided additional homework where they deemed it necessary. Another notable finding in Xu's study was the diversity of the kinds of literacy experiences among the children and their parents and across the six families participating in the study. Xu's study was inspired in part by teachers' questions about the children's home literacy practices, and upon sharing the results with them, Xu noted the importance of the teachers' learning of the support for literacy and diversity of activity in the homes and of the subsequent need for "each child to be perceived as a unique individual from a unique home environment with varying home literacy experiences and knowledge in English and the native language" (p. 61).

The conclusion by Xu just cited is particularly interesting and useful when seen in the context of one of the most notable home–school literacy studies of Asian ELLs (or any ELL population): Ellen Skilton-Sylvester's (2002) exploration of the literacy practices and experiences of an elementary school age Cambodian girl named Nan. What stood out for Skilton-Sylvester was the "mismatch between her home and school practices" (p. 63). At home Nan was an avid writer in English, where she had free rein to draw from a wide range of sources to practice literacy in various creative, story-telling modes. At school she was an entirely different writer because of the limited, controlled nature of academic writing compared to what Skilton-Sylvester called the "social work" of her out-of-school writing. The restrictions of school-based writing did not allow Nan to tap into the creativity found in her out-of-school writing. As Skilton-Sylvester observed:

> When I compared Nan's in-school and out-of-school literacy practices, one of the first things I noticed was how her oral, visual, and creative focus was often at odds with what mattered most in the school writing she encountered. Whereas at home her strengths as a speaker, an artist, and storyteller were assets, at school such strengths did not help her master the powerful discourse in which the written word is more valued than speech, words are more important than pictures, and accuracy often matters more than meaning. (p. 67)

Here, as suggested earlier by Xu, it would be invaluable for those in the school environment to have a greater awareness of the world of home literacy experienced by students like Nan and to incorporate that into school-based experiences and instruction.

Sze, Chapman, and Shi (2009) extend our understanding of the home–school comparison in their exploration of the home and school-based writing of four grade 2 Chinese children in Canada. The children's parents were all immigrants from China and Hong Kong. Cantonese was the language spoken at home, where the parents engaged in informal heritage language instruction but also encouraged the children to develop their English literacy skills. The authors analyzed the writing produced at home and in school by the four children and were struck, in particular, by the wider range of functions and genres of writing generated in the home setting, where the children wrote frequently, and of their own volition, in English, such as composing notes to their parents. Noting the value of this kind of out-of-school literacy experience to overall literacy development, the authors concluded, like Xu and Skilton-Sylvester, that it is important for teachers not only to be aware of the literacy practices occurring at home, but also to find ways to link those to the literacy activities enacted in the school setting so as to create richer grounds for literacy development.

Studies of School-based Literacy

Several recently published studies of ELLs' school-based reading and writing have provided a rich picture of how second language learning unfolds for these learners in the context of academic literacy development. They also reveal an intriguing mix of theoretical frameworks by which their literacy activities are analyzed.

Working with the theoretical lens of critical pedagogy, Souryasack and Lee (2007) investigated the writing in an after-school literacy program of a rarely studied Asian population: Laotian students. Their three middle-school participants had been born and raised in the United States and were unmotivated, struggling writers while trying to write within the narrow conventions of standard academic writing in English despite strong oral fluency in English. As in the case of Nan cited earlier, for these students, what they perceived as the rigid, formulaic nature of academic writing prevented them from being interested in writing or drawing on the resources they possessed. Participation in an after-school enrichment program that featured a writing workshop approach in which the participants were part of a community of writers collaborating in writing about their own lives and identities changed their perception of writing in English. Working in small groups and talking about writing with others sharing their Asian background had an empowering and motivating effect that opened the world of literacy to them. Thus, like Nan, they had to circumvent the official school curriculum in order to be opened to the world of literacy.

Jayoung Choi (2009) also reveals the benefits of ELLs' out-of-school literacy activity in her discussion of three Asian boys' participation in a voluntary, after-school literacy club she formed. Much of their activity revolved around responses to multicultural literature they read; these responses occurred on a Wiki site she created. As the boys interacted on this site, they explored issues in their own lives related to themes and events in the literary texts, engaged in identity construction, and developed their English literacy skills.

An earlier study by Duff (2001) brings these results into even sharper focus. Duff looked at the experiences of a wide variety of Asian students (Chinese, Korean, Japanese, Indonesian) enrolled in two sections of a 10th grade social studies course at a Canadian high school. Duff found that the group project and structured debate and discussion sessions that were a major part of the course activity and that relied on cultural knowledge and norms not familiar to the students disadvantaged them: "ESL students appeared to be onlookers or voyeurs in discussions, peripheral or marginal participants who were at times amused, puzzled, and alienated by the talk around them" (p. 121). She also found that, despite the importance placed on language use in performing the genres and activities common in the course, "very little explicit attention was paid overtly to text structures and vocabulary that students read, heard, or were asked to produce" (p. 121), thereby denying these English language learners the opportunity they needed to acquire important academic discourse knowledge. Thus, the students were unable to display knowledge or ideas they possessed or to further develop their academic literacy skills. Here, similar to Li's 2004 study cited earlier, there was a kind of discontinuity between what the ELLs needed and what the school structure provided. This is where, as we saw in Choi's (2009) and Souryasack and Lee's (2007) studies cited earlier, after-school literacy programs appear to mitigate against such discontinuities to some extent.

A study by Margaret Hawkins (2005) of two kindergarten students, a boy from Peru and a boy from Korea, further problematizes issues surrounding ELLs in school settings. Working within the framework of identity formation, which she defines as "an ongoing negotiation between the individual and the social context or environment, with particular attention paid to operant cultural and power relations" (p. 61), Hawkins examines the boys' early encounters with academic literacy in English. The Peruvian boy, Anton, struggled in terms of social interaction, but he carefully observed how to use language for academic purposes and in the process developed an identity for himself within this new school setting, thus enabling his language proficiency to increase significantly. By contrast, the Korean boy, William, was outgoing, confident, and socially adept, yet his level of English proficiency fell far short of Anton's by the end of the school year. While William was a popular classmate, he failed to gain the necessary knowledge of the early genres of school discourse and expression unfolding at that grade level; by contrast, Anton was remote from his peers but gained the genre and discourse knowledge that eluded William. Seeing this surprising contrast, Hawkins raises questions about the approach to learning adopted in this setting, asserting that

> there needs to be a shift in the teacher's role: from designing lessons to designing ecologies. This shift might entail varying participation patterns across classroom activities and designing instruction such that students must

collaboratively negotiate content- and genre-specific language and perform-ances. This approach would allow for both practice and scaffolding. (p. 79)

For Hawkins this means providing more overt instruction that shows "children how to do performances and how to recognize and use forms of language that fit with types of practices . . . teachers, even teachers of very young children, must focus on academic literacies and not just vocabulary and generalized grammatical proficiency" (p. 80). Thus, a young learner like William, who resisted meaningful engagement in academic interactions, must be drawn into them through a peda-gogy that encourages successful participation among all learners.

Finally, two studies first-authored by Sarah McCarthey provide valuable and yet somewhat contrasting pictures of the literacy activities, especially writing, of Asian elementary school students. The McCarthey, Garcia, Lopez-Velasquez, Lin, and Guo (2004) study looks at 4th and 5th grade Chinese (as well as Spanish-speaking) students in an American elementary school in which they read and wrote in three different settings: ELL classes, content-courses, and native language courses. The purpose was to compare the opportunities for writing across these contexts. Because the students "had to interact with at least three different teachers in different settings, each involving different tasks, expectations, and rules governing interaction . . . [their] views of writing at school were somewhat fragmented" (p. 384). On the whole, the students had, on the one hand, numerous opportun-ities to write, with writing generally related to reading, but the nature of their writing was limited, with the primary emphasis on summarization of what they had read. Thus, they were unable to engage in writing that might have been more meaningful to them, such as writing about their own experiences. Nor were there meaningful opportunities to talk about writing. In addition, it was only in the Chinese and Spanish classes where the students could write in their native lan-guage, thus limiting their opportunities to examine their bilingual identities. Interestingly, these apparent limitations did not stand in the way of the students' learning how to successfully negotiate the demands of their wide-ranging curric-ulum across the three contexts they experienced, and they managed to find ways to write about what interested them. However, the authors questioned whether there was sufficient support for the students' fuller development as writers.

In McCarthey and Garcia (2005), the focus is once again on Chinese- and Spanish-speaking students, but this time with an emphasis on both home- and school-based writing across a two-year time period. Here the authors found a wide variety of writing activities across the home and school environments as well as varying attitudes toward writing among the participants. In the case of school-based writing, they discovered a mixed picture with respect to opportun-ities for the students to experience different forms of writing and to develop positive attitudes about writing. For the most part, year two was more favorable than year one. They also observed shifting positive views toward writing (in English and Chinese) across the two years of the study as well as changes in how well the students wrote in their native language, Chinese. A key variable in the Chinese writing was whether the students would eventually be returning to live in a Chinese setting.

Taken together, these two studies, as well as the others cited in this section, reveal a complex picture with respect to academic literacy development among ELLs. There appears to be no consistent pattern in terms of what and how often they write, and there is no clear evidence as to how well they learn to write academically in English.

Out-of-School Literacy Research

A recent and intriguing development in research on ELLs is the shift in focus from the classroom to the students' voluntary or self-selected literacy activities that have little or no connection to academic literacy acquisition. Two studies by Eva Lam are especially noteworthy in this line of research. In Lam (2000) she describes a case study of a high-school-age immigrant student from Hong Kong, Almon, and how he addressed his difficulties with writing in English through his creation of an English-language website devoted to a popular Japanese singer. Lam shows how Almon's online interaction with an international group of what she calls "transnational peers" enabled him to restructure his engagement with writing in English. By personalizing his use of written English within the domain of computer-mediated communication (CMC), Almon found an important identity for himself and in turn shifted to a more positive outlook on literacy activity in English. In a later study, Lam (2004) once again works within the framework of ELLs operating voluntarily within a community of transnational peers. She shows how her high-school-age participants, Yu Qing and Tsu Ying, both immigrants to America from southern China, participated actively in a bilingual (English and Cantonese) online site called Hong Kong Chatroom and, like Almon, underwent a process of language socialization that strengthened their identities and their relationship with English (as they had intended by joining the chatroom). Here, too, computer-mediated literacy activity in an out-of-school setting contributed to the development of literacy skills.

Rebecca Black (2005) reported a similar success story in the context of ELLs' participation in an online "fanfiction" community in which they either reacted to fictional stories posted by other members of the community or contributed their own stories. For instance, she analyzes the written interaction of a 14-year-old native speaker of Chinese who, in introducing her story to her community, acknowledges her ELL status and the mistakes this may cause her to make and explains how her participation in this computer-mediated site will hopefully enable her to improve her written English. She moves from this short, casual introduction where she relies somewhat on colloquial English to a more formal-sounding summary of her story, followed by the story itself, which, like the summary, features more careful, precise, formal English. In discussing this and other examples found in her study, Black notes the many ways in which the participants use voluntary literacy activity in English, ranging from composing stories to responding to them to peer review intended to help others improve their stories.

The studies of out-of-school or voluntary literacy activity among ELLs suggest that this is an important domain for such activity (as it is for HLLs, as we saw earlier). This is likely to be an important site for future ELL research.

English Language Learners Transitioning to College

In this section I look at a handful of studies that examined ELLs in their transition from high school to college-level literacy. It is important to note here that there is in fact a rich body of literature that examines the college-level writing of English as a Second Language (ESL) students, that is, as explained earlier, international students studying in Anglophone universities. Many of these studies have focused on Asian students. However, as noted previously, these students operate in different circumstances with respect to English than ELLs. Thus, I have chosen not to write about that literature.

In this "transitions" literature about ELLs, we once again see a heavy emphasis on qualitative research. Furthermore, a key feature of the "transitions" literature is its focus on "1.5 generation" or immigrant students. These are students, who in the case of North America, immigrated to Canada or the United States after receiving some education in their home country and who expect to reside permanently in North America. Thus, they pass through the North American education system with a vested interest in learning English for both personal and practical purposes and yet retain ties of one kind or another to their home culture and perhaps literacy. As the "transitions" research shows, the movement from high school to college is often complex and unpleasant, though in many cases ultimately marked by success.

Linda Harklau (2000), in one of the most discussed studies of this kind, sheds important light on this complex trajectory. Her study, which tracks three ELLs (two Asian students and one Turkish student) from their senior year in an American high school through their first year of community college study, adopts as a framing device the notion of representation. By this she means the ways in which schools define students and their expectations for them, such as through stereotypes (as opposed to, say, the students' self-representation). At the high school level, the ELLs are seen as the "good kids" because of their considerable work ethic and determination to succeed academically. As a result, they are popular among teachers. However, Harklau also observes a subtle deficit model at work within this "good kids" representation: the students' dedication and perseverance are seen, in subtle ways, as indications that the students lack necessary academic ability and English proficiency and must compensate through their "good" behavior. Teachers then lower their expectations for these students and modify the amounts and kinds of school work expected of them. Then, when they enter a community college or university, they become the "worst kids" who are viewed within another deficit model. In this case, they are seen as ill-prepared academically, especially as writers, an outcome of the lowered expectations and simplified work assigned them in high school. Here we see some of the reasons why the transition from high school to college-level literacy is complex and often problematic for ELLs.

Marilyn Sternglass (1997), too, has provided important insight into this transitions trajectory. Her longitudinal study focused on nine undergraduates at an American university, including one Asian participant, Jacob, a Korean 1.5 generation student whose pre-college education had taken place mostly in Australia. He brought with him from those years a core set of writing skills and a deep interest in creative writing. For Jacob, learning to write at the college level was largely a matter of developing appropriate strategies for meeting the writing-related challenges he faced in various courses. What was interesting was Jacob's primary motivation for developing these strategies: not to succeed, but rather to meet course requirements with the least amount of effort and commitment he could expend and still make it through the courses. Sternglass laments the way in which Jacob used his "talents to 'fool' his instructors by providing the minimal amount of work and thinking, padding and stretching out small amounts of information to fulfill length requirements" (p. 288).

A longitudinal study by Herrington and Curtis (2000) produced somewhat similar results regarding an Asian student, Nam, among their four participants. Like Jacob, Nam, an undergraduate immigrant student from Vietnam who was studying at an American university, was initially unwilling to invest more than was necessary to perform assigned writing tasks. His experiences in high school had generally been unhappy ones, and he had come to view the learning of writing as a matter of imitation, not creation. Eventually, however, he did demonstrate greater flexibility in how he approached writing. When he encountered discourse practices that he deemed valuable to achieving his goals as a college student, he displayed a facility for appropriating them and using them in ways he considered constructive. However, he resembled Jacob in the sense that "when he encountered a discourse that conflicted with ways of writing and knowing that he valued, he distanced himself from that discourse, mimicking it in order to pass the course, but separating it from 'his way' " (p. 57).

Linda Blanton's oft-cited (2005) article, "Student Interrupted: A Tale of Two Would-be Writers," is yet another intriguing exploration of the transitions experienced by ELLs moving on to college. She provides case studies of students from Ethiopia and Vietnam. Tran, the Vietnamese immigrant, successfully passed through ELL and mainstream English courses in high school and then ran into serious roadblocks while attempting to complete required ESL writing courses as a college student. While failing the ESL courses several times, particularly because of linguistic issues that undermined his written performance, he went on to take (and pass) as many other college courses as he could, until he could proceed no further without successful completion of the ESL requirement. In exploring this dilemma, Blanton writes about the "interrupted" literacy background of students like Tran, who leave their native country before establishing full command of literacy in their L1. Because of the relatively undemanding literacy environment in high school, where, as Tran maintained, he mostly had to "fill in blanks" with respect to writing, as well as the fluency of his spoken English, his interrupted literacy development was not a significant detriment to success. However, he left high school with an unfinished notion of literacy and major weaknesses in the grammatical domain of writing. Here Blanton addresses what she sees as the failure of ESL writing administrators and instructors to account meaningfully for students' interrupted literacy acquisition. Her conceptualization of interrupted literacy development and its implications for second-language writing instruction have provided significant food for thought in the design of college ESL writing course curricula.

Blanton's findings and conclusions resemble those in an earlier study by Susan Bosher (1998), who compared the college-level writing of a student from Vietnam who had completed high school there and two students, one from Laos and the other from Cambodia, who had immigrated to the United States and graduated from high school there. Bosher compared the writing processes and products of the three students. As in Blanton's study, the two 1.5 generation students struggled with the transition to college-level writing, while the Vietnamese student made a smoother transition from her high school experience in Vietnam despite considerably less fluency in her spoken English than the two participants who had attended high school in the United States. While not overtly citing Blanton's notion of "interrupted" literacy development, Bosher, too, was struck by the negative impact on literacy development of students moving to L2 writing before fully developing their L1 writing (and reading) ability, as was the case with her two 1.5 generation students. Similar to Blanton's study, in her research Bosher found that high school literacy experiences were not sufficient to prepare 1.5 generation students for college-level literacy activities.

Another study that sheds light on these issues is Frodesen and Starna's (1999) exploration of the high school–college transition of a 1.5 generation immigrant from China named Min. Min's experiences echoed Tran's in Blanton's study cited earlier. Min had performed well in high school, but, having left China at the age of 13, he had not fully developed his Chinese literacy skills and thus lacked an overall foundation in literacy. And, like Tran, he had significant problems with the grammatical dimension of writing in English. Nor was he challenged by the nature of the literacy activities common in high school. Indeed, he left high school believing he was a good writer in English. In college he struggled with writing in his ESL courses, especially because of his difficulties with the linguistic aspects of writing. However, unlike Tran, he eventually committed himself to overcoming his grammatical errors and finally achieved success. As his grammatical command increased, the overall quality of his writing did as well, in that his better use of language complemented other aspects of writing. However, it was only through a major commitment to improvement on his part that his progress occurred, a commitment not easy for many 1.5 generation students to make.

One more study worth noting in this context is Christina Ortmeier-Hooper's (2008) examination of three 1.5 generation students' reactions to their high school and college experiences, including their literacy experiences, relative to their status as ELLs. One of her participants, Jane, had immigrated from Hong Kong and spent much of her life in the United States, so much so that she considered English to be her native language. Despite her long residence in the U.S., Jane had been branded an ELL/1.5 generation student and had spent five years in ELL courses prior to her university study. As a college student, she was so afraid of being "outed" as a 1.5 generation student that, in her first-year English composition assignments where she was expected to write a literacy autobiography and in other ways explore her background, she avoided, as much as she could, descriptions or discussions of her bicultural and biliterate identity. Having been singled out as an ELL student by teachers in her high school (and stigmatized by this, from her point of view), Jane sought to conceal that side of herself as much as she could, thus depriving herself of opportunities to further her development as a writer by essentially bypassing important components of her background that she brought to her writing.

The research on ELLs' transition from high school to college-level literacy has, thus far, provided a complex picture of what takes place. On the one hand, many seem to struggle; on the other hand, many find ways to succeed. However, success in these studies tends to be defined by grades obtained by the students and by graduation. What is not clear is how much their literacy skills actually improve or what they can really do with literacy. It is interesting to note, though, the indications that they develop a notion of writing as a tool for learning, not as an end in itself.

Conclusion

Ann Raimes, a key figure in the development of the second language writing field as an autonomous domain of scholarship, once remarked that "There is no such thing as a generalized ESL student" (1991, p. 420). Likewise, this review is a reminder that "there is no such thing as a generalized Asian student" or a generalized account of how Asian students engage literacy. Across and within the two general realms examined—heritage language learning and English language learning—we have seen that literacy practices unfold in very different ways, and for different reasons, among the Asian students inside those realms. In addition, there is now a wide range in terms of the settings in which literacy research involving these populations takes place: in the home, in the community (including locally organized heritage language schools), in the mainstream school context, in after-school programs, and in online environments. There is indeed considerable diversity in the world of literacy as it is experienced by Asian populations in the North American context. While there is one significant thread that runs across all of the populations and all of the settings in which they engage literacy—their relationship with literacy is situated in dual linguistic, rhetorical, cultural, and social worlds—it is clear that their literacy practices and encounters are manifested in complex ways. A concluding remark cited earlier in Li's (2004) study captures some of this complexity and is thus worth revisiting:

> They [his research participants] not only had to acquire their first language literacy at home while learning second language literacy at school, but they also had to constantly negotiate between school and home practices that were embedded in different cultural values. Their parents and teachers held different cultural beliefs about literacy and how it should be taught, and these differences were reflected in their differences in making sense of the two children's struggles. (p. 60)

We gain from Li's remark a sense of how many factors must be considered in attempting to understand these populations' passage through literacy (and biliteracy) development and in developing appropriate theory, pedagogy, and research that accounts meaningfully for them.

Stephen Kucer (2005) reminds us that "Literacy involves more than a text and a mind" (p. 224) and that "literacy does not necessarily have an endpoint" (p. 287). In other words, it involves a host of learning variables and entails an ongoing process of acquisition. These observations ring especially true with respect to Asian populations as we attempt to capture what takes place within the cognitive, social, cultural, and academic domains in which they engage in literacy activity for both formal (school-based) and informal (out-of school or voluntary) purposes and with two languages as their key contact point with literacy. This enormous diversity reinforces key points cited earlier by Gutierrez and Orellana regarding research on these populations: that there is danger in trying to create norms that reflect their common experiences, and that the (perhaps understandable) temptation to gain larger perspectives on their literacy practices based on studies of narrow sites for their literacy activity via "selected exemplification" may ultimately restrict what is learned about them. Clearly, more attention must be given to how research about these populations should be conducted and what theoretical frameworks should guide that research, especially given the ever-present danger of essentializing them or reinforcing (unintentionally or otherwise) deficit models of literacy development by comparing literacy acquisition between languages and cultures. And, as the observation by Raimes cited above suggests, we must be particularly careful about attempting to represent "Asian" students as one collective body.

While researching and theorizing about these populations as well as developing pedagogies that enhance their literacy and biliteracy development may seem daunting given these perspectives, we have also seen in this selected review that there is a rich body of studies providing important information about what happens to them within the various research sites that have been explored. With its qualitative orientation and its reliance on case studies that penetrate deeply into the daily and ongoing realities of life within the multiple literacies experienced by these populations, the research in this area has opened important doors toward uncovering what it means to acquire literacy and become literate relative to the biliterate, bicultural, and bilingual circumstances they face. We have learned a great deal about what literacy means to these populations and what variables are in play as they negotiate the world of literacy, and we have seen how literacy unfolds in different ways within the heritage language learning and English language learning realms that are the focus of such research. In short, important progress has been made.

At the same time, there is a need for more research of this kind, that is, extensions of what has been done thus far. As Yi and Hirvela (2009) observe in a recently published special issue of the *Journal of Asian Pacific Communication* which focuses on Asian students in the North American context, "In order to better understand these uniquely positioned individuals who regularly juggle languages and cultures and perhaps competing needs and expectations across them as they move between home, school, and community, we need research that explores the world of shifting, and perhaps overlapping, literacies as these young people traverse it" (p. 3).

One of the newer lines of research—investigating out-of-school literacy practices—looks particularly valuable given the ubiquitous world of electronic literacy that many, if not all, of these learners inhabit via their involvement in homepages, text messaging, and other computer-mediated activities popular among young people. There is also a need for more research related to identity construction as it relates to these students, whose cultural affiliations are apparently in flux as they move through various stages of development in both their in- and out-of-school literacy practices. Yi's (2009) study, cited earlier, in which she uses the "transnational perspective" to investigate Korean 1.5 generation adolescents' voluntary, online composing activities, represents an important step in this identity construction research. As Yi asserts, the transnational framework is best suited to capture the "two-way back-and-forth movements" 1.5 generation students experience as they traverse the literacies, cultures, and languages that are part and parcel of their daily lives (p. 101). Learning more about the increasing numbers of heritage language schools (concomitant with the steady rise in the numbers of Asian students) and the literacy-based teaching and learning practices within them also appears to be an area worthy of expanded research. Along related lines, a strong need remains for further research exploring pedagogy as it impacts on the two different populations this review has examined. Fortunately, in all of these areas a foundation to work from has been established.

On the other hand, there is a notable lack of research that explores the important world of assessment as it relates to the Asian populations. How to assess their literacy skills and knowledge in valid and reliable ways when they circulate between languages and literacies is a complex question deserving much greater attention. This can be tied to research that explores pedagogical practices and how they are related to assessment practices. Another as yet undeveloped area of research involves their use of literacy in occupational settings upon completion of school and of opportunities to develop academic literacy skills. As we have seen, some attention is now being paid to out-of-school literacy practices. This could be expanded to vocational and community-based literacy activity that occurs beyond school boundaries.

Collectively, what we have seen over the past 20 years, and particularly in more recent years, is that momentum is growing in terms of the amount of research being conducted on Asian populations' literacy practices. We have learned much about the nature of their literacy practices, about the settings in which they take place, about the stakeholders involved (particularly the learners themselves), about the issues to be addressed, about the ways of conducting such research, and about the diversity present in all of these areas. Thus, we find ourselves in a dynamic period of growth and understanding as we explore what literacy means for these Asian populations, with opportunities abounding for further research within and across the two populations discussed in this review.

References

Black, R.W. (2005). Access and affiliation: The literacy and composition practices of English language learners in an online fanfiction community. *Journal of Adolescent and Adult Literacy, 49(2)*, 118–128.

Blanton, L. (2005). Student, interrupted: A tale of two would-be writers. *Journal of Second Language Writing, 11(2)*, 295–310.

Bosher, S. (1998). The composing processes of three southeast Asian writers at the post-secondary level: An exploratory study. *Journal of Second Language Writing, 7(2)*, 205–241.

Canagarajah, S. (1997). Safe houses in the contact zone: Coping strategies of African-American students in the academy. *College Composition and Communication, 48(2)*, 173–196.

Chevalier, J.F. (2004). Heritage language literacy: Theory and practice. *Heritage Language Journal, 2(1)*. Retrieved August 11, 2008 from http://www.heritagelanguages.org/

Chinen, K. (2005). Heritage language development: Understanding the roles of ethnic identity and Saturday school participation. *Heritage Language Journal, 3(1)*. Retrieved August 11, 2008 from http://www.heritagelanguages.org/

Chinen, K., & Tucker, G.R. (2005). Heritage language development: Understanding the roles of ethnic identity and Saturday school participation. *Heritage Language Journal, 3(1)*. Retrieved August 11, 2008 from http://www.heritagelanguages.org/

Choi, J. (2009). Asian English language learners' identity construction in an after school literacy site. *Journal of Asian Pacific Communication, 19(1)*, 130–162.

Curdt-Christiansen, X.L. (2006). Teaching and learning Chinese: Heritage language classroom discourse in Montreal. *Language, Culture and Curriculum, 19(2)*, 189–207.

Duff, P.A. (2001). Language, literacy, content, and (pop) culture: Challenges for ESL students in mainstream courses. *The Canadian Modern Language Review, 58(1)*, 103–132.

Fishman, J. (1991). *Reversing language shift*. Clevedon, UK: Multilingual Matters.

Frodesen, J. & Starna, N. (1999). Distinguishing incipient and functional bilingual writers: Assessment and instructional insights gained through second language writer profiles. In L. Harklau, K.M. Losey, & M. Siegel (Eds.), *Generation 1.5 meets college composition: Issues in the teaching of writing to U.S.-educated learners of ESL* (pp. 61–80). Mahwah, NJ: Lawrence Erlbaum.

Gee, J.P. (1996). *Social linguistics and literacies: Ideology in discourses* (2nd edition). London: Taylor & Francis.

Gutierrez, K.D., & Orellana, M.F. (2006). The "problem" of English learners: Constructing genres of difference. *Research in the Teaching of English, 40(4)*, 502–507.

Guzetti, B.J., & Gamboa, M. (2004). Zines for social justice: Adolescent girls writing on their own. *Reading Research Quarterly, 39(4)*, 408–436.

Haneda, M., & Monobe, G. (2009). Bilingual and biliteracy practices: Japanese adolescents living in the United States. *Journal of Asian Pacific Communication, 19(1)*, 7–29.

Harklau, L. (2000). From the "good kids" to the "worst:" Representations of English language learners across educational settings. *TESOL Quarterly, 34(1)*, 35–67.

Hawkins, M.R. (2005). Becoming a student: Identity work and academic literacies in early schooling. *TESOL Quarterly, 39(1)*, 59–82.

Herrington, A.J., & Curtis, M. (2000). *Persons in process: Four stories of writing and personal development in college*. Urbana, IL: National Council of Teachers of English.

Hornberger, N.H. (1989). Continua of biliteracy. *Review of Educational Research, 59(3)*, 271–296.

Hornberger, N.H., & Skilton-Sylvester, E. (2000). Revising the continua of biliteracy: International and critical perspectives. *Language and Education, 14(2)*, 96–122.

Jensen, L. (2007). Heritage language reading in the university: A survey of students' experiences, strategies, and preferences. *Heritage Language Journal, 5(1)*. Retrieved August 1, 2008 from http://www.heritagelanguages.org/

Jia, L. (2009). Contrasting models in literacy practice among heritage language learners of Mandarin. *Journal of Asian Pacific Communication, 19(1)*, 56–75.

Joo, H. (2009). Literacy practices and heritage language maintenance: The case of Korean-American immigrant adolescents. *Journal of Asian Pacific Communication, 19(1)*, 76–99.

Ke, C. (1998). Effects of language background on the learning of Chinese characters among foreign language students. *Foreign Language Annals, 31(1)*, 91–100.

Kim, S.H. (2007). Heritage and non-heritage learners of Korean: Sentence processing differences and their pedagogical implications. In K. Kondo-Brown & J.D. Brown (Eds.), *Teaching Chinese, Japanese, and Korean heritage language students: Curriculum needs, materials, and assessment* (pp. 94–113). Mahwah, NJ: Lawrence Erlbaum.

Kondo, K. (1998). Social-psychological factors affecting language maintenance: Interviews with *Shin* Nisei university students in Hawaii. *Linguistics and Education, 9(4)*, 369–408.

—— (1999). Motivating bilingual and semibilingual university of Japanese: An analysis of language learning persistence and intensity among students from immigrant backgrounds. *Foreign Language Annals, 32(1)*, 77–88.

Kondo-Brown, K. (2003). Heritage language instruction for post-secondary students from immigrant backgrounds. *Heritage Language Journal, 1(1)*. Retrieved August 11, 2008 from http://heritagelanguages.org/

—— (2005). Differences in language skills: Heritage language learner subgroups and foreign language learners. *The Modern Language Journal, 89(4)*, 563–581.

Kondo-Brown, K., & Fukuda, C. (2007). A separate track for advanced heritage language students? Japanese inter-sentential referencing. In. K. Kondo-Brown & J.D. Brown (Eds.), *Teaching Chinese, Japanese, and Korean heritage language students: Curriculum needs, materials, and assessment* (pp. 134–152). Mahwah, NJ: Lawrence Erlbaum.

Kucer, S.B. (2005). *Dimensions of literacy: A conceptual base for teaching reading and writing in school settings* (2nd edition). Mahwah, NJ: Lawrence Erlbaum.

Lam, E.W.S. (2000). L2 literacy and the design of the self: A case study of a teenager writing on the internet. *TESOL Quarterly, 34(3)*, 457–483.

—— (2004). Second language socialization in a bilingual chat room: Global and local considerations. *Language Learning & Technology, 8(3)*, 44–65.

Lee, J.S. (2006), Exploring the relationship between electronic literacy and heritage language maintenance. *Language Learning & Technology, 10(2)*, 93–113.

Li, G. (2002). *East is east, west is west? Home literacy, culture, and schooling.* New York: Peter Lang.

—— (2004). Perspectives on struggling English language learners: Case studies of two Chinese-Canadian children. *Journal of Literacy Research, 36(1)*, 31–72.

—— (2006a). Biliteracy and trilingual practices in the home context: Case studies of Chinese-Canadian children. *Journal of Early Childhood Literacy, 6(3)*, 355–381.

—— (2006b). What do parents think? Middle-class Chinese immigrant parents' perspectives on literacy learning, homework, and school–home communication. *The School Community Journal, 16(2)*, 27–46.

Luo, S.J., & Wiseman, P.L. (2005). Ethnic language maintenance among Chinese children in the United States. *International Journal of Intercultural Relations, 24(3)*, 307–324.

Maguire, M.H., & Curdt-Christiansen, X.L. (2007). Multiple schools, languages, experiences and affiliations: Ideological becomings and positionings. *Heritage Language Journal, 5(1)*. Retrieved August 11, 2008 from http://heritagelanguages.org/

Matsunaga, S. (2003). Instructional needs of college-level learners of Japanese as a heritage language: Performance-based analyses. *Heritage Language Journal, 1(1)*. Retrieved August 11, 2008 from http://heritagelanguages.org/

McCarthey, S.J., & Garcia, G.E. (2005). English language learners' writing practices and attitudes. *Written Communication, 22(1)*, 36–75.

McCarthey, S.J., Garcia, G.E., Lopez-Velasquez, A.M., Lin, S., & Guo, Y-H. (2004). Understanding writing contexts for English language learners. *Research in the Teaching of English, 38(4)*, 351–394.

Orellana, M.F., & Gutierrez, K.D. (2006). What's the problem? Constructing different genres for the study of English learners. *Research in the Teaching of English, 41(1)*, 118–123.

Ortmeier-Hooper, C. (2008). "English may be my second language, but I'm not ESL." *College Composition and Communication, 59(3)*, 389–419.

Raimes, A. (1991). Out of the woods: Emerging traditions in the teaching of writing. *TESOL Quarterly, 25(4)*, 407–430.

Schiefflin, B., & Ochs, E. (1986). *Language socialization across cultures.* Cambridge: Cambridge University Press.

Schultz, K. (2002). Looking across space and time: Reconceptualizing literacy learning in and out of school. *Research in the Teaching of English, 36(3)*, 356–390.

Schuman, J.H. (1978). The acculturation model for second language acquisition. In R.C. Gingras (Ed.), *Second language acquisition and foreign language teaching* (pp. 27–50). Arlington, VA: Center for Applied Linguistics.

Shen, H. (2003). A comparison of written Chinese achievement among heritage learners in homogeneous and heterogeneous groups. *Foreign Language Annals, 36(2)*, 258–266.

Skilton-Sylvester, E. (2002). Literate at home but not at school: A Cambodian girl's journey from playwright to struggling writer. In. G. Hull & K. Schultz (Eds.), *School's out! Bridging out-of-school literacies with classroom practice* (pp. 61–92). New York: Teachers College Press.

Souryasack, R., & Lee, J.S. (2007). Drawing on students' experiences, cultures and languages to develop English language writing: Perspectives from three Lao heritage middle school students. *Heritage Language Journal, 5(1)*. Retrieved August 11, 2008 from http://www.heritagelanguages.org/

Sternglass, M.S. (1997). *Time to know them: A longitudinal study of writing and learning at the college level.* Mahwah, NJ: Lawrence Erlbaum.

Street, B. (1993). *Cross-cultural approaches to literacy.* Cambridge: Cambridge University Press.

Sze, C., Chapman, M., & Shi, L. (2009). Functions and genres of ESL children's writing at home and at school. *Journal of Asian Pacific Communication, 19(1)*, 30–55.

Tse, L. (2001). Resisting and reversing language shift: Heritage language resilience among U.S. native biliterates. *Harvard Educational Review, 71(4)*, 676–708.

Valdes, G. (2001). Heritage language students: Profiles and possibilities. In J.K. Peyton, D.A. Ranard, & S. McGinnis (Eds.), *Heritage languages in America: Preserving a national resource* (pp. 37–80). New York: Delta Systems.

Valdes, G., & Figueroa, R.A. (1994). *Bilingualism and testing: A special case of bias.* Norwood, NJ: Ablex.

Veltman, C. (1983). *Language shift in the United States.* Berlin: Mouton.

Warschauer, M. (2000). The changing global economy and the future of English teaching. *TESOL Quarterly, 34(3)*, 511–536.

Weger-Guntharp, H. (2006). Voices from the margin: Developers of a profile of Chinese heritage language learners in the FL classroom. *Heritage Language Journal, 4(1)*. Retrieved August 11, 2008 from http://www.heritagelanguages.org/

Wen, X. (1997). Motivation and language learning with students of Chinese. *Foreign Language Annals, 30(2)*, 235–251.

Wong Fillmore, L. (1991). When learning a second language means losing the first. *Early Childhood Research, 6(3)*, 323–346.

Xiao, Y. (2006). Heritage language learners in the Chinese language classroom: Home background. *Heritage Language Journal, 4(1).* Retrieved August 11, 2008 from http://www.heritagelanguages.org/

Xu, H. (1999). Young Chinese ESL children's home literacy experiences. *Reading Horizons, 40(1),* 47–64.

Yi, Y. (2005). Asian adolescents' out-of-school encounters with English and Korean literacy. *Journal of Asian Pacific Communication, 15(1),* 57–78.

—— (2007). Engaging literacy: A biliterate student's composing practices beyond school. *Journal of Second Language Writing, 16(1),* 23–39.

—— (2008a). Relay writing in an adolescent online community. *Journal of Adolescent and Adult Literacy, 51(8),* 870–880.

—— (2008b). Voluntary writing in heritage language: A study of biliterate Korean heritage adolescents in the U.S. *Heritage Language Journal, 6(1).* Retrieved November 8, 2008 from http://www.heritagelanguages.org/

—— (2009). Adolescent literacy and identity construction among 1.5 generation students: From a transnational perspective. *Journal of Asian Pacific Communication, 19(1),* 100–129.

Yi, Y., & Hirvela, A. (2009). Composing in and out of school: Biliterate Asian students' encounters with heritage and second language literacy. *Journal of Asian Pacific Communication, 19(1),* 1–6.

Yu, W.H. (2007). Developing "a compromise curriculum" for Korean heritage and non-heritage learners. In K. Kondo-Brown & J.D. Brown (Eds.), *Teaching Chinese, Japanese, and Korean heritage language students: Curriculum needs, materials, and assessment* (pp. 217–239). Mahwah, NJ: Lawrence Erlbaum.

Zhou, M., & Kim, S.S. (2006). Community forces, social capital, and educational achievement: The case of supplementary education in the Chinese and Korean immigrant communities. *Harvard Education Review, 76(1),* 1–29.

Part II

Integrating Ethnolinguistic Diversity into Schooling

6 Dialect Awareness, Cultural Literacy, and the Public Interest [1]

Walt Wolfram

Introduction

A few years ago I was asked to conduct a workshop for a school system in Maryland, one of the hundreds I have conducted over the past few decades. The reaction of the participants was predictable. While the teachers understood the need to be tolerant and respectful of different cultures and the diverse ways of speaking represented by their students, they firmly insisted that their primary if not exclusive task as educators was to get their students to speak "correct," "proper," or "Standard English"—and that any compromise of this objective was at best frivolous and at worst misguided education. What I did not realize as I was conducting the workshop, however, was that I had done a similar workshop at the same school two decades earlier. I had completely forgotten my previous workshop until a participant observed, "I remember you doing a workshop like this about 20 years ago." The most startling revelation was not my forgetfulness, but the fact that there was no indication from the responses of the participants that my earlier workshop had any effect on the perspective or the policy of the school with respect to dialect diversity. Language ideology is among the most entrenched belief systems in society, rivaling religion, morality, and nationalism, and change does not take place rapidly.

Almost a half century after the advent of the field of sociolinguistics and the inception of the extensive study of sociocultural dialects of American English, little has changed in terms of the public perception of dialect diversity. This is not to say that some professional organizations and selected individuals have not made substantive progress in terms of recognizing the legitimacy of language differences. Certainly, organizations such at the National Council of Teachers of English (NCTE), the American Speech-Language-Hearing Association (ASHA), Teaching English to Speakers of Other Languages (TESOL), and other prominent professional organizations have endorsed policies and practices that recognize the naturalness of language diversity. By the early 1980s, for example, the American Speech Language and Hearing Association, the world's largest and most influential speech pathology organization, issued a sociolinguistically informed position on social dialects (Asha, 1983, pp. 22–23) along with an attendant set of competencies for speech and language pathologists with respect to language differences:

1. knowledge of the particular dialect as a rule-governed linguistic system
2. knowledge of nondiscriminatory testing procedures
3. knowledge of the phonological and grammatical features of the dialect
4. knowledge of contrastive analysis procedures
5. knowledge of the effects of attitudes toward dialects
6. thorough understanding and appreciation for the community and culture of the nonstandard speaker

Notwithstanding this policy, the practical implementation is still sometimes an unrealized ideal. As Supple (1993, p. 24) notes, "The sociolinguistic model has now become firmly entrenched within the field of communication disorders. However, while this fact is acknowledged, it is unfortunately often not given the necessary focus in the day-to-day clinical setting."

By the same token, the National Council of Teachers of English (NCTE) was an early advocate of "students' right to their own patterns and varieties of the language—the dialects of their nurture or whatever dialects in which they find their own identity and style" (Committee on College Composition and Communication Language Statement, 1974, p. 2). Furthermore, the NCTE/NCATE (National Council for Accreditation of Teacher Education, 2003) standards for teacher training programs include specific objectives for the preparation of secondary teachers related to language diversity. Consider, for example, the target goals for language diversity in the standards for teacher training shown in Table 6.1.

Table 6.1 NCTE/NCATE Standards for the Initial Preparation of Teachers in Secondary English Language Arts

	NOT ACCEPTABLE	ACCEPTABLE	TARGET
3.1.4	Show a lack of respect for, and little knowledge of diversity in language use, patterns, and dialects across cultures, ethnic groups, geographic regional, and social roles;	Know and respect diversity in language use, patterns and dialects across cultures, ethnic groups, geographic regions and social roles and show attention to such diversity in their teaching;	Show extensive knowledge of how and why language varies and changes in different regions, across different cultural groups, and across different time periods and incorporate that knowledge into instruction and assessment that acknowledge and show respect for language;
4.4	Show limited ability to create learning environments that promote respect for, and support of, individual differences of ethnicity, race, language, culture, gender, and ability;	Create and sustain learning environments that promote respect for, and support of, ethnicity, race, language, culture, gender, and ability;	Create opportunities for students to analyze how social context affects language and to monitor their own language use and behavior in terms of demonstrating respect for individual differences of ethnicity, race, language, culture, gender, and ability;

Despite these admirable NCTE/NCATE ideals, teacher-training programs rarely achieve "acceptable" and "target" standards in terms of these goals. Furthermore, student curricula focusing explicitly on language diversity are virtually non-existent in formal public education programs. Again, we see dissonance between idealistic policy and practical implementation.

The Challenge of Dialect Awareness

On the one hand, language variation is so transparent that it can be assumed that most speakers of English will readily notice language differences. On the other hand, there is a public presumption that anyone can make valid observations about language diversity. Not only do people notice language diversity; they feel free to make pronouncements about the status of these language differences, thus creating a good-news–bad-news scenario in which natural observations about language diversity are often countered by uninformed opinions espoused as fact. Despite the significance of language in all spheres of public life and at least twelve years of compulsory public-school education in English and/or language arts, there is still no tradition of English language study that includes the examination of language diversity as a regular part of this education. Programs targeting language diversity are also conspicuously absent from informal public education, apart from the sporadic language controversies that afford linguists their proverbial fifteen minutes of media exposure for a "teachable moment." In the past two decades, only two national public TV documentaries related to language diversity have aired, *American Tongues* in 1986 (Alvarez & Kolker, 1986) and *Do You Speak American?* in 2005 (MacNeil & Cran, 2005). In complementary ways, both of these productions fulfilled an important mission in public education, but two decades passed between the appearance of these documentaries.

The lack of public discussion about language diversity does not appear to be a simple matter of oversight. Instead, it affirms Fairclough's observation that beliefs about language need not be made explicit and that language ideology is most effective when its workings are least visible (Fairclough, 1989, p. 85). The application of the "correctionist model," in which language differences are explicitly noted only for correction to prescriptivist norms, still dominates the public interpretation of language.[2] Indeed, most public discussions of English dialect differences are still consumed by the discussion of the right and wrong way to use the English language. The sustained application of prescriptive labels such as "correct," "proper," "right," and "grammatical" when speaking of language differences is hardly accidental; it directly reflects the underlying belief that non-mainstream and minority varieties of English are simply unworthy approximations of the standard variety. A half-century after the advent of sociolinguistics, the most persistent challenge in all venues of public education continues to be the widespread application of the so-called "principle of linguistic subordination" (Lippi-Green, 1997), in which the language of socially subordinate groups is interpreted as linguistically inadequate and deficient by comparison with the language of socially dominant groups.

Though popular culture has resisted large-scale change in language attitudes, it is essential for sociolinguists to recognize that primitive belief systems—those related to religion, politics, morality, and language—take generations to change. Authentic change will not come overnight, and sociolinguists should not be alarmed that negative language attitudes exposed decades ago are still alive and well. At the same time, it is difficult to imagine wide-scale change in language attitudes and understanding without systematic dialect awareness programs that target multiple levels of formal and informal education. The use of the term "dialect awareness program" refers to activities that are intended to promote an understanding of and appreciation for language variation. Unfortunately, there is still no tradition in English language studies or in related programs of study (e.g., social studies, history, etc.) that regularly includes the examination of language diversity as a regular part of this education. The need for informed knowledge about language variation and the dissemination of essential knowledge to the public thus remains an imposing challenge for sociolinguistics that has intensified rather than receded over the decades. Sociolinguistics is a very small, largely invisible professional field that can be overwhelmed by popular perception and dominant opinion. Accordingly, the public impact of sociolinguistics is severely limited if it does not effectively use a range of media venues to communicate its message.

Rationale for Dialect Awareness

Most educational systems claim to be committed to a search for fundamental truths about matter, nature, and society. When it comes to dialects, however, there is an educational tolerance of misinformation and folklore that is matched in few subject areas. As noted, there is an entrenched mythology about dialects that pervades the understanding of this topic, particularly with respect to the nature of standard and vernacular varieties. At the very least, then, the educational system and society at large should assume responsibility for replacing the entrenched myths about dialects with factual information about the authentic nature of dialect diversity.

From a humanistic standpoint, dialect awareness programs help us understand similarities and differences in human behavior. They also offer an opportunity to see how language reflects and helps shape different historical and cultural developments. In this context, it is somewhat surprising that the current emphasis on multicultural education in the U.S. has, for all practical purposes, excluded the study of linguistic diversity, since language is so integral to cultural identity. Understanding language differences as a manifestation of cultural and historical differences provides an important rationale for studying the nature of dialect differences on a formal and informal level.

Another rationale for examining dialect differences is related to the nature of intellectual inquiry. The study of dialects affords a fascinating window through which we can see how language works. Certainly, an important aspect of understanding language in general, and the English language in particular, is the development of an appreciation for how language changes over time and space and how various dialects arise. Studying dialects formally and informally provides a wealth of information for examining the dynamic nature of language. Given people's inherent interest in dialects, this type of study has great potential for piquing students' and community members' interest in how language works.

The study of dialects offers another enticement. Language, including dialects, is a unique form of knowledge in that speakers know a language simply by virtue of the fact that they speak it. Much of this knowledge is not on a conscious level, but it is still open to systematic investigation. In examining dialect differences, students can hypothesize about the patterning of language features and then check these hypotheses by carefully studying and describing a set of data on people's actual usage patterns. This process is, of course, a type of scientific inquiry. Though this rationale for studying dialects may seem a bit esoteric at first glance, hypothesizing about and then testing language patterns is quite within the grasp even of younger students. In fact, I have led classes of students in the mid-elementary grades through the steps of hypothesis formation and testing by using exercises involving dialect features. As illustrated later in this chapter, students may inductively learn how to formulate and test hypotheses at the same time that they learn about the intricate nature of patterned dialect differences. The inner workings of language are just as readily observed in examining dialects and their patterning as through the exclusive study of a single standard variety.

Finally, there is a utilitarian reason for studying dialects. Information about dialects should prove helpful to students as they work to develop the language skills required as a part of the educational process, including the use of the standard variety (Sweetland, 2006). Vernacular dialect speakers may, for example, apply knowledge about dialect features to composing and editing skills in writing. I have personally witnessed students who studied third-person singular -s absence in a unit on dialects transfer this knowledge to their writing when called upon to write standard English. The studying of various dialects hardly endangers the sovereignty of standard English in the classroom. In fact, if anything, it enhances the learning of the standard variety through heightened sensitivity to language variation.

An Approach to Cultural Literacy

Language variation holds broad-based, inherent intrigue for general audiences. People notice language differences and they frequently comment on them or discuss them without prompting from sociolinguists. Accordingly, any approach to broad-based public education must seize upon this intrinsic curiosity. The notion that presentations about language should be entertaining may seem somewhat superficial to scholars focused more on the transmission of knowledge than the entertainment value of sociolinguistic information, but informal, public education does indeed compete with other types of entertainment. One of the reasons that the now-dated documentary *American Tongues* (Alvarez & Kolker, 1986) remains effective after two decades is due to its high entertainment value. The use of striking dialogue and humor also serve as a non-confrontational method for opening up candid discussions about language attitudes.

A series of recent documentaries on language diversity produced for public TV in North Carolina and beyond (Hutcheson, 2001, 2004, 2005, 2006, 2009) has shown that it is quite possible to pique the public's interest in language differences if it is framed in an appropriate, natural cultural setting. The airing of *Voices of North Carolina* (Hutcheson, 2005) had a rating of 2.3 per 1,000 viewing homes, significantly higher than the regular programming in the time slot. Perhaps just as importantly, the viewing audience did not turn the program off; the audience at the beginning and the end of the program was stable. While a viewer rating of 2.3 may pale by comparison with the rating of a popular major network program, it does demonstrate that presentations about dialect diversity can compete at least within the restricted audience of potential viewers who watch public television. In fact, the public television station, the state affiliate of PBS, was so impressed by the viewer response to the program that they offered a DVD of *Voices of North Carolina* as an incentive give-away item in their annual fundraising campaign. To my knowledge, this is the only language documentary ever used in this way.

In presenting language difference in public venues, it is also essential to portray language as a proxy for deeper cultural and sociopolitical representations. In effect, language is simply a symbolic token of more fundamental social and cultural issues. The connection between language and more broadly based social and cultural themes is an underlying theme in our documentaries and museum exhibits that focus specifically on language. As one of the Cherokee speakers in the documentary *Voices of North Carolina* put it, "Language is culture and culture is language." In such a context, receding language varieties are portrayed as reflections of vanishing cultural traditions, and ethnolinguistic varieties may be portrayed as a reflection of persistent racial and ethnic boundaries and identities. Or, as Gloria Anzaldúa (1987, p. 59) put it, "Ethnic identity is twin skin to linguistic identity—I am my language." One of the most persistent messages portrayed in our language documentaries for public television is, in fact, the notion that language is merely a reflection of underlying sociohistorical and cultural traditions and trends.

The themes that frame our public presentations of language diversity are typically related to cultural legacy and historical heritage. When language diversity is associated with historical and cultural traditions such as settlement history, social developments, and other cultural traditions, a meaningful context for broader cultural and social issues is established for the presentation of language differences. The framing of language diversity in a historical, regional, and cultural context is one of the reasons that our dialect awareness curriculum targets the eighth-grade social studies program (Reaser & Wolfram, 2007a, 2007b; Reaser, 2006), the grade level when students study state history. The rationale for the choice is straightforward: an important component of the state's historical and cultural development is reflected in language diversity, ranging from endangered or lost Native American languages to the development of distinct regional and sociocultural varieties of English. Accordingly, our program naturally fits in with the state's mandated course of study for eighth-grade social studies (http://ncsu.edu/linguistics/research_dialecteducation.php) that includes curricular themes of "culture and diversity," "historic perspectives," and "geographical relationships." In this context, the goals of the dialect awareness curriculum neatly dovetail with social studies competency goals such as "Describe the roles and contributions of diverse groups, such as American Indians, African Americans, European immigrants, landed gentry, tradesmen, and small farmers to everyday life in colonial North Carolina" (Competency Goal 1.07) or "Assess the importance of regional diversity on the development of economic, social, and political institutions in North Carolina" (Competency Goal 8.04). Though students and the general public may neither understand nor value the seemingly myopic obsession of linguists with technical structural detail, they can appreciate and identify with the symbolic role that language plays in its representation of historical, regional, and cultural development.

One of the attributes of our public outreach programs and formal educational curriculum is the focus on the positive dimensions of language diversity rather than on the controversies sometimes associated with language differences. Despite deep-seated ideological differences between sociolinguistic axioms and public interpretations of language differences, we take the position that positively framed presentations of language differences hold a greater likelihood of being received by the public than the direct confrontation of unassailable ideologies. Once a few fundamental sociolinguistic premises about language diversity are established inductively, the discussion of more sensitive social issues related to the conflict between folk theories and sociolinguistic premises may become more meaningful.

Our experience in framing language differences positively has helped avoid some of the traditionally contentious discussions associated with highly controversial, stigmatized varieties such as African American English (AAE). For example, the vignette on AAE in the documentary, *Voices of North Carolina*, is introduced with the statement, "Language is an important part of all cultural and social groups, but it seems to have a special place in the African American experience." Perhaps as important as the introductory narrative is the narrator selected for the documentary. In a strategic decision to provide credibility to the presentation, we enlisted William C. (Bill) Friday, President Emeritus of the University of North Carolina University system and arguably the most highly respected and noncontroversial public figure in North Carolina, to narrate the documentary. In a concluding, unscripted remark Friday notes, "We now know the value of history, we now know why we should preserve buildings, and languages, and people, and traditions—because they become a part of what you really are." In the presentation, AAE is treated simply as one of the significant sociocultural varieties of English that complements other sociocultural and regional varieties of English. *Voices of North Carolina* includes entire segments on two Native American varieties (the Cherokee language and Lumbee English), Spanish, and several regional varieties to complement the vignette on AAE. In fact, AAE is sequentially presented only after several regional and other sociocultural varieties have been portrayed. There has sometimes been so much focus on AAE to the exclusion of other legitimate varieties that it runs the risk of being interpreted as a special condition of being black in American society. It is important neither to exaggerate nor minimize the status of any particular variety, including AAE, in representing the natural development of sociolinguistic diversity within the English language. It is noteworthy that we have yet to receive any negative reactions from the public about our presentation of AAE in the documentary. We attribute this primarily to the highly contextualized, positive representation of AAE along with other sociocultural and regional language differences in the documentary.

Finally, it should be noted that the most effective and permanent education always takes place when learners discover truths for themselves. Inductive, scaffolded education that begins with a positive, non-threatening perspective on language diversity provides a much more effective opportunity for an authentic discussion of linguistic diversity than the direct opposition to entrenched positions. Deductive linguistic proclamations about the legitimacy of language diversity tend only to result in the balkanization of entrenched sociopolitical positions rather than open an honest discussion of language differences. Though sociolinguists may, in fact, be ideological brokers who are heavily vested in their position, audiences ultimately must come to understand the truth about language diversity for themselves.

Venues for Formal and Informal Sociolinguistic Education

Opportunities for public education extend from opportunistic-based, teachable moments that naturally arise from current news events to planned programs that systematically target specific or broad-based public audiences. On an occasional basis, sociolinguists are called upon by the media to provide perspectives and opinions on language-related stories. These stories may range from long-standing national debates about amendments to adopt English as the official language of the United States to local stories that involve comments or observations about language or dialect. When a prominent, nationally recognized linguist such as Deborah Tannen talks about the role of language in social interaction or when John Baugh talks about linguistic profiling (see Alim & Baugh's chapter in this volume for the details of the linguistic profiling) on a national network news program, it paves the way for teachable moments in public education. I have, for example, effectively used the "20/20 Downtown" news program on linguistic profiling (ABC News, 2002) and the subsequent U.S. Fair Housing Commission's 60-second public advertisement (Ad Council, 2003) about the role of linguistic profiling in housing discrimination as important illustrations of the subtle but significant role of language in discrimination with audiences that extend from traditional middle-school classrooms to community-based civic groups.

Though news events involving language provide an opportunity for public education, such occasions are typically reactive rather than proactive, and linguists have little control over the presentation format or editing their response to a convenient, abbreviated soundbite. Our current proactive efforts have attempted to be more deliberate, detailed, and diverse, ranging from documentaries produced for public television to dialect awareness curricula for teachers and public school students.

Documentary productions of the North Carolina Language and Life Project have ranged from those for local communities to those produced for general public television audiences, mostly for the state affiliate of PBS, or, in one case,

PBS nationally. Some of these productions have focused exclusively on language (Blanton & Waters, 1996; Hutcheson, 2001, 2004, 2005, 2009), while others have followed local interests to the point of having little to do directly with language (Hutcheson, 2006; Rowe & Grimes, 2006). The documentary on Lumbee English titled *Indian by Birth: The Lumbee Dialect* (Hutcheson, 2001) illustrates a production specifically focused on language though it naturally frames this discussion within a cultural context, a regional setting, and a sociohistorical background. It includes a vignette on the ancestral language background of the Lumbee Indians and the English roots of Lumbee English, a sociocultural section about the symbolic cultural role of language in community life, a cognitive component that depicts some of the linguistic structures of the dialect, and an affective section about the attitudes, stereotypes, and misconceptions that often characterize the public perception of this ethnolinguistic variety. The goal is to educate the general public, including local community members, about the role of language in its community setting and the emblematic function of Lumbee English as a marker of socioethnic identity. The sociohistorical and sociocultural legacy of language is of particular significance on a local, community level as well as for outsiders who know little about the Lumbee as a Native American tribe. Language differences are presented in terms of cultural identity and historical heritage rather than language ideology, though issues of linguistic subordination are addressed in indirect ways.

One of our most successful documentaries on public TV in North Carolina, *Voices of North Carolina*, provides an overview of a number of different language situations in the state. These include the status of the Cherokee language, an endangered Native American language, and the varieties of Spanish brought to North Carolina with Latino immigrants in the last decade. Different regional dialects of English are also featured, including Outer Banks English and Appalachian English, along with ethnic varieties such as Lumbee English and African American English. It further features a vignette on language change in metropolitan areas of the South by comparing older, lifetime residents of Charlotte, North Carolina, with younger residents and outsiders who are now predominant in the city's population. As the promotional blurb reads, "*Voices of North Carolina* is a unique journey through the dialects and language of this diverse Southern state, from Hoi Toider speech on the Outer Banks to the Highland Speech of the Smoky Mountains" (Hutcheson, 2005).

Although the North Carolina Language and Life Project has had the good fortune of having a highly creative, full-time videographer (Neal Hutcheson), it should be noted that some projects can be done on a modest budget by students who are interested in film-making and/or documentary production. In fact, the first documentary ever produced under the aegis of the North Carolina Language and Life Project was done by undergraduate students in a linguistics class who were more interested in documentary production than in linguistic analysis. They had no prior experience in film-making and production, no equipment of their own, and no budget to carry out the project. We set up an independent study, borrowed equipment from the film laboratory of the Communication Department at the university, and operated on a shoe-string budget of less than $1,500, mostly for travel and supplies. More than a decade later, the 23-minute production, *The Ocracoke Brogue* (Blanton & Waters, 1996), about the dialect spoken on Ocracoke Island, in the North Carolina Outer Banks islands, remains one of the most well-known and economically successful documentaries we have ever produced. Furthermore, it has become a staple feature in the Ocracoke Preservation Society's museum, where it runs continuously whenever the museum is open to the public. Current digital video technology available at most universities makes these types of low-budget, public education projects even more accessible for student production.

The museum exhibit is another venue for the public presentation of language diversity. With the cooperation of community-based museums and preservation societies, we have now constructed three permanent museum exhibits that high-light language diversity in North Carolina. The exhibition at the museum of the Ocracoke Preservation Society includes panels on the history and development of the dialect, its current moribund status, and an illustrative list of some distinctive lexical items of the variety, along with the continuously playing documentary that is the center of the so-called "Dialect Room" at the museum.

We also constructed a permanent exhibit on Lumbee language for the Museum of the Native American Resource Center in Pembroke, North Carolina. The exhibit, funded by a grant from the Informal Science Education program of the U.S. National Science Foundation, features four panels highlighting the ancestral Native American language heritage of the Lumbee, the development of their unique Lumbee English dialect, the representation of Lumbee identity through dialect, and the presentation of some distinctive lexical items of Lumbee English. The exhibit also includes an interactive, touch-screen monitor that allows visitors to select from a menu of two-minute video vignettes that range from segments on the development and status of Lumbee language to an interactive vocabulary quiz on Lumbee English. In addition to visitors and community residents, each year thousands of schoolchildren in Robeson County visit the museum to view the exhibition.

A third exhibit was recently constructed in the gallery of the Outer Banks History Center located at the Lost Colony Festival Park on Roanoke Island, one of the most popular tourist attractions in North Carolina. This exhibit, titled "Freedom's Voice: Celebrating the Black Experience on the Outer Banks," is by far the most inclusive and extensive of our exhibitions, extending far beyond language variation on the Outer Banks. It includes images, a documentary (Sellers, 2006), interactive audiovisuals, and artifacts and panels that highlight the Freedmen's Colony on Roanoke Island during the Civil War, African Americans' involvement in the maritime industry, and African Americans' role in education, religion, and community life on the Outer Banks. A half-dozen different listening stations feature the voices of local residents who were a part of our research study on language variation and change in Roanoke Island (Carpenter, 2004, 2005). In an important sense, this exhibition combines history, culture, and language in narrating the story of the "other lost colony" on Roanoke Island. Exhibits such as these offer a permanent venue for public education that can be used in both formal and informal education. Such presentations can also be adapted or designed as virtual museums so that their education potential extends well beyond their local, physical community site.

One of our most ambitious programs in public education involves the development of formal curricular materials on language diversity in the public schools. We have experimented with curricular programs in a number of communities throughout North Carolina and taught a program annually for more than a decade in the public school in Ocracoke. Unfortunately, formal education about dialect variation is still a relatively novel, and, in some cases, controversial idea. The pilot program focuses on a middle-school curriculum in social studies that connects with language arts (Reaser, 2006; Reaser & Wolfram, 2006a,b), but similar units might be designed for other levels of K–12 education as well. The curriculum is based on a humanistic, scientific, and a social science rationale as specified above, and engages students on a number of different participatory levels. In the process, students learn about dialect study as a kind of scientific inquiry and as a form of social science research. The examination of dialect differences offers great potential for students to investigate the interrelation between linguistic and social diversity, including diversity grounded in geography, history, and cultural beliefs and practices. In a separate section, we illustrate some of the activities and exercises that are incorporated into the curriculum, which is now being piloted more extensively throughout North Carolina.

One of the greatest advantages of a curriculum on dialects is its potential for tapping the linguistic resources of students' indigenous communities. In addition to classroom lessons, students learn by going into the community to collect current dialect data. In most cases, the speech characteristics of the local community should make dialects come alive in a way that is unmatched by textbook knowledge. Educational models that treat the local community as a resource to be tapped rather than as a liability to be overcome have been shown to be quite effective in other areas of language arts education, and there is no reason why this model cannot be applied to the study of dialects. A model that builds upon community strengths in language, even when the language is different from the norm of the mainstream educational system, seems to hold much greater potential for success than one that focuses exclusively upon conflicts between the community language and school language.

We are currently expanding our pilot program with the eventual goal of providing such materials for all eighth-grade social studies students throughout the state. As previously described, our decision to target eighth-grade social studies is based in part on the fact that this level is dedicated to the study of state history and culture, a topic that dovetails neatly with the study of language variation over time and place (Reaser 2006; Reaser & Wolfram, 2006a,b). The rationale is straightforward: an important component of the state's historical and cultural development is reflected in language diversity that ranges from the endangered or lost Native American languages to the development of distinct regional and sociocultural varieties of English.

A further consideration in targeting the social studies curriculum is the fact that it tends to have more flexibility in innovative materials than language arts, which is traditionally constrained by year-end, standardized performance testing.

The subject of language diversity may converge naturally with language arts and even science at points where the focus is on language analysis as a type of scientific inquiry. Students are not the only ones who profit from the study of dialect diversity. Teachers also find that some of their stereotypes about languages are challenged and that they become more knowledgeable and enlightened about language diversity in the process of teaching the curriculum. In fact, the classroom teachers who piloted the curriculum were among its most enthusiastic supporters because of the new knowledge they had acquired in teaching the curriculum to their students.

One of the most effective sources for disseminating information about language diversity is magazine articles and books for general audiences. Deborah Tannen (1990, 1995) has demonstrated that popular books about language use in social interaction can, in fact, be quite intriguing to the public and provide an effective venue for public education about the role of language in everyday life, though her popular recognition is certainly the exception rather than the rule among academics. One of the more successful popular writing ventures related to dialect diversity is *Spoken Soul: The Story of Black English* (2000), co-authored by sociolinguist John R. Rickford and his son, Russell John Rickford, then a journalist with the *Philadelphia Inquirer*. Winner of an American Book Award for outstanding literary achievement, this book demonstrates that the presentation of language diversity can, in fact, reach very broad audiences, though again it is notably the exception in sociolinguistic writing.

Our own efforts to write for general audiences have met with more modest, regional success. The book, *Hoi Toide on the Outer Banks: The Story of the Ocracoke Brogue* (Wolfram & Schilling-Estes, 1997), received considerable publicity on the Outer Banks and the North Carolina mainland as well, and the first run of almost 4,000 copies sold out within several months of its release. A decade after its original publication, the book is still available at tourist sites, in popular bookstores, lighthouses, and museums throughout the Outer Banks. Another trade book, *Fine in the World: Lumbee Language in Time and Place* (Wolfram, Dannenberg, Knick, & Oxendine, 2002), is distributed through the Museum of the Native American Resource Center in Pembroke and through the North Carolina State University Extension/Publications program. Though its appeal is fairly local, residents and teachers in Southeastern North Carolina have found its presentation of the role of dialect in Lumbee life informative. A more recent effort to educate the general public about the status of dialects in American society is the collection *American Voices* (Wolfram & Ward, 2006), a book of brief essays for non-experts that aims to demonstrate that everyone speaks a dialect and that they are all interesting and valuable. It attempts to translate the research of professional dialectologists and sociolinguists into brief, readable descriptions for those who are curious about language differences but have neither the background nor the desire to be professional linguists. The success of this attempt, co-edited by a sociolinguist and career journalist, is yet to be determined, but it may ultimately have to do as much with its marketability as with its readability. Popular literary venues for the presentation of language diversity hold great potential, although the process of writing for such audiences is a formidable challenge that requires writing skills quite different from those typically exhibited by linguists. Furthermore, such ventures are probably best undertaken with professional journalists and/or by those accustomed to writing for popular audiences. Perhaps just as importantly, such literary ventures need aggressive marketing plans that ensure that they will reach their intended audiences.

Some Illustrative Activities

In various workshops, dialect curricula, and other public presentations, we use a wide variety of activities and exercises to educate the public about the nature of dialect diversity. These activities are supported by a full set of audiovisual vignettes. In one of the exercises in the dialect curriculum (Reaser & Wolfram, 2007a, 2007b), we directly ask students to confront the issue of language prejudice by having them view the one-minute ad on linguistic profiling and housing discrimination prepared by National Fair Housing Alliance, U.S. Department of Housing and Urban Development, and Leadership Conference on Civil Rights Education (Ad Council, 2003). The activity below, adapted from Reaser and Wolfram (2006b), is presented as shown in Figure 6.1.

This reflective activity has a humanistic goal, while other activities have complementary objectives related to social science and to linguistic science. Exercises on grammatical patterning can go a long way towards dispelling the notion that dialects are simply imperfect renditions of the standard variety. Working with dialect patterning sets the stage for a non-patronizing respect for the complexity of systematic differences among dialects. The advantage of the *a*-prefixing exercise shown in Figure 6.2, which I have used effectively in public presentations as well as textbooks (e.g., Wolfram, 1991; Wolfram & Schilling-Estes, 2006) for a few decades now, involves a form whose patterning is intuitive to both those who use the form in their vernacular dialect and those who do not (Wolfram, 1982). This fact makes the exercise appropriate for participants regardless of their native dialect. Working through exercises of this type is the most effective method for confronting the myth that dialects have no rules of their own; at the same time, such exercises effectively demonstrate the underlying cognitive patterning of

---

During phone conversations, it is often possible to tell a number of things about a person based on the characteristics of their voice. You will see a 1-minute commercial produced by the U.S. Department of Housing and Urban Development (HUD). The purpose of this commercial is to raise awareness of how discrimination can occur over the phone. As you watch the video, think of answers to the following:

1. How common do you think it is for people to be discriminated against on the phone?

2. How strong are people's prejudices about language?

3. Why do you think people have such strong prejudices about language?

Figure 6.1 Video Exercise: Examining Language Prejudice.

In traditional rural dialects of the South, some words that end in *-ing* can take an *a-*, pronounced as *uh*, in front of the word. We call this *a-* prefix because it attaches to the front of the *-ing* word. The language pattern or rule for this form allows the *a-* to attach to some words but not to others. We will try to figure out this fairly complicated rule by looking at the kinds of *-ing* words *a-* can and cannot attach to. We will do this using our inner feelings about language. These inner feelings, called **intuitions**, tell us where we **CAN** and **CANNOT** use certain forms. Our job as linguists trying to describe this dialect is to figure out the reason for these inner feelings and to state the exact pattern.

Look at the sentence pairs in **LIST A** and decide which sentence in each pair sounds better for attaching the *a-*. For example, in the first sentence pair, does it sound better to say, *A-building is hard work* or *He was a-building a house*? For each sentence pair, just choose one sentence that sounds better with the *a-*.

LIST A: Sentence Pairs for *a-* Prefixing
1. a. __ Building is hard work.
    b. __ She was building a house.
2. a. __ He likes hunting.
    b. __ He went hunting.
3. a. __ The child was charming the adults.
    b. __ The child was very charming.
4. a. __ He kept running to the store.
    b. __ The store was shocking.
5. a. __ They thought fishing was easy.
    b. __ They were fishing this morning.
6. a. __ The fishing is still good here.
    b. __ They go fishing less now.

Examine each of the sentence pairs in terms of the choices for the *a-* prefix and answer the following questions:

- Do you think there is some pattern that guided your choice of an answer? You can tell if there is a definite pattern by checking with other people who did the same exercise on their own.
- Do you think that the pattern might be related to parts of speech? To answer this, see if there are any parts of speech where you CANNOT use the *a-* prefix. Look at *-ing* forms that function as verbs and compare those with *-ing* forms that operate as nouns or adjectives. For example, look at the use of *charming* as a verb and adjective in sentence 3.

The first step in figuring out the pattern for *a-* prefix is related to the part of speech of the *-ing* word. Now let's look at another difference related to prepositions such as *from* and *by*. Based on the sentence pairs in **LIST B**, say whether or not the *a-* form can be used after a preposition. Use the same technique you used for **LIST A**. Select the sentence that sounds better for each sentence pair and say whether it is the sentence with or without the preposition.

Figure 6.2 Understanding Linguistic Patterns: The Use of *a*-Prefix.

language. The version of the *a*-prefix exercise presented here is adapted from Reaser and Wolfram (2007b, pp 7–9).

In another exercise, we extend the notion of linguistic patterning to African American English (AAE), arguably the variety of English most affected by the stereotype that vernacular varieties are simply unworthy approximations of Standard English. While most people are familiar with the association of a finite form of *be* with AAE, few are familiar with the patterning that governs the use of this form. The exercise demonstrates further that the linguistic notion of

LIST B: A Further Detail for _a_- Patterning
1. a. __ They make money by building houses.
    b. __ They make money building houses.
2. a. __ People can't make enough money fishing.
    b. __ People can't make enough money from fishing.
3. a. __People destroy the beauty of the island through littering.
    b. __ People destroy the beauty of the island littering.

Now we have another detail for figuring the pattern for the _a_- prefix use related to prepositions. But there is still another part to the pattern for _a_- prefix use. This time, however, it is related to pronunciation. For the following _-ing_ words, try to figure out what it is about the pronunciation that makes one sentence sound better than the other. To help you figure out the pronunciation trait that is critical for this pattern, the stressed or accented syllable of each word is marked with the symbol ´. Follow the same procedure that you did in choosing the sentence in each sentence pair that sounds better.

LIST C: Figuring out a Pronunciation Pattern for _a_- Prefix
1. a. __ She was discóvering a trail.
    b. __ She was fóllowing a trail.
2. a. __ She was repéating the chant.
    b. __ She was hóllering the chant.
3. a. __ They were fíguring the change.
    b. __ They were forgétting the change.
4. a. __ The baby was recognízing the mother.
    b. __ The baby was wrécking everything.
5. a. __ The were décorating the room.
    b. __ They were demánding more time off.

Say exactly how the pattern for attaching the _a_- prefix works. Be sure to include the three different details from your examination of the examples in **LISTS A**, **B**, and **C**.

In **LIST D**, say which of the sentences may attach an _a_- prefix. Use your understanding of the rule to explain why the _-ing_ form may or may not take the _a_- prefix.

LIST D: Applying the _a_- Prefix Rule
1. She kept handing me more work.
2. The team was remémbering the game.
3. The team won by playing great defense.
4. The team was playing real hard.
5. The coach was charming.

grammaticality is different from social acceptability. No sociolinguistic axiom is more critical to the study of AAE than the systematic patterning of its grammatical and phonological forms.

Another exercise, shown in Figure 6.3 (from Reaser & Wolfram, 2006b, pp. 36–37), examines language change in dialects in apparent time. Participants listen to different speakers representing different generations from an isolated rural area in coastal North Carolina (Wolfram & Thomas, 2002) and consider how regional AAE and European American English have changed over several generations. Students listen to the different segments while they view a transcript of the passage that highlights some of the features illustrating the changing regional and ethnolinguistic configuration in this region. The goal of this exercise is both historical and cultural, to promote an understanding of the dynamic nature of language and to examine why ethnolinguistic varieties may be sustained.

Finally, there are various kinds of culminating activities that review the

You will hear four different generations of speakers who lived all of their lives in mainland Hyde County. All of the speakers are members of the same family, a long-standing African American family of Hyde County. In this region of Eastern North Carolina, European Americans and African Americans have been living in close proximity since the early 1700s. Because the county is 80 per cent marshland, residents have been more isolated here than in many other areas of North Carolina. The first paved roads into the county arrived in the mid-1900s, and dramatically changed life for the younger generations of Hyde County residents. Listen closely to the speakers and follow along with the transcripts on the screen. Think about the following questions as you listen to the passages.

1. How does the oldest speaker sound compared with the younger speaker? What changes do you see across the generations?

2. What differences in speech take place from generation to generation? What do you think is happening to the Outer Banks Brogue over time in this family?

3. Why do you think that some of these changes are taking place?

Now listen to two European American residents of Hyde County: A middle-aged male and a teenager. Do these two speakers sound similar? Compare the speech of the young European American male to the speech of the youngest speaker in the African American samples that you just listened to. Answer the following questions.

1. What differences do you hear between the younger European American male and the youngest African American speaker you just listened to?

2. Were the two European American speakers more or less similar to each other than the older and younger African American speakers?

3. What does this comparison tell you about the way language is changing in mainland Hyde County for European Americans and for African Americans?

4. Why do you think these differences in language change are taking place?

Figure 6.3 Listening Exercise: Hyde County.

naturalness of dialects. One of the effective interactive activities for public audiences involves a review of regional and sociocultural dialect lexicon. Regardless of background, everyone understands the dialectal significance of lexical items. While a variety of formats may be used to engage students of all ages in understanding lexical variation, the use of a relatively straightforward sentence placement task invariably captures the interest of participants. Figure 6.4 shows a task that we have used effectively for North Carolina residents in venues ranging from middle-school students to Elderhostel participants.

Dialect vocabulary is often very important to dialect speakers. It is also the level of language that is most likely to differ between dialects; and it is the easiest level of dialect difference to understand.

One of the most entertaining activities we developed involves a PowerPoint version of *Jeopardy* based on the popular television game show by the same name. This activity may serve as a culminating activity for a dialect awareness curriculum

A lot can be learned by listening to the special words that a particular group uses. Oftentimes, these words describe the history, life, and language of a group. Examining the special words of communities throughout the state paints a picture of the diversity of North Carolina that includes Outer Banks English, Appalachian English, and Lumbee English. Fill in the blanks in the following sentences with the appropriate dialect words.

Word Bank

juvember	mommuck	boomer	gaum
airish	poke	slam	
sigogglin	dingbatter	token	

Sentences

1. They used a _____ for target practice.
2. That _____ is from New Jersey.
3. Put those groceries in a _____ and I'll take them home.
4. When I got up this morning it was right _____ outside.
5. I saw a _____ in the field last night and it scared me.
6. They worked so hard that they were _____ wore out.
7. Last night a _____ got in the attic.
8. They road going up there sure is _____.
9. She used to _____ him when he was a child.
10 Don't _____ up the radiator with that stuff.

Answers: 1. juvember; 2. dingbatter; 3. poke; 4. airish; 5. token; 6. slam; 7. boomer; 8. sigogglin; 9. mommuck; 10. gaum

Figure 6.4 North Carolina Dialects Vocabulary Exercise.

or, at any point, an entertaining way to present fundamental notions about dialects to popular audiences. The format for this activity is given in Figure 6.5, along with some samples of items from each of the categories.

Examples like the dialect quiz, *Jeopardy*, or playing the game of Charades with dialect lexicon, are just a few of the ways in which instructors can engage and inform students interactively. After almost four decades of involvement in informal and formal education efforts related to dialect diversity, I am convinced that the most effective methods for dialect awareness education mix entertainment and learning within or outside of the classroom.

Conclusion

The selection of venues for informal and formal public education in language diversity should not be limited by past traditions or standard frames for public education. Mitigating the effects of the dominant language ideology and the widespread application of the principle of linguistic subordination involves long-term, proactive formal and informal re-education on both a local and global level.

Though it may seem like a relatively minor and incidental step, mainstreaming the discussion of language differences would constitute a major accomplishment in public education. For all of the natural curiosity that language differences raise, there is little informed public discussion of language as a reflection of historical legacy, regional affiliation, and cultural background. Entire television channels

---

Dialect Levels: *100 Points*

"It's hoi toid on the sound soid" would be an example of this level of dialect

Answer: What is pronunciation?

Dialect History: *200 Points*

This is the current name of the Lost Colony

Answer: What is Roanoke Island (Manteo)?

Language Attitudes: *500 Points*

This type of discrimination is illegal and involves telling someone they cannot rent an apartment because they have a particular accent

Answer: What is Linguistic Profiling?

Say it Our Way: *500 Points*

"We play basketball everyday" (African American English)

Answer: What is, "We be playing basketball (everyday)"?

Definition: *500 Points*

This is a simplified language used for communication between two groups with no common language.

Answer: What is a pidgin?

Figure 6.5 Answer Key.

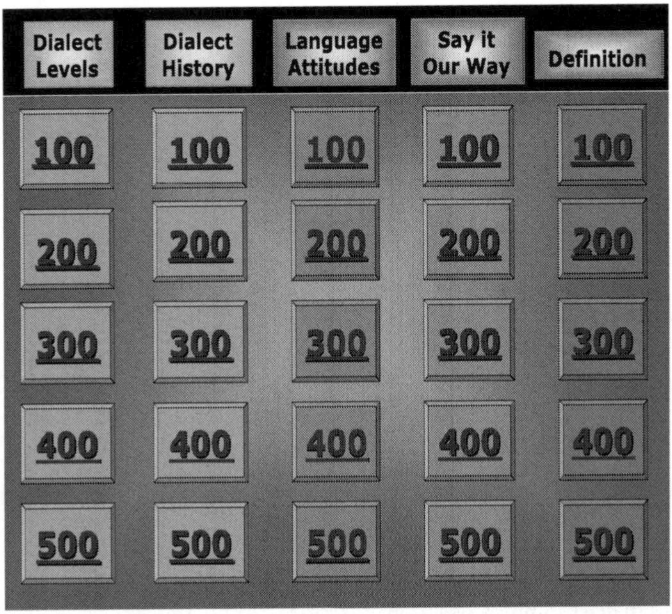

are dedicated to history, geography, and the public interest, but language diversity is rarely represented despite its emblematic role in the development of peoples and cultures in time and place. Though society and the educational system claim to be committed to a search for fundamental truths about matter, nature, and society, when it comes to language variation there is an educational tolerance of misinformation and conventional beliefs that is matched in few subject areas. At the very least, then, the educational system and society at large should assume responsibility for replacing entrenched myths about dialects with factual information about the authentic nature of dialect diversity. Realistically, fundamental change in popular language ideology will take generations to accomplish, and we must utilize the full range of formal and informal educational venues to tell the story of the most fundamental and essential manifestation of human behavioral differences. It is of course more than curious information and entertaining vignettes; the effects of racism, classism, and ethnocentrism remain more evident in language than in any other form of human behavior. Promoting cultural literacy about dialects for the public interest requires our most encompassing, creative, and entrepreneurial endeavors.

Notes

1 Funding for research and the development of informal science education programs reported here was provided by NSF grants BCS-0542139, BCS-0535438, and ESI-0354711.
2 As used here, the prescriptivist tradition refers to a set of rules designed that give instructions about regarding the socially acceptable or "correct" way to speak or write whereas the descriptivist tradition refers to a grammar based on how language is actually used by speakers.

References

ABC News. (2002). *20/20 Downtown*. February 6, 2002.
Ad Council. (2003). *Accents*. Washington, DC: National Fair Housing Alliance, U.S. Department of Housing and Urban Development, and Leadership Conference on Civil Rights Education Fund.
Adger, C., Wolfram, W., & Christian, D. (2007). *Dialects in schools and communities*, second edition. Mahwah, NJ: Erlbaum.
Alvarez, L., & Kolker, A. (1986). *American tongues*. New York: Center for New American Media.
Anzaldúa, G. (1987). *Borderlands/la frontera: The new mestiza*. San Francisco: Aunt Lute Books.
Asha. (1983). Position Statement on Social Dialects. *Asha* 25(9): 24.
Baugh, J. (2003). Linguistic profiling. In C. Makoni, G. Smitherman, A.F. Ball, & A.K. Spears (Eds.), *Black linguistics: Language, society, and politics in Africa and the Americas* (pp. 155–68). New York: Routledge.
Blanton, P. & Waters, K. (Producers). *The Ocracoke Brogue*. Raleigh: North Carolina Language and Life Project.
Carpenter, J. (2004). *The lost community of the Outer Banks: African American speech on Roanoke Island*. MA thesis. Raleigh: North Carolina State University.

—— (2005). The invisible community of the lost colony: African American English on Roanoke Island. *American Speech* 80: 227–55.

Committee on College Composition and Communication Language Statement. (1974). Students' rights to their own language. *College Composition and Communication* 25 (special issue, separately paginated). Champaign-Urbana: National Council of Teachers of English.

Fairclough, N. (1989). *Language and power.* London/New York: Longman.

Hutcheson, N. (Producer). (2001). *Indian by birth: The Lumbee dialect.* Raleigh: North Carolina Language and Life Project.

—— (2004). *Mountain talk.* Raleigh: North Carolina Language and Life Project.

—— (2005). *Voices of North Carolina.* Raleigh: North Carolina Language and Life Project.

—— (2006). *The Queen family: Appalachian tradition and back porch music.* Raleigh: North Carolina Language and Life Project.

—— (2009). *The Carolina Brogue.* Raleigh: North Carolina Language and Life Project.

Lippi-Green, R. (1997). *English with an accent: Language, ideology, and discrimination in the United States.* London/New York: Routledge.

MacNeil, R., & Cran, W. (2005). *Do you speak American?* New York: McNeil/Lehrer Productions.

NC Public Schools Standard Course of Study (2004). Eighth grade Social Studies. Retrieved on July 6, 2009, from http://www.dpi.state.nc.us/curriculum/socialstudies/scos.

NCTE/NCATE. (2003). NCTE/NCATE Program Standards: Program for the Initial Preparation of Teachers in Secondary English Language Arts. Urbana: National Council of Teachers of English.

Reaser, J.L. (2006). *The effect of dialect awareness on adolescent knowledge and attitudes.* Ph.D. dissertation. Durham: Duke University.

Reaser, J.L, & Wolfram, W. (2007a). *Voices of North Carolina: Language and life from the Atlantic to the Appalachians, instructor's manual.* Raleigh: North Carolina Language and Life Project.

—— (2007b). *Voices of North Carolina: Language and life from the Atlantic to the Appalachians, student workbook.* Raleigh: North Carolina Language and Life Project.

Rickford, J.R., & Rickford, R.J. (2000). *Spoken soul: The story of Black English.* New York: John Wiley & Sons.

Rowe, R., & Grimes, A. (Producers). (2006). *This side of the river: Self-determination and survival in Princeville, N.C.* Raleigh: North Carolina Language and Life Project.

Sellers, J. (Producer). (2006). *If you could cross the creek.* Raleigh: North Carolina Language and Life Project.

Supple, M. (1993). Sociolinguistics: the clinical perspective. In M. Leahy and J.L. Kallen (Eds.) *International Perspectives in Speech and Language Pathology* (pp. 24–29). Dublin: Trinity College.

Sweetland, J. (2006). *Teaching writing in the multicultural classroom: A sociolinguistic approach.* Ph.D. dissertation, Stanford University, Palo Alto, CA.

Tannen, D. (1990). *You just don't understand: Women and men in conversation.* New York: Ballantine.

—— (1995). *Talking from 9 to 5: Women and men at work.* New York: Quill.

Wolfram, W. (1982). Speaker knowledge and other dialects. *American Speech* 57: 3–18.

—— (1991). *Dialects and American English.* Englewood Cliffs: Prentice Hall.

Wolfram, W, & Schilling-Estes, N. (1997) *Hoi toide on the Outer Banks: The story of the Ocracoke brogue.* Chapel Hill/London: University of North Carolina Press.

—— (2006). *American English: Dialects and variation,* second edition. Malden/Oxford: Blackwell.

Wolfram, W,. & Thomas, E.R. (2002). *The development of African American English.* Malden/Oxford: Blackwell.

Wolfram, W., & Ward, B. (Eds.) (2006) *American voices: How Americans speak from coast to coast.* Malden/Oxford: Blackwell.

Wolfram, W., Dannenberg, C., Knick, S., & Oxendine, L. (2002). *Fine in the world: Lumbee language in time and place.* Raleigh: NC State Humanity Extension Program/Publications.

7 Ethnosensitivity in Time and Space

Critical Hip Hop Language Pedagogies and Black Language in the U.S.[1]

H. Samy Alim and John Baugh

> Let's imagine, for example, a populist teacher who refuses this right of correction [correcting students' language] and says "Anyone who wants to speak should just speak; the most beautiful French is street French" ... When it comes to defining the laws of the specific market of his classroom, the teacher's freedom is limited, because he will never manage to create "an empire within an empire," a sub-space in which the laws of the dominant market are suspended.
>
> (Bourdieu 1993 [1977], p. 63)

> I have suggested that teachers should be about the serious business of educating young black minds to deal with (and if necessary, on) a society of power politics and incredible complexity ... As agents of change, teachers can work to help mold American society into a humane and pluralistic social universe. Effectuating changes in language attitudes and policies, in the classroom and beyond, is a major step in this direction. What teachers would be doing, then, amounts to a social and political act, which, like charity, begins at home. Can I get a witness?
>
> (Smitherman 1977, p. 241)

Introduction

This chapter has two related goals. The first is to address the daily cultural tension, or cultural combat, that linguistically profiled and marginalized students engage in as they form their linguistic identities in creative and often unexpected (by teachers) ways through their participation in Hip Hop Culture. The second goal is to present a critical language pedagogy while speaking broadly to the field of sociolinguistics about its involvement in language pedagogy, policy-making, and politics. By providing insights of sociolinguistic involvement in language pedagogies, we will be simultaneously addressing ways in which we can interrogate and reverse (rather than merely "suspend" as Bourdieu wrote above) the laws of the dominant linguistic market through the development of critical pedagogies rooted in students' diverse cultural-linguistic realities, in this case, critical Hip Hop language pedagogies (CHHLPs).

Our sociolinguistic approach is overtly political. Rather than divorce language usage from the contexts in which it is produced, we have gathered data as participant observers: Baugh (1983) gathered interviews among Black adults in Southern California while working at a recreational facility in Los Angeles at an inner-city public park, typically gathering speech from the same adult consultants over a span of years during formal-to-informal speech events. Alim (2004a) taught at Sunnyside High School in Northern California, and integrated ethnolinguistic assignments into various classroom and homework activities. Participant observation alone does not account for our extensive and prolonged contact (and friendship) with various consultants who have provided us with the gifts of data reported herein; rather, we were mindful of our roles in the respective communities where we engaged, and, at times, challenged various consultants about their linguistic claims and observations.

The Los Angeles studies, begun during the 1970s, attempted to replicate Labov's (1972) "Contextual Styles," which compare different reading styles with speed from interviews. Since Labov's carefully controlled experimental methods require higher degrees of literacy than were common among many of the less fortunate African American adults who were often educated in inferior schools where their literacy skills were never adequately developed, and they were subsequently reluctant to "read aloud," it became necessary to modify data collection in ways that did not call for any reading. Therefore, the undue consultant embarrassment that resulted from Baugh's (1980) desire to replicate Labov's experimental methods and findings gave rise to an alternative longitudinal study that defined (in)formality in terms of how (un)familiar participants are during any given speech event (Baugh, 1983). Whereas many sociolinguists advocated the importance of fieldworkers establishing a positive rapport with their informants, Baugh's research among African American adults confirms that some of his experimental "researcher requests" caused considerable discomfort and were antithetical to obtaining recorded samples of (nearly?) natural speech (Wolfson, 1976). Based, in part, on first-hand lessons learned in Los Angeles, to say little of the insights cited above from Bourdieu and Smitherman, Alim's (2005) ensuing curriculum development functioned on multiple levels (i.e., pedagogy, policy, and politics) in the various contexts where learning occurs (i.e., within and beyond classrooms). The rise of Hip Hop Culture coincided with Smitherman and Bourdieu's focus on language, power, and education; stated in other terms, our pedagogy, policy, and politics all address social disparities that have been disproportionately suffered by U.S. slave descendants, which are confirmed through language usage.

Data Collection and Methodology

Data collection was enhanced by our occupational circumstances; we weren't merely fieldworkers who recorded interviews. Baugh's efforts were often challenged by those who were quite suspicious of tape recordings during the Nixon presidency and in the post-Watergate era. Alim's role as a high school teacher provided a perfect context to introduce ethnolingusitic research methods to his students, who, in turn, were introduced to sociolinguistics through their own independent research and classroom assignments. Both approaches did not merely rely on establishing a "rapport" with our consultants; rather, we attempted to gather data in an ethnosensitive manner.

> Ethnosensitivity requires the fieldworker to collect the data, in this instance linguistic interviews, in such a manner that the values and cultural orientation of the native consultants are taken into account. (Baugh, 1983, p. 40)

In much the same way that Goffman's (1961) research in asylums and casinos was enhanced by his employment in a mental hospital or as a card dealer in Las Vegas, our employment (as a lifeguard or teacher) provided greater access to African American consultants who might otherwise be very reluctant to offer personal recordings that could "put they business on the streets."

Baugh always began interviews employing the following question: "Do you feel that Blacks have made an important contribution to the development of music in the United States?" Although this question could evoke a "Yes" or "No" reply, nearly every consultant answered this question in the affirmative, before providing various examples. This question did more than "break the ice" during interviews; it provided further insight into the cultural orientation of the consultant. Younger adults would routinely refer to contemporary artists, whereas older adults would often refer to historical African American musical icons such as Scott Joplin, Louis Armstrong, Billie Holiday, or Duke Ellington.

Drawing upon modified ethnosensitive procedures, Alim began to develop Critical Hip Hop Language Pedagogies as a holistic approach aimed at both students *and* teachers, incorporating theory *and* practice, so that innovative approaches might begin to be implemented in classrooms. He began by locating the school as a primary site of language ideological combat, and situating CHHLPs within the frame of critical language awareness. Alim further argued (as Smitherman did in the opening quotation) that linguists and educators are obligated to present the current social and linguistic reality to students who are economically, politically, and culturally subjugated in mainstream institutions. To this end, Alim and his students developed various pedagogical approaches, including the "Real Talk" project, the "Language in My Life" project, the "Hiphopography: the Ethnography of Hip Hop Culture and Communication" project, and the "Linguistic Profiling in the Classroom" project. All of these approaches were crafted employing ethnosensitivity; that is, to enhance development of CHHLPs.

We shall conclude this chapter with a vision for critical, reflexive language pedagogies and a call to mobilize the full body of language, social, and cultural theory to produce consciousness-raising pedagogies. As sociolinguists, we must reconsider both our roles and our goals in studying educational institutions.

Old Heads from the Old School: Evidence of African American Adult Language Awareness

African American adults in Los Angeles during the 1970s were keenly aware of the linguistic dimensions of Du Bois' (1903) "Double Consciousness," resulting from

Blacks occupying both integrated and segregated circumstances. Consultants easily describe their linguistic navigation between Black and White cultures:

J: Have you come in contact with any other situations where you could see the difference [in dialect]?

R: O.K. . . . yesterday . . . O.K. . . . in my apartment building there are some New York poor White people . . . O.K. now, I know they didn't live the best of their lives . . . like most Whites . . . O.K . . . they can relate [to Black people] more than the California White person . . . let's say like that . . . O.K.?

So, I'm sitting over there talking to them . . . right? Two of my girl-friends come in, right? . . . they come in, they come to their house [the Whites' house] . . . right? O.K. . . . We introduce everybody . . . I would sit there and see them try to make the Black girls comfortable when it wasn't really necessary . . . Y'know . . . they want . . . they try to make lots of conversation, lots of laughter . . . and that's not necessary.

J: So, what did the Sisters do? How did they handle it?

R: The Sisters . . . they felt . . . I could sit there . . . I saw them . . . yeah, "Here some more White people trying to make us feel comfortable when it's not really necessary."

J: No . . . but how was their reaction?

R: O.K. Their reaction was kinda like . . . sit back and watch the show cause if you get up and try to dance with them [the Whites] they just gonna sit back and watch you act-a-fool . . . So, it's kind of hard to sit in the middle of a situation like that. You can feel two-faceded.

This informal conversational setting, in a private home, differs considerably from the demands of academic language usage in schools, and Alim's students confirm other cultural and linguistic conflicts that they have encountered in schools.

"I Ain't Tryna Get Caught Up In That No More:" Hip Hop Language Ideologies and Droppin That Catch-22

As speakers of non-dominant languages can testify, the politics of language often leave linguistically profiled and marginalized groups in a "cultural catch-22." Smitherman (1977, pp. 206–7), shocking the American sociolinguistic establish-ment by soundly obliterating the false distinction between "difference" and "def-icit" theorists, explained that difference theorists merely "pay lip service" to the "systematic" and "highly verbal" linguistic practices of Blacks. At the same time, these theorists indirectly maintain the position of the "dominant culture," *not* by believing in its superiority, but rather by tacitly accepting that "the white middle class either cannot or will not accept" Black Language (BL) and continuing to tell the "gross lie" that "speaking White English guarantees economic advancement." We still see the continued telling of this lie thirty years later. In much the same way as economic and political institutions are gentrifying Black communities around the nation and offering unfulfilled promises of economic independence, one can also say that educational institutions have been attempting to gentrify and remove BL from its speakers with similarly unfulfilled promises of economic mobility. In both cases, the message is: "Economic opportunities will be opened up to you if you just let us clean up your neighborhoods and your language."

Most Blacks in the U.S. since integration can testify that they have experienced teachers' attempts to eradicate their language and linguistic practices (see Morgan, 2002 on "outing schools") in favor of the adoption of White cultural and linguistic norms. Many U.S. Blacks can also testify that their desire for group solidarity and identification—as well as linguistic creativity (as with much of the Hip Hop generation)—has rendered this coercive process of cultural and linguistic norming all but irrelevant. Morgan (2001, p. 188) describes the language ideology of the Hip Hop Nation as "consciously and often defiantly based on urban African American language norms, values, and popular culture constructed against dominant cultural and linguistic norms." The Hip Hop Nation's language ideology, she writes, "relies on the study, knowledge, and use of African American English (AAE) and General American English (GAE) linguistic features and principles of grammaticalization." This ideology, which claims urban, working-class BL as its prestige variety, has led to a dramatic increase of localized lexicon and, as Latasha points out below (as did Morgan), a greater emphasis on phonology as a cultural, class-based, regional identifier within Black America:

Latasha: Yeah, like the way I talk to my teacher ain't the same way I talk with the 3L Click.

Alim: 3L Click? What's that?

L: All of our names begin with "L," so we named our clique after that, the 3L Click. It's me, LaToya and Lamar . . .

A: And how is the way y'all talk different from the way you talk to the teacher?

L: Well, it's like, you know that rapper, Nelly?

A: Yeah, yeah.

L: How he say everything like "urrrr," like for "here" he'll be like "hurrrr"?

A: Yeah! [Laughing] "I ain't from round hurrrr!"

L: [Laughing] That's how we try to talk!

A: Why, though?!

L: Cuz we like it!

When Latasha's favorite rappers, Nelly and the St. Lunatics, burst onto the Hip Hop scene, they were among the first rappers to represent St. Louis, Missouri on an (inter)national scale. Language was an essential part of establishing their identity in the fiercely competitive world of Hip Hop. In a popular single, they emphasized every word that rhymed with "urrrr" to highlight a well-known (and sometimes stigmatized) aspect of southern/midwestern pronunciation (also popularized by St. Louis' Chingy and New Orleans' Mystikal, among others). By intentionally highlighting linguistic features associated with their home turf, they established their tenacity through language, as if to say, "We here now!" As we see from the dialogue above, northern California-based Latasha and the 3L Click borrow this phonological feature of BL and fashion themselves as multiregional and multilectal Hip Hop Heads.

This phenomenon of Hip Hop Heads borrowing regionally-marked phonology is occurring around the nation and has been noted by Perry (2004) in her literary criticism of Hip Hop. She describes an "uncanny experience" of visiting a movie theatre in Boston only to encounter employees speaking as if they were from the "Deep South." She writes: "It wasn't until after I left the theatre that it occurred to me that this phenomenon of southern language entering Boston might have something to do with the massive success of hip hop artists from the South such as the Cash Money Millionaires, Master P, and the 504 Boys. That region had taken center stage nationally" (pp. 22–23). What these instances demonstrate is that Hip Hop language ideologies are often more concerned about playing with and exploiting interregional differences in BL than they are with remaining trapped in that "catch-22." Or as one of my students put it, they "ain't tryna get caught up in that no more."

"Everything Is Just 'Was':" The School as a Primary Site of Language Ideological Combat

CHHLPs build upon research in the field of language ideologies, brought into focus by Schieffelin, Woolard, and Kroskrity (1998) and Kroskrity (2000). Those who have conducted long-term research in schools are well aware that teachers' language ideologies are remarkably consistent in their elevation of the "standard" language variety and their devaluation of all other varieties (Alim 2004a, 2004b). In fact, one could argue that most members of any society (even linguists are not immune) have purchased and are deeply, if unconsciously, invested in the hegemony of the "standard" language (DeBose, 2007). Teachers are the shared focus of CHHLPs because they are the ones charged with the awesome responsibility of educating culturally and linguistically diverse students. They hold the same deeply-entrenched set of folk linguistic mythologies and ideologies of language as most citizens, yet they are required to enforce "rules" which reproduce the current sociolinguistic order in a very direct way through language teaching, thus placing them in a tremendous position of power.

The teacher, by virtue of the education system's dialectical relationship to the labor market, is a primary conduit of the cultural reproduction of prescriptive and sometimes prejudicial language ideologies. Writing about the construction, legitimation and imposition of an official language, Bourdieu (1991, pp. 48–49) ascribes a decisive role to the educational system:

> Georges Davy goes on to state the function of the schoolmaster, a *maitre a parler* (teacher of speaking) who is thereby also a *maitre a penser* (teacher of thinking): "He [the primary school teacher], by virtue of his function, works daily on the faculty of expression of every idea and every emotion: on language. In teaching the same clear, fixed language to children who know it only vaguely or who even speak various dialects or *patois*, he is already

inclining them quite naturally to see and feel things in the same way; and he works to build the common consciousness of the nation."

Bourdieu articulates language education in much broader terms than the mere acquisition of a "standard variety"—in fact, he places language education as central to the construction of a common national consciousness. Many teachers still view their role as one in which they "work daily on the faculty of expression" in order to "build the common consciousness of the nation." The establishment of that "same clear, fixed language" to speakers of diverse linguistic varieties is, as one teacher put it, "the thing that teachers . . . *combat* the most." (See dialogue below)

In this context, CHHLPs view the school as a primary site of language ideological combat, and begin with efforts to uncover and understand the complex and conflicting language ideologies within particular educational institutions. The school is a key site for the construction, legitimation, and imposition of an "official language." One of the goals of CHHLPs is to uncover both the official, articulated language ideologies of the school, as well as the unofficial, unarticulated language ideologies of teachers and students. From the two opening quotations in this chapter, we can already get a sense of how these ideologies may be at odds. Whereas teachers consistently engage in behaviors that aim to produce a homogenous "academic language," many students are busy celebrating, highlighting, and consciously manipulating diverse language varieties.

CHHLPs create a Freireian critical pedagogy (Freire, 1970) of language that educates linguistically profiled and marginalized students about how language is used and, importantly, how language can be used against them. Questions central to the overall project are: "How can language be used to maintain, reinforce, and perpetuate existing power relations?" And, conversely, "How can language be used to resist, redefine and possibly reverse these relations?" CHHLPs engage in the process of consciousness-raising, that is, the process of actively becoming aware of one's own position in the world and what to do about it (as in the Black, Chicana/o, Women's, and LGBT Liberation movements). By learning about the full scope of their language use (see below) and how language can actually be used against them (Baugh, 2003; see Bertrand & Mullainathan, 2003), students become more conscious of their communicative behavior and the ways by which they can transform the conditions under which they live.

Bearing critiques of critical language awareness in mind (Reagan, 2006), the remainder of this chapter will focus specifically on pedagogical approaches that can empower diverse students. Although each project is really a unit, and can be described at much greater length, the following sections introduce the main pedagogical initiatives and provide sample exercises. This pedagogical framework furthers what Gutierrez (2005) refers to as "sociocritical literacy" by providing a progression of language learning experiences that illustrate a developmental approach, one that brings a theoretically grounded and socioculturally rich pedagogy alive. Moreover, as Morrell (2004) has shown, engaging students in critical research relating to popular culture can be particularly effective, especially when deep and meaningful learning is too often preserved for more privileged others.

"Mostly in Slang, or Ebonics, but Sometimes in Standard English:" Language Learning Through Reflexive, Ethnographic Analyses

After teaching about the systematic nature of spoken speech, and that socio-linguistic variation refers to the variable frequencies of certain features within a linguistic system, we introduce the concept of variation in terms of language use, or "ways of speaking." The "Language in My Life" project begins by introducing students to Dell Hymes' (1964, 1972) theory of the "Ethnography of Speaking" and ends with student-conducted, reflexive, ethnographic analyses of their own speech behavior. The goal is for students to answer the question: How do I use language in my life? They are given an "Ethnography of Speaking" reference sheet that they keep in their binders throughout the unit. The sheet reviews basic concepts in this area, such as *speech situation, speech event,* and *speech act,* as levels of analysis in a communicative encounter. (In this case, the speech situation is a Hip Hop concert in Oakland, CA; the speech event is an interview with the rapper Juvenile; and speech acts include greetings, jokes, etc.)

Students are presented with another sample of "Real Talk"—this time with New Orleans rapper Juvenile (in order to use a speaker who is *not* from their local community)—and are guided through an "ethnography of speaking" analysis of an interview, which they learn is a "speech event." A small sample from the interview is used to create a worksheet (full interview appears in Spady, Alim, & Meghelli, 2006):

J = Juvenile
A = Alim

A: Wassup, Juve?
J: Wassup, woadie?
A: What's goin on?
J: Chillin, you know me. I'm chillin.
A: How would you describe the last year/year and a half for you?
J: Spectacular, man! I've been blessed you know.
A: It's a blessin, ha?
J: Workin real hard, you know. Just a lot of things. A lot of things have been goin on and so far everything's been goin right. I've been makin the right moves...

Figure 7.1 Interview with Juvenile.

Students are encouraged to notate the transcript in detail. They are usually adept at identifying a certain level of informality (through the use of "slang" like "wassup," "chillin," "you know what I'm saying?") as well as regionalisms in the New Orleans based-rapper's speech (such as "woadie," which can mean, "man," homie," etc.; "It's all gravy!" for the commonly used "It's all good."), and my use of "ha?" as an attempt to build rapport with (or "be cool with") the rapper by using one of his most famous expressions.

But, of course, the students are told that they cannot gather so much information by reading a transcript—they have to "go out into the field." After introducing the theory and doing a hands-on ethnography of speaking analysis, I wanted the students to be able to analyze their own communication behavior in their everyday environments, from their actual lived experiences. After challenging students and asking them if they thought that *they* could do an ethnography of speaking with their own language data, I introduced the "Language in My Life" project. In this project, the students were instructed to analyze their own communication behavior as it shifted across contexts and situations. As ethnographers, they were charged with carrying an ethnography notebook and documenting their communicative encounters. The notebook consisted of grids that were to be filled in throughout the day. An example from an eighth-grader is shown in Table 7.1.

Immediately, this project validates the language practices that students engage in outside of the classroom—e.g., *rappin* or *battlin*—by allowing the students to see their speech behavior taken as a subject of analysis. Further, after collecting data on their own speech, students gain a much higher level of metalinguistic awareness (speaking of themselves as style shifters possessing multiple languages and a range of speech styles) that allows them to not only better understand the abstract theory of "speaking," but also to better understand the linguistic landscape of their social worlds. These worlds are not marginalized in the classroom, or "checked-in at the door," as some teachers would have it. They are made central to the students' language learning experience.

Table 7.1 Language in My Life

Date:	**Time:**
November 22nd	Early in the morning, like, 7am

Mode of Language (reading, speaking, writing, listening, etc.):

Speaking, listening, rappin

Name of Language:

Mostly in slang, or Ebonics, but sometimes in standard English because my aunt was there and she talks like that.

Context (who's involved, where is it happening, what's happening):

I was sitting in the kitchen with my dad, eating cereal before I had to go to school. Before that, I was reading this rap I had wrote over and over again in my room, so I wanted to rap it for my dad. I did, and he was feelin it! He said the he could do a better one, so he tried, but it wasn't better. He called my mom and aunt over from the other room and told me to rap for them and I did. My mom was like, "Wow, Lamar! You bad!" I said, "I know." (Being cocky, as I am!) And my aunt said, "What a talented young man." My dad said he was gonna battle me after school.

Comments on the style(s) of language used:

The language with me and my dad was mostly in slang, or Ebonics, as I like to call it. Nah, I mostly say slang. And my mom, too. But my aunt, she talks standard English. I don't know, maybe because she's older.

"Aight, Rogue:" Hiphopography—The Ethnography of Culture and Communication

After the students have learned about and conducted sociolinguistic and ethnographic analyses of their own speech behavior, we expand the scope of the pedagogy and encourage students to "go back into the field" to study their social worlds through an analysis of their peer group and peer culture. As seen in the example that follows, one of the primary ways to accomplish this is through the study of localized lexical usage. We begin by raising students' awareness of the variety of lexical innovations within Hip Hop Culture (of course, most students are already aware of this, since they actively participate in these innovations). To pique their interest, as well as to localize the dialogue by focusing on the Bay Area, we provide a specific example of a research interview about the language of Hip Hop Culture with JT the Bigga Figga. In this short excerpt, JT provides an "emic" view of Hip Hop's evolving lexicon (the full interview appears in Spady et al., 2006).

[J = JT the Bigga Figga; A = Alim]

A: What does it mean to be certified with game?

J: **Certified** mean you official . . . How it got incorporated into our language in the streets, from my first experience with the word in the streets, was from **mobb** cars. And the mobb cars is Caprice Classics or Chevy Impalas '87 to '90. Them three years right there. And if you get a mobb car and it don't have a certain seal on it, it's not certified. So when dudes buy the car, it have to have that seal. You want yo car to be certified, you know what I'm saying? And that's just like if you into the collectors' cars and if it don't have the same steering wheel or if you change something it's not certified no more. So it's original, you know what I'm saying? *And* another meaning for certified meaning that you *official* . . . If I say, "Man, Alim's gon handle it. If he said he gon handle it, he certified, man. He gon handle it." So somebody who word is good.

Upon reading the transcript aloud as a class, students immediately respond by critiquing phrases, calling some out-of-date, providing new or similar phrases, comparing with other regional phrases, etc. This excitement is channeled into further training in ethnographic methods. For this particular case, we borrow from the introduction to linguist Geneva Smitherman's *Black Talk: Words and Phrases from the Hood to the Amen Corner* (1994 [2000]). The following worksheet translates academic language into a familiar Hip Hop-stylized way of writing (again, validating both academic language and the language of Hip Hop Culture).

ETHNOGRAPHIC METHODS USED BY GENEVA SMITHERMAN TO WRITE *Black Talk: Words and Phrases from the Hood to the Amen Corner.* We should use all of these methods in writing our own book (by the way, we need a title—what's up?)

(1) *Written language surveys and word lists* completed by Black people. She made up surveys and gave them to some folks that she knew, and many that she didn't, and asked them to fill out the surveys. What would a survey look like?

(2) *Songs and hit recordings.* Basically, she blocked out 30 minutes or so in her daily schedule to play some of her CDs and tapes. As the songs played, she listened really closely for any unique words and phrases. Most of us listen to music way more than 30 minutes a day, right? I know I do.

(3) *Radio shows.* My radio stay *locked* on KMEL, so this one should be easy. Whether you listen to Chuy in the morning or Big Von in the evening for the 7 o'clock Drop, you'll hear tons of slang words and phrases.

(4) *Movies and television.* You can block out 30 minutes to watch your favorite TV show (*106ᵗʰ and Park, Rap City, BET*, whatever) and catch all the slang that's being used. If you happen to be watching a movie that day, or that week, pay extra attention to the slang. You can probably get *hecka* words from one movie.

(5) *Collecting words* from community bulletins, leaflets, magazines, announcements or other written material. Can you think of any that you might use?

(6) *Face-to-face interviews.* You can literally ask people if they know any slang words or phrases that you can include for your slang dictionary. Sometimes we can't think of all of these terms by ourselves, right, so we need some help from our people. How would you ask somebody to help you? Who would you ask?

(7) *Eavesdropping.* I ain't gotta tell y'all about that one. Mmm-hmmmm . . .

(8) *Participant observation.* Participant observation means that you are not only *observing* the event or the scene, but you are also *actively participating* in it. In what events or scenes do you hear lots of slang talk? I bet you the talk at lunch time is full of slang words and phrases, huh? This is your first official ethnographic assignment. You are to be a participant observer at lunch tomorrow (Thursday) and at least one other day before we meet again next Wednesday. Keep your lil notebooks handy so you can jot words down as you hear them. I know some of you are dying to ask, so yeah, you can combine this with *eavesdropping*, but if you get popped in the eye, I'ma be like Silkk the Shokker and say, "OOOOOH, it ain't my fault!"

Students are given further training in these methods as we move through the unit. This type of assignment generates intense interest in ethnographic fieldwork and some students go above and beyond expectations by interviewing peers, family members, neighbors, and others until they completely run out of tape! One thing that needs to be emphasized is that this is not just a way to "get students excited" about language, but rather, students are told that they are contributing to the body of scholarly literature on BL. They are charged with the historical responsibility of archiving Black culture—in this case, Hip Hop Culture—through words.

In our experience, students have contributed much to the literature. One example is the term *rogue*, a localized example of semantic inversion that highlights a very specific regionalism, as it is used *only* within the 2.5 square miles of Sunnyside (Alim, 2004a).

"My Problem with English:" From Language Use to Language Discrimination

Thus far, we have outlined projects that develop students' metalinguistic awareness, particularly in the area of language use. As we stated earlier, our goal is to develop CHHLPs that do more than provide students with the tools to analyze language and to theorize its use in their local, social worlds (which is a substantial development in its own right). But beyond this, we are also obligated to expose the nature of power relations vis-à-vis language that exists within and beyond our students' social worlds. Many of our students, particularly those who speak marginalized language varieties, are already acutely aware of the fact that people can use language to discriminate against "others"—they and their families are often those "others." Other students, those for whom a more "standard" variety of English is native, may not have had similar experiences—yet, as Baugh (1998) has already argued, those students also need an education that makes linguistic discrimination explicit, one that recognizes the privileged status of native "standard" English speakers in relation to linguistically profiled and marginalized groups.

In an effort to incorporate the full range of what linguists know about language and its use in society, we begin this lesson by drawing from sociolinguistic research conducted on *linguistic profiling*. Baugh (2003) describes linguistic profiling as the auditory equivalent of racial profiling. This type of profiling (usually occurring over the phone), for example, can prevent potential homeowners from moving into certain neighborhoods. Linguistic profiling covers the full range of discriminatory practices based on racial, geographic, gender, class, and sexuality inferences made from speech alone.

Students are introduced to this compelling research by watching a video of recent cable news coverage of the Linguistic Profiling Project (LPP in Alim, 2005). The LPP research findings (Purnell, Idsardi, & Baugh, 1999), which show that the overwhelming majority of us can make correct racial inferences based on the pronunciation of the single word "Hello," inspire an entire unit of activities designed to investigate this phenomenon. After introducing *linguistic profiling* research as "applied linguistics," the students collect data from the community about similar experiences.

It is at this point in the developmental progression of CHHLPs that students begin to explore the relationships between language and discrimination, as well as the connective marginalities across linguistically profiled and marginalized populations. One brief example illustrates this point. While one Black American student interviewed his aunt and discovered that she had a very painful experience of discrimination in the housing market (that is, she would often be told that units were "still open" only to be turned away upon arrival), a Latina student shared a narrative from her father in which he was fired from his truck-driving job because of "phony" charges of tardiness. In the first case, the Black American aunt spoke "proper" on the phone, but she was still often denied access to housing based on the visual representation of her race ("when they saw I was a Black person"). And in the second case, the Latino father spoke English as a second language and believed that he was fired *not* because of his job performance (or his race) but because of his "problem with English," as he put it. These narratives are sites of exploration and critical interrogation of the links between language, discrimination, and power.

Conclusion: The Role of the Sociolinguist

Before designing pedagogies, we need to seriously consider the language ideological combat that is being waged inside and outside of our classroom walls. Otherwise, we will continue to produce language pedagogies that fail our students. Explanations of academic failure as the result of students' ideological opposition to formal schooling and "acting White" often miss the complexity and multi-directionality of ideological combat. More directly, ethnographic studies (e.g., Alim, 2004a; Carter, 2005) reveal that teachers can spend as much time devaluing students' language and culture as students spend rejecting that devaluation (which is not the same as rejecting "acting White"). Further, while Bourdieu (1993 [1977]) insists that students will continue to maintain the laws of the dominant linguistic market despite the intentions of "radical" and "populist" teachers, actual teaching experience suggests otherwise. The irony is that even as some teachers spend an inordinate amount of time "focusing on English grammar," and as some social theorists spend an equally inordinate amount of time on macro-phenomena, our students are busy *takin* English to a *whole nother level*, i.e., "grammaticalizing" it (see Alim, 2006).

In order to keep it real with our students, we need to recognize that the full body of available research on language, its structure, its use, and its role in constructing identities and mediating intergroup relations, is not produced solely for the consumption of scholars. Rather, this knowledge can be used to develop pedagogies that create high levels of metalinguistic awareness through reflexive ethnographic and sociolinguistic analyses of speech. In this way, CHHLPs operationalize the vast body of research on language for the purposes of raising the linguistic and social consciousness of all students.

Finally, as we read above, students ain't the only ones that's strugglin. Teachers of linguistically profiled and marginalized youth often struggle with the contradictions emerging from their own ideological positions, training, lived experiences, and sometimes overwhelmingly anti-democratic school cultures and practices. To this end, more research on teachers' language ideologies and experiences is needed. CHHLPs aim to use this research to engage teachers in the same type of critical language pedagogies outlined for students in this article. Teachers, too, can benefit greatly from reflexive analyses of their own language behaviors and ideologies. In fact, it is only when teachers develop a meta-ideological awareness that they can begin to work to change their ideologies—and be more fully prepared to teach all students more effectively.

Arriving at this awareness is seen as the first step in challenging a given social order (including the structure of the dominant linguistic market), a "wake-up call" that encourages students and teachers to interrogate received discourses on language, which are always connected to issues of race, class, gender, sexuality, and power. As Fairclough (1989, in Reagan, 2006, p. 14) has pointed out, critical language pedagogies have a "substantial 'shock' potential" and "can help people overcome their sense of impotence by showing them that existing orders of discourse are not immutable." Training in critical language issues can help teachers be not only well-meaning but also well-informed enough to address student questions about the imposition of dominant language norms. With such an approach, teachers can stop apologizing for "the way things are," and begin helping their students envision the way things *can be*. As sociolinguists and scholars of language, we can help teachers become those "agents of change" whom Smitherman wrote so passionately and eloquently about in the opening quotation. Armed with this knowledge, and these approaches, teachers can work to push the limits of a Bourdieuian analysis—that is, they *can* create "an empire within an empire" by creating a subspace in which the laws of the dominant market are more than suspended—they are interrogated and, over time, dismantled with the goal of providing equal language rights for all.

For too long, scholars of language have studied educational settings for the purposes of addressing "the most fundamental questions in the sociology of language (or sociolinguistics)" (Bourdieu 1993 [1977], p. 61) while choosing not to get their hands dirty with the practical processes of teaching and learning. Following Pennycook (2001, p. 176), we must recognize that language teaching and learning, as well as the study of these practices, is "always already political and, moreover, an instrument and a resource for *change*, for challenging and changing the wor(l)d." Change begins with one teacher, one classroom, one school, one district, and this cannot be overemphasized. Important social changes have been initiated and bolstered through the active work of educational institutions. Understandings of gender, racial and sexual identification and orientation, for example, have benefited greatly through changes in the official discourses of schools. Change from the school outwards carries the potential of creating a deeper understanding of linguistic diversity. As sociolinguists, we must do more than study the relationships between language, society and power—we must do what we can to alter those relationships for the betterment of humanity.

Acknowledgements

We would like to acknowledge the support of the Spencer Foundation and the Ford Foundation, without which we would not have been able to complete this chapter. This chapter has also benefited from comments by Kris Gutierrez, Austin Jackson, David Kirkand, Ernest Morrell, Marjorie Orellana, Geneva Smitherman, Charla Larrimore Baugh, and Stephanie Biermann, all of whom made excellent suggestions. Conversations with Candy Goodwin and Paul Kroskrity have also greatly enhanced this chapter. Last but not least, much love to all the Sunnysidaz out there *DO*in it real BIG and gettin they grown self on! (Yeah, yee yee!)

References

Alim, H.S. (2004a). *You know my steez: An ethnographic and sociolinguistic study of styleshifting in a Black American speech community.* Publications of the American Dialect Society, 89. Durham, NC: Duke University Press.

—— (2004b). Hearing what's not said and missing what is: Black language in White public space. In C.B. Paulston & S. Keisling (Eds.), *Discourse and intercultural communication: The essential readings.* Malden, MA: Blackwell.

—— (2005). Critical language awareness in the United States: Revisiting issues and revising pedagogies in a resegregated society. *Educational Researcher* 34(7), 24–31.

—— (2006). *Roc the mic right: The language of Hip Hop culture.* London & New York: Routledge.

Alim, H.S., & Baugh, J. (Eds.). (2007) *Talkin Black talk: Language, education, and social change.* New York: Teachers College Press.

Baugh, J. (1980). A reexamination of the Black English copula. In W. Labov (Ed.), *Locating Language in Time and Space* (pp. 106–133). New York: Academic Press.

—— (1983). *Black street speech: Its history, structure, and survival.* Austin: University of Texas Press.

—— (1998). Linguistics, education, and the law: Educational reform for African American language minority students. In S. Mufwene, J. Rickford, G. Bailey, & J. Baugh (Eds.) *African-American English: Structure, history and use.* London and New York: Routledge.

—— (2000). *Beyond Ebonics: Linguistic pride and racial prejudice.* New York: Oxford University Press.

—— (2003). Linguistic profiling. In S. Makoni, G. Smitherman, A.F. Ball, and A.K. Spears (eds.), *Black linguistics: Language, politics and society in Africa and the Americas* (pp. 114–126). London: Routledge.

Bertrand, M., & Mullainathan, S. (2003). Are Emily and Greg more employable than Lakisha and Jamal?: A field experiment on labor market discrimination. NBER Working Paper No. 9873.

Blommaert, J. (ed.). (1999). *Language ideological debates.* Berlin: Mouton de Gruyter.

Bourdieu, P. (1993 [1977]). What talking means. Paper delivered to the *Associacion Française des Enseignants de Français,* Limoges, 30 October 1977. Published in P. Bourdieu (1993). *Sociology in Question.* London: Sage Publications.

—— (1991). *Language and symbolic power.* Edited and Introduced by J.B. Thompson. Translated by G. Raymond and M. Adamson. Cambridge, MA: Harvard University Press.

Carter, P. (2005). *Keepin' it real: School success beyond Black and White.* New York: Oxford University Press.

Collins, J. (1999). The Ebonics controversy in context: Literacies, subjectivities, and language ideologies in the United States. In J. Blommaert (Ed.) *Language ideological debates* (pp. 201–234). Berlin: Mouton de Gruyter.

DeBose, C. (2007). The Ebonics phenomenon, language planning, and the hegemony of standard English. In H.S. Alim and J. Baugh (Eds.) *Talkin Black talk: Language, education, and social change.* New York: Teachers College Press

Du Bois, W.E.B. (1903). *The souls of Black folk: Essays and sketches.* Chicago: A.C. McClurg & Co.

Fairclough, N. (1989). *Language and power.* London: Longman.

—— (1995). *Critical discourse analysis: The critical study of language.* London: Longman.

Freire, P. (1970). *Pedagogy of the oppressed.* New York: Seabury Press.

Goffman, E. (1961). *Asylums: Essays on the social situation of mental patients and other inmates.* New York: Doubleday Anchor.

Gumperz, J. (1982a). *Discourse Strategies.* Cambridge: Cambridge University Press.

—— (1982b). *Language and Social Identity.* Cambridge: Cambridge University Press.

Gutierrez, K. (2005). Building sociocritical literacies: A decolonizing tool for contemporary demographics of inequality. Paper presented at the American Educational Research Association.

Heath, S.B. (1983). *Ways with words: Language, life, and work in communities and classrooms.* Cambridge: Cambridge University Press.

Hornberger, N.H. (1988). *Bilingual education and language maintenance: A southern Peruvian Quechua case.* Berlin: Mouton.

Hymes, D. (1964). Introduction: Towards ethnographies of communication. In J. Gumperz & D. Hymes (Eds.). The ethnography of communication. *American Anthropologist* 66(6), 1–34.

—— (1972). Models of interaction of language and social life. In J. Gumperz & D. Hymes (Eds.), *Directions in Sociolinguistics* (pp. 35–71). New York: Holt, Rinehart and Winston.

Jaffe, A. (1999). *Ideologies in action: Language politics in Corsica.* Berlin: Mouton de Gruyter.

Kroskrity, P. (Ed.). (2000). *Language ideologies: The cultures of language in theory and practice.* Santa Fe, NM: School of American Research.

Labov, W. (1972). *Sociolinguistic Patterns.* Philadelphia: University of Pennsylvania Press.

Morgan, M. (2001). "Nuthin' but a G thang:" Grammar and language ideology in Hip Hop identity. In S. Lanehart (Ed.). *Sociocultural and Historical Contexts of African American Vernacular English.* Athens: University of Georgia Press.

—— (2002). *Language, discourse and power in African American culture.* Cambridge: Cambridge University Press.

Morrell, E. (2004). *Becoming critical researchers: Literacy and empowerment for urban youth.* New York: Peter Lang.

National Council of Teachers of English/International Reading Association. (1996). *Standards for the English language arts.* Newark, DE: IRA/NCTE.

Pennycook, A. (2001). *Critical applied linguistics: A critical introduction.* Mahwah, NJ: Lawrence Erlbaum Associates.

—— (2004). Performativity and language studies. *Critical Inquiry in Language Studies* 1(1), 1–19.

Perry, I. (2004). *Prophets of the hood: Politics and poetics in hip hop.* Durham, NC: Duke University Press.

Purnell, T., Idsardi, W., & Baugh, J. (1999). Perceptual and phonetic experiments on American English dialect identification. *Journal of Language and Social Psychology* 18: 19–30.

Reagan, T. (2006). The explanatory power of critical language studies: Linguistics with an attitude. *Critical Inquiry in Language Studies* 3(1), 1–22.

Rumsey, A. (1990). Word, meaning, and linguistic ideology. *American Anthropologist,* 92(2), 346–361.

Schieffelin, B.B., Woolard K., & Kroskrity, P. (Eds.). (1998). *Language ideologies: Practice and theory.* New York: Oxford University Press.

Smitherman, G. (1977 [1986]). *Talkin and Testifyin: The language of Black America.* Houghton Mifflin; reissued, with revisions, Detroit: Wayne State University Press.

—— (1994 [2000]). *Black talk: Words and phrases from the hood to the amen corner.* Boston and New York: Houghton Mifflin.

Spady, J.G., Alim, H.S., & Meghelli, S. (2006). *Tha Global Cipha: Hip Hop Culture and Consciousness.* Philadelphia: Black History Museum Press.

Wodak, R. (1995). Critical linguistics and critical discourse. In J. Verschueren, J. Ostman, & J. Blommaert (Eds.), *Handbook of pragmatics* (pp. 204–210). Philadelphia: John Benjamins.

Wolfram, W. (1993). A proactive role for speech-language pathologists in sociolinguistic education. *Language, Speech and Hearing Service in Schools* 24: 181–5.

Wolfram, W., Adger, C.T., & Christian, D. (1999). *Dialects in schools and communities.* Mahwah, NJ: Lawrence Erlbaum.

Wolfson, N. (1976). Speech events and natural speech. *Language in Society.* 5: 81–96

8 Standardized Assessment of African American Children

A Sociolinguistic Perspective

Anne H. Charity Hudley

Introduction

The No Child Left Behind Act of 2001 (Public Law 107–110) resulted in a greater emphasis on standardized testing in U.S. schools. This chapter provides a sociolinguistic perspective on critical issues concerning standardized assessments used to measure the aptitude and achievement of African American children. I emphasize the linguistic issues that arise from lexical choices in the testing stimuli and the cultural assumptions that test writers make about test takers. I suggest ways that current assessment practices may be ameliorated to minimize bias, and I also present several assessment practices that are more equitable for children of different linguistic and cultural backgrounds.

History of Testing

Standardized assessment in the United States has relied on tests that are scored based on mathematical norms and deviation from these norms. Intelligence Quotient (IQ) testing, created by Alfred Binet and his colleagues in late-nineteenth-century France, was originally developed to determine if students needed extra assistance in a particular subject or cognitive area. In contrast to this original aim, standardized tests are currently used to measure students' aptitude and achievement in comparison to a set of objectives and the results of other students' performances. The early development of assessment tests in the United States as conceived by Lewis Terman, the developer of the Stanford-Binet test (Terman, 1916), was tied to ideas of the heredity of intelligence and the assessment of intelligence but was measured through tests that assessed education and achievement through cultural norms. Essential to the understanding of the use of standardized tests in the United States is the idea of the promotion of the U.S. meritocracy (Lemann, 1999). Tests were envisioned as a method for unrecognized talent to be discovered in the population, even when social and cultural opportunities varied.

Broad-scale testing in the U.S. was intended to be both a system for selecting an elite and a way of providing universal opportunity (Lemann, 1999). The underlying idea of the selection and preservation of the meritocracy was central to the early creation and administration of the Stanford-Binet tests. Terman stated that high scorers should be more eligible for higher-ranking positions and occupations, while lower scorers were destined for lower performing jobs or living off the welfare of the state (Terman, 1916).

Gould (1996) asserts that standardized tests are a valid way to identify and concentrate on the success of those with talent and consign those who score poorly to lower strata of school and society. The realization of this ideal, however, was not open to everyone in the U.S. African Americans could not fully participate in the meritocracy or in the development of the tests designed to maintain it because until 1972, African Americans and all other non-European Americans were excluded from the standardization sample of the Stanford-Binet test. The social treatment of African Americans yielded the assumptions of early test makers: African Americans had always been relegated to lower social and economic status, so the inference was that African Americans would generally be lower scorers on standardized tests.

The most popular and widely known standardized test in the United States is the College Board Scholastic Achievement Test (now officially named the SAT). The College Board was founded in 1900 by twelve university presidents led by Nicholas Murray Butler, president of Columbia University, and Charles Eliot, president of Harvard University. Examinations were administered in chemistry, English, French, German, Greek, Latin, history, mathematics, and physics. The tests were administered mostly in the northeast and were difficult to pass if the test taker had not attended boarding schools with the specific curricula on which the boards were based (Lemann, 1999). Examinations originally contained no multiple-choice questions. Students demonstrated their knowledge by writing extended essays or displaying their solutions to problems. For example, in preparation for the English examination, ten classic works of literature were assigned in advance for students. Every two or three years, the standards and reading lists were revised, and high school teachers knew well in advance which works would be covered.

The Scholastic Achievement Test was first given in 1926 and was made mandatory at Harvard University in 1936. The American College Testing Program began in 1959 with what is now known as the ACT test, which still is used widely by students who live west of the Mississippi River. Today the SAT and the ACT serve as the gatekeepers to colleges and universities across the United States, although there is a growing movement to abolish the taking of the SAT as a prerequisite for college admission (see http://www.fairtest.org/optstate.html for a list of colleges and universities that do not require a standardized test as part of their admissions criteria). Similar standardized testing has now been expanded to all levels of schools and to a wider range of functions. Whereas standardized testing in secondary schools was once used to inform the teachers of the progress and weaknesses of their students, it is now used to measure student, teacher, and school progress. Students may fail an entire school year based on the results of their test scores. Individual superintendents, principals, and teachers may be held responsible for the scores of a class, a district, or an entire school system. In many school systems, school funding is tied to test scores.

One plausible reason for the expansion in testing is that it is a profitable business. A handful of companies dominate the secondary school testing market: Harcourt Educational Measurement, CTB McGraw-Hill, Riverside Publishing (a Houghton Mifflin company), and NCS Pearson. Harcourt, CTB McGraw-Hill, and Riverside Publishing write the majority of the exams administered at the state level, while NCS Pearson is the leading scorer of standardized tests that are used to measure school and school system success (Educational Marketer, 2001, 2005).

African Americans as a Test-Taking Population

The racial characterization of test takers is most often absolute; with few exceptions in aggregate data reports, each test taker is defined as a member of one racial group. Governmental classifications for race, however, have expanded. The Census 2000 classification system allowed for individuals to choose two or more races and to mark Latino ethnicity as a category separate from race (U.S. Census Bureau, Population Division, 2008). The method of racial classification for African American test takers lies in sharp contrast with methods of classification for Native Americans, Latinos, and other ethnic categories. For example, Native American classification policies center on the individual having enough Native American heritage to claim tribal membership, whereas Latino classification often centers on the test taker's classification as both non-European American and non-African American. In contrast, test takers having one drop of blood from a line of African descent are considered to be African American. As anthropologists and psychologists in the nineteenth and the first half of the twentieth centuries looked for links between race and species, brain size and intelligence, and racial motivation for social and cultural traits, European American supremacy was upheld overall, and racial mixtures were seen as degenerate and abnormal (American Anthropological Association 1998). Lemann (1999) asserts that the development of assessment testing directly contributed to this racial agenda. Many people still implicitly use this classification system today and those who are mixed race and do not fit into a specific racial group such as African American, European American, or Latino, are seen as inauthentic and as not belonging to any group (i.e., "other").

The social results of the intersection of wealth, race, and intelligence testing thus far are clear and are as follows: because you are poor and go to racially and economically segregated schools, you score lower. Because you score lower, you must take fewer subjects and get fewer opportunities in school. Beliefs about race and IQ persist to this day as gross racial classifications and are correlated with intelligence scores and academic performance (Jensen, 1969; Herrnstein & Murray, 1994). Schools themselves also suffer. Poorer schools with fewer resources continue to receive even fewer resources due to their low performance on tests. In many areas, schools also lose their autonomy, with the state government stepping in over local officials when test scores dip too low. This punitive-based system may make some groups strive to achieve more, but for many, the forces that cause their students to fail in the first place have not been ameliorated (Kozol, 2005).

Issues of IQ assessment can be, in even more direct ways, questions of life or death. IQ test scores are used to determine if defendants are eligible to stand trial for capital crimes. In many states death penalty laws require a defendant to have a score of 70 or above on the IQ test before he or she can stand trial for a capital crime (Atkins vs. Virginia, 536 U.S. 304, 2002). A disproportionate number of those being tested for their eligibility to stand trial are African American. Certain states have responded to the unfair nature of IQ tests; for example, in the state of California, IQ tests alone cannot be used to determine if a student should be placed in special education classes (Larry P. vs. Riles, 793 F. 2nd 969 9th Cir., 1984). In an earlier ruling of Larry P. vs. Riles (No. C-71-220 R F P (N.D. Cal., 1979)), Judge Robert Peckham stated that standardized intelligence tests "are racially and culturally biased, have a discriminatory impact against black children, and have not been validated for the purpose of essentially permanent placements of black children into educationally dead-end, isolated, and stigmatizing classes for the so-called educable mentally retarded."

Understanding the social context of assessment is essential for understanding children's reactions to tests and the test-taking environment. Many African Americans devalue tests because they are known to inaccurately represent the aptitude and achievements of African Americans. As shown in Hare and Castenell (1985), African American boys in particular find greater value in activities outside of school, and by extension, outside of the testing situation, because of long-term discouragement within the school setting. Unfortunately, tests are now greatly emphasized as the center of the school experience. In my work with four- and five-year-olds in several cities in the U.S. (Charity, 2007), many children wondered if just talking with me would somehow cause them to be put back a grade if they did not do a good job in our conversations. The high level of anxiety towards school may greatly impede the creation of a school environment that fosters learning, which inevitably involves the freedom to make mistakes. While the creation of more equitable tests could ultimately ensure that children of all backgrounds are being taught adequately and are learning what they need to know to become well educated, the use of high-stakes testing as prompted by the No Child Left Behind Act has created a culture of immediate reliability and liability among teachers and supervisors that holds them directly responsible for the success of their students even when the reasons for their students' struggles are not completely their fault.

Lloyd (1995) notes that the performance of African American students may indicate differences in knowledge and achievement, but this problem can only be rectified by improvements in teaching. He challenges the reader to see testing as purpose driven. Lloyd notes that with a greater emphasis on testing, scholars must question the purpose of education and the purpose of teaching. Lloyd notes five key ways in which racism has affected the purpose of education, the purpose of teaching, and therefore the testing of African American children. According to Lloyd, racism has deprived African Americans of the experiences that develop rich cultural backgrounds, deprived African Americans of employment opportunities that enrich home life and social experience, misdirected African Americans' work habits, instilled negative self-concept and lack of self-confidence, and distorted school performance by blatant failure to provide equal school facilities.

In order to address inequities in testing, these legacies of institutionalized racism in the educational system must be rectified. Lloyd notes that while students are tested within school and within the framework of the school, there are few tests that examine how well these same students function in society. Lloyd also notes that key life and employment skills often are not tested in schools. He directs attention to fundamental questions regarding the purpose of education and the purpose of teaching. Lloyd concedes that the tests are so institutionalized that we must examine those who test how well students function in society and how key information about how to do well on standardized test success is acquired by students of different backgrounds and socioeconomic statuses.

African American English

African Americans are discriminated against regardless of the language they produce, and the use of African American English often further contributes to the discrimination, which causes academic disparity. Decades of linguistic research have demonstrated that the linguistic features of African American English (AAE) are systematic and regular (Rickford, Sweetland, & Rickford, 2004). The systematic nature of AAE as a linguistic system must be reflected in the assessment of its speakers, and yet research-based knowledge about AAE is not written into standardized tests that speakers of AAE must take. Adger, Wolfram, and Christian (2007) argue that knowing more about the unique language patterns of students can help with the acquisition of reading and with overall school performance.

We cannot assume, of course, that all African Americans speak (only) AAE. Baugh (1983) explains that African American speakers who have greater contact with non-speakers of AAE also do not necessarily use many features of AAE. In addition, every language difference that an African American speaker produces is part of the linguistic speech patterns of AAE. As a result, AAE speakers lie along a continuum according to their frequency of use of AAE features. Wolfram (1994) provides a useful paradigm for understanding how to characterize AAE speakers who have language differences that are not considered part of AAE. Wolfram suggests that children's speech be analyzed for features that are consistent with AAE and features that are consistent with Standard American English (SAE), and that each set of features should be measured against the assessor's understanding of the language norms of the given community. Some features of AAE are more frequent than others (e.g., consonant cluster reduction (ex: best produced as "bes") and production of interdental fricatives as labiodentals and stops (ex: with produced as "wit")) and thus are more easily measurable. Features such as double negatives ("I don't know nothing" and optional subject–verb (ex: "They is happy") agreement occur less frequently over a given sample of speech and thus need to be measured qualitatively rather than quantitatively in a given speech sample and across samples.

Hilliard (1995) describes the variety of linguistic and cultural differences between the perceived audience of most achievement and aptitude tests and the AAE-speaking test taker. Hilliard calls for a multidisciplinary approach to addressing inequalities in testing. Taylor and Lee (1995) note the reliance on communicative behavior on standardized tests. Hoover, Politzer, and Taylor (1995) add that on many tests, communicative behavior is being directly tested or is the method of assessment used to test a specific subject. Hoover et al. expand on the linguistic notions of communicative behavior by categorizing different types of linguistic biases. They note that the AAE features identified by many sociolinguists, such as vowel mergers (ex: "pen" and "pin' " rhyme for most AAE speakers) and consonant variation (ex: consonant cluster reduction such as "best" as "bes" results in a greater number of homophones), cause adverse results on assessment tests. Hoover et al., moreover, note that such communicative style issues manifest due to the rapid answer format of many tests. Many African American speakers (especially children) produce narrative forms both in conversation and in school discourse that are less valued than the forms that characterize academic prose (Labov, 1972; Ball, 1995). Hoover et al. (1995) and Scott and Rogers (1996) note that African Americans also use more pronouns instead of nouns and more non-verbal language and elliptical and topic-associated sentences. Such sentences assume that the listener or reader shares some information with the speaker (ex: "She is my friend") rather than the topic-centered (ex: "Angela, a classmate of mine from school, is my friend") and more elaborate, even if less contrived, sentences that assume that the listener or reader does not share experiences with the speaker and are more like sentences that the tests demand (Scott & Rogers, 1996).

Macro and Micro Aspects of Test Assessment

In this section I examine the assessment of African American children on the macro and micro levels. The macro level analysis concerns what it means for an African American to be assessed using a test that seeks to measure deviation from a norm that is based on criteria largely established outside of the African American population. The micro level concerns the specifics of the test that present extreme or unfair challenges to African American populations. Examples are given from major tests currently used in the United States.

Macroanalysis of Testing

The macro analysis of assessment concerns the examination of the key concepts that are central to the creation of most major standardized tests. The notion of what constitutes an average test taker and an average test score, for example, is central to test evaluation. Binet's first tests, by his own description, were designed only for healthy, motivated subjects who were from mainstream French culture (Becker, 2003). The specifics of testing must be examined with respect to the general ideology or motivation of the test type. Although batteries of tests specifically designed for assessing African Americans exist, the U.S. educational system continues to use the same major standardized tests for all cultural populations. It is a challenge, in any event, to create a situation in which a member of any minority group is in any sense average. This reality must be respected in the test design stage and not just in measures to balance and correct for inequities in the scoring and result-interpretation process, which is most often the case with tests that have been created and administered thus far.

Normalization of Tests

Norm-referenced tests rely on a statistical average that is established by a sample group of students. Sampling of students is a great challenge for test developers. Average test scores are set in relation to the distribution of scores, and this relationship is often represented as a curve, the most common of which is the bell curve. Although samples of African American students that comply with normalization standards may be used to establish norms for African American populations, the tests are still designed, in many cases, to comply with the ideal European American, middle-class academic target.

Washington (1996) describes special challenges to language assessment for AAE-speaking children who have other physical and mental differences (e.g., Down's syndrome, fetal alcohol syndrome, and lead poisoning). These populations have few normalized samples against which to compare their language variation, whereas European American populations do have alternate norms to use for testing purposes. In light of the absence of such information, Washington argues for the necessity of understanding the individual child's language patterns and the language patterns of the community to compensate for the lack of normative samples.

Validity

Standardized tests are evaluated on the basis of their validity and reliability. Various kinds of validity concern how well a test measures what it purports to examine. Content validity measures the relationship between what has been taught and what is being tested. Construct validity measures how well the test evaluates the particular psychological domain (e.g., IQ) that it seeks to assess. Criterion-related validity examines how the test taker's performance on a particular test is correlated with an external standard. Such standards can be based on past performances of similar students or be predictive of performances in the future based on the test results of similar students.

Test-taking conditions also must be taken into consideration when analyzing validity. For test results to be considered valid, the test manufacturer's instructions must be followed exactly when the test is given, ensuring that testing conditions are basically the same both for the groups on which the test was normalized and for all present testers. A test can be deemed reliable yet not valid due to possibilities for variation in the testing administration process.

Reliability

Reliability concerns the extent to which a test can capture accurately and replicate what it is measuring over several test-taking populations. For a test to be reliable, it must be fairly easy to administer in different places at different times. Reliable tests report similar results when taken by similar groups at a different point in time. As indicated in the previous section on racial classification, however, it is difficult to determine what a similar group consists of without using racial classification systems that are known to be faulty, since genetic differences within supposed racial groups are greater than those across such groups (Blakey, 1999). Moreover, impoverished and working-class children do not always have the same social and educational opportunities as middle-class children, yet both groups take the same tests and the tests are deemed reliable for all students.

All tests have measurement errors. Test takers' scores may vary from day to day due to changes in testing conditions or the mental or emotional state of the test taker. As a result of such measurement errors, many individuals' scores could frequently be wrong. Test anxiety and underperformance on tests because of social and racial expectations have been well documented among African American test takers (Steele & Aronson, 1995).

Microanalysis of Testing

Differences in test construction can put the test taker at an advantage or disadvantage. The microanalysis of assessment tests describes the specific purpose that a test serves and how, in light of that purpose, test performance is evaluated. Ideas about what test takers need to know to do well on the test are central to the microanalysis of tests.

African American children, especially those in lower socioeconomic status schools, have higher rates of classroom overcrowding. Overcrowding of children at test time can cause a lack of concentration on the test and also set up an environment where cheating is more likely to occur. Classrooms are also subject to disturbance by unruly children and outside noise, and such disturbances do not always cease at test time. Social issues such as poor nutrition, lack of sleep, and attention disorders may present greater challenges for some test takers. These environmental issues, however, are not taken into account when the tests are validated, leaving children and their teachers to blame for disparities in test scores that they themselves cannot alleviate.

Test Reference

Norm-referenced tests compare a test taker's abilities to other individuals who are taking the test concurrently or who have taken it previously. Social and cultural differences across test takers are reflected in the deviations from the norm. Criterion-referenced tests compare the test taker's abilities to an established standard, such as a body of knowledge or a teaching rubric. Issues with criterion-referenced tests among African Americans arise with the accessibility of the body of knowledge and how it is assessed as well as with the comparison of the test results to those of other test takers. Many members of minority groups are by definition deviant from the larger European American norm in American society, so tests must be carefully normalized for minority groups.

Achievement Tests

Achievement tests measure what the test taker learned in a particular subject area as directly taught in a curriculum. They are often criterion-referenced. Achievement tests assume that the material tested has been delivered in a way that is equitable across all test takers. In reality, however, there are huge differences in teacher instruction and in the books and resources that are available in schools across the United States. Inequalities in education, especially for African American populations, often violate the basic assumptions that standardized achievement tests must make regarding the equality of instruction and learning in the test population.

Aptitude Tests

Aptitude tests are designed to predict future performance, so they may not include information that was directly taught in a specific curriculum. These tests are most often norm-referenced, so that African American populations are compared to non-parallel populations. Most proclaimed aptitude tests, such as the SAT, are actually more like achievement tests. For example, the relationship between performance on the SAT and the verbal portion of IQ tests are more highly correlated than SAT performance and first year college grades (Lemann, 1999).

Reliability, Validity, and Cultural Considerations of Test Administration

Many challenges in the assessment of AAE-speaking children are the result of linguistic and cultural ignorance. Conventional testing situations have been shown to cause African American and other children to become hesitant and taciturn. Labov (1972) explains that the following general conclusions may be drawn about the impact of linguistic and cultural differences (pp. 229–230):

1. The low SES child's verbal response to a formal and threatening situation is used to demonstrate his lack of verbal capacity, or his verbal deficit.
2. This verbal deficit is declared to be a major cause of the lower-class child's poor performance in school.
3. Since middle-class children do better in school, middle-class speech habits are said to be necessary for learning.
4. Class and ethnic-related differences in grammatical form are equated with differences in the capacity for logical analysis.
5. Teaching the child to mimic certain formal speech patterns used by middle-class teachers is seen as teaching him to think logically.
6. Children who learn these formal speech patterns are then said to be thinking logically, and it is predicted that they will do much better in reading and arithmetic in the years to follow.

Every time a child is tested, generations of social and cultural capital are being scrutinized, and more than simply racial factors are examined. Macintosh (1988) describes the social and cultural capital that children bring to school as the "invisible knapsack." The invisible knapsack that more privileged European American children bring with them includes social and cultural tools that are needed to succeed in school. These tools, while necessary for academic success, are not readily acquired at school, thus leaving children from lower socio-economic backgrounds at a great disadvantage. Popham (2002) summarizes the relationship of the invisible knapsack and test success quite succinctly in an interview with the PBS program Frontline:

> What's most disturbing to me is in traditionally constructed standardized achievement tests, many of the items, such as those that are linked to inherited academic aptitudes or socioeconomic status, do not measure at all what is supposed to be taught in classrooms. . . . They measure things that children bring to school. They measure how smart a kid is when he walked through the door, and not what he was supposed to learn in that school.

The persistence of the black–white achievement gap has met with some mystery due to the fact that the gap still prevails even among students of different social classes. The complicated nature of the relationship between race, social class, and testing is highlighted in my own experience, especially in the differences between my maternal and paternal grandmothers' respective experiences and the items they were later able to place in my invisible knapsack.

Self-Cultural Analysis

By most measures, I would be classified as having an upper-middle-class upbringing. My paternal grandmother was raised working-class. She was at the top of her class at the Virginia Randolph School, but because segregation limited her educational options, she was not able to attend college. Due to these limited options, she had a limited vocabulary and limited educational experiences, but she made the best of what she had, even practicing with me the French vocabulary that she still remembered from her high school days. Her experience and what she passed on contrasts greatly with the social capital and history of my maternal grandmother, who held master's degrees in both English and History.

My maternal grandmother was also raised working-class but due to different opportunities available to African Americans in North Carolina was able to attend college and graduate school. She taught me to read by the age of three and had me reciting poetry and conversing on topics in African American history by the age of eight. I carried her annotated copies of Maya Angelou and John Milton with me to Harvard, where I studied poetry with Helen Vendler.

This anecdote from my family illustrates that the conventional assessment of the black–white achievement gap, which assumes that social class categories for European Americans and African Americans are parallel is not completely accurate. Simple measures of race and social class do not begin to indicate inequalities that are not simply attributable to wealth but also to local policies of segregation and institutional racism. The diachronic and synchronic effects of racism and segregation in this country are real for all African Americans, and wealth alone does not mitigate these effects.

Language and Reading Assessment

While other forms of assessment could be addressed, the language and reading assessment of African American students is of the most crucial concern. African American children are put in special education classes at higher rates than other groups of children, and lower literacy rates among African Americans often preclude further education. In this section, I delineate different forms of language and reading assessment and highlight a few assessment tests and what they measure. The tests described are representative of the difficulties faced by test takers.

Washington (1996) examines the factors leading to African American children's greater rate of referral for language services and placement into special education classes based on language differences. Washington notes that clinicians must be sure of the child's specific dialect status, even though the assessment of the individual child's language is a challenging task. Reliable samples for both the child and the child's target speech population must be available for such results to be valid. Stockman (1996) asserts that it is important to know what the general way of speaking is in the child's community; yet macroexaminations of AAE are limited. Charity (2007) shows that regional differences in AAE use by children on sentence imitation and story recall centered on the frequency of the use of certain features and not the number of unique features that a child uses. Such quantitative differences would cause AAE to look structurally the same for speakers across regions but could account for the type of variation that would cause a speaker to do worse on a test than other children who are supposedly in the same demographic group.

AAE-speaking children may have more or less the same phonetic inventory as other children, but their rate of AAE usage causes their language to pattern differently than that of other speakers. Many developmental guides rely instead on binary assessments of linguistic features in a speaker's language: either the feature is assessed to be in the language or not. For example, all children may have the *th* phonemes (voiceless *th* as in *with* or voiced *th* as in *this*), but AAE speakers use these phonemes at different frequencies, so assessment of the feature with respect to word-initial or word-final position is essential. African American children may use the phoneme at the beginning of words, as in *this*, but use it less frequently at the end of the words, as in *with*. If the phonetic inventory is tested using a word that asks the child to produce *th* word-finally, the item may be missed in the assessment of the child's inventory.

Washington also notes that several of the major tests used with children, including the Peabody Picture Vocabulary Test and the Peabody Picture Vocabulary Test—Revised, oversample African American children as needing special services. Washington cautions that examination of the population on which the test was normalized and the suitability of the testing instrument based on the performance of the population examined must be taken into account when determining if a test is appropriate for that population.

Washington further notes that scoring adjustments can be made for some tests. The Black English Sentence Scoring (BESS) procedure was designed to accommodate the language of African Americans as analyzed by Developmental Sentence Analysis (DSA), a popular language sample procedure. Washington explains, however, that the BESS data is largely based on African American adult speech and therefore advocates for the creation of new criterion-based tests, such as Stockman's Minimal Competency Core (Stockman, 1996), as tests that are comprehensively more reflective of the dialect variation found in African American children.

Hart and Risley (1995) examine the speech of African American and European American children of different social backgrounds and suggest that the speech of low-SES African American children is more linguistically impoverished than the speech of European American and middle-class children. They focus on inequalities in the vocabulary and syntactic complexity of speech samples of children speaking with their caregivers. Hart and Risley do not include, however, an assessment of the linguistic structure of AAE. Instead, they compare the speech of the African American children to the norms of the European American children, without considering linguistic and cultural differences in verbal discourse. There is no doubt that the lexical usage of African American children differs from that of other groups of children and does not fit the expectations of the school, but this fact must be separated from the idea that expressive language can only be produced within the linguistic definitions that the authors present. Hart and Risley use "textbook definitions" (p. 138) to define utterances and vocabulary. For example, they report that they used "a standard dictionary to define words as nouns, verbs, modifiers, and functors." The use of such general definitions for parts of speech does not readily take dialect variation into account.

As indicated in Labov (1972), as well as many other studies of African American children (e.g., Craig & Washington, 2006), differences in the nature of relationships between African American children and the adult who observed them may have greatly influenced the assessment situations described by Hart and Risley. In Hart and Risley's study, research assistants who visited the families' homes once a month observed parents and children. These assistants were distanced from the children's family units and the children's social and cultural worlds. It is likely that African American family units are more guarded during outside observation than European American middle-class family units. This guardedness may cause less interaction between parent and child when another person is in the room. This difference in the outward presentation of the family unit is one of the lingering effects of segregation—and of the higher rates of intrusion by governmental agencies into the social life of African Americans (higher rates of police contact, incarceration, judgment by social services)— such that language use might be more greatly monitored by both the child and parent being examined. This is an extreme example of the Observer's Paradox

(Labov, 1966) that the observation of an event or experiment is influenced by the presence of the observer/investigator.

Nonetheless, the assessment of the productive vocabulary of African American children has been a challenge. Basic assessments rely on comprehension-based measures to test vocabulary. Scarborough, Charity, and Griffin (2004) examine the comprehension of relational terms by low-SES kindergarteners and first graders in three major cities. The terms examined were commonly found on standardized aptitude tests as well as in classroom discourse and instruction. The test included terms describing physical space, including *to the left* and *beneath*; terms describing time and order, including *beginning* and *middle*; terms describing quantity, including the ordinal numbers; and terms describing logic, including *exactly the same, different,* and *every.* The children in this study acquired many of the terms during the first grade, but they did not come to school knowing the terms. Many logic terms, including *most, each, a few of,* and *almost all of,* were not acquired by first grade, indicating that more direct instruction of such terminology would help children master the accompanying concepts. The authors found it distressing that many of these terms are employed on widely used tests of school and reading readiness. Thus children without this vocabulary might be deemed not "ready" for school or learning to read, when this is not at all the case, and it is simply a matter of learning the vocabulary, which they do during first grade.

In response to such linguistic issues, non-verbal assessment measures and tests that do not require use of the vocabulary that is so directly tied to academic instruction, which advantaged children often receive at home or in preschool (McCallum, Bracken, & Wasserman, 2000) have been developed. Non-verbal assessments thus provide a way to avoid some of the linguistic biases found in verbal assessments and also are useful for speakers of other languages. Yet even non-verbal norms are culturally and socially based, so care must be used when assessing the validity and reliability of non-verbal tests.

Psychological and Emotional Batteries

The Diagnostic Analysis of Nonverbal Accuracy (DANVA) measures emotions and paralinguistic judgments of children (Nowicki, 2001a). Collins and Nowicki (2001) demonstrate that African American children's recognition of European American paralinguistic features on the DANVA correlates with teacher perceptions of students' academic and social achievement in school. The test consists of 24 photographs of adult facial expressions. The pictures depict different emotions using adult and child faces that are meant to represent the following emotions in both high and low intensities: happy, sad, angry, and fearful. The same emotions are then measured using the sentence, "I'm going out of the room now but I'll be back later," calling for what the authors label "paralanguage" features. Then children are supposed to link emotions with each stimulus. Other studies involving the DANVA, including Nowicki and Carton (1993) find that African American girls score higher on the paralinguistic section of the DANVA than do African American boys. In addition, Collins and Nowicki (2001) find that 84 African

American children enrolled in a private school, average age ten years old, were not as adept as their public-schooled European American peers at judging differences in emotions. There was a significantly different interpretation of the adult voices by the African American children, and African American children did not as readily perceive the intended emotions. Collins and Nowicki found no effects by gender of the test taker.

In light of their findings, it follows that recognizing emotions and judging responses may be analyzed as part of a student's emotional IQ, and thus students who do better on tests such as the DANVA may also do better in school. Accordingly, Collins and Nowicki found that the ability to read emotion in adult and child voices as well as in adult faces was significantly related to greater academic achievement. They hypothesize that girls who are better able to recognize adult emotions form better relationships with adults, and having greater chances of building better relationships increases the students' rate of learning and achievement. Collins and Nowicki call for more research to be done on African American non-verbal and paralinguistic cues, so that the DANVA can be made culturally and linguistically sensitive and more specifically based on research gathered about emotional expression in various cultural groups rather than on European American norms.

Reading Assessment

As described by the National Teacher Quality Survey (Walsh, Glaser, & Wilcox, 2006), five components are crucial to reading success. Those elements are: phonemic awareness, phonics, fluency, vocabulary, and reading comprehension. Reading assessment is important because it allows teachers and parents to know what reading strategy to use with their children. Children are generally evaluated and ascribed to one of three levels of reading instruction. Students assessed to be at tier one receive general education that focuses on whichever reading instruction approach the school system has adopted: a whole-language approach, a phonics-based approach, or a mix of the two. Tier two students often undergo a more specialized reading approach with intensive training, such as the Wilson Reading System (Wilson, 1998). Students who are assessed at tier three receive special education services; they may be placed in special education classes or kept in mainstream classes. These children meet with reading specialists when the rest of the class is receiving generalized reading instruction, and they also meet with instructors after school.

Contemporary aptitude and achievement tests, especially those designed to assess the aptitude of beginning readers, have attempted to respond to commonly known dialect differences by including in the directions a caveat that instructs the test scorer not to take off points for dialect differences. But if the tester is not well versed in the features of AAE, then it is very difficult to make the needed accommodations. Several tests have diligently attempted to respect dialect variation in the administration and the assessment of the tests. The instructions that follow are for the DIBELS test, a web-based assessment test used to monitor students' reading skill and accuracy. DIBELS features a web-based database that allows schools and districts to enter their DIBELS data online and generate automated reports. The DIBELS test states the following as part of its instructions:

#7 Articulation and dialect:

The student is not penalized for imperfect pronunciation due to dialect, articulation, or second language interference. For example, if the student consistently says /th/ for /s/ and pronounces "thee" for "see" when naming the letter "C," he/she should be given credit for naming the letter correctly. This is a professional judgment and should be based on the student's responses and any prior knowledge of his/her speech patterns.

The instructions call for the test giver to be sensitive to the dialect variation that the test giver notices, but it does not include common dialect differences and even the example given is not explicitly referenced as a specific dialect, articulation, or second language interference difference. Since no test giver could be held responsible for identifying every dialect of English and judging the student accordingly, specific guidelines must be established as to what features are most likely for a given population, and that list must be checked against non-standard speech production of any given student.

Woodcock-Johnson Mastery Tests

Broad reading assessment is a goal of the Woodcock-Johnson Mastery Tests (WJMT) (Woodcock, McGrew, & Mather, 2006). The writing of letter sounds, word identification, sound/grapheme correspondence, and reading fluency are just a few of the areas that versions of the Woodcock-Johnson battery of tests cover. The WJMT relies heavily on cloze analysis, or a fill in the blank test, for word identification, word attack, and, unfortunately, reading comprehension. Fill in the blank assessment poses many different linguistic issues. Language processing has been shown to be closely related to context cues. When items are presented without context, learners who process language contextually are at a marked disadvantage. Speakers with non-standard discourse and syntactic patterns are also at a severe disadvantage.

Sounding out words is an important part of the WJMT. The "arr" sound is the expected pronunciation for the letter "R," yet many African American speakers may not always produce the sound "R" in this manner, if they produce the form at all. In the sentence comprehension section of the WJMT, there is a photo of a steaming bowl of soup with two crackers on the plate below the soup bowl. The picture is labeled: The soup ____ hot. In African American English there is variation between realization of the copula as "is" and copula absence. Therefore the sentence could be seen as correct without having to fill in the blank at all. So in this instance, the sentence confounds the measuring of comprehension with the measuring of dialect.

The reading fluency section of the WJMT also presents dialect and language development issues that interfere with the actual assessment of the skill that the test seeks to measure. The first section asks the readers to answer yes or no to a series of statements. An example of such a statement is, "You can eat an apple." The word "can" has two main meanings, which may confound the test taker on this item: can, to allow or to permit, and can, to be physically able. In this instance, the definition of "can" may also be interpreted literally by the test taker, and is confusing. At the time of taking the test, the taker is not permitted to eat an apple (e.g., no eating in the classroom). Children also don't know if the existential "you" is physically able to eat an apple or not. Context clues are not available for many of the test items either; at the start of the sentence comprehension section on the WJMT, the "stories" are just two sentences long, so there is no context for the child to adhere to. As the texts get longer and become more story-like and advanced, students possessing specific cultural knowledge may have an advantage that children who are more socially distanced from the test do not share.

Measuring Reading Comprehension

Reading comprehension is widely considered difficult to measure by test makers and educators alike. There are two main types of questions that are used to assess comprehension of a reading passage. Passage-dependent questions can only be answered correctly by using information from the text (e.x., What time did Bill eat dinner?). Passage-independent questions could be answered by using information the reader already knows (e.x., What color is the broccoli?). The designation of a question as passage-dependent or passage-independent may vary based on the social and cultural information that the test taker brings to the test. Students with limited social and cultural knowledge may rely more on information presented in the passage than readers with a wider social and literary background.

Sociocultural Responses: Good Intentions

As a response to calls for more sensitivity to the diversity of the test-taking population, many standardized tests now include passages that deal with multicultural themes and issues. The following example is taken from the DIBELS third grade benchmark assessment test and is representative of such passages:

We Celebrate Kwanzaa
One holiday celebrated by African Americans is Kwanzaa. Kwanzaa means a gathering time like Thanksgiving. It means not only the gathering of foods for the winter, but also the gathering of family. It began in Africa many years ago. The holiday reminds us of the way of life of the first African Americans.

In America, houses are decorated in black, red, and green for Kwanzaa. Black stands for the color of the people. Red reminds us of our struggle. Green is for Africa and hope. Seven candles are on the table, one for each rule for how to live. An ear of corn for each child in the family is on the table. Everyone wears colorful African clothes.

The party lasts for seven days, from the day after Christmas to New Year's day. We do not eat during the day. Every night we feast and light a new candle. For dinner we have chicken and catfish. We add greens, black-eyed peas and corn bread. For dessert we have sweet potato pie and carrot cake. After dinner we play music and dance.

Kwanzaa is also a time for older family members to tell stories. We remember those who have lived before us. On the sixth night we give presents to each other. Kwanzaa is a very special time for our family.

While the subject of Kwanzaa is benign in nature and representative of a positive aspect of African American culture, the piece makes gross generalizations about African American practices. Many African American children may not even be familiar with Kwanzaa, and few celebrate the holiday with the diligence suggested by the reading passage. Non-African American children may assume that all African Americans celebrate the holiday. Regardless of the information provided, what really is at issue is the fact that social generalizations, such as the foods presented at the Kwanzaa feast, and cultural burdens, such as red for struggle, should not be placed on students in a test-taking situation. An African American child should not be unduly burdened with cultural and social generalizations while trying to take tests.

Assessments that address social and cultural innovations may also put the low-SES reader (African American or otherwise) at an unfair disadvantage. The following passage is taken from the grade six DIBELS assessment test; it highlights the unfair advantage that children who are familiar with middle-class social practices have on such tests:

Yoga for Kids

What's your favorite type of exercise? For many kids, it's soccer, basketball, tennis, swimming, or maybe pressing the buttons on a computer game, but another form of exercise that's becoming more popular is yoga.

Yoga is a great way to exercise the whole body, regardless of your physical ability. Yoga exercises consist of poses, or postures, that help strengthen, stretch, and tone the body.

In addition, they promote balance and relaxation. No special equipment is required to practice yoga. Some people use exercise mats, but you can always use the bare floor and a towel. When practicing yoga, you should wear comfortable clothes such as tights or shorts and a loose shirt.

You can purchase or check out books and videotapes that teach the basics of yoga, or you can attend a class. The best way to learn yoga is from an experienced instructor who enthusiastically practices yoga. If you were to attend a yoga class, you might begin by warming up with some gentle stretches. Next, you might do special work poses such as the "tree pose." In this pose, you stand on one leg with the foot of the other leg placed on the inside thigh of the standing leg. Then you slowly raise your arms above your head, placing your palms together.

Some poses may be sitting or squatting poses, or you might lie on your back with your legs stretched over your head. Some yoga poses may look strange, but they feel great, like a nice long yawn.

Breathing deeply and steadily is quite important in yoga, because it helps you stretch your body and relax into the poses. Speaking of relaxing, an essential part of a yoga session is lying still and quiet for several minutes at the end. "Allow your body to melt into the floor," a yoga instructor might say. This is a time of rest and making room for the calm, silent part of us that sometimes gets lost in the noise of everyday life. No wonder this is the most popular part of a yoga session!

Children who are not familiar with yoga or do not agree with the idea that it is an important exercise are at a clear disadvantage when reading this passage. If a child is already familiar with yoga, reading the passage is easier, as familiarity with the subject matter makes decoding and comprehension easier.

Case Study: Virginia Standards of Learning Tests

The Virginia Department of Education Standards of Learning (SOL) tests are administered in the following subjects in the following grades:

English: 3–6, 8–11
Math: 3–6, 8–10
Science: 3, 5, 8, 10
Social Studies: 3, 5, 8, 10

The American Federation of Teachers (AFT) considers the Virginia standards strong. Both multiple choice and extended response type questions are used on the tests, and students do have to pass the tests to graduate from high school. Rubrics are given online, and teachers are provided materials and continuing education training.

The narratives used on the SOL tests are often built around issues of morality, including the morality of sharing, the morality of standing out and apart from others, especially from family members, and the morality of working together. Such stories can be seen as constructing and testing for a strong middle-class set of values. Stories also often involve the expression and evaluation of emotions. Many stories also emphasize the value of history and tradition, especially that of Virginia. These historical and traditionally based stories include information about American (especially Virginian) culture and history, and they presume that children have been exposed to certain cultural themes. New immigrants are at a particular disadvantage in this type of localized testing, as are children who have not had the advantage of visiting the many historical sites, such as Williamsburg, Jamestown, and Monticello, that are so prominently featured in U.S. and Virginia history. As found on the DIBELS and on other standardized tests, the Virginia SOLs also use racial topics on reading comprehension sections. The fifth grade reading test in 2001 featured a story about Martin Luther King, which placed a specific moral and racial burden on African American test takers in that they have to think about their race during the test in the name of test diversity while there are not passages that talk about whiteness in such a directly racialized manner.

Virginia SOL makers have offered a glimpse of how the information for the SOLs is chosen. In a video clip presented in a Frontline special on high-stakes testing (http://www.pbs.org/wgbh/pages/frontline/shows/schools/standards/virginia.html), test makers themselves demonstrate that much of the knowledge that children are tested on is not based solely on survey or research but on personal opinion concerning what children should know.

Testing and Other Language Minorities: Lessons Learned from African American Test Takers

When there are inequities in the education system, it will be the poor and disenfranchised members who feel them first. While the focus in this chapter has been on speakers of African American English, speakers of other varieties of English who are from lower socioeconomic status backgrounds will face many of the challenges that African American and English Language Learner students encounter. Speakers of Creoles and other languages, especially those from lower-SES backgrounds, face similar difficulties when taking standardized tests. Taking dialect and cultural differences into account will result in fairer tests for all students. Regardless of his or her background, the average student should be able to succeed at tests that that are appropriate for him/her. Ultimately, it is crucial to examine how all educators can help minority children succeed in standardized tests.

Helping the Test Makers

There are two major ways that educators and researchers can work toward the success of African American children: changing the tests and helping children be better prepared for them. This section will focus on what readers of this book can do in both arenas.

Educators and researchers can work with psychometricians to create test items that are less biased. Linguists can help test creators to become more familiar with the dialect and language varieties that various test takers bring to the test. Hoover et al. (1995) mention three areas of concern that can be immediately addressed: phonological bias, syntactic bias, and lexical bias. Test makers can address phonological bias by using forms that are not variable across dialects. If such forms are used, dialect-influenced answers still must be taken into account in the test-norming process and not just in the individual scoring process. Syntactic bias can be addressed by helping test makers understand which items syntactically discriminate against African American children.

Information about AAE syntax will help test makers avoid items that may be misconstrued by the African American test taker, such as cloze test items involving the copula or auxiliaries. Lexical bias can be addressed by helping test makers use vocabulary items that are more familiar to all children and that do not draw too heavily on the middle-class European American experience. Linguists can help inform test makers when there are multiple or different interpretations of items, or when items (even made-up words) closely resemble words that are found in the vernacular.

Linguists can also help test makers understand the root of sociocultural differences, so that they are not just seen as pathologies or deficiencies. For instance, African Americans have been shown to travel less than other groups. This is not due to lack of desire but rather to the constraints that segregation historically put on free movement, as well as to the current economic situations of many African Americans such that they have less expendable income for travel. Paktose, Stokes, and Cook (2003) explain that African Americans also are likely to visit casinos, gamble, enjoy fine dining, go to theme parks, experience nightclubs and stage shows, visit historic sites and churches, go to beach resorts, and visit museums, art galleries, nightclubs, and stage shows.

The preferred destinations of most African American travelers thus contrast with the academic ideal of more intellectual or international travel, but in such places African Americans' safety and rights are not as guaranteed as they are in domestic, protected environments. Scholars outside of the test-developing industry can also play a crucial role in helping test makers to understand the social and cultural backgrounds of the test takers and therefore eliminate bias that might result from social opportunities and experiences.

Changing the Test

Test makers can use language and concepts that are more universal across racial and cultural groups. For instance, in the assessment of reading on the Virginia SOL, the elimination of references to historical situations that children may interpret differently based on their own cultural backgrounds would reduce cultural and social bias on the SOL tests. Test writers could replace these stories with general stories that do not reward children with a more detailed grasp of American history and culture. If the information provided is central to the questions asked, all children from all backgrounds will have a better chance at success. For example, items that are seemingly general to American education can be very specific to geography: "a cherry tree" can be replaced with items such as "a pair of shoes," which would be more universal to all children.

In response to concerns that dialect use directly influences test results, The Diagnostic Evaluation of Language Variation™ Screening Test (Seymour, Roeper, de Villiers, & de Villiers, 2003) has been created; this instrument takes the developmental stages and dialect differences of the AAE-speaking child into account. The DELV is both norm- and criterion-referenced with representative samples of African American children from across the United States. The development of more tests such as the DELV that directly serve the African American population is needed.

Helping Teachers

Linguists can work with classroom teachers to educate them about linguistic and social bias to help their children better prepare for standardized testing.

Few teachers have had the opportunity to gain the insights that sociolinguistic approaches to testing can provide. With respect to linguistic-specific aspects of learning, linguists can help teachers understand how to prepare students to face the specific language bias that they encounter on tests. Examples of such approaches are given below.

Phonological Bias

Teachers can be made aware of the language and dialect differences that their students have in order to help them with items that may be obscured by these differences in standardized tests. The argument can be made that in the case of reading achievement tests, the children do need to know the standard sound-to-letter correspondences in order to achieve reading success. It is necessary to teach AAE-speaking children the contrasts between African American and Standard American English grapheme–phoneme relationships since the knowledge of standard forms is ultimately needed for overall academic success and the knowledge of African American forms is needed for social and cultural success.

Syntactic Bias

Teachers can learn about the different types of syntactic complexity that discriminate against dialect-speaking children and use this to help them with the acquisition of forms that are found on standardized tests while showing them the contrasts with the forms that the children naturally produce.

Lexical Bias

Teachers can devise ways to systematically introduce students to concepts and vocabulary that the educational system presently assumes children are acquiring. Following Hoover et al. (1995), teachers can help students with lexical acquisition in three main ways. Teachers can introduce items that may be unfamiliar due to class or geographical differences (e.g., toboggan) and items that may have different orientations or interpretations in different dialects (e.g., house). Teachers can help students understand the differences between similar items that may be confusing (e.g., train vs. subway). In addition, as demonstrated in Scarborough et al. (2003), the teaching of the language used in test questions is essential.

Researchers can help teachers emphasize the teaching of sociocultural aspects of education and literacy. Vocabulary is often measured through picture prompts on standardized tests. Teachers can ensure knowledge of educational imagery including stylized drawings, cartoon figures, and antiquated photographs. Teachers can make sure that students are familiar with photographs and pictures of scenes and places that they might not have encountered in their daily lives. Urban teachers should introduce students to suburban and rural imagery. Likewise, rural and suburban teachers should introduce students to urban imagery and imagery of diverse scenes and people who may not populate the local area. For example, low-SES inner city students in the south rarely ski, and students in more tropical areas are more familiar with just two seasons. Therefore, linguists can also help with strategies for the teaching of taxonomies and cultural scenes, especially with the teaching of lexical and social items related to places where stories or test items may be set, including: beach, pool, city, desert, and weather-related scenes. Unfortunately, many of the images that appear on standardized assessments are not culturally relevant to particular student populations, but they are necessary for test success. In another popular national test, an Asian American family is presented as cross-eyed, which means that minority children might also need to be aware of the social burdens that caricaturized images of racial and minority groups could have on test takers.

Helping Children

Students who have attended school since the passing of the No Child Left Behind Act are now accustomed to taking great numbers of tests, so they simply need the tools to perform better. Linguists can provide metalinguistic training for students so that they can achieve a better understanding of the language of testing and the communicative styles that tests demand. Children should be made aware of the challenges of dialect interference in test-taking situations (see Wolfram, this volume).

Linguists can aid with the creation of programs to help students with the processing of complex sentences. The students should then learn to devise methods to translate syntactically complex questions into forms that are more familiar and easily comprehensible to them. Once the students themselves form strategies to understand what the test is looking for and how they should answer, they will be better prepared to demonstrate their knowledge in the forms that are required on standardized tests.

Helping Parents

African American parents, as well as other low-SES adults and those not so familiar with the college application and matriculation process, need help to understand the educational and social significance of the tests. Fewer African American parents have been to college than European American parents. Many African American parents do not understand the importance of taking the test more than once to obtain the best score. These parents may have fewer resources to invest in pre-test measures such as training courses and online test preparation materials, and they do not understand why money should be invested in this way.

Parents must also understand what the tests mean in the future of their children's lives. When conducting research with teachers in schools, I was dismayed by an African American high school principal who told me that his top student had to sit out a year after high school because he didn't take the proper standardized tests required by the school he wished to attend. The guidance counselor had missed the fact that he hadn't taken the tests, and his parents, not having been to college themselves, didn't know which tests were required. Often it is not that the parents do not care about their child's future, but that the parents are unfamiliar with the college application process and trust that the child will receive the guidance and help he or she needs from the school. As this story demonstrates, it is not only the young, academically struggling children who are affected by this high testing environment; African American students who are trying their best and are doing well in their classes are also suffering in this testing climate.

Conclusion

This chapter has demonstrated the discriminatory nature of standardized tests by tracing their historical development into more recent forms. The basic concept of "deviation from the norm" that is central to much test creation, normalization, and scoring puts the African American test taker at a disadvantage because African Americans in the United States are never the norm.

Delineating the academic, linguistic, and social demands of testing will help educators and researchers assist both test makers and test takers so that accurate assessment can occur. It is very important to remember that, in many cases, tests are not being used for the purposes for which they were historically designed. Test design, however, has not responded to the change in the demands of the test-taking population. The emphasis in many classrooms has been taken off of the "how" to learn and has been put on the "what" must be learned for a given test. Alon and Tienda (2007) show test scores to be an increasingly important barrier for minorities' chances to attain a bachelor's degree, thus restricting their opportunities to become leaders in all walks of life. Alon and Tienda recommend that universities concentrate instead on high school grade point average and class rank in admissions decisions, noting that these measures of academic success have been shown to be as good as, if not better than, standardized test scores as predictors of success in college.

Additional funding is needed to train teachers on coaching for the tests in order to help them become more familiar with the methods used by successful test-training services. It is important to remember, however, that many of the same methods that work for wealthier students (such as a great amount of drill and practice taking the tests) might not work for poorer children. Cole (1995) notes that there is a huge industry built around the coaching and cramming for standardized tests even though many test makers insist that aptitude tests and achievement tests cannot be studied for in such a manner. Students who cannot afford test preparation services are at a clear disadvantage. In the absence of funding for students to attend commercial test preparation courses, programs can be set up as partnerships between universities and high schools to provide many of these services.

The biased nature of assessment in U.S. schools highlights the challenges that the African American student faces on the path to academic success. Linguists have years of research-based information on African American English which can be shared with parents and teachers in order to help prepare students for the demands of specific tests. Students can learn more about the cultural and social histories of the tests so that they can better prepare socially and academic-ally for test taking. Researchers and educators can work together to change the unfair nature of the testing situation. If practices are not changed, the tests will continue to be measures of how African Americans students understand and interpret language and culture that is largely not their own.

References

Adger, C.T., Wolfram, W., & Christian, D. (2007). *Dialects in schools and communities* (2nd ed.). Mahwah, NJ: Lawrence Erlbaum.

Alon, S., & Tienda, M. (2007). Shifting meritocracy in higher education. *American Sociological Review 72*(4): 487–511.

American Anthropological Association. (1998). *Statement on race*. Retrieved June 30, 2009, from http://www.aaanet.org/stmts/racepp.htm.

American College Testing Program (ACT). (2007). *ACT, Inc.* Retrieved June 30, 2009, from http://www.act.org/.

Atkins vs. Virginia, 536 U.S. 304 2002.

Ball, A.F. (1995). Text design patterns in the writing of urban African American students: Teaching to the strengths of students in multicultural settings. *Urban Education, 30*(3).

Baugh, J. (1983). *Black street speech: Its history, structure and survival*. Austin: University of Texas Press.

Becker, K.A. (2003). History of the Stanford-Binet intelligence scales: Content and psychometrics. (*Stanford-Binet Intelligence Scales, Fifth Edition Assessment Service Bulletin No. 1*). Itasca, IL: Riverside Publishing.

Blakey M.L. (1999). Scientific racism and the biological concept of race. *Literature and Psychology, 4*, 529–43.

Charity, A.H. (2007). Regional differences in low-SES African American children's speech in the school setting. *Language Variation and Change, 19*(3), 281–293.

Charity, A.H., Scarborough, H.S., & Griffin, D.M. (2004). Familiarity with school English in African American children and its relation to early reading achievement. *Child Development, 75*(5), 1340–1356.

Cole, B. (1995). College admissions and coaching. In A.G. Hilliard III (Ed.), *Testing African American students*, (2nd rev. ed.) (pp. 97–110). Chicago: Third World Press.

College Board. (2007). *SAT website*. New York: College Board. Retrieved June 30, 2009 from http://www.collegeboard.com.

Collins, M., & Nowicki, S., Jr. (2001). African American children's ability to identify emotion in facial expressions and tones of voice of European Americans. *The Journal of Genetic Psychology, 162*(3), 334–346.

Craig, H.K., & Washington, J.A. (2006). *Malik goes to school: Exploring the language skills of African American students from preschool–5th grade*. Mahwah, NJ: Lawrence Erlbaum.

Dynamic Indicators of Basic Early Literacy Skills (DIBELS). (2007). *University of Oregon Center on Teaching and Learning*. Retrieved on June 30, 2009 from http://dibels.uoregon.edu/

Educational Marketer. (2001). Publishers suffer growing pains as testing market mushrooms. 32(29). Simba Information. R.R. Bowker. New Providence, New Jersey. pp. 4–7.

——. (2005). Pearson, CTB, ETS benefit most from $1b in testing contracts awarded in 2005. 37(2). Simba Information. R.R. Bowker. New Providence, New Jersey. pp. 1–2.

Gould, S.J. (1996). *The mismeasure of man*. New York: Norton.

Hare, B., & Castenell, L.A., Jr. (1985). No place to run, no place to hide: Comparative status and future prospects of black boys. In M. Spencer, G. Brookins, & W. Allen (Eds.),

Beginnings: The social and affective development of black children (pp. 201–214). Hillsdale, NJ: Lawrence Erlbaum.

Hart, B., & Risley, T.R. (1995). *Meaningful differences in the everyday experience of young American children.* Baltimore: Paul Brookes.

Herrnstein, R.J., & Murray, C.A. (1994). *The bell curve: Intelligence and class structure in American life.* New York: Free Press.

Hilliard, A.G., III (Ed.). (1995). *Testing African American students,* (2nd rev. ed.). Chicago: Third World Press.

Hoover, M.R., Politzer, R.L., & Taylor, O. (1995). Bias in reading tests for Black language speakers: A sociolinguistic perspective. In A.G. Hilliard, III (Ed.), *Testing African American students,* Second Revised Edition (pp. 51–68). Chicago: Third World Press.

Jensen, A. (1969). How much can we boost IQ and scholastic achievement? *Harvard Educational Review, 39*(1), 1–123.

Kozol, J. (2005). *The shame of the nation: Restoration of apartheid schooling in America.* New York: Crown.

Labov, W. (1966). *The social stratification of English in New York City.* Washington, DC: Center for Applied Linguistics.

———. (1972). The logic of nonstandard English. In *Language in the inner city* (pp. 201–240). Philadelphia: University of Pennsylvania Press.

———. (2001). *Principles of linguistic change, volume 2: Social factors.* Oxford: Blackwell.

Larry P. vs. Riles, 793 F. 2nd 969 (9th Cir. 1984).

Lemann, N. (1999). *The big test: The secret history of the American meritocracy.* New York: Farrar, Straus and Giroux.

Lloyd, R. (1995). Editor's comments. In A.G. Hilliard, III (Ed.), *Testing African American students,* Second Revised Edition (pp. 9–11). Chicago: Third World Press.

Macintosh, P. (1988). *White privilege and male privilege: A personal account of coming to see correspondences through work in women's studies.* Wellesley, MA: Wellesley College, Center for Research on Women.

McCallum, R.S., Bracken, B.A., & Wasserman, J. (2000). *Essentials of nonverbal assessment.* New York: Wiley.

Nowicki, S. (2001a). *Diagnostic analysis of nonverbal accuracy 2 (DANVA2).* Emory University. Retrieved June 30, 2009, from http://www.psychology.emory.edu/clinical/interpersonal/danva.htm.

Nowicki, S., & Carton, J. (1993). The measurement of emotional intensity from facial expressions. *Journal of Social Psychology, 133*(5), 749–750.

Patkose, M., Stokes, A.M., & Cook, S.D. (2003). *The Minority Traveler.* Washington, DC: The Research Department of the Travel Industry Association of America. Article retrieved on July 6, 2009, from http://www.tia.org/uploads/research/pdf/summMinority03.pdf.

Popham, J. (2002). Testing our schools, Interview. *PBS Frontline.* Retrieved June 30, 2009, from http://www.pbs.org/wgbh/pages/frontline/shows/schools/interviews/popham.html.

Rickford, J.R., Sweetland, J., & Rickford, A.E. (2004). African American English and other vernaculars in education: A topic-coded bibliography. *Journal of English Linguistics, 32,* 230–320.

Scarborough, H.S., Charity, A.H., & Griffin, D.M. (2003). *Linguistic challenges for young readers.* SSSR Presentation, Boulder, CO, June 15, 2003. Retrieved June 30, 2009, from http://www.triplesr.org/conference/archive/2003/03ProgB.htm.

Scott, C., & Rogers, L. (1996). Written language abilities of African American children and youth. In A. Kamhi, K. Pollock, & J. Harris (Eds.), *Communication development and disorders in African American children* (pp. 307–332). Baltimore: Paul Brookes.

Seymour, H.N., Roeper, T., de Villiers, J.G., & de Villiers, P.A. (2003). *Diagnostic Evaluation of Language Variation (DELV)—Screening Test.* San Antonio, TX: Pearson Assessment. Retrieved July 8, 2009, from http://pearsonassess.com/HAIWEB/Cultures/en-us/Productdetail.htm?Pid=015-8092-112&Mode=summary.

Steele, C.M., & Aronson, J. (1995). Stereotype threat and the intellectual test performance of African Americans. *Journal of Personality and Social Psychology, 69*(5), 797–811.

Stockman, I. (1996). Phonological development and disorders in African American children. In A. Kamhi, K. Pollock, & J. Harris (Eds.), *Communication development and disorders in African American children: Research, assessment, and intervention* (pp. 117–153). Baltimore: Paul Brookes.

Taylor, O., & Lee, D. (1995). Standardized tests and African Americans: Communication and language issues. In A.G. Hilliard, III (Ed.), *Testing African American students,* (2nd rev. ed.) (pp. 37–50). Chicago: Third World Press.

Terman, L.M. (1916). *The measurement of intelligence: An explanation of and a complete guide for the use of the Stanford revision and extension of the Binet-Simon Intelligence Scale.* Boston: Houghton Mifflin.

U.S. Department of Education. (2001). *No Child Left Behind Act.* Retrieved June 30, 2009, from http://www.ed.gov/nclb/landing.jhtml.

U.S. Census Bureau, Population Division (2008). Racial and ethnic classifications used in Census 2000 and beyond. Retrieved June 30, 2009 from http://www.census.gov/population/www/socdemo/race/racefactcb.html.

Virginia Department of Education. (2007). *Standards of Learning (SOLs).* Retrieved June 30, 2009, from http://www.doe.virginia.gov/VDOE/Superintendent/Sols/home.shtml.

Walsh, K., Glaser, D., & Wilcox, D. (2006). *National teacher quality survey: What schools aren't teaching about reading and what elementary teachers aren't learning.* National Council on Teacher Quality. Retrieved June 30, 2009 from http://www.nctq.org/nctq/images/nctq_reading_study_exec_summ.pdf.

Washington, J.A. (1996). Issues in assessing the language abilities of African American children. In A. Kamhi, K. Pollock, & J. Harris, (Eds.), *Communication development and disorders in African American children: Research, assessment, and intervention* (pp. 35–54). Baltimore: Paul Brookes.

Wilson, B. (1998). *Wilson Reading System.* Millbury, MA: Wilson Language Training.

Wolfram, W. (1994). The phonology of a socio-cultural variety: The case of African American vernacular English. In J.E. Bernthal & N.W. Bankson (Eds.), *Child phonology: Characteristics, assessment, and intervention with special populations* (pp. 227–244). New York: Thieme Medical Publishers.

Woodcock, R., McGrew, K.S., & Mather, N. (2006). *Woodcock-Johnson III NU Complete.* Rolling Meadows, IL: Riverside Publishing. Retrieved June 30, 2009, from http://www.riverpub.com/products/wjIIIComplete/index.html.

9 Latino Language Practices and Literacy Education in the U.S.

Ofelia García

Introduction

Few issues are as important in U.S. education circles today as how to promote the literacy practices of language minority students, and in particular those of U.S. Latinos, the largest language minority. With this in mind, this chapter focuses on the growing dissonance between the complex sociolinguistic reality of U.S. Latinos and the monoglossic[1] literacy policies and practices enacted to educate them. As Hudelson (1994) has said, "Literacy is language and language is literacy" (p. 102). All processes of reading, writing, listening and speaking are interrelated and mutually supportive. Thus, they need to be considered and developed holistically. In this chapter, therefore, I argue that the lack of understandings of the complex language practices of U.S. Latinos, and the inability of schools to build on them, is responsible for much academic failure.

The chapter starts out by reviewing traditional concepts of language and bilingualism. Focusing on the language practices that are readily observable among bilinguals, new conceptualizations are proposed that are helpful to understand the changes that are necessary to develop the academic language of U.S. Latinos. The chapter then reviews traditional models of teaching literacy to Latinos, and proposes other ways of teaching and assessing complex pluriliteracies by taking into account Latinos' social language practices, rather than focusing on a discrete set of skills.

From Language to Languaging

The discourse surrounding the language practices of U.S. Latino communities often has to do with whether they are monolingual or bilingual. But we are proposing here that the language practices of U.S. Latino children cannot be reduced to a simple dichotomy. To understand this argument, we have to question traditional concepts of language and bilingualism.

Many have proposed that the notion of a discrete language makes little sense in most multilingual societies where "people engage in multiple discursive practices among themselves" (Mühlhäusler, 2000, p. 358), and that language is a "European cultural artifact fostered by procedures such as literacy and standardization" (Romaine, 1994, p. 12).

That language was "invented" by states that wanted to consolidate political power, and in so doing encouraged the preparation of grammars and dictionaries and the institutionalization of schooling to strengthen these practices, is the central thesis of Makoni and Pennycook (2007).

Standardization is not an inherent characteristic of language, but an "acquired or deliberately and artificially imposed characteristic" (Romaine, 1994, p. 84). Wright (2004, p. 54) clarifies:

> A standard language is the means by which large groups become and remain communities of communication. The norm is decided and codified by a central group, disseminated through the institutions of the state such as education and then usage is constantly policed and users dissuaded from divergent practices, both formally and informally.

Standardization occurs by fixing and regulating such features as the spelling and the grammar of a language in dictionaries and grammar books which are then used for prescriptive teaching of the language.

Despite the fact that what schools call "English" or "Spanish" has little to do with the language practices of real U.S. Latino schoolchildren, it is important to acknowledge the importance of "standard language" and its consequences for U.S. Latinos. In schools, even bilingual schools, it is a standard that is valued for teaching, learning, and especially to assess what is being learned. The school's insistence in using only "the standard" to teach, learn, and assess, has much to do with the concept of *governmentality* as proposed by Foucault (1991). Foucault focuses on how language practices have much to do with "regulating" the ways in which language is used and establishing language hierarchies in which some languages, or some ways of using language, are more valued than others. This has to be interpreted within the framework of *hegemony* developed by Antonio Gramsci (1971) which explains how people acquiesce to invisible cultural power, thus limiting the life chances of members of stigmatized groups. Our routine language practices become "regulatory" mechanisms which unconsciously create categories of exclusion.

In general, languages have been constituted separately "outside and above human beings" (Yngve, 1996, p. 28) and have little relationship to the ways in which people use language, their discursive practices, or what Yngve calls their "languaging." *Languaging*, Merril Swain (2006) tells us, emphasizes language as an action, as it becomes an integral part of our meaning-making selves. Languaging, says Swain, is how we regulate our social, emotional, and cognitive behavior as well as that of others, and how we transform our thoughts into a shareable resource. Language is then a social notion that cannot be defined without reference to its speakers and the context in which it is used. It is thus more useful to speak of the languaging of Latinos, rather than their languages.

Reconstituting Bilingualism

Despite the advances of macro-sociolinguistics since the 1960s, scholarship on bilingualism, based on traditional language constructs and focused on school bilingualism, continues to define bilingualism as simply 1 + 1 = 2, and to uphold the notion of *balanced bilingualism* which views a bilingual as two persons, each fluent in one of the two languages. But *bilinguals are not double monolinguals*, and as Grosjean (1982) and Romaine (1995), among others, have repeatedly stated, they cannot be studied (or taught and assessed) as monolinguals. Bilingualism is not about 1 + 1 = 2, but about a plural which mixes different aspects or fractions of language behavior as they are needed to be socially meaningful.

Generally, only two models of bilingualism, both having been developed in response to traditional bilingual schooling, are acknowledged in the scholarly literature. Bilingualism could be *subtractive* and resulting in monolingualism, or it could be *additive*, with the two languages added and maintained (see Figure 9.1).

Responding to the disinvention of language considered above, and the resulting "*languaging*" of speakers, I have proposed (García, 2009a) that bilingualism needs to be also seen as *recursive* and moving back and forth as it blends its components, or as *dynamic* with both languages coming in and out and mixing.

These last two models of bilingualism suggest the fluid relationship between the multiple ways of languaging with the many interlocutors and the multiplicity of settings in which bilinguals interact. *Recursive* bilingualism reflects situations of *language revitalization* spurred especially by a renewed emphasis on language rights of many minorities in the twenty-first century. For example, U.S. Latinos beyond the first generation who are in the process of revitalizing their languaging practices to include what we know as Spanish, do so by recapturing bits and

Subtractive Bilingualism	Additive Bilingualism
L1 + L2 - L1 = L2	L1 + L2 = L1 + L2

Figure 9.1 Subtractive and Additive Bilingualisms.

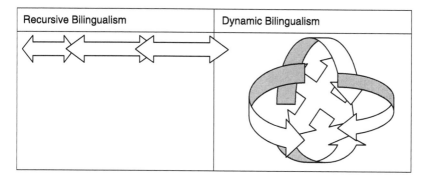

Figure 9.2 Recursive and Dynamic Bilingualisms.

pieces of their ancestral linguistic practices, as they're reconstituted for new functions. They do not start as monolinguals, nor do they add a second language. They simply recover bits and pieces of language practices that exist within their fluid bilingual social context.

Dynamic bilingualism is consonant with the new ways in which bilingualism is being constructed for a globalized world. The concept of dynamic bilingualism has much to do with the notion of *plurilingualism* that has been advanced in the European Union. For the purposes of communication and to take part in intercultural action, a plurilingual person "viewed as a social agent, has proficiency, of varying degrees, in several languages and experience of several cultures" (Council of Europe, 2000, Common European Framework of Reference for Languages, p. 168). It is not about "adding" a "second" language; it is about developing complex language practices that encompass several social contexts. The new discourse contact that comes about from the complex communication that takes place with different interlocutors on diverse planes using various language abilities in simultaneous ways leads to the deconstruction of monolingual realities.

The bilingualism of U.S. Latinos cannot be seen as a simple continuum with monolingualism at either end. With language interaction taking place in different planes that include multilingual multimodalities,[2] U.S. Latino schoolchildren engage in multiple complex communicative acts that do not in any way respond to the linear traditional models of subtractive or additive bilingualism. And yet, U.S. schools continue to insist on learning and assessing standard language, especially a Standard English, without regard to the multiplicities of language practices in U.S. Latino communities. The failure of Latinos in U.S. schools has much to do with the ignorance regarding their complex languaging practices.

Insisting on Language Characteristics

The lack of understanding of U.S. Latinos' bilingualism, as well as the insistence on seeing language as an autonomous skill separate from sociocultural practices, has led the U.S. government and educators to describe U.S. Latino schoolchildren as being English Language Learners or English monolingual, rather than recognizing their ability to negotiate their languages and varieties.

The U.S. Census gives us information on whether U.S. Latinos speak English only or not at home, as well as their degree of English language proficiency. According to the U.S. Census, 80 percent of U.S. Latinos over five years of age are very fluent in English—30 percent of them are monolingual in English,[3] while 50 percent of them speak English very well (see Table 9.1).

The limitations of self-report data are well known, but the problem of reducing language use to a "language" category as if this was a monolithic particular skill is problematic. Beyond the difficulties of reporting on "language" itself, there are other ways in which the U.S. Census shows its disinterest in the bilingualism of U.S. Latinos. For example, although the U.S. Census asks about English language proficiency, it doesn't do so for Spanish, signaling that English is the only language of importance for U.S. society and schools.

Table 9.1 U.S. Latinos' English Language Proficiency 5-17 Years

Eng Monolingual	3,055,667	30%
Eng Very Well	4,891,303	50%
Eng Less Than Very Well	1,930,387	20%
TOTAL	9,877,357	100%

Source: American Community Survey, 2005.

Of course, the number of U.S. Latino schoolchildren who the U.S. Census classify as speaking English less than very well—almost 2 million—is an important reason why educators need to pay attention to this population. But educators also need to notice the eight million U.S. Latino schoolchildren, who, despite being fluent in English and sometimes even monolingual in English, still fail in the nation's schools. Eighty percent of U.S. Latino schoolchildren speak English only or English very well. Despite the enormous attention paid to school-aged Latinos who speak English less than very well—those often referred to as *English Language Learners* in the literature and *Limited English Proficient* by the federal government—U.S. Latinos are, for the most part, English speakers. Students who are in the process of acquiring English are "only the tail of the elephant" (García, 2006a).

Schools, products of governmental authorities, also create language categories that parallel the educational options that they offer, rather than the close observation of the language practices of Latino schoolchildren themselves. Those classified as "Limited English Proficient" by the federal government and "English Language Learners" by most educators end up in special programs—either English as a Second Language or Bilingual Education. The categorization of "Spanish Dominant" or "English Dominant" has emerged to place Latino schoolchildren into transitional bilingual education programs that use more or less English. The label of "English monolingual" is applied to U.S. Latinos who seem to speak English fluently, as if traces of bilingualism disappear completely in Latino families and communities. Seldom is the category of "bilingual" used by educators, since this category has little to do with success in U.S. schools that is increasingly measured by high-stakes English-only assessments. In fact, there is a lack of recognition that by acquiring English, those considered "limited" in English or "learners" of English, are in effect "emergent bilinguals."[4] It is precisely this misunderstanding about bilingualism itself that leads to the increased failure of U.S. Latino schoolchildren, and most especially those who continue to be categorized as "Limited English proficient" or "English Language Learners" (see García, Kleifgen, & Falchi, 2007). The language practices of U.S. Latinos are a lot more fluid than government and schools recognize, and this fact is increasingly understood by language scholars.

Language Practices of U.S. Latinos

Especially in the last decade, the more dynamic and hybrid language practices of U.S. Latinos have received increased attention from scholars. In *Growing Up*

Bilingual, Zentella (1997) described the language use in *el bloque* by five New York Puerto Rican girls who were raised in the same tenement in El Barrio. The girls grew up in bilingual homes where varieties of Spanish such as popular and standard Puerto Rican Spanish, as well as popular and standard English, and everything in between were spoken to them. The girls also participated in networks where other varieties of Spanish and English were spoken, including African American Vernacular English and Dominican Spanish. Other language scholars have described the same complex language uses in other U.S. Latino communities (see, for example, Martínez (2006) for a description of the linguistic complexity of Mexican Americans; González (2001) on their language practices in Phoenix; Schecter and Bayley (2002) of those in northern California and San Antonio). Farr and Guerra (1995) have examined the interplay between English and Spanish language and literacy strategies among transnational populations as they moved between Mexico and Chicago. In addition, Farr (2006) has recently described the ways of speaking of rancheros in Chicago. The language use and learning across home and school among Mexican origin families in Eastide, California, has also been described (Pease-Alvarez & Vásquez, 1994). Kalmar (2000, p. 1) records how undocumented immigrants decided to help each other write down English *"como de veras se oye"* (as it really sounds). They thus developed a hybrid unique alphabet that coded the two languages and enabled them to make sense of their new language.

A *dynamic understanding of language socialization* (Bayley & Schecter, 2003), beyond that originally proposed by Schieffelin and Ochs (1989), is needed to understand how it is that U.S. Latino children acquire and use language. Schieffelin and Ochs (1989) proposed that children are socialized through language (how they learn the group's ways of being and doing via language) and to language (how they become speakers of the languages of their community) at the same time. But language socialization is not smooth and unilinear, directed from parents or teachers to children. Language socialization is dynamic because it is steeped in participation, and responds to the negotiation with the social context and the participants in which the interaction takes place. In this process, children exhibit considerable *agency*, choosing among options offered, and sometimes *resisting* and *constructing* new languaging practices and new identities (Bayley and Schecter, 2003). The hybrid discourse of U.S. Latino children responds to the construction of the multiplicity of identities in which multiple factors like age, race, social class, generation, sexual orientation, geopolitical situation and institutional affiliation come to bear (Pavlenko & Blackledge, 2004).

U.S. Latinos have been shown to have language practices that violate the traditional concept of *diglossia* (Fishman, 1972) with only one language being used in one domain (Pedraza, Attinasi, & Hoffman, 1980). Their language practices tap into their different dialects and languages in *functional interrelationship* for communicative and social benefit (Martí et al., 2005) in what García (2009a) has called *transglossia.* U.S. Latino schoolchildren pragmatically access their multiple linguistic and cultural resources as they participate in plural social networks. Their speech acts are, as Le Page and Tabouret-Keller (1985) have observed, "acts of projection." Their language practices are not direct manifestations of their identities; instead they perform their multiple identities through their hybrid language practices (for the concept of "performativity," see Pennycook, 2003). Gutiérrez and her colleagues (2001) have described these hybrid language practices as "a systematic, strategic, affiliative, and sense-making process" (p. 128). A binary view of the languages of U.S. Latinos has been increasingly rejected, as there has been increased recognition that their linguistic repertoire is a complex phenomenon comprising multiple codes and modes or channels of expression (see Zamel & Spack, 1998, for bilinguals).

The language practices of children in U.S. Latino communities and homes is multiple and mixed, as they draw creatively from their linguistic and cultural systems in innovative combinations. I have referred to these socially complex language practices of bilinguals as *translanguaging* (García, 2009a).[5] Although translanguaging encompasses code-switching and other features of language practices that sociolinguists often study as "language contact," it differs in that the starting point is not language as an autonomous skill. Bilingual people translanguage as they make meaning in speech communities that are, in the twenty-first century, no longer attached to a national territory, and thus to a single national language. Bilingual communities often experience transnational lives, shuttling between states, as diasporic communities. But most of the time, bilingual people shuttle between communities that are hybrids themselves, a product of postmodern societies.

The language practices of bilinguals in the twenty-first century go beyond simply using what is considered one language for certain situations and with different people. Bilinguals mix and choose different features that may be considered parts of different autonomous languages, as they discursively perform their meanings. They use language practices associated with one or another autonomous language to perform different languaging acts, sometimes mixing uses for different modalities of communication (listening, speaking, reading, writing, signing; image, icon and sound production, etc).

That immigrant youth are experts at translanguaging as they translate or paraphrase for their parents has been shown by Orellana, Reynolds, Drner, and Meza (2003) who claim that this language practice could be used to support the within-language paraphrasing that is important in schools. U.S. Latino families are usually *multi-bilingual-tasking*, as they watch television in one language, listen to a radio in another one, read lists, labels, books, and newspapers in different languages, write to different interlocutors using both and sometimes one or the other, at the same time that the young child, the older child, the parents, the relatives are speaking not only in different ways, but also using different codes, varieties and languages. It is almost impossible to live within a U.S. Latino family or community and not engage in translanguaging practices. The language practices of U.S. Latino children have little to do with the ways in which language and bilingualism are framed in school.

These heteroglossic language practices, however, are often debased as inferior. Even when Latino non-English language practices are considered, their way of using Spanish is characterized as deficient, a "patois" referred to as *Spanglish* (Stavans, 2004). And yet, their translanguaging practices reflect greater choice of expression than each monolingual separately can call upon or that schools can ever accept. Their translanguaging conveys not only linguistic knowledge, but also combined cultural, social, and political understandings that come to bear upon language practices. Sandra María Esteves (1997) expresses this in a poem to the Puerto Rican woman when she says: "I speak two languages broken into each other but my heart speaks the language of people born in oppression" (p. 384).

Monoglossic Miseducation for U.S. Latinos

One of the biggest controversies over the education of U.S. Latinos today has to do with whether it should be in English only or also use what is viewed as their "mother tongue," Spanish.[6] Especially since the advent of *No Child Left Behind* and the emphasis on high-stakes tests in English that has followed, most U.S. schools use English only in teaching and assessing U.S. Latinos (Crawford, 2004; Zehler et al., 2003). In fact, Hopstock and Stephenson (2003) have confirmed that even U.S. Latinos who are in the process of acquiring English are, for the most part, in English-only programs.[7] But, as we will argue below, even when bilingual approaches are used, the understandings of the language and literacy practices of U.S. Latinos are considered from a monoglossic angle.

The inappropriate education of U.S. Latinos, whether monolingual or bilingual, often has to do with misunderstanding their sociolinguistic complexity. As a result, U.S. Latino students experience more remedial instruction, greater probability of assignment to lower curriculum tracks, higher dropout rates, poorer graduation rates, and over-referral to special education classes (Artiles & Ortiz, 2002; Cummins, 1984; De Cohen, Deterding, & Chu Clewell, 2005). Few school leaders, and not enough teachers, are well versed in issues surrounding the language and literacy practices of U.S. Latinos. As the number of emergent bilinguals rises, along with the attendant increase in accountability, the crisis of a shortage of qualified teachers for these students has been exacerbated. For example, in 1986 there was one bilingual teacher to every seventy students in California. By 1996 there was one to 98 (Gándara et al., 2003). In California, less than 8 percent of the school psychologists are bilingual and capable of assessing bilingual students (Gándara et al., 2003). Misunderstanding U.S. Latinos' language practices is a major cause of failure in schools.

Despite the substantial research evidence that it takes between five to seven years to develop academic proficiency in standard academic English (Cummins, 2000), many states insist that emergent bilinguals may stay in special programs for only one year (e.g., California, Arizona, and Massachusetts) or for a maximum of three years (e.g., New York State and Washington). The *No Child Left Behind Act* has established strict Annual Measurable Achievement Objectives (AMAOs) to increase the percentage of "Limited English Proficient" (LEPs) progressing toward and attaining English proficiency. In 2005–6, New York State established AMAOs that required that 60 percent of all emergent bilinguals in a school district advance from one proficiency level to the next, and that 84 percent of LEP students with three years in programs, 14 percent with two years, and 10 percent with one year score at the proficient level. In 2005–6, only 23 percent of school districts in the state met the objective (New York State, AMAOs, 2006). Clearly, emergent bilinguals and programs to educate them are being deemed as school failure at alarming rates. But is the failure that of the children, or is it that of the educational establishment that refuses to understand the intricacies of their bilingualism and their translanguaging practices?

Schooling Practices for U.S. Latinos

As we said before, most U.S. Latino students attend programs in English only. Only a few attend bilingual education programs. The programs in English only sometimes, although not always, include *English as a Second Language* instruction for those who are emergent bilinguals. The programs in bilingual education are usually of three kinds: 1) *transitional bilingual education*, where the instruction is increasingly in English as students acquire more proficiency and which targets emergent bilinguals; 2) *developmental bilingual education*, which includes U.S. Latinos with different linguistic profiles and where students are educated in both English and Spanish; and 3) *two-way bilingual education programs* (increasingly called "dual language"[8]) that include U.S. Latino students with different linguistic profiles, as well as non-Latinos. The first type of bilingual education, transitional bilingual education, responds to a subtractive bilingualism model, with English only as the goal. The second type, developmental bilingual education, reflects a belief in bilingualism being additive. Only the third type, two-way bilingual education, breaks out of the traditional bilingualism mold, although it continues to insist on the separation of languages for instruction. But it is precisely in the mix of linguistically diverse students that is present in those classrooms where traditional definitions of language and bilingualism start breaking down, with children's language use increasingly showing the multiple discursive practices that Mühlhäusler (2000) describes for multilingual communities (for more on this, see García, 2006b and García et al., forthcoming).

Because these two-way bilingual education classrooms often use progressive pedagogies, there is much collaborative social practice in which students try out ideas, actions and language (Lave & Wenger, 1991). The abundant talk present in these classrooms among children with different linguistic profiles often demonstrates the hybrid language practices that characterize multilingual communities. Thus, there is much potential in those classrooms, although often this hybrid talk is contested by teachers and administrators who insist that children use one language or the other, and by the federal government, which persists in measuring progress through high-stakes tests in English only.

Literacy, Biliteracy and Pluriliteracy Practices for U.S. Latinos

Most U.S. Latinos are taught to read exclusively in English through heavily phonics-based approaches, a way to "regulate" their bilingualism, often blamed for their educational failure. And yet, research on teaching and learning has validated the importance of *collaborative social practices* (Lave & Wenger, 1991) to socially construct learning (Vygotsky, 1978). Effective classrooms, research tells us, include a great deal of talk or what Tharp et al. (2000) call _instructional conversation_, that is, talk in which relevant ideas are explored and students are engaged in extended discussions among themselves and with the teacher.

Most schools consider literacy to be simple mastery of reading and writing. And thus, many consider biliteracy a simple mastery of reading and writing in both English and Spanish (see, for example, Brisk & Harrington, 2000; Carrasquillo & Segan, 1998; Freeman & Freeman, 1996). But not all bilingual education programs have this kind of biliteracy as a goal. A more useful definition of biliteracy is that by Hornberger (1990), who defines it as "any and all instances in which communication occurs in two or more languages in or around writing" (p. 213). Hornberger's definition takes into account Brian Street's New Literacy Studies (1985) (more on this below), and emphasizes literacy as a series of social practices, and not simply a monolithic construct made up of a discrete set of skills.

There are four types of biliteracy pedagogy that are used in bilingual education programs:

1. A _convergent bimedial model of biliteracy practices_ which uses both English and Spanish in oral communication to transact with a text written in English. Here, teachers and students communicate orally in both Spanish and English _around writing_ in English, but Spanish is _not used in writing_. It corresponds to subtractive theoretical frameworks of bilingualism and is prevalent in transitional bilingual education. Only English is assessed. It can be diagrammed as in Figure 9.3.

Language A and Language B ———→ Language B written text

Figure 9.3 Convergent Bimedial Model of Biliteracy Practices.

2. A _convergent model of biliteracy practices_ which uses English and Spanish in communication to transact with a text written in each of the two languages, but with Spanish literacy practices calqued on English literacy practices. It is often found in transitional bilingual education programs where literacy is expected and assessed only in English, but Spanish literacy is used to assist in that development. In these cases, the Spanish literacy practices are calqued from (or copied from) those of English. It can be diagrammed as in Figure 9.4.

Language B and
Language A calqued on Literacy B ———→ Language B written text

Figure 9.4 Convergent Model of Biliteracy Practices.

3. A _separation model of biliteracy practices_ which uses English and Spanish to transact with a text written in one language or the other according to their own sociocultural and discourse norms. Children and teachers _match_ the language in which they are communicating around writing to the language of the written text. Students are encouraged to "think" in the language in which they are reading or writing. One language or the other is used around writing and in writing in the same language. Both English and Spanish are assessed and it is expected that students engage in literacy practices in one or the other language according to monolingual standards. Bilinguals are expected to behave and use language

as two monolinguals. Usually, bilingual education programs that adhere to an additive bilingual education theoretical framework follow this model of biliteracy practices. It can be diagrammed as in Figure 9.5.

Figure 9.5 Separation Model of Biliteracy Practices.

4. A *flexible multiple model of biliteracy practices* which uses both English and Spanish in communication to transact with texts written in both languages and in other media according to a bilingual flexible norm, capable of both integration and separation, and allowing *cross-overs.* That is, both languages and media are used in literacy practices around a text in one or the other language or in multiple media. Teachers encourage children to use all linguistic codes and modes as resources in order to engage in literacy practices in one or the other language. For example, when planning to write in English, Latino children could use Spanish to build the background, to question the text, to think about strategies; and they use not only print, but also signs, images, videos. Translanguaging is encouraged and supported. Although both languages are assessed, it is expected that students' engagement with written texts would differ from that of their monolingual counterparts. It can be diagrammed as in Figure 9.6.

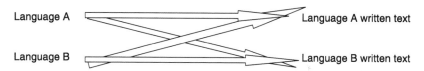

Figure 9.6 Flexible Multiple Model of Biliteracy Practices.

It is this type that most closely resembles the hybrid language cross-overs of U.S. Latino communities. And yet, it is seldom used in bilingual education and is much contested (for a notable exception, although not aiming for biliteracy, see Fu, 2003).

Brian Street (1985, 1996, 2005) has maintained that the uses of academic language are a series of *social practices*, and he views literacies as multiple and embedded in a web of social relations that maintain asymmetries of power. Hornberger and Skilton-Sylvester's revision of the *continua of biliteracy* (2003) integrates a critical perspective, positing that biliteracy is better obtained when learners can draw on all points of the continua (Hornberger 1989, p. 289). The interrelated nature of Hornberger's continua supports the potential for positive transfer across literacies, but its nested nature also shows how transfer can be promoted or hindered by different contextual factors (Hornberger 2003, p. 25). Martin-Jones and Jones (2000) have gone beyond the continua model in proposing the term *multilingual literacies* to refer to the "multiplicity and complexity of individual and group repertoires" (p. 5) and the "multiple ways in which people draw on and combine the codes in their communicative repertoire when they speak and write" (p. 7).

Bilingualism and biliteracy are not sufficient to understand the language and literacy practices of U.S. Latinos. Elsewhere (García, Bartlett, & Kleifgen, 2007) we have referred to *pluriliteracy practices* as a more fruitful concept that includes *literacy practices in sociocultural contexts*, the *hybridity* of literacy practices afforded by new technologies, and the increasing *interrelationship of semiotic systems*. Gutiérrez and her colleagues (Gutiérrez, Baquedano-López, & Tejada, 1999; Gutiérrez, Baquedano-López, & Alvarez, 2001), as well as Reyes (2001) have demonstrated the diversity of, and interplay between, linguistic codes and literacy practices in bilingual classrooms. Manyak (2001, 2002), working in a primary grade English immersion class in California post-proposition 227, examined the blending of not only Spanish and English but also home and school registers in an elementary classroom, although he warned that hybrid literacy pedagogy did not benefit all students equally. And Gutiérrez et al. (1999) have shown how the "commingling of and contradictions among different linguistic codes and registers" (p. 289) offered significant resources for learning.

A *pluriliteracy practices* approach moves away from the dichotomy of the traditional English/Spanish pairing, emphasizing instead that language and literacy practices are interrelated and flexible, positing that all literacy practices have equal value, and acknowledging the *agency* involved in communicating around writing. Although grounded in the social and the political, pluriliteracy practices have the potential for *transformation and change*, precisely because of the dynamism and flexibility of integrated hybrid practices and the agency of those involved. What is important in pluriliteracy practices is that students develop the agency to use both languages in an integrated or separate fashion, depending on the sociocultural context in which they perform the literacy practice.

Promising Pluriliteracy Pedagogies and Assessment for U.S. Latinos

The New London Group (1996) has identified four factors in meaningful literacy pedagogy:

1. *Authentic situated practice* and immersion of students in such practice;
2. *Overt instruction* to develop awareness and understanding of practice;
3. *Critique of practices* so that meanings are related to students' social contexts and purposes;
4. *Transformed practice* in which students transfer and re-create their designs of meaning from one context to another through experimentation with innovative practices.

We believe that these are important blocks; but a meaningful pluriliteracy pedagogy for U.S. Latino bilinguals would have to build on their translanguaging practices to enable them to think deeply, imagine widely, create broadly, as well as approximate acceptable academic "standard" languages. Following Freebody and Luke (1990), U.S. Latino students must (1) *break the code* of written texts in one or the other language by recognizing and using fundamental features of language;

(2) *participate in understanding and composing* meaningful written, visual, and spoken texts using all the modes and varieties of languaging practices at their disposal, including translanguaging; (3) *use texts* functionally by knowing about and acting on the different linguistic, cultural and social functions that various texts perform inside and outside school; and (4) *critically analyze and transform texts* by understanding that texts, whether written in standard academic language or not, are not ideologically natural or neutral.

More than simple adaptation of the New London Group recommendations and the roles proposed by Freebody and Luke would be needed if U.S. Latino students were to develop strong pluriliteracies. For that, schools would have to let go of their traditional understandings of language and bilingualism and would have to take notice of the hybrid language practices of U.S. Latino communities—their translanguaging. Some schools around the world are already paying heed and supporting translanguaging practices. In Wales, Cen Williams encourages teachers to involve students in hearing or reading the lessons in one language and developing the work (the oral discussion, the writing of passages, the development of projects and experiments) in another language, and vice versa (Baker, 2001; García, 2009a). In countries of Africa, where the switch to the dominant language, usually English, typically occurs in the third or fourth grade, causing the miseducation of most African children who do not understand the language of instruction, educators who had previously banned code-switching from the classroom have started to defend what they are calling "responsible code-switching" (Van der Walt, 2006; for more on this see García, 2009a). In the United States, Gutiérez and her colleagues (1999) have suggested that bilingual classrooms can use the "commingling of and contradictions among different linguistic codes and registers" (p. 289) of bilingual communities as resources for learning. Instead of holding the two languages separate and ignoring the translanguaging practices that U.S. Latino schoolchildren engage in outside of classrooms, schools could develop ways of using them, making students aware of their potential and their distance from the use of "standard" languages that schools uphold. Incorporating these practices, rather than ignoring them, might go a long way towards solving the problem of the continued miseducation of Latinos in the United States.

Despite educators' efforts to silence these practices, they are rampant in most bilingual classrooms whenever children are asked to work collaboratively. In the growing two-way bilingual education programs that pride themselves in being "dual language," thus keeping the two languages separate, the prevalent practice to teach literacy to linguistically integrated groups is the "workshop model." This method of reading and writing instruction combines language and literature-rich authentic activities aimed at enhancing meaning, understanding, and the love of language and literacy, with explicit teaching skills (Honig, 1996). This approach does not privilege either *top-down processing* (where high-level processing strategies[9] are used to make predictions about text and inferences about characters and events in a text) or *bottom-up processes* (starting with precise bits of knowledge about language, writing, and processing strategies that permit readers to "turn the squiggles on the page into meaningful symbols"

(Birch, 2002, p. 2), but balances both. During the literacy workshop, children freely incorporate their own language practices, and not the "artificial" ones of the teacher. And it is those translanguaging practices that negotiate their learning. The potential of the workshop literacy model for these students is great precisely because it builds on their own hybrid language practices.

But no amount of translanguaging as classroom practice will undo the monoglossic language ideologies of U.S. school assessment. Every assessment is an assessment of language (American Educational Research Association, American Psychological Association, & National Council on Measurement in Education, 1985), and thus, unless some recognition is made of the different ways of using languages, U.S. Latino schoolchildren will continue to perform poorly and be foreclosed of meaningful educational opportunities. We know that test translations and accommodations do not solve the problem for bilingual students (Abedi & Lord, 2001; Abedi, Hofstetter, & Lord, 2004). Assessments that claim to be in the child's "native language" demonstrate monoglossic biases and misunderstandings about children's bilingualism and have little validity since there is nonequivalence of vocabulary difficulty between languages, making comparisons for content proficiency between tests given in different languages totally inappropriate (August & Hakuta, 1998). Assessments conducted in different languages are not psychometrically equivalent (Anderson, Jenkins, & Miller, 1996). But there could be ways for assessments, even standardized ones, to take the translanguaging of U.S. Latinos and their pluriliteracies into account.

U.S. Latino students could be *assessed via a bilingual mode*, a way of rendering their bilingual competence an accepted part of their identity and knowledge. For example, questions may be put in the two languages and responses allowed in any. Or the written text could be produced by the learner in their language of choice and the oral presentation in another. If U.S. schools insist that only English be used, assessment could still follow a *bilingual tap mode*, a way of tapping the students' different language practices in order to produce a target language of assessment. That is, rather than negate the students' bilingualism, this type of assessment would, for example, give instructions and questions in English and Spanish and ask students to respond solely in English. In this way, the children's Spanish and their bilingualism would be used to activate knowledge for assessment. This *bilingual-tap assessment* builds on recent work on bilingual language processing by Dufour and Kroll (1995) and Kecskes and Papp (2007). Van der Walt (2006, 2007) has shown how an explicit bilingual task affected the performance of a group of bilingual higher education students in South Africa, compared to another group of bilingual students who were given the same, but monolingual task. Although rarely used, *bilingual-tap assessment* holds much promise, for it builds on the ways in which languages and literacies are naturally used in U.S. Latino communities.

Although translanguaging and pluriliteracy practices are readily observable in U.S. schools with Latino bilingual students, teachers and administrators continue to insist on using language as monolingual bounded systems. In both teaching and assessment, the results continue to be disastrous, as Latino schoolchildren's multiple voices are ignored within the school walls.

Conclusion

Despite the potential to build on the integrated plurilingual literacy practices that are prevalent among peoples in the twenty-first century and facilitated through new media, schools in the United States reflect a national monolingual and monoglossic ideology. The core of the resistance lies in the lack of will to change the status quo of situations in which dominant languages and literacies hold power and privilege. An important question is whether schools, regarded as the most influential educational domain, will continue to protect literacy in standard national languages and in traditional media, or will begin to build on the flexible and multi-modal plurilingual literacy practices that are sorely needed by ALL U.S. citizens in the world today.

Notes

1 I use monoglossic to refer to treating each of the languages as separate and whole bounded autonomous systems. In contrast, heteroglossic refers to multiple language practices in interrelationship, as the multiple voices in Bakhtin (1981).

2 By multimodalities, I mean that linguistic modes of meaning are intricately bound up with other visual, audio, and spatial semiotic systems. For more on this concept, see, for example, Jewett & Kress (2003) and the New London Group (1996).

3 This figure, taken from the U.S. Census, has to be interpreted with caution. The U.S. Census asks what language is spoken at home. Those who reply that they speak English only are here considered English monolingual, although it is possible that some of them might have bilingual proficiency.

4 For more information on this topic, see García, Kleifgen, and Falchi, 2007, and García, 2009b.

5 I borrow the term "translanguaging" from Cen Williams who used it only to refer to a pedagogical approach that alternates language modes. For more on that use of trans-languaging, see Baker, 2001. I have extended its meaning.

6 The concept of mother tongue is contested. For different dimensions of mother tongue, see Skutnabb-Kangas, 1981. See also García, 2009a.

7 A significant use of the native language was provided for only 16 percent of those who were learning English, and of these, most were Spanish speakers. Zehler et al. (2003) report that in 2001–2, 12 percent of emergent bilinguals were receiving no special services whatsoever, and only 36 percent were receiving appropriate services. According to the survey, only 52 percent of those identified as "ELLs" were receiving an educational program substantially different from that of their monolingual counterparts.

8 This has to do with the negative connotations that the word "bilingual"—what Crawford (2004) has called "the B-word"—has acquired in the U.S., but also of insisting on the separation of the two languages. Increasingly in the U.S. the term "dual language" is also used to refer to bilingual education programs other than transitional ones.

9 These strategies refer to making meaning out of stories, paragraphs or sentences.

References

Abedi, J., Hofstetter, C.H., & Lord, C. (2004). Assessment accommodations for English language learners: Implications for policy-based empirical research. *Review of Educational Research* 74, 1–28.

Abedi, J., & Lord, C. (2001). The language factor in mathematics tests. *Applied Measurement in Education*, 14(3), 219–234.

American Educational Research Association, American Psychological Association, & National Council on Measurement in Education (1985). *National Council on Measurement in Education standards for educational and psychological testing.* Washington, DC: American Psychological Association.

Anderson, N.E., Jenkins, F.F., & Miller, K.E. (1996). *NAEP inclusion criteria and testing accommodations: Findings from the NAEP 1995. Field test in Mathematics.* Princeton, NJ: Educational Testing Service.

Artiles, A.J., & Ortiz, A.A. (Eds.) (2002). *English language learners with special education needs: Identification, assessment, and instruction.* Washington, DC and McHenry, IL: Center for Applied Linguistics and Delta System.

August, D. & Hakuta, K. (Eds.) (1998). *Educating language-minority children.* Washington, DC: National Academy Press.

Baker, C. (2001). *Foundations of bilingual education and bilingualism,* 3rd edn. Clevedon, UK: Multilingual Matters.

Bakhtin, M. (1981). *The Dialogic imagination: Four essays.* Austin: University of Texas Press.

Bayley, R. & Schecter, S.R. (Eds.) (2003). *Language socialization in bilingual and multilingual societies.* Clevedon, UK: Multilingual Matters.

Birch, B.M. (2002). *English L2 reading. Getting to the bottom.* Mahwah, NJ: Lawrence Erlbaum.

Brisk, M.E. & Harrington, M. (2000). *Literacy and bilingualism.* Mahwah, NJ: Lawrence Erlbaum Associates.

Calkins, L. (1994). *The art of teaching writing,* 2nd edn. Portsmouth, NH: Heinemann.

Carrasquillo, A. & Segan, P. (Eds.) (1998). *The teaching of reading in Spanish to the bilingual student.* Mahwah, NJ: Lawrence Erlbaum.

Council of Europe (2000). *Common European framework of reference for languages: Learning, teaching, assessment.* Language Policy Division, Strasbourg. Retrieved July 17, 2007, from http://www.coe.int/t/dg4/linguistic/CADRE_EN.asp.

Crawford, J. (2004). *Educating English learners: Language diversity in the classroom,* 5th edn. (formerly *Bilingual education: History, politics, theory, and practice*). Los Angeles: Bilingual Educational Services.

Cummins, J. (1984). *Bilingualism and special education: Issues in assessment and pedagogy.* Clevedon, UK: Multilingual Matters.

—— (2000). *Language, power and pedagogy: Bilingual children in the crossfire.* Clevedon, UK: Multilingual Matters.

De Cohen, C.C., Deterding, N., & Chu Clewell, B. (2005). *Who's left behind? Immigrant children in high and low LEP schools.* Washington, DC: Program for Evaluation and Equity Research. Urban Institute.

Dufour, R. & Kroll, J.F. (1995). Matching words to concepts in two languages: A test of the concept mediation model of bilingual representation. *Memory and Cognition* 23(2): 166–180.

Esteves, S.M. (1997). A la mujer Borrinqueña. In H. Augenbraum & M. Fernández Olmos (Eds.), *The Latino reader* (p. 384). Boston: Houghton Mifflin.

Farr, M. (2006). *Ways of speaking and identity: Rancheros in Chicagoacán.* Austin: University of Texas Press.

Farr, M. & Guerra, J. (1995). Literacy in the community: A study of Mexicano families in Chicago. *Discourse Processes* 19: 7–19.

Fishman, J. (1972). *The sociology of language: An interdisciplinary approach to language in society.* Rowley, MA: Newbury House.

Foucault, M. (1991). Governmentality. In G. Burchell, C. Gordon, & P. Miller (Eds.)

The Foucault effect: Studies in governmentality (pp. 87–104). Chicago: University of Chicago Press.

Freebody, P. & Luke, A. (1990). Literacies programs: Debates and demands in cultural context. *Prospect: Australian Journal of TESOL* 5(7): 7–16.

Freeman, Y.S. & Freeman, D.E. (1996). *Teaching reading and writing in Spanish in the bilingual classroom*. Portsmouth, NH: Heinemann.

Fu, D. (2003). *An island of English: Teaching ESL in Chinatown*. Portsmouth, NH: Heinemann.

Gándara, P., Rumberger, R., Maxwell-Jolly, J., & Callahan, R. (2003). English learners in California schools: Unequal resources, unequal outcomes. *Education Policy Analysis Archives*. Retrieved July 1, 2003, from http://epaa.asu.edu/epaa/v11n36/

García, O. (2006a). Equity's elephant in the room. Multilingual children in the U.S. are being penalized by current education policies. *TC Today* (Fall 2006), p. 40.

—— (2006b). Lost in transculturation: The case of bilingual education in New York City. In M. Putz, J.A. Fishman, & Neff-Van Aertselaer (Eds.) *Along the routes to power: Exploration of empowerment through language* (pp. 157–178). Berlin: Mouton de Gruyter.

—— (2009a). *Bilingual education in the 21ˢᵗ century: A global perspective*. Oxford: Basil Blackwell.

—— (2009b). Emergent bilinguals and TESOL. What's in a name? *TESOL Quarterly* 43(2).

García, O., Bartlett, L., & Kleifgen, J.A. (2007). From biliteracy to pluriliteracies. In P. Auer & L. Wei (Eds.) *Handbook of applied linguistics*. Vol. 5: *Multilingualism* (pp. 207–228). Berlin: Mouton/de Gruyter.

García, O., with Makar, C., Starcevic, M. and Terry, A. (forthcoming) Translanguaging of Latino kindergarteners. *Sociolinguistic Studies*, special issue on child Spanish speakers in English speaking societies edited by J. Rothman, K. Potowski and M. Niño-Murcia.

García, O., Morín J.L., & Rivera, K. (2001). How threatened is the Spanish of New York Puerto Ricans? Language shift with vaivén. In J.A. Fishman (Ed.) *Can Threatened Languages be Saved? Reversing language shift revisited* (pp. 44–73). Clevedon, UK: Multilingual Matters.

García, O., Kleifgen, J.A., & Falchi, L. (2007). *Equity in the education of emergent bilinguals: The case of English language learners*. Teachers College, Columbia University: Campaign for Educational Equity. Retrieved July 1, 2009 from http://www.tc.columbia.edu/i/a/document/6468_Ofelia_ELL__Final.pdf.

González, N. (2001). *I am my language: Discourse of women and children in the borderlands*. Tucson: University of Arizona Press.

Gramsci, A. (1971). *Selections from the prison notebooks*. (Translated and edited by Q. Hoare & G.N. Nowell-Smith) New York: International Publishers.

Grosjean, F. (1982). *Life with two languages*. Cambridge, MA: Harvard University Press.

Gutiérrez, K., Baquedano-López, P., & Tejada, C. (1999). Rethinking diversity: Hybridity and hybrid language practices in the third space. *Mind, Culture and Activity* 6 (4), 286–303.

Gutiérrez, K., Baquedano-López, P., & Alvarez, H.H. (2001). Literacy as hybridity: Moving beyond bilingualism in urban classrooms. In M. Reyes & J.J. Halcón (Eds.) *The best for our children: Critical perspectives on literacy for Latino students* (pp. 122–141). New York: Teachers College Press.

Honig, B. (1996) *Teaching our children to read: The role of skills in a comprehensive reading program*. Thousand Oaks, CA: Corwin Press.

Hopstock, P.J. & Stephenson, T. (2003). *Descriptive study of services to LEP students and LEP students with disabilities. Special Topic Report* #2: Analysis of Office of Civil Rights Data related to LEP students. OELA, U.S. Department of Education.

210   *Ofelia García*

Hornberger, N. (1989). Continua of biliteracy. *Review of Educational Research* 59: 271–96.
—— (1990) Creating successful learning contexts for bilingual literacy. *Teachers College Record* 92 (2), 212–229.
—— (Ed.) (2003). *Continua of biliteracy: An ecological framework for educational policy, research, and practices in multilingual settings.* Clevedon, UK: Multilingual Matters.
Hornberger, N. & Skilton-Sylvester, E. (2003). Revisiting the continua of biliteracy: International and critical perspectives. In N. Hornberger (Ed.). *Continua of biliteracy. An ecological framework for educational policy, research, and practices in multilingual settings* (pp. 35–70). Clevedon, UK: Multilingual Matters.
Hudelson, S. (1994). Literacy development of second language children. In F. Genesee (Ed.) *Educating second language children: The whole child, the whole curriculum, the whole community* (pp. 129–158). Cambridge: Cambridge Univesity Press.
Jewett, C. & Kress, G. (2003). *Multimodal literacy.* New York: Peter Lang.
Kalmar, T.M. (2000). *Illegal alphabets and adult biliteracy: Latino migrants crossing the linguistic border.* Mahwah, NJ: Erlbaum.
Kecskes, I. and Papp, T. (2007). Foreign language learning affecting mother tongue. Actas do i Simposio Internacional sobre o Bilinguismo. Retrieved July 1, 2009 from http://webs.uvigo.es/ssl/actas1997/03/Kecskes.pdf.
Lave, J. & Wenger, E. (1991). *Situated learning: Legitimate peripheral participation.* Cambridge: Cambridge University Press.
Le Page, R.B. & Tabouret-Keller, A. (1985). *Acts of identity: Creole-based approaches to language and ethnicity.* Cambridge: Cambridge University Press.
Makoni, S. & Pennycook, A. (2007). *Disinventing and reconstituting languages.* Clevedon, UK: Multilingual Matters.
Manyak, P. (2001). Participation, hybridity, and carnival: A Situated analysis of a dynamic literacy practice in a primary-grade English immersion class. *Journal of Literacy Research* 33(3), 423–65.
—— (2002). "Welcome to Salon 110:" The consequences of hybrid literacy practices in a primary-grade English classroom. *Bilingual Research Journal* 26(2), 421–42.
Martí, F., Ortega, P., Idiazabal, I., Barreña, A., Juaristi, P., Junyent, C., Uranga, B., & Amorrortu, E. (Eds.) (2005). *Words and worlds. World languages review.* Clevedon, UK: Multilingual Matters.
Martínez, G.A. (2006). *Mexican Americans and language. Del dicho al hecho.* Tucson: University of Arizona Press.
Martin-Jones, M. & Jones, K. (2000). *Multilingual literacies. Reading and writing different worlds.* Amsterdam: John Benjamins.
Mühlhäusler, P. (2000). Language planning and language ecology. *Current Issues in Language Planning* 1 (3), 306–367.
New London Group (1996). A Pedagogy of multiliteracies: Designing social futures. Harvard Educational Review 66(1): 60–92.
New York State AMAOs (2006). 2005 and 2006 Title III AMAO status. Retrieved August 15, 2007 from http://www.emsc.nysed.gov/biling/0506TIIIAMAO.htm [website no longer active following revision of policy].
Orellana, M.F., Reynolds, J., Drner, J., & Meza, M. (2003). In other words: Translating or "para-phrasing" as a family literacy practice in immigrant households. *The Reading Research Quarterly* 38 (1): 12–35.
Pavlenko, A. & Blackledge, A. (2004). *Negotiation of identities in multilingual contexts.* Clevedon, UK: Multilingual Matters.
Pease-Alvarez, L. & Vásquez, O. (1994). Language socialization in ethnic minority communities. In F. Genesee (Ed.), *Educating second language children: The whole child, the*

whole curriculum, the whole community (pp. 82–102). Cambridge: Cambridge University Press.

Pedraza Jr., P., Attinasi, J., & Hoffman, G. (1980). Rethinking diglossia. In R.V. Padilla (Ed.) *Ethnoperspectives in bilingual education research: Theory in bilingual education* (pp. 76–97). Ypsilanti, MI: Department of Foreign Languages and Bilingual Studies. Eastern Michigan University.

Pennycook, A. (2003). Global Englishes, rip slyme, and performativity. *Journal of Socio-linguistics* 7(4), 513–33.

Reyes, M. (2001), Unleashing possibilities. Biliteracy in the primary grades. In M. Reyes & J.J. Halcón (Eds.) *The best for our children: Critical perspectives on literacy for Latino students* (pp. 245–248). New York: Teachers College Press.

Romaine, S. (1994). *Language in society : An introduction to sociolinguistics.* Oxford: Oxford University Press.

—— (1995). *Bilingualism* (2nd ed.) Oxford: Basil Blackwell.

Schecter, S.R. & Bayley, R. (2002). *Language as cultural practice: Mexicanos en el Norte.* Mahwah, NJ: Erlbaum.

Schieffelin, B.B. & Ochs, E. (1989). Language socialization. *Annual Review of Anthropology* 15: 163–191.

Skutnabb-Kangas, T. (1981) *Bilingualism or not: The education of minorities.* Clevedon, UK: Multilingual Matters.

Stavans, I. (2004). *Spanglish: The making of a new American language.* New York: Rayo.

Street, B.V. (1985). *Literacy in theory and practice.* Cambridge: Cambridge University Press.

—— (1996). Academic literacies. In D. Baker, J. Clay, & C. Fox (Eds.), *Alternative ways of knowing: Literacies, numeracies, sciences* (pp. 101–134). London: Falmer Press.

—— (Ed.). (2005). *Literacies across educational contexts: Mediating, learning and teaching.* Philadelphia: Caslon Press.

Swain, M. (2006). Languaging, agency and collaboration in advanced second language learning. In H. Byrnes (Ed.), *Advanced language learning: The contributions of Halliday and Vygotsky* (pp. 95–108). London: Continuum.

Tharp, R.G., Estrada, P., Dalton, S.S, & Yamauchi, L.A. (2000) *Teaching transformed: Achieving excellence, fairness, inclusion and harmony.* Boulder, CO: Westview Press.

Van der Walt, C. (2006). University students' attitudes towards and experiences of bilingual classrooms. *Current Issues in Language Planning* 7(2,3): 359–376.

—— (2007). Bilingual assessment strategies in higher education. Unpublished manuscript.

Vygotsky, L.S. (1978). *Mind and society.* Cambridge, MA: Harvard University Press.

Wright, S. (2004). *Language policy and language planning. From nationalism to globalisa-tion.* New York: Palgrave.

Yngve, V. (1996). *From grammar to science: New foundations for general linguistics.* Amsterdam: John Benjamins.

Zamel, V. & Spack, R. (Eds.) (1998). *Negotiating academic literacies: Teaching and learning across languages and cultures.* Mahwah, NJ: Lawrence Erlbaum.

Zehler, A., Fleischman, H., Hopstock, P., Stephenson, T., Pendizick, M., & Sapru, S. (2003). *Descriptive study of services to LEP students and LEP students with disabilities.* Volume 1. Research Report. Washington, DC: NCELA.

Zentella, A.C. (1997). *Growing up bilingual: Puerto Rican children in New York.* Malden, MA: Blackwell.

10 Language, Literacy, and Pedagogy of Caribbean Creole English Speakers

Shondel Nero

Introduction

The most certain outcome of continued immigration into the United States in the twenty-first century is the fact that ethnolinguistic diversity will become the norm. By every metric, according to recent census data (www.census.gov), the U.S. will continue to be the principal receiving country of linguistically diverse immigrants, especially from the Caribbean and Latin America. As a consequence, U.S. public schools will be charged with the task of educating school-age immigrant children from this region whose language and literacy needs will challenge traditional paradigms, research, and practice with respect to the nexus of language, literacy, and culture. Although a significant body of work has examined the educational needs, issues, and academic performance of Spanish-speaking children from the Caribbean and Latin America in U.S. schools (Farr, 2005; García & Menken, 2006; Torres-Guzmán et al., 2002; Valdés, 2001, among numerous others), research on the language, literacy, and culture of children from the English-speaking (Anglophone) Caribbean[1] in North American schools has been far less widespread or more regionally focused (Clachar, 2004a, 2004b; Coelho, 1991; Nero, 2001, 2006; Pratt-Johnson, 2006; Winer, 2006). The research on the latter reflects the settlement patterns of Anglophone Caribbean immigrants, who are disproportionately located on the east coast of the U.S., specifically New York City (home to the largest Anglophone Caribbean population outside of the Caribbean), New Jersey, Maryland, Washington, DC, Atlanta, and Miami. However, as immigration from the Anglophone Caribbean continues to increase exponentially, and shows no signs of abating, it will become necessary for educators to deepen understanding of the language and literacy issues of this population, as teachers grow more likely to encounter Anglophone Caribbean children in their classrooms in other parts of the U.S. and Canada. This chapter attempts to add to that understanding by exploring the language of the majority of recent immigrants from the English-speaking Caribbean, hereafter called Caribbean Creole English (CCE);[2] the extent to which their language practices impact their literacy development in school; and the degree to which teacher training and professional development in sociolinguistics as well as the history, structure, and use of CCE might influence pedagogical approaches in order to enhance the literacy development of CCE speakers.

Background

New York City (NYC) is home to approximately one million Anglophone Caribbean immigrants, who comprise some 20 percent of the city's foreign-born population. Immigration from the Anglophone Caribbean to the U.S., especially to NYC, dates back to the early twentieth century, but the last thirty years have witnessed the arrival of an unprecedented number of Anglophone Caribbean immigrants to the city, unmatched in any of the previous waves of immigration (Foner, 2001). Of the top five countries that are sources of immigration to NYC, Jamaica and Guyana rank third and fourth respectively. Many of these recent immigrants are CCE-speaking school-age children, who attend the city's public schools. The language, literacy, and culture of CCE speakers in NYC public schools, then, can serve as an illustrative case in terms of how educators might constructively address the educational needs of this population elsewhere in the U.S.

One characteristic of a large percentage of recently arrived CCE-speaking children—that is, those who came in the last ten years as compared to earlier arrivals—is that they are reading and writing significantly below grade level and are having difficulty meeting the writing demands of New York State's English Language Arts (ELA) curriculum.[3] From the perspective of many teachers, the spoken and written language of CCE speakers seem at variance with standardized academic language. However, because CCE speakers are categorized as native speakers of English, they are not eligible for English as a Second Language (ESL) services. Many teachers are therefore unsure how to respond to the language and literacy needs of students who are classified as native speakers of English but whose spoken and written language appear non-native or unfamiliar. Furthermore, with the exception of ESL and bilingual teachers, most pre- and in-service general education K–12 teachers are not sufficiently trained in language diversity to the degree necessary to effectively address the language and literacy needs of linguistically diverse children, particularly the unique needs of those who speak non-American varieties of English.

CCE speakers are such a unique group. Their language use outside of school and their educational experiences in the Caribbean are largely unfamiliar to American teachers. Many teachers hold what Winer (2006) calls a "sun and fun" view of the Caribbean, mostly based on tourist experiences there, and, at best, know that in the English-speaking Caribbean, some form of English is spoken with what they perceive as a lilting accent. American teachers' encounters with CCE speakers in the classroom, then, might be their first experience of having to teach students classified as native speakers of English, but who speak other than an American variety of English. Specifically, Caribbean speech ranges bidirectionally along a continuum that includes Creole (patois), Creole English, and standardized Caribbean English (all of which is called English), depending on the speaker's socioeconomic class, education level, rural/urban provenance, topic, context, desire for solidarity, and so forth (Nero, 2001; Rickford, 1987; Roberts, 1988). Generally speaking, Creole-dominant speech is associated with lower socioeconomic class, less formal education, and rural residence; conversely, English-dominant speech is linked to higher socioeconomic class, more formal education and urban residence. In terms of syntax, pronunciation, lexicon, and discourse norms, the CCE speaker's language spans a wider range, and appears at greater remove from standardized American English than speakers of most American varieties of English, including African American Vernacular English (AAVE). As I have argued elsewhere (Nero, 2001; 2006), teachers' encounters with CCE speakers, especially those whose speech is Creole dominant, call into question the notion of the native speaker, what counts as English, and the extent to which, as Roberts (1988) notes, two varieties may be sufficiently different and still be considered as part of the same language.

CCE speakers, not unlike other children, come to school with deeply embedded language and literacy practices that may or may not align with many school-based literacy practices depending on a host of factors, including many of those noted above that account for language variation. For CCE-speaking students who are reading and writing below grade level, this chapter examines the specific gaps that exist between their literacies and the expectations of the ELA curriculum, and what pedagogical approaches might be appropriate with this population.

The specific group of CCE speakers discussed here are at the middle and high school level, which means adolescents. This age group is targeted for four reasons: (1) adolescents already have their first language speech habits, including accent, ingrained; thus, recent arrivals from the Caribbean who are adolescents are likely to exhibit more CCE features in their speech; (2) adolescents are also heavily influenced by peer pressure, which can impact their language use. I hypothesize that Anglophone Caribbean immigrant youth's language will be somewhat influenced by their interaction with American peers such as those who speak AAVE and other varieties; (3) recently arrived adolescent immigrants have already experienced, and have been impacted by, schooling and literacy practices in their home countries, which can influence their literacy practices in U.S. schools; (4) adolescents are expected to read and write in the content areas, including literature, social studies, math, and science, which puts a greater demand on the students and their teachers to develop their literacy skills.

A Pilot Project: CCE-Speaking Students in Middle and High Schools in New York City

In an attempt to begin to address the language and literacy needs of CCE-speaking adolescents, I designed a pilot project involving two public schools in NYC with large Caribbean populations. The project had two objectives:

1. To analyze the language use and literacy practices of CCE speakers in middle and high schools.
2. To raise teacher awareness of the unique linguistic practices and needs of CCE speakers through ongoing professional development and training in sociolinguistics with a view to improving student literacy development.

Given that the project combined both exploration of student language and literacy practices as well as teacher training, it is important to foreground the theoretical re/conceptions around language and literacy practices as well as language attitudes that informed the project before examining the data. Many of the challenges faced by the teachers of CCE-speaking students in the project call up deeper attitudes and beliefs about language vs. dialect, standard language ideology, language use in school, and definitions of, and expectations regarding school-based literacy practices. These are taken up in the following section.

Reconceptualizing Languages and Dialects

CCE is but one variety of English, which, as a modern language, has been unparalleled in the speed and scope of its simultaneous spread and change over the last fifty years. Changes in the structure and uses of English, not to mention the diversity of its users around the world, force us to reject a static view of English and of languages in general. McArthur (1998) uses the phrase *the English languages* to illustrate the pluralistic and dynamic nature of modern English, and in so doing creates a space to debunk some of the myths about language that have impacted, and in many ways constrained, educational practice. The first myth is that language structures are fixed and don't change. The second is that there is only one standard variety, and that it is inherently superior. Lippi-Green (1997) has written eloquently of the dangers of what she calls "standard language ideology," which is most strongly enforced in schools. The ideology not only suggests that only one standardized variety exists, but it privileges it in almost all school-based activities, especially writing tasks, and perpetuates a culture whereby speakers of nonstandard language varieties such as CCE bear (or are made to feel that they bear) the sole responsibility of making linguistic adjustments, lest they jeopardize their academic success. CCE speakers, in fact, have varying degrees of receptive and productive knowledge of standardized forms of Caribbean English, which is merely different and part of the family of the English languages, but Lippi-Green notes that through the lens of standard language ideology, *different* is often framed as *deficient*, and for that reason she is right to suggest that this ideology must ultimately be rejected.

CCE speakers' language is particularly apt to be framed as deficient or deformed versions of English because of the interaction of Creole and standardized English along the continuum. This perception is reinforced in North American classrooms where CCE speakers call *all* of their language use English, regardless of how creolized it might be, while teachers may be judging their language against a standardized American variety of English, and finding it wanting. Over the years, linguists and educators (Adger, Wolfram, & Christian, 2007; Delpit, 1998; Devonish & Carpenter, 2007; Labov, 1981; Rickford, 1999; Smitherman, 2000) have worked to dispel dialect myths and simultaneously suggest ways to validate dialect use in schools, but such work has repeatedly been challenged by a larger culture, and an educational culture in particular, that sees dialect use or validation in school as problematic.

Dialect or vernacular use in schools is controversial because, as already noted, schools have historically been the custodians of standard language and standard language ideology. Siegel (2006) notes some of the typical arguments against use of the vernacular in school: (1) it is seen as interfering with the acquisition of the standard; (2) its use might undermine the integrity of the standard; (3) its use by students marks them as lesser (linguistically, educationally, and socioeconomically); (4) there is a fear that dialect use might further ghettoize historically marginalized groups (p. 46). These were the identical arguments used in the 1996 Ebonics controversy, and the same arguments against bilingual education. But Siegel's work makes a persuasive case against these arguments, buttressed by the research of other scholars (Craig, 2006; Simpkins & Simpkins, 1977; Wheeler & Swords, 2006), showing instead that validation of the home language in school facilitates literacy development.

Rethinking the Language User

A more pluralistic stance on languages and dialects, as suggested in the previous section, inevitably leads to a rethinking of the language user. Speakers of non-American varieties of English such as CCE expose the wide range of use and users of English, and in so doing have challenged the traditional construct of the native speaker. In fact, a significant body of work has already challenged the narrowly defined, Chomskyan view of the native speaker (Brutt-Griffler & Samimy, 2001; Cook, 1999; B. Kachru, 1986; Paikeday, 1985; Pennycook, 1994, and others), so that will not be discussed here. Leung, Harris, and Rampton's (1997) work in England showed that the complex linguistic identities and language practices of their British-born students of various language minority backgrounds defy what they call the "idealised native speaker" that schools tend to imagine. Reinforcing this view, Cook (1999) suggests that educational practice can no longer start from the presumption of the monolingual/monodialectal language user. The ethno-linguistic diversity resulting from immigration and demographic shifts guarantees that many language users will enter classrooms today at least bidialectal or bilingual. Furthermore, many immigrants today are transnationals by virtue of the ease with which they are now able to travel back and forth between the U.S. and their home countries (see Farr's chapter in this volume). Modern technology also facilitates international communication in a more efficient way. This transnational lifestyle reinforces the home language, but also takes U.S. varieties of English to their home countries as well. Transnationalism is particularly visible among Caribbean immigrants, given the proximity of the Caribbean to the U.S. In addition, adolescent immigrants in particular pick up the language of their peers, who may include European American, African American, Hispanic American, and/or Asian American teenagers. As a consequence, the linguistic repertoire of a Caribbean adolescent immigrant might include CCE, AAVE, and other varieties of English, all used in different domains for different purposes. In accepting this reality, Cook (1999) suggests that educational practice should begin not from a native/non-native dichotomy but rather from the presumption of a multi-competent language user. I would argue that many language users today facilitate their multi-competence by transcending borders literally, figuratively, culturally, linguistically, and digitally. Literacy practitioners would do well, then, to harness this multi-competence in creative and productive ways in the classroom.

Literacies in the Twenty-First-Century Classroom and Beyond

The historical debate over the two dominant models of literacy—autonomous vs. ideological—should have been resolved by now. Adherents to the autonomous model believe that literacy is a neutral set of skills, mostly acquired in school. Street (1995), Gee (1990), Kress (1997) and others counter the autonomous model by proposing the ideological view, which sees literacy as a social practice situated in culturally embedded contexts influenced by the confluence of race, class, gender, and power structures. The emergence of newer forms of literacies in the twenty-first century—digital, multimodal, semiotic—has further complicated literacy debates, and by extension how to facilitate the literacy development of adolescents who come to school with a multidialectal repertoire and who regularly engage in newer forms of literacies within and beyond the classroom. In fact, there appears to be an ongoing tension between curricular goals that appear to engage literacies in the broadest sense and assessment practices that are narrowly defined. The New York State ELA curriculum is a case in point. It spells out four broad learning standards as follows:

1. Students will read, write, listen, and speak for information and understanding.
2. Students will read, write, listen, and speak for literary response and expression.
3. Students will read, write, listen, and speak for critical analysis, and evaluation.
4. Students will read, write, listen, and speak for social interaction.[4]

Each standard is accompanied by a set of "literacy competencies" and "grade-specific performance indicators" that demonstrate evidence of having met the standard. The performance indicators appear to be wide in range. For example, a performance indicator for grade 7, standard 3 reads: "Evaluate the validity and accuracy of information, ideas, themes, opinions, and experiences in text to identify cultural and ethnic values and their impact on content." Another indicator for grade 11, standard 2 reads: "compare a film, video, or stage version of a literary work with the written version." Yet, in practice, academic achievement continues to be measured narrowly on competence in the essayist genre, and on standardized tests such as the New York State Regents Exam or the eighth grade ELA test, which privilege only standardized American English, and rarely take into account newer forms of literacies practiced by students, or some of the very competencies listed in the curriculum. To be fair to teachers, they feel a professional obligation to ensure that their students pass state-mandated tests, as this is the principal measure of their students' academic success; thus, teachers must essentially teach to the test. Consequently, there are ongoing tensions between curriculum, instructional, and assessment practices of what O'Brien & Bauer (2005) call the Institution of Old Learning (IOL) and new literacy practices of today's youth. In fact, newer forms of literacies are often positioned in opposition, or even as a threat, to traditional print literacy (readings of books and documents). This, I would argue, is a false dichotomy, as all literacy practices draw on key learning strategies and critical thinking skills, regardless of how those practices are enacted. CCE speakers present a special case because they bring literacy practices from their home countries, communities, and interactions with other immigrant youth, expressed through a multidialectal repertoire. It is this unique set of circumstances that spurred the pilot project.

The guiding questions of this project are as follows:

1. What are the typical patterns of language use as well as literacy practices of CCE speakers in NYC middle and high schools?
2. What are the current beliefs and state of knowledge of teachers of CCE speakers about their students' culture, language, and literacy practices?
3. To what extent does raising language diversity awareness through teacher training in sociolinguistics and professional development impact the academic performance of CCE speakers in middle/high school English language arts classes?

Setting and Participants

School A

This is a combined middle/high school, located in a very Caribbean neighborhood in the borough of Brooklyn. It was chosen as one of the project sites because many of its students are reading and writing below grade level, as evidenced by their standardized test scores and the recent School Report Card issued by the New York State Department of Education.[5] Most students at this school are eligible for free lunch. It was founded five years ago, as one of several specialized middle and high schools in NYC. Specialized schools are named for a theme such as "Diplomacy" or "Leadership," on which the school's mission, vision, and teaching practices are premised. On any given day, School A is teeming with the energy of talkative and energetic adolescents shuttling between classes, "trash talking" with each other in the hallways. Sometimes the students are physically indistinguishable from their mostly young and enthusiastic teachers, including the principal, who work hard to fit in with their adolescent population while challenging them to do their best academically. This school includes grades 6 to 12, and has a population of approximately 550 students, 85 percent of whom are of English-speaking Caribbean background of African descent. The racial/ethnic identification is an important point, as it contrasts with Indo-Caribbean students whose ancestors came from India, and whose language practices show different lexical items, cultural references, and cadences from Afro-Caribbean students. A large number of the CCE-speaking students at School A are recent immigrants to NYC, while others migrated to the city at an earlier age.

At this school, there were four participating ELA teachers in the pilot project, all of whom are female. Three are white: Ann (8th grade), Beth (11th grade), and Eva (12th grade); and one is a nonwhite Hispanic: Paula (7th grade).[6] Each of the four teachers was asked to identify two Caribbean students from their respective classes who were particularly challenged by school-based language and literacy practices or who had a keen sense of his/her varied language use. The eight students that were subsequently identified were: two Jamaicans (Theresa and Len), two Trinidadians (Jim and Kevin), one Guyanese (Tina), one Grenadian (Ted), one St. Lucian (Tom), and one Vincentian (Janet). See profiles of all participants in Appendix B.

School B

This is a traditional middle school located in Queens, the most linguistically and culturally diverse borough in NYC. At this school, about one third of the population is reading below grade level, and students are also eligible for free lunch. The neighborhood in which the school is located is largely made up of immigrants from South Asia, the Middle East, and the Caribbean. This is a large school, occupying an entire block in the neighborhood. In contrast to School A, the school is extremely quiet on a typical day, students move from class to class in an orderly fashion, teachers are older and more experienced, and the African American principal runs a tight ship of discipline and tough love. The school includes grades 6 to 8 and has a population of approximately 1,300 students, about 70 percent of whom are immigrants and about half of them of Caribbean background. These are mainly Indo-Caribbean students from Guyana and Trinidad.

The participating teachers at this school are one African American female teacher, Dina (7th grade), and two literacy teachers—one white female (Susan) and one white male (Steve)—who co-teach what is called a "Newcomer Class," made up of very recently arrived immigrants who are low-literacy-level non-native speakers of English as well as CCE speakers. The Newcomer Class includes students from grades 6 to 8. At this school, there were four participating students, two Jamaicans from Dina's class (Derek and Coleen), and two Indo-Guyanese from the Newcomer Class (Devi and Dookie).

Data Sources

- Weekly classroom observations from September 2008 to May 2009
- Questionnaires completed by participating teachers and students
- Recorded interviews with teachers and students
- Samples of reading/writing assignments
- Samples of students' written work and tests
- Teachers' reflective journals
- Professional development workshops for participating teachers
- New York State ELA curriculum grades 6–12.

Data Analysis

The first guiding question was intended to gather information about the actual language and literacy practices of CCE-speakers. To address this question, questionnaires were completed by the students and recorded interviews were conducted with them and analyzed to gauge their self-perception of their language, literacy practices, and educational experiences in both the Caribbean and New York. Samples of their reading and writing assignments and tests were also collected, coded, and analyzed for emerging themes (Miles & Huberman, 1994). Evidence of CCE features in students' written language was particularly noted.

The second question was addressed by having the teachers complete questionnaires, which provided biographical as well as other information on whether or not they had received formal training in sociolinguistics. Tape-recorded interviews were also conducted with teachers to gauge their prior knowledge of Caribbean history, culture and language; their perceptions of their CCE-speaking students' language and literacy practices; and their students' strengths and weaknesses with respect to school-based literacies.

The third question was addressed by having teachers participate in professional development training workshops conducted by this author, where they engaged in readings and discussion on sociolinguistics, language and dialect variation, language attitudes, the history, structures, and uses of CCE, as well as broader readings on the sociocultural contexts of literacy, and culturally responsive pedagogy. Additionally, teachers read articles on the dynamics of Caribbean migration and its impact on the academic performance of Caribbean adolescents. Teachers were provided with models of alternative literacy activities that might be used with students within the parameters of the ELA curriculum. They were asked to reflect on and assess their training and ongoing pedagogical practice in journals. Teacher training has been a recursive process of reading, reflection, and revised practice based on my ongoing classroom observations of the teachers and CCE-speaking students as well as analysis of the language demands of the New York State ELA curriculum for middle and high schools.

Findings and Discussion

Student Voices: Oral Language

Most of the students in both schools defined their native language as English, except Len and Tom, who said "patois," Ted, who said he spoke "patois and English," and Theresa, who characterized her speech as "a mix of patois/broken English." All of the students had a clear sense that they spoke differently at home than in school, especially given that they lived in homes surrounded by CCE speakers. Even in school, there was a marked difference between their speech with peers and their speech with teachers. As Kevin pointed out, "Yeah, I make switches all the time." Devi said she tries to "talk good" with her teachers but with her aunt at home she goes into "Guyana talk." Theresa gave a specific example of the way she switches into Jamaican Patois when she gets emotional or angry, which would be different from someone showing anger in Standard English: "You know when you say to someone, 'Leave me alone.' Instead, I say 'Lef me alone' or 'Come outta mih face!' " (3/12/09)[7]

It was interesting to note on the recorded interviews how the students' speech gradually became more accented in the Creole direction as each interview progressed. My sense is that as they became more comfortable with me, knowing that I am Guyanese, their speech (and to a certain degree mine as well) converged into the vernacular. At these points, I noted more distinct features of Creole syntax and pronunciation, for example:

Plurality: "I would just ask my sisters *and dem.*" (Kevin)
"But the teachers, Ms. P *and dem*, they could understand me." (Ted)

Object in subject position; also progressive verb form without the verb "to be:" "The *book taking* a long time to finish." (Ted)

Deletion of word initial "h:" "Back home I neva '*ave* to take test all the time." (Derek)

Students' interviews revealed distinct differences in the degree of Creole or English features in their spoken language, which, as noted in the literature (Nero, 2001; Rickford, 1987; Roberts, 1988), is related to race/ethnicity, socioeconomic class, years and quality of education, and rural/urban provenance. As mentioned above, the students at School A are all Afro-Caribbean and live in a community of mostly Afro-Caribbean residents in Brooklyn while the two Guyanese students at School B are of Indian descent and live in a community of mostly Indo-Guyanese in Queens. This ethnic separation of settlement patterns in NYC between Afro- and Indo-Caribbean immigrants reflects a similar separation in the Caribbean, especially in Guyana and Trinidad, the two countries with the largest Indian-descent populations. Settlement patterns have linguistic consequences, as Afro-Caribbean adolescents live close to, and interact more socially with, their African American peers, and in so doing pick up AAVE features as well as other elements of urban vernacular in their speech. Theresa and Coleen, who migrated to the U.S. at ages 3 and 5 respectively, showed the strongest evidence of AAVE influence in their speech, given that they have had the longest residence in the U.S. and thus more exposure to AAVE. Some examples are:

Habitual *be*: "Like when I *be* in school and I be like 'Give me the book!' and they *be* like 'What you just say to me?' and I *be* like 'Forget it.' " (Theresa 3/12/09)

Multiple negation: "Cause ain' nobody don' tell me nothin' when I come up in here, you know what I'm sayin?" (Coleen 3/23/09)

By contrast, Indo-Caribbean immigrants in NYC, many of whom hail from rural communities in Guyana and Trinidad, live in neighborhoods among themselves, and thus maintain more Creole features in their speech. Not surprisingly, the two Indo-Guyanese students at School B, Devi and Dookie, who had both migrated within the last two years, showed strong evidence of rural, Creole features in their speech, especially deletion of word initial "h," e.g., "I does do mih 'omework in dih aftanoon" (Dookie 4/6/09).

Consistent with the literature, the students all expressed ambivalent feelings about their vernacular, at once celebrating it as a way of asserting their Anglophone Caribbean identity, and denigrating it in the classroom setting as "not proper" English, a phenomenon characterized by Kachru and Nelson (2001) as "attitudinal schizophrenia" (p. 14). Many students noted that they did not like reading aloud in class because their accent was sometimes difficult to understand. Len laments, "When I have to read to myself, it's okay, but when I have to read to others, they can't understand me. It's kind of challenging. I don't like that" (3/26/09). Another negative view of reading was echoed by Devi: "I'm not really good at reading. In Guyana, I wasn't so good at reading because . . . uhm . . . like it's too hard for me to pronounce dih word dem and know what's in dih book to read" (3/23/09).

As Delpit (1998) notes, however, reading aloud is not a fair assessment of reading comprehension. It is rather an oral performance, and dialect speakers are often negatively evaluated in read aloud situations because their accent is judged against a standardized pronunciation. It is important, therefore, to look at students' interaction with text to get a better gauge of their reading ability. The next section takes up the CCE students' reading and writing practices.

Student Voices: Reading and Writing

In my observation of, and interviews with, the students, it was clear that their reaction to reading depended on whether the book was chosen by them or assigned by the teacher, and if assigned, what they were asked to do in response to the reading. Many students said they liked reading stories that involve high drama (Janet and Theresa), or crime and detective stories (Kevin), or fiction and biographies (Len), or horror stories (Tom), giving personal responses to the texts in terms of relating to specific characters, or making connections to their lives. Some teachers asked students to write post-it notes in response to texts, or compare and contrast books they are currently reading with books they previously read. Students viewed these types of reader response tasks favorably and they generally spurred lively class discussion.

On the other hand, several students expressed an instinctive resistance to reading and responding to traditional texts like Shakespeare, which are often required in the ELA curriculum and on standardized tests. Theresa states candidly:

> I'm just saying that certain books that the teacher give you, like not every student want to read it. Like right now we're reading *Othello*, my mind want to drift away from it but you can't, cause every day you have to do something with this book so it's like I have to sit down there and try to focus on it. (3/12/09)

The students also expressed displeasure at having to do typical academic language functions like summarizing, making inferences, or writing a critical response to a text, functions that their teachers insisted were important for them to know, these are central tenets of the middle and high school ELA learning standards alluded to earlier.

In regard to writing, students were asked to share what they saw as their strengths and weakness in writing. Consistently, a number of them saw their creative ability in writing, including coming up with good ideas, creating a good story, or writing a poem as their strengths. In creative writing, students could effectively draw on their multidialectal repertoire. Janet proudly stated that she likes to make up stories using "big words," but Theresa captured it best:

> I'm good with coming up with ideas for writing. Like if I could put my mind to it, I could write anything. I could write about it. It could be the stupidest thing in the world, I could write about paper, gum, something . . . (3/12/09)

Theresa and Len, who are both in Beth's 11th grade class, also noted that they liked two types of writing that Beth taught. These were the *controlling idea* essay and the *critical lens* essay, both of which are tested on the Regents Exam. The first involves reading two passages, finding a controlling idea that is shared by the passages, then using evidence from both passages to develop the idea into a unified essay. The critical lens essay usually begins with a famous quote given to the student by the teacher. The student must first critically analyze the quote then relate it to a text they are reading and/or something in their lives, and develop an essay from it. Theresa and Len particularly liked the critical lens essay because they interpreted it as a free-writing activity, even though Beth saw it as practice for the essayist writing demanded in the Regents Exam. The quotes below shed light on their understanding of the critical lens essay:

> Theresa: "With the critical lens, you have a quote and you can do whatever you like—it's a freewrite." (3/12/09)

> Len: "And critical lens idea, they give you a quote and you gotta put it in your own words and write an essay about it." (3/26/09)

Yet, when it came to identifying their weaknesses, several students did not characterize writing in this holistic way. Instead, they mostly focused on mechanics and grammar. Jim, Tom, Kevin, Devi, Dookie, Derek, and Len specifically identified spelling as their main weakness. Others lamented their poor grammar. Theresa only briefly mentioned her difficulty writing conclusions. In fact, with the exception of creative writing, the students viewed classroom-based writing as largely a mechanical exercise focused on correctness and test preparation, instead of a meaning-making process. Moreover, an examination of selected students' writing samples reflected starkly different qualities of writing, depending on whether they were doing creative pieces or more traditional classroom assignments. The following examples are from Theresa, Len, and Dookie respectively:

Assignment in Beth's 11th grade class: Rewrite Iago's soliloquy [from Shakespeare's *Othello*] in modern English. Do not do a direct translation. Make the soliloquy sound real.

Theresa's response begins as follows:

1   Yo this nigga is so dum yo. I betta watch how I hang out with him before I
2   be dum. Roderigo dum son, but hey it's kind of fun son; dhis nigga does
3   put a lot of cake in my pocket. And Othello think he some god around
4   here. I hate dhis nigga, he get me so tight. I swear he sleeping with my
5   wifey, but I don't know yo shit really got me bussin my head, but dhis
6   what I think so dhat's what I'm going by. (3/12/09)

The most striking characteristic of this excerpt is the fact that it is written entirely in AAVE. There are AAVE lexical items such as "nigga" (lines 1 & 2); "tight" and "wifey" (lines 4 & 5); and phrases such as "put a lot of cake in my pocket" (line 3); "bussin my head" (line 5). Theresa also shows a good ear for dialect pronunciation by writing "betta" (line 1) or "dhis" (line 2).

It should be noted that Theresa chose to interpret the term "modern English" in the assignment in the broadest sense of the word. By drawing on her own multidialectal repertoire of Englishes, which includes AAVE, she has defied the classroom expectation that modern English might only mean standardized modern English. I observed the class in which Theresa made a persuasive case for her dialect choice in this assignment, telling the teacher that her rendering is, in fact, her idea of modern English. She also did an excellent oral reading of this piece. Instead of the class discussion focusing on Theresa's rich, creative rewriting of the soliloquy, which showed she understood the text, the discussion veered into a heated debate about whether the use of the word "nigga" should be permitted in class. The discussion reflected deeply held language attitudes on both the teacher's and students' part. The teacher allowed a fair hearing of all views, then skillfully directed the discussion back to the assignment and to the question of language variation and modern English(es).

Another assignment by Beth produced a very different kind of writing from Theresa:

Assignment: In response to Tennessee Williams, *A Streetcar Named Desire*, answer one of the following questions with specific evidence from the text:

1.   What is Tennessee Williams' message about the world?
2.   Is Blanche a victim or a villain?
3.   Do you agree or disagree with Stella's decision at the end of the play?
4.   Is Stanley a hero or a villain?
5.   Does Blanche's character change over the course of the play?

Theresa's response:

1   "Blanche's character change over the period of time that she has been at
2   her sister's house. She comes to her sister's house looking disgust with the
3   house and why does she live in a place like this. Then acting so high class
4   with fanasy clothing and despecting Stella's home and Stella's husband
5   calling him a polack.
6   Blanche's gives these false stories that she taking a vacation knowing that

7   she running from her life. Blanche character changes as she drinks liquior
8   and lies more than ever. (3/19/09)

Theresa's writing is more formal in the piece above, as required by the assignment. The writing, however, lacks the liveliness of the first example. There is
evidence of her oral language influence in the syntax such as zero -*ed* inflection
on "disgust" (line 2); the embedded direct speech question "why does she live in a
place like this" (line 3); and the zero verb *to be* in progressive phrases "she taking"
and "she running" (lines 6 & 7). Elsewhere (Nero, 2001), I have characterized this
type of writing as *academic interlanguage*—a student's attempt at standardized
writing, influenced by vernacular forms. It appears that such writing is more apt
to appear in formal assignments. An excerpt from Len's critical lens essay below
shows a similar phenomenon:

1   Fredrick Douglas once said, without struggle there is no progress. This
2   means that in order to become successful in life you must overcome
3   struggle and obstacle. "Sonny's Blue" and "Dead Man" prove that you
4   must overcome an obstacle or struggle to become successful in life.
5   Sonny's blue proves that you must overcome an obstacle or struggle to
6   become successful in life. In the story sonny the character was hooked on
7   drugs. "He was trapped in a darkness which roared outside; he was even
8   pick up and evening in a raid at an apartment down-town for peddling and
9   using heroin." Sonny wanted to stop but he is addicted and that make him
10 feel very bad about himself. (10/10/2008)

Len is attempting here to analyze Douglas's quote as required by the assignment.
We see his marked repetition of the phrase "overcome an obstacle and struggle"
in lines 2–5, as he struggles to express his ideas in essayist form. He is obviously
following the teacher's instruction to provide evidence from the text to support
his point; hence, the incorporation of the quote in lines 7–9. There is also some
morphosyntactic oral language influence in the zero inflections on the verbs
"pick up" (line 8) and "that make him" (line 9).
    By contrast, when Len is creative, he writes a heartwarming poem about his
native Jamaica entitled "My Jamaican Poem," in which the rhyme and writing
flow easily. The following is an excerpt:

1   You're the ackee in my saltfish
2   Condensed milk in my tea
3   The patty in my cocobread
4   Without you there is no me

5   Just like coconut water
6   You're good for my heart
7   And Mr. Wray without his nephew
8   Is like when we are apart (2/5/09)

All of Len's references in the first stanza refer to Jamaican food items. In line 1, "ackee and saltfish" is a classic reference, as it is considered the national dish of Jamaica. In the second stanza, he refers to "Mr. Wray without his nephew" ("Wray and Nephew" is the name of the major Jamaican rum). It is interesting that Len offers no footnote or explanation for his references. Yet, in a sense none is needed. The title of the poem and the pairing of food items as a metaphor for love speak for themselves.

Finally, a writing excerpt from Dookie at School B shows his attempt at academic writing by summarizing a fable as part of a unit on fables in his Newcomer Class:

> The frog and the chipmunk
> 1   There once was a chipmunk and it living a tree and lean across the river
> 2   and chipmunk are looking for nut for winter and chipmunk have found
>   lots
> 3   of nut and the chipmunk have put all the nut in the tree he have found and
> 4   the chipmunk was in the tree and a hard breeze blow and the leam brake
> 5   and all the nut the chipmunk have put in the tree fell in to trench and the
> 6   chipmunk fell off the tree and hit himself heard. (2/9/09)

In this piece, Dookie attempts school-based writing by beginning with a conventional, formulaic fable opener, "There once was a . . ." It is clear that he understands the gist of the story. His episodic narrative style linked by multiple uses of the paratactic combining word "and" shows strong oral language influence. His writing also shows Creole influence such as "a hard breeze blow" (line 4), meaning a strong breeze blew; and "fell in to trench" (line 5), which is a word more likely to used by rural Guyanese folk for a small, stagnated river. There were also phonetic spellings such as "leam brake" (limb break) in line 4.

For Dookie's teachers, however, their first comment on this piece was the fact that there was no punctuation in the story, his subject/verb concord was consistently incorrect (e.g., "he *have* found" in line 3), and there was an absence of proper formatting, including paragraph indentation. Because Dookie is in the 8th grade and must take the 8th grade ELA test this year, this is a legitimate concern, because his teachers know that his writing as it stands will likely fail the test. The curriculum still demands standardized presentation of ideas in very specific formats.

Classroom Experiences

Reflecting on their classroom experiences, most of the students stated that by comparison to their schooling experience in the Caribbean, they felt that they received more personalized attention from their teachers in the U.S., which they saw as generally positive. The question of teacher attention, however, merits further discussion. On the one hand, the students felt that in the Caribbean, teachers left it up to students to motivate themselves to do their schoolwork:

"The teachers don' care if you don' come to school." (Dookie—4/6/09)

"Like if you don't care, the teachers don't care. If you don't do the work, they don't push you to do it. And you can't make up anything that you miss. It's already passed." (Len—3/26/09)

"They paid attention but they didn't usually come and talk to you and sit down and tell you what you need. They didn't pay attention to you in that way. They talk to you in class and that's it. After that, the day's over." (Kevin—3/12/09)

On the other hand, the students felt that Caribbean teachers' leaving students to figure things out on their own was part of a general "tough love and strict discipline" approach to education in the Caribbean, which includes the use of corporal punishment. The students contend that this approach made for a more orderly classroom environment in the Caribbean based on fear of the teacher, as compared to what they considered the "too easy" approach of their American teachers, which led to lack of discipline in the classroom. Perceptions of Caribbean approaches to education are discussed among other views expressed by teachers of CCE-speaking students in the following section.

Teachers' Perspectives

In attempting to understand the teachers' state of knowledge and beliefs about their CCE-speaking students' culture, language, and literacy, recorded interviews first sought information on the teachers' knowledge about the Caribbean itself, either through visiting the region or through interaction with the students. Four of the teachers, two from School A and two from School B, had visited the Caribbean as tourists, but noted correctly that their tourist experience did not give them a realistic gauge of life in the Caribbean. They all felt that they learned more about the Anglophone Caribbean culture from interacting with their students. As Paula notes in reflecting on her visit to Jamaica:

"I was doing more tourist things, and I feel like the relationship between tourists and like natives of a country is so interesting, often really uncomfortable. I feel like I'm a lot more able to understand my students and understand the culture from being here than being on the beach in Montego Bay." (12/4/08)

The teachers' interactions with, and observations of, the Caribbean students significantly influenced their views of the students' language. All of the teachers with the exception of Susan at School B felt that the students were native speakers of English, albeit a nonstandard variety or dialect thereof. Some of their answers to the question of defining their students' spoken language are as follows:

"I definitely would say they're native English speakers but you know there are two different ways that they might speak." (Paula—12/4/08)

"Yes, I feel they are native speakers of English." (Beth—11/6/08)

"English, or I guess I've heard the word 'patois' . . . I just don't know how to define it necessarily—but my impression is that in school, they've been learning something that is Standard English but that at home they may speak like a different dialect." (Ann—11/20/08)

"I would say yes, I think they are native speakers of English in the same way that you know anyone is a native speaker of English. Just there are some dialects that are recognized as or are validated automatically as native English and some aren't." (Eva—11/6/08)

"Their spoken language is a derivative of English. It's not the English that is taught in school. We might say that it's not proper, but to their ears it is. They understand the whole purpose of language is to communicate, and they can communicate." (Steve—12/15/08)

The quotes above reflect the teachers' trying to characterize their students' language within the family of Englishes while acknowledging dialect variation in actual use. Steve makes an important point that what is "proper" English is relative to the speaker and hearer, and that ultimately language use succeeds as long as it serves its communicative function. Susan took a more extreme position about the CCE students' language:

"Nah, I wouldn't [call it English] . . . now when they speak to each other . . . when they speak to each other and quickly, there's no way I would . . . but I guess if I went to parts of England I would probably say the same thing. But, no, when they speak to each other quickly, I don't understand hardly any of it." (12/15/08)

It is curious that Susan forcefully rejects her CCE speakers' vernacular as not English and as unintelligible while simultaneously acknowledging that she may have no easier time understanding speakers in some parts of England. Still, she implies that she would not think of the latter as non-native speakers of English. The irony here is that Susan recognizes her own socially constructed native speaker hierarchy, and the fact that the judgment is more on who the speaker is than any measure of intelligibility.

In terms of literacy practices, the teachers consistently noted that their CCE-speaking students wrote the way they spoke. Ann and Dina talked about the word order in the students' written language mirroring their speech. But a larger concern for the teachers was their sense that the Caribbean students seemed to focus disproportionately on correctness in writing to a negative degree. This they attributed to what they felt was an internalized philosophy of education in the Anglophone Caribbean that focused on getting things right in a very structured and formulaic way, and a notion that the teacher, invested with absolute authority, is always right. Eva, who had spent a year studying in England, noted this structured, "get it right" approach to teaching, and suggested that the Anglophone Caribbean way of teaching might have been influenced by their British colonial legacy. Eva stated in her interview:

> "The British instruction in reading and writing is so much more scaffolded and structured anyway than I feel like American instruction in reading and writing. When I went to British schools I felt like there was an expectation that there was a right answer, there was a meaning inside the text that you had to . . . your teacher would eventually tell you what it was and um, there is just sort of a rigidity in how I was expected to react to the text." (11/7/08)

Ann shares her views on this emphasis among her Caribbean students:

> ". . . there's an emphasis on correctness—what is correct, which is sort of good and bad . . . I find it's positive and negative. The positive is that there's a will to do it right. The negative is that . . . and I try to emphasize this with them . . . is that in English class there's not always a right or wrong answer. It's about how you say it . . . how you communicate it . . . So teaching them to get off this there's always a right and wrong answer. And what I say is always right. When it comes to the spelling of a word, yes, I will tell you the right spelling of a word, but your ideas . . . we can differ on." (11/20/08)

Beth echoes Ann's sentiment when she says:

> "There's a general resistance to generating their own theory; they've been so used to, which I do, give them an outline and this is how you do it. To them, there is one way to do it and that way is sort of not in me—I need to look to my teacher." (11/6/08)

The teachers in School A in particular lamented the fact that this perceived dependence on the teacher stifled students' ability to express their critical thinking and weakened their self-confidence as thinkers, learners, and writers. Beth explains:

> "I don't think critical thinking is an issue: I think *expressing* critical thinking is an issue . . . we get so bogged down in skills and processes that there's very little room in my curriculum for just talking about meaning, which I feel like is all I did in English class in high school." (11/6/08)

Eva pointed out that her students haven't really been taught to think through writing. They've been "taught to write to *express* [my emphasis] their thinking as opposed to using writing as a *way* of thinking" (Eva—11/6/08). These comments are consistent with the autonomous view of literacy alluded to earlier. Moreover, this view is part of a larger culture of a transmission model of learning and literacy, which is test driven and non-engaging for learners. Beth sums it up thus:

"I think most kids actually have a real desire to . . . achieve success which can be harnessed very positively but I think what's happened to them is this notion of success isn't entangled with a notion of learning; it's been entangled with this notion of passing the test, passing the class, so there is in a lot of students a reluctance to engage for engagement's sake." (11/6/08)

Even before I began to work with these teachers, Ann, Beth, and Eva took steps to redress what they saw as a curriculum too constrained by skills, processes, and narrowly defined products, by deciding to engage students with language in a more constructive way. First, Ann encouraged her students to read an entire novel and construct meaning on their own in their journals. Beth took this idea one step further by having students express their ideas through internet blogs, then used the blogs as a starting point to revise their writing to different audiences. Eva took the boldest step by designing an entire unit around language variation, dialects, and code switching. Of all the teachers, she had the most formal training in dialects of English, as she took a course in graduate school on dialect speakers and the implications of teaching Standard English as a Second Dialect. She also did a workshop on code switching and language. Yet, it took her two years before she could muster the courage to actually teach her unit on language. She noted that she wanted to "get a handle on things" and do "a lot of thinking about how I wanted to teach language" before she began. Still, she admitted the trepidation of many of her colleagues on the idea of teaching a unit on language variation: "You know, a lot of my co-workers are a little bit nervous about teaching language especially that like I'm not African American, I'm not Caribbean at all. And my own language experiences are very different" (11/06/08).

It is ironic that so many ELA teachers are hesitant to make language the object of study. This can be largely attributed to Lippi-Green's (1997) notion of standard language ideology alluded to earlier, which often puts English teachers in the position of gatekeepers of the standard language variety only rather than as providers of opportunities to engage with language in creative and meaningful ways.

When Eva introduced her language unit to her students, she said she was careful not to be condescending to her students. She began by discussing the history and evolution of English, its mixed nature as a language (influenced by German, French, etc.), its spread through colonization, its standardization and diversity. She discussed various dialects of English including Pennsylvania Dutch, AAVE, and Creoles. After working through the students' initial negative attitudes towards dialects, including their own, which is socially constructed and deeply engrained, Eva noted that her students came to a deeper awareness, understanding, and appreciation of their own language use, and language variation in general. Once, after doing a bidirectional translation exercise between AAVE and Standard English, Eva pointed out that one of her students said, "This is how I speak, oh my God!" Overall, Eva concluded that the unit was an extremely positive experience; that the students engaged with language in a way that is often lacking with the traditional prescriptivist approach of English teaching.

The unit brought out what Eva saw as a strength of the Anglophone Caribbean students—their natural love of language, especially words. The unit allowed them the freedom to experiment with language both in speech and in writing. Ann also pointed out that her students love to learn new words: "big words," as she put it. At School B, Dina spends a lot of time teaching the students what she calls "sophisticated words," and the students seem to enjoy learning them and using them in their writing.

Also at School B, Susan and Steve spend an inordinate amount of time teaching their students new words, mostly by labeling pictures and diagrams on handouts downloaded from internet sites. But their reason for teaching words is more to make up for what they see as a serious deficit in the students' vocabulary rather than to expand the already rich language repertoire of the students. The Newcomer Class which they co-teach is essentially a remedial class, and they have taken a very basic approach to literacy that is focused on vocabulary building, and having students read simple books and write summaries of what they read. Teaching approaches are taken up further in the following section.

Teacher Training

An important component of this project was professional development (PD) training for the participating teachers consisting of three workshops, selected readings, implementation of suggested reading and writing activities within the parameters of the ELA curriculum, and reflecting on the training in their journals. The readings addressed a number of areas: (1) sociolinguistics, focusing on language and dialect variation; (2) the history, structure, and uses of CCE; (3) culturally responsive pedagogy, which includes addressing the sociocultural contexts of literacy; and (4) Caribbean migration and its impact on Caribbean students' academic performance (see Appendix C for a list of relevant readings for each topic).

The first PD workshop held at both schools in Fall 2008 focused on language attitudes. I chose to begin training by focusing on language attitudes, as attitudes and beliefs undergird practice in critically important ways. The teachers began by completing a language attitude survey that asked for their thoughts on words like "dialect," "accent," "standard English," and "Caribbean Creole English." This workshop unearthed deeply held attitudes about language and dialect and spurred a heated debate on the role of the vernacular and standard English in school. Several teachers felt strongly that no vernacular use by students should be permitted in speech or writing in the classroom while others felt it might be permissible in less formal writing. At the same time, many teachers pointed out the inevitability of vernacular use in the classroom: "This is their language. They speak it no matter what we say," Steve asserted in one of the workshops. It was noted that teachers who had previous training in dialects and education, such as Eva, or Beth, who had a more meaning-making approach to language teaching, were more open to vernacular use in the classroom, and to challenging the standard language ideology (Lippi-Green, 1997) that pervades English language teaching. Still, there was no illusion that one workshop would change attitudes, nor was that the goal. The idea was to begin a conversation and re-examination of how teachers think about language and dialect.

The second half of the workshop introduced teachers to the history, structure, and uses of CCE. According to the information the teachers provided on their questionnaires, none of them had had any formal training in CCE, so for them this information was all new. Their encounters with CCE were mostly through their students, as only a few of them had visited the Anglophone Caribbean, and mainly as tourists, where their encounters with the vernacular were very superficial, as Paula noted earlier. The teachers' examination of CCE as a rule-governed language variety, then, began to open a dialogue about language structure, rules, and variation in a more informed way. This became a point of departure to encourage them to make language an object of study in their classroom—not in purely prescriptivist ways, but rather to take the students' language as a starting point to talk about ways to engage language difference. To this end, teachers were asked to design a writing assignment that would allow students to express themselves naturally, then to discuss ways that their written piece may be adjusted for various audiences. Beth, as noted earlier, asked students to write blogs, drawing on their internet literacies. One blog described a student explaining his absence from class to a friend. The student was asked how he would change the blog to explain the same content to his teacher and to justify his changes. Eva, who had already begun her unit on language, asked her students to write found poems. Ann used students' post-its to foster discussions on emerging themes in their readings.

At School B, Susan and Steve did not do this assignment. They felt strongly that their students were low-functioning new arrivals who needed to focus on getting used to routines in an American classroom, learning basic skills of decoding, building vocabulary, and writing simple answers to fill-in-the-blank questions. As literacy specialists, they both rejected the ideological view of literacy as social practice. They both firmly espouse a skills-and-drills approach to literacy, as evidenced by having their students complete fill-in-the-blank handouts almost on a daily basis. For Susan and Steve, their participation in the project was mainly to gain cultural knowledge and understanding of their Caribbean students' background. Thus, in the workshops and in my classroom visits, they both raised many critical questions about Guyanese culture, socioeconomic class structure, the educational system, and migration patterns, as their focal students, Devi and Dookie, hailed from Guyana. These questions were addressed in the assigned readings, as well as through my own experience as a Guyanese native. The questions spawned spirited discussion among the teachers, as they wrestled with the same topics in regard to their students from other Anglophone Caribbean countries.

As the Fall 2008 semester progressed, however, teachers expressed a tension that they felt between implementing some of the activities suggested in PD, validating their students' vernacular in class, and the need to prepare their students for upcoming standardized tests in January such as the Regents Exam or the 8th grade ELA test. The second workshop was thus dedicated to designing reading and writing activities that would include language variation _and_ attend to the language functions that students needed to master in preparation for standardized testing. Beth came up with a brilliant idea for her class to use the speeches of then presidential candidate Barack Obama to discuss and write about language variation, audience, and language use in persuasive essays. Given that the students were highly engaged in the general election campaign, they were easily motivated to read excerpts from Obama's speeches. Students read excerpts from three of Obama's speeches to three different audiences: (1) People who paid $200 per ticket to listen to Obama debate economic policy; (2) a group of students on a college campus in Massachusetts; (3) a congregation at Ebeneezer Baptist church in Atlanta. Students were first told about the audiences without seeing the speeches, and were asked to predict each audience's knowledge, education, gender, age, interests, and what they might want to hear from a potential president. Specifically, they were asked to predict what kind of vocabulary and subject matter might persuade the audience. After making their predictions, students were then asked to look at the excerpts and match each one with the appropriate audience based on the language. This activity was highly successful as it forced students to attend to language closely and to look for the differences in vocabulary, syntax, tone, and rhetorical devices used by Obama to persuade different audiences. Students could then apply these same strategies to their own persuasive essays required on the Regents Exam.

Other teachers like Paula, Ann, Dina, and Eva used Caribbean literature as a way to motivate students while developing critical reading skills. They found that by having students read books that are related to their culture such as Jean Rhys's classic text *Wide Sargasso Sea*, set in Dominica, students bring strong prior knowledge to the text that enriches their reading and informs their writing. At the same time, they fulfill the New York State ELA curriculum that requires students to read at least 25 books of high quality per year.

The third workshop took place in the Spring 2009 semester after the testing period in January was over. The teachers seemed more relaxed that testing was over but continued to lament in their journals that their teaching is still largely driven by the standardized tests, and that there is neither enough time nor opportunity to engage their students' out-of-school literacies in class. Still, their participation in the project began to have a positive effect. They began to confront language attitudes with their students more directly; they employed contrastive approaches in writing pedagogy, and sensitive error correction strategies using handouts given in the workshops. Most importantly, they began to focus on the language and culture of their Caribbean students in a more substantive way.

Conclusion

This chapter examined the language and literacy practices of CCE-speaking students, and the ways in which teacher training might engender more effective pedagogical practices for this population. The participating students and teachers in the pilot project discussed herein shed light on the complex nature of language, dialect, language attitudes, and literacy practices. The project showed that CCE-speaking students have both positive and negative views about their languages and literacies, are fully aware of their multidialectal repertoire and code-switching practices, and are strongly influenced by their educational experiences in the

Caribbean. The teachers, for their part, are challenged to find creative ways to harness the students' linguistic abilities while working within a narrowly prescribed curriculum that privileges essayist literacy. Students and teachers also grapple with the sociological issues of migration adjustment that impact the academic performance of Caribbean immigrant adolescents.

Looking ahead, this pilot project paves the way for future research to develop new paradigms in the curriculum more aligned with the twenty-first-century literacy practices of Caribbean and other immigrant youth and to design assessment tools that take dialect diversity and new literacies into account.

Acknowledgements

My gratitude to New York University Steinhardt's Challenge Fund for financial support of this project. Special thanks to my graduate assistant, Heather Finn, who spent countless hours in the field with me doing observations, and transcribing interview data. My appreciation to the principals and staff at Schools A and B for allowing me access to their schools. Finally, I owe a profound debt to the participating teachers and students at both schools for generously giving of their time and energy to deepen understanding of, and better serve, our Caribbean students.

APPENDIX A
Prototypical Features of Caribbean Creole English

Pronunciation

- Vowels pronounced differently from Standard English, e.g., "mistah" for "mister"
- In basilectal speech, "h" is often dropped or added differently at the beginning of words, e.g., "ouse" for "house" or "honion" for "onion"
- Voiceless "th" pronounced as "t," e.g., "tink" for "think"
- Voiced "th" pronounced as "d," e.g., "dem" for "them"
- Syllable-timed pronunciation as opposed to stress-timed pronunciation of Standard English, e.g., cóndémn vs. condémn

Other Features That May Show Up In Writing

Grammar

- Sentence structure is flexible. Subject and object can switch positions, e.g., "Me tell she fuh come."
- Zero inflections for:
  - Plurals if plurality already indicated e.g., "five dollar." If plurality not indicated, use of plural marker "dem," e.g., "My cousin and dem."
  - Possession—e.g., "My friend house."

- Subject–verb agreement—e.g., "She live in Brooklyn."
- Tense—e.g., "They call me yesterday."

- Zero use of the verb "to be" if:

  - The predicate is an adjective, e.g., "She fat."
  - There's a phrase showing location, e.g., "She in the kitchen."
  - The verb is in the progressive form, e.g., "She working today."

- No use of the passive voice:

  - e.g., "The food cook quick" = "The food was cooked quickly"

Vocabulary

- Creole words., e.g., "nyam" means "eat"
- Standard English words with Creole meanings, for example:

  - "hand" means everything from the shoulders to the fingers
  - "foot" means everything from the thighs to the toes.
  - "waiter" means a "tray"
  - "tea" can mean any hot beverage.

- Occasional use of British spellings e.g., "theatre" for "theater"

Narrative Style

- Episodic narrative style (topic associating) based on oral discourse norms.
- Predominant use of paratactic structures for cohesion (e.g., frequent use of "and" and "but" for connecting sentences)

APPENDIX B
Profile of Participants

School A Students

Name	Gender	Age	Race/ ethnicity	Grade level	Country of origin	Rural/urban provenance	Year of arrival in the U.S.
Theresa	F	17	Black	11	Jamaica	Rural	1995
Len	M	17	Black	11	Jamaica	Rural	2007
Kevin	M	18	Black	12	Trinidad	Urban	2004
Tina	F	18	Black	12	Guyana	Urban	2003
Ted	M	13	Black	7	Grenada	Urban	2008
Janet	F	14	Black	7	St.Vincent	Urban	2004
Tom	M	15	Black	8	St. Lucia	Rural	2004
Jim	M	14	Black	8	Trinidad	Rural	2007

School A Teachers

Name	Gender	Age	Race/ ethnicity	Current grade level teaching	Years of teaching	Subject
Eva	F	27	White	12	4	English
Beth	F	26	White	11	4	English
Paula	F	31	Nonwhite Hispanic	7	5	English
Ann	F	29	White	8	5	English

School B Students

Name	Gender	Age	Race/ ethnicity	Grade level	Country of origin	Rural/urban provenance	Year of arrival in the U.S.
Devi	F	13	Indian	7	Guyana	Rural	2008
Dookie	M	16	Indian	8	Guyana	Rural	2007
Derek	M	13	Black	7	Jamaica	Rural	2003
Coleen	F	12	Black	7	Jamaica	Urban	2002

School B Teachers

Name	Gender	Age	Race/ ethnicity	Current grade level teaching	Years of teaching	Subject
Dina	F	30	Black	7	4	English
Susan	F	59	White	6–8	19	Literacy
Steve	M	60	White	6–8	20	Literacy

APPENDIX C
Reading List for Teacher Training

(See References for full citations)

Creole English History and Features

Peter Roberts (1988)
Dennis Craig (2006)
Hubert Devonish & Karen Carpenter (2007)

Differences Between CCE and ESL Writing

Arlene Clachar (2004a; 2004b)

Academic Language/Discourse

Michael Halliday (1994)
Mary Schleppegrell (2004)

Literacies

James Gee (1990)
Gunther Kress (1997)
Brian Street (1984; 1995)

Language in the Content Areas

Ana Uhl Chamot & J. Michael O'Malley (1994)

Language Socialization and Classroom Discourse

Courtney Cazden (2001)
Lisa Delpit (1996)
James Gee (1990)
Shirley Brice Heath (1983)

Reflective Teacher Practice

Jack Richards & Charles Lockhart (1994)

Culturally Responsive Pedagogy

Geneva Gay (2000)

Working with Caribbean Students in North American Schools

Elizabeth Coelho (1991)
Shondel Nero (2000; 2006)
Yvonne Pratt-Johnson (2006)
Lise Winer (2006)

Language Attitudes and Dialects

Carolyn Temple Adger, Walt Wolfram & Donna Christian (2007)

Caribbean Migration

Nancy Foner (2001)

Notes

1 The Anglophone Caribbean (commonly known as the West Indies) includes all of the following islands: Anguilla, Antigua and Barbuda, Barbados, Dominica, Grenada and Carriacou, Jamaica, Montserrat, Nevis, St. Kitts, St. Lucia, St. Vincent, Trinidad and Tobago, as well as Guyana on the mainland of South America, and Belize in Central America. Guyana and Belize are included because of their shared history of British colonization with other Caribbean islands.
2 Caribbean Creole English (CCE)—a general term for the range of English used in the Anglophone Caribbean countries listed above. In a narrow sense it covers English alone; in a broad sense it covers English and Creole (Carrington, 1992). CCE spans a creole continuum, which is a continuous spectrum of speech varieties, ranging from the *basilect* (creole or patois) to the *mesolect* (midrange, less creolized varieties) to the *acrolect* (the standard variety with some local phonological and lexical features). There is no sharp cleavage between the basilect and the acrolect. Prototypical features of CCE are listed in Appendix A.
3 New York City Department of Education, Division of Assessment and Accountability: http://schools.nyc.gov/Accountability/DOEData/default.htm.
4 New York State English Language Arts Resource Guide: http://www.emsc.nysed.gov/ciai/ela/pub/ccela.pdf.
5 New York State Report Cards are issued annually by the New York State Education Department for each district and school. They consist of three parts: (1) the Accountability and Overview Report, which shows district/school profile data, accountability statuses, and data on accountability measures like English language arts, mathematics, science, and graduation rate; (2) the Comprehensive Information Report, which shows non-accountability data; and (3) the Fiscal Accountability Supplement, which shows expenditures per pupil and some information about students with disabilities: http://www.emsc.nysed.gov/irts/reportcard/
6 Pseudonyms are used for all teachers and students to protect their identity.
7 The date in parentheses indicates the date of the interview with the participant.

References

Adger, C.T., Wolfram, W., & Christian, D. (2007). *Dialects in schools and communities*, 2nd ed. Mahwah, NJ: Erlbaum.

Brutt-Griffler, J. & Samimy, K. (2001). Transcending the nativeness paradigm. *World Englishes 20*(1), 99–106.

Carrington, L. (1992). Caribbean English. In T. McArthur (Ed.). *The Oxford companion to the English language* (pp. 191–193). Oxford: Oxford University Press.

Cazden, C. (2001). *Classroom discourse: The language of teaching and learning*, 2nd ed. Boston: Heinemann.

Clachar, A. (2004a). The construction of Creole-speaking students' linguistic profile and contradictions in ESL literacy programs. *TESOL Quarterly 38* (1), 153–165.

—— (2004b). Creole discourse effects on the speech conjunctive system in expository texts. *Journal of Pragmatics 36*, 1827–1850.

Coelho, E. (1991). *Caribbean students in Canadian schools. Book II*, Ontario: Pippin Publishing.

Cook, V. (1999). Going beyond the native speaker in English language teaching. *TESOL Quarterly 33* (2), 185–209.

Craig, D. (2006). *From vernacular to standard English: Teaching language and literacy to Caribbean students*. Miami, FL: Ian Randle Publishers.

Delpit, L. (1996). *Other people's children: Cultural conflict in the classroom*. New York: New Press.

—— (1998). What should teachers do? Ebonics and culturally responsive instruction. In T. Perry & L. Delpit (Eds.). *The real Ebonics debate* (pp. 17–28). New York: Beacon Press.

Devonish, H. & Carpenter, K. (2007). Full bilingual education in a Creole situation. The Jamaican Bilingual Primary Education Project. *Occasional Paper, No. 35.* St. Augustine, Trinidad: Society for Caribbean Linguistics.

Farr, M. (Ed.). (2005). *Latino language and literacy in ethnolinguistic Chicago.* Mahwah, NJ: Erlbaum.

Foner, N. (Ed.). (2001). *New immigrants in New York,* 2nd rev. ed. New York: Columbia University Press.

García, O. & Menken, K. (2006). The English of Latinos from a plurilingual transcultural angle: Implications for assessment and schools. In S. Nero (Ed.). *Dialects, Englishes, Creoles, and education* (pp. 167–183). Mahwah, NJ: Erlbaum.

Gay, G. (2000). *Culturally responsive pedagogy: Theory, research, and practice.* New York: Teachers College Press.

Gee, J. (1990). *Social linguistics and literacies: Ideology in discourses.* London: Falmer Press.

Halliday, M.A.K. (1994). *An introduction to functional grammar,* 2nd ed. London: Edward Arnold.

Heath, S.B. (1983). *Ways with words: Language, life and work in communities and classrooms.* Cambridge: Cambridge University Press.

Kachru, B. (1986) *The alchemy of English: The spread, function, and models of nonnative Englishes.* Oxford: Pergamon Press (Reprinted, 1990, University of Illinois Press).

Kachru, B. & Nelson, C. (2001). World Englishes. In A. Burns & C. Coffin (Eds.). *Analysing English in a global context* (pp. 9–25). London and New York: Routledge.

Kress, G. (1997). *Before writing: Rethinking the pathways to literacy.* London: Routledge.

Labov, W. (1981). *The study of nonstandard English,* Urbana, IL: NCTE.

Leung, C., Harris, R., & Rampton, B. (1997). The idealised native speaker, reified ethnicities, and classroom realities. *TESOL Quarterly 31* (3), 543–560.

Lippi-Green, R. (1997). *English with an accent.* New York: Routledge.

McArthur, T. (1998). *The English languages.* Cambridge: Cambridge University Press.

Miles, M. & Huberman, M. (1994). *Qualitative data analysis: An expanded sourcebook,* 2nd ed. Thousand Oaks, CA: Sage Publications.

Nero, S. (2000). The changing faces of English: A Caribbean perspective. *TESOL Quarterly 34* (3), 483–510.

—— (2001). *Englishes in contact: Anglophone Caribbean students in an urban college.* In series on Writing, edited by M. Farr. Cresskill, NJ: Hampton Press.

—— (Ed.). (2006). *Dialects, Englishes, Creoles and education.* Mahwah, NJ: Erlbaum.

O'Brien, D.G., & Bauer, E.B. (2005). New literacies and the institution of old learning. *Reading Research Quarterly 40* (2), 120–131.

Olson, D. (1994). *The world on paper: The conceptual and cognitive implications of writing and reading.* Cambridge: Cambridge University Press.

Paikeday, T. (1985). *The native speaker is dead!* Toronto: Paikeday.

Pennycook, A. (1994). *The cultural politics of English as an international language.* London: Longman.

Pratt-Johnson, Y. (2006). Teaching Jamaican Creole-speaking students. In S. Nero (Ed.). *Dialects, Englishes, Creoles, and education* (pp. 119–136). Mahwah, NJ: Erlbaum.

Richards, J. & Lockhart, C. (1994). *Reflective teaching in second language classrooms.* Cambridge: Cambridge University Press.

Rickford, J. (1987). *Dimensions of a Creole continuum.* Stanford, CA: Stanford University Press.

—— (1999). *African American vernacular English: Features, evolution, educational implications.*

Roberts, P. (1988). *West Indians and their language.* Cambridge: Cambridge University Press.

Schleppegrell, M. (2004). *The language of schooling: A functional linguistics perspective.* Mahwah, NJ: Erlbaum.

Siegel, J. (2006). Keeping Creoles and dialects out of the classroom. Is it justified? In S. Nero (Ed.). *Dialects, Englishes, Creoles, and education* (pp. 39–67). Mahwah, NJ: Erlbaum.

Simpkins, G.A., Holt, G., & Simpkins, C. (1977). *Bridge: A cross-cultural reading program.* Boston: Houghton Mifflin.

Smitherman. G. (2000). *Talkin that talk: Language, culture, and education in African America.* New York: Routledge.

Street, B. (1984). *Literacy in theory and practice.* Cambridge: Cambridge University Press.

—— (1995). *Social literacies: Critical approaches to literacy in development, ethnography, and education.* London: Longman.

Torres-Guzmán, M., Abbate, J., Brisk, M., & Minaya-Rowe, L. (2002). Defining and documenting success for bilingual learners: A collective case study. *Bilingual Research Journal 26* (1), 1–22.

Uhl Chamot, A. & O'Malley, J.M. (1994). *The CALLA handbook.* New York: Addison Wesley.

Valdés, G. (2001). *Learning and not learning English: Latino students in American schools.* New York: Teachers College Press.

Wheeler, R. & Swords, R. (2006). *Code-switching: Teaching standard English in urban classrooms.* Urbana, IL: NCTE.

Winer, L. (2006). Teaching English to Caribbean English Creole-speaking students in the Caribbean and North America. In S. Nero (Ed.). *Dialects, Englishes, Creoles and education* (pp. 105–118). Mahwah, NJ: Erlbaum.

11 From Outside Agitators to Inside Implementers

Improving the Literacy Education of Vernacular and Creole Speakers[1]

Angela E. Rickford and John R. Rickford

Introduction

Forty years ago, linguists working in the United States and the Anglophone Caribbean (e.g., Labov, 1968, p. 1; Le Page, 1968) observed that students who spoke African American Vernacular English (AAVE) or Caribbean Creole English performed poorly on achievement tests of reading and the language arts relative to their peers who spoke varieties closer to the standard English that was expected and rewarded in schools. For almost as long, linguists and tertiary level educators have also served as critics of existing approaches to literacy education for vernacular and Creole speakers in schools, from the elementary to the university level. But vernacular and Creole speakers continue to underperform academically,[2] and there are increasing opportunities now for us to propose and implement changes from the inside.[3] So what do we need to know and do to move our contributions to a higher and more successful level—from that of outside agitators to inside implementers?

In addressing this question, we will draw on four recent experiences of ours (and the work of others) in which the role of the linguist/educator has been more like that of an inside resource person or implementer than an outside critic or agitator:

- Participating in research on the University of California Subject A *writing* placement exams of African American students in 2000–2001;
- Lecturing on AAVE and Education to California teachers, instructional supervisors and administrators between 2001 and 2009;
- Observing the implementation of the University of the West Indies' experimental Creole education project in a Jamaican classroom, in 2006;
- Observing and supervising the teaching of reading and language arts (phonemic awareness, phonics, comprehension, vocabulary development, and spelling) in Northern California schools from 1994 to 2007, and serving as consultants to an elementary textbook publisher seeking to meet the new California language arts requirement to provide additional support to AAVE speakers in mastering reading and academic English.

We will discuss these experiences in turn, focusing on at least one "lesson" we learned from each of them.

Research on African American Student Performance on the Analytical Writing Placement (Subject A) Examination at the University of California (2000–1)

The University of California has a long-standing, university-wide writing require-ment for its freshmen that reads as follows:[4]

> ALL STUDENTS who will enter the University of California as freshmen must demonstrate their command of the English language by fulfilling the Entry Level Writing Requirement (formerly known as Subject A requirement).
> [...]
> THE FACULTY of the University of California intends this ... University-wide ... Examination ... to publicize the standard and kind of writing competence necessary for success in the University's introductory courses.

But, as indicated by Figure 11.1, which summarizes data from 1995 to 1999, the number of African American students passing this exam is usually lower than that of White students by about twenty percentage points each year.

In 2000 and 2001, we were both part of a small "Action Research" group of tertiary level educators that met regularly at the University of California (U.C.) Office of the President in Oakland to consider the "Writing Development Needs of African American College-Bound High School Students." The specific focus of this group was to attempt to discover why African American students were underperforming on this gate-keeping "Subject A" exam and develop recom-mendations for improvement. Among other things, we examined several U.C. "Subject A" practice essays submitted to the U.C.'s Diagnostic Writing Service (DWS) by African American high school (11th grade) students.[5] In this section of

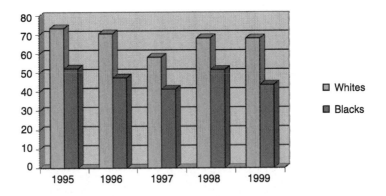

Figure 11.1 Percentages of Blacks and Whites Passing U.C. Subject A Writing Exam, 1995–99.

our chapter, we will discuss one such essay, but we need first to explain the essay question on "The Appeal of the Democracy of Goods" to which the student was responding.

For this essay question, students were given a 1985 excerpt from a book by Roland Marchand analyzing the advertising strategies used to sell products in the U.S. from the 1920s to the 1940s. The chief advertising strategy was to show wealthy people using products like Cream of Wheat or Ivory Soap to which ordinary people had equal access through the concept of "The Democracy of Goods." Students were asked to identify what American ideals and desires underlay the appeal of the 1920s–40s concept of the "Democracy of Goods," and to say whether they thought today's advertising was based on the same ideals and desires, or other ones. The question prompt included the note: "To develop your essay, be sure to discuss the appeals of specific advertisements."

Here is one Subject A practice essay written by an African American student about to go into the 11th grade:

> In this world, money is the ideal and desires that appeal [?] the concept of the democracy of goods. To me, without money you have very little power and that's kind of unfair. The people that start off wealthy just get more wealthier and the people that's lower class struggle to pay the bills. Money play[s] a big role in society, but it's not everything. If you have God by your side, you can't complain. For example, Michael Jordan wants to advertise some shoes and so do[es] a college ball player. Michael Jordan would sale more shoes because he had more money to put out advertisements everywhere, commercial[s], magazines, billboards and of course the shoe books and like I was saying Jordan [would] get richer while the college player spent a grip to just make such a litle profit. Back in the 1920's it seems like 100% money was the key, now days who you know have to do with a little bit of your success. You can barely be able to pay your rent, but if you have a cousin that's rich he or she could probably blow you up. For instance, [if] you happen to be able to rap really good and you hook up with the biggest record lable in the rap industry you would become successful because you would have some of the best rappers featuring on your CD. Sometimes you will run into a lot of things that's unfair, but if you want to use advertisements to make it big like the next company and it's not working it may [END OF ESSAY]

Several of the mechanical "errors" in this essay may be interpreted as transfers from AAVE, including third person present tense singular -*s* absence (*money play*, so *do* *a college ball player*), plural -*s* absence (*commercial*), and subject–verb agreement (*people that's* instead of *people that are*). One could recommend that teachers use Contrastive Analysis and related strategies (e.g., Wheeler and Swords, 2006) to minimize transfers from AAVE at school when academic or standard English is required. However, previous studies (e.g., Godley, 2004; Smitherman, 2000; Sweetland, 2006; Whiteman, 1981) have suggested that the rate of such incursions from AAVE in the academic English *writing* (vs. speech) of African American students is relatively low,[6] and this was pretty much what we found to be true of this essay and others submitted to the Diagnostic Writing Service.

The larger and more important conclusion we reached, however, is that, even if its AAVE features and punctuation and other mechanical infelicities were to be edited out, this essay would still be a relatively weak piece of writing, in terms of its *ideas* and *structure* or *organization*. For instance, it does not address, in its opening sentences, the *first* requirement of the essay prompt, that students identify the American ideals and desires (for instance, the ideal of equality, or the desire for everyone to have access to some of the same opportunities, goods and services, regardless of wealth and power) that underlay the appeal of the 1920s–40s concept of the "Democracy of Goods." Instead, it begins with the essay-writer's own opinion that "without money you have very little power." This is in fact the exact opposite of what advertisers of the 1920s–1940s tended to suggest, according to Marchand. Such advertisers asserted, instead, that Chase and Sanborn coffee, or Ivory soap, were the best products of their kind available anywhere, and that since they were reasonably priced, they were equally available to bourgeoisie and proletariat alike.

The essay goes on to develop the essay-writer's idea that "without money you have very little power," but not without mis-steps. For instance, two sentences later, we encounter the claim that while money is important, "it's not everything." The only support for this qualification is the undeveloped argument that "If you have God by your side, you can't complain." Indeed, the entire point of the longish example that follows next, the contrast between Michael Jordan and a college basketball player trying to sell shoes, is that Jordan would do better "because he had more money." So money IS everything.

The essay-writer does try to address the essay prompt (especially the part that requires you to compare advertising strategies from the early twentieth century with those of today) by going on to argue that while money might have been "100%" in the 1920s, now "who you know" might also be important. The first example is not too felicitous, since it is the rich cousin's wealth (money once again) that would help to make up for your own financial deficiencies. The second example is somewhat more promising, suggesting that skill in rapping could lead you to success if it leads you to a recording contract and endorsements by other rappers. (This presumably picks up on the belief among some of today's youth that rapping is a viable means of moving from rags to riches.) But the focus on *advertising strategy* (as against individual upward mobility) is not central in this argumentation, and time runs out before the essay-writer can develop his or her conclusion.

Moreover, the essay as a whole follows an elementary *list* structure in the text structure model of Calfee and Chambliss (1987), simply enumerating the benefits that money or contacts make possible. The use of more complex alternatives such as the Hierarchy, in which sets of attributes are linked by superordination and subordination, might help to shape the student's logical argumentation more successfully and reveal his or her expository writing skills more effectively. See Figure 11.2 for other alternatives in the text structure model of Calfee and Chambliss (1987), as modified by Ball (1992).

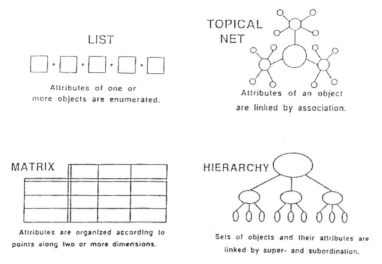

Figure 11.2 Diagrams of Descriptive Expository Text Structures.

Source: Ball (1992), adapted from Calfee and Chambliss (1987, p. 364).

Talking to Oakland, California Teachers about AAVE and Education (2001–9)

A second project on which we've collaborated is lecturing to teachers, literacy coaches and instructional supervisors in the Oakland Unified School District about AAVE and Education, and strategies for teaching narrative, exposition, and comprehension. We did this over several months in 2001, and at an all-day session in 2009.

Here, in the district where the Ebonics controversy erupted in 1996, we found the audience receptive to and interested in what we had to say about the systematic phonological and grammatical structures of AAVE, and about ways in which this could be taken into account in teaching reading and writing. But as interested as they were, the educators we talked to wanted two things: (a) evidence of the *effectiveness* of the linguistically informed methods we were describing; and (b) *specific, detailed lesson plans and examples* to use in their reading/language arts classrooms.

In relation to (a), we would point, among other things, to the increased gain in mean reading scores achieved by fifth and sixth grade students in Kelli Harris-Wright's Bidialectal Communication program in DeKalb county, outside Atlanta, between 1994 and 1997. As shown in Table 11.1, students in this program, which involves Contrastive Analysis and other innovative techniques, showed relatively large increases in their reading scores every year, *more so* than students in a Control Group who were taught by traditional techniques that did not involve explicit comparisons between vernacular and standard English. (Note, indeed,

Table 11.1 Reading Composite Scores for Bidialectal and Control Groups, DeKalb County, Georgia, on Iowa Test of Basic Skills

Group	1994–95	1995–96	1996–97
Bidialectal Post-test	42.39	41.16	34.26
Bidialectal Pre-test	39.71	38.48	30.37
GAIN by Bidialectal Students	**+2.68**	**+2.68**	**+3.89**
Control Post-test	40.65	43.15	49.00
Control Pre-test	41.02	41.15	49.05
GAIN by Control Students	−0.37	**+2.0**	−0.05

Source: Kelli Harris-Wright, personal communication.

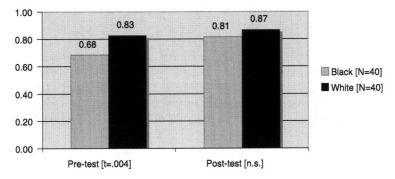

Figure 11.3 Progress in Reducing the Minority Differential: The Effect of 40 Hours of Instruction with the Individualized Reading Program.

Source: Reprinted, with permission, from http://www.ling.upenn.edu/~wlabov/

Note: Proportion read correctly of 25 words with final -CCC spelling (eg., *thought, catch, hands, branch, works, didn't, might*. . .), before and after instruction in California schools, grades 2–4, 2001–4.

that Control Group students actually did more poorly on their post-tests in two years of the program than they had on their pre-tests, while students in the bidialectal program showed positive gains, and greater ones, every year.)

Another example of effectiveness that we have used recently comes from a presentation in which we participated with William Labov, at a session for administrators and textbook publishers sponsored by Voices for African American Students (VAAS) in Los Angeles in September 2006. In his talk, entitled "Spotlight on Reading," Labov presented the dramatic result shown in Figure 11.3, in which African American students taught by the Invidualized Reading Method (now "Reading Road") developed by Bettina Baker and himself improved substantially, so much so that the differences between their scores and those of White students, significant on the pre-test, were no longer so on the post-test.[7]

In relation to (b), it is important to remember that, as practitioners, teachers tend to be less interested in theoretical constructs and more excited by hands-on strategies and techniques that can be implemented immediately.

There are not many materials of this kind that one could recommend. Older materials like California's (1970s) *Proficiency in Standard English for Speakers of*

Black Language [*SEP*] or the "Talk Across" program of Crowell et al. (1974) use outdated terminology (like "Nonstandard" English), and depend too heavily on tedious drills, Moreover, since they were never published in the conventional sense, they are difficult if not impossible to obtain. Sweetland (2006) developed twelve excellent dialect awareness lesson plans for teachers in Cincinnati who participated in her dissertation research, but they are not yet published. One of her lessons, dealing with the use of Sandra Cisneros' story, *Hairs*, to teach standard English possessive -s, is included as an appendix, with her permission.[8] Note the level of detail at which the lesson has been developed—including time estimates, materials needed for each activity, and the specification of objectives—and the fact that the lesson specifies the NCTE/IRA standards for English Language Arts it satisfies.

The only publicly available, linguistically informed lesson plans that take AAVE into account are ones that have emerged very recently, including the *Reading Road* program of Labov and Baker (2009, available on Labov's website (http://www.ling.upenn.edu/~wlabov/PRI/index.html), Seymour, Roeper & de Villiers (2005), Wheeler and Swords (2006 and forthcoming), and Brown (2009). Meier (2007) also contains a number of specifics—particularly helpful since they build on AAVE conversational and discourse patterns rather than just its phonological or grammatical features—that could be used in lesson plans for teachers. We need more publications like these,[9] and they should be more integrated with the basal reader textbooks and language arts standards that schools use.

Observing One Implementation of the University of the West Indies' Experimental Creole Education Project in a Jamaican Classroom (2006)

A third experience that we shared was observing a 2006 class session in a Jamaican elementary school that was participating in the highly innovative Creole/English bilingual program developed by the Linguistics Department at the University of the West Indies, Mona, Jamaica (see Devonish & Carpenter, 2007). The particular lesson we observed involved translating an expository text about the Ostrich, and the specific excerpt we will focus on is the translation of the first sentence in the class text ("The ostrich is a strange animal") from English to Jamaican Creole (JC).

The teacher had prepared the students for the sentence translation exercise by bringing to class a number of flashcards, each of which had one word from the text in its original English orthography, e.g., *story*. He also had a second set of cards, each of which had a Jamaican equivalent in the phonemic orthography developed by Cassidy (1961) and Cassidy and Le Page (1967), e.g., *tuorii*. He had given students on one side of the class one "English" card each, and students on the other side of the class—facing the first set across a narrow gap—one "Jamaican" card each. At a given signal, students had to get up and find the student who had the translation equivalent of the word on their card, and when they were successful, they took the pair of cards to the teacher, who then taped them to the board so that everyone could see and learn the appropriate "translations," e.g.:

because / bikaaz
people / piipl
ostrich / aschriij
parts / paats

We should note here that the immediate buzz of activity this exercise generated was one of the plusses of this teacher's pedagogical technique. The atmosphere was one of a treasure hunt, and the students were active, engaged, and clearly enjoying themselves as they tracked down their translation equivalents, and took them with pride to the teacher.

Moving then from the <u>lexical</u> translation to the <u>sentence</u> translation task, the teacher read the first sentence of the story "The ostrich is a strange animal," and asked for volunteers to translate it into JC. A male student offered the following translation, converting the <u>pronunciation</u> into JC (e.g., the interdental fricative / ∂/ to the dental/alveolar stop /d/) but not the <u>grammar</u> (e.g., English copula "is" to its Creole equivalent, /a/):

De ostrij is a strange animal
/di <u>aa</u>strij iz a streenj aniimal/

The teacher's negative reaction indicated that he was not satisfied with this, and a female student, one of several eager volunteers who vigorously stuck their hands in the air, competing for selection, offered this alternative:

De ostrij a one 'trange animal
/di <u>aa</u>strij a wan (s)treenj aniimal/

This translation, which met with the teacher's warm approval, included not only the phonetic features changed by the male student, but another phonetic feature (/st/ > /t/ in the onset of "strange") and the following grammatical conversions as well:

- Replacement of the English copula *iz* by the JC prenominal copula *a*
- Replacement of the English indefinite article *a* by the JC indefinite article *wan*

The lesson, overall, was commendable in several respects. The teacher was fluent in both languages, he was well prepared, he was active and enthusiastic, and he kept the students engaged throughout the class by his animated instructions and performance and by the small-group activities in which he asked them to engage. His lesson also required translating from standard English to the vernacular as well as translating from the vernacular to the standard; most U.S. contrastive lessons, to their detriment, only involve translation to the standard, which conveys to students the not-so-subtle message that their home variety is not of equal value (see J. Rickford 2002, p. 39). Moreover, the teacher had prepared the students well for the phrasal/sentence translation task by having them first engage in the animated lexical flashcard exercise. In these and other respects, the teacher's bilingual lesson was very, very good.

On the crucial point of the grammatical differences between English and Creole, however, the teacher repeated the girl's correct translation, but did not write it on the board nor explain in detail the specific differences between it and the male student's mesolectal or phonetics-only translation, as the "Repetition and Reinforcement" pedagogical principle (see A. Rickford, 2005) would require. As a result, the male student (and others in the class) may NOT have understood exactly WHY his response was wrong, and he/they might not be able to produce the "correct" answers in the future. In addition, the lesson had no writing component. One of the basics of language arts instructional pedagogy is to try to include all four elements—Listening, Speaking, Reading, Writing [LSRW]—in each lesson where possible. This approach helps teachers check for understanding and helps students remember what they've learned. It would have been good practice to have at least involved the students in a writing exercise in which they copied in their books a short table listing the Creole words, structures and pronunciations side by side with their standard English counterparts. Furthermore, the teacher could have asked content-based questions of them in standard English, and had them reply in Creole, and vice versa, again, to reinforce their knowledge of the differences being taught.

What is at stake here is not only the success of one lesson, but the success of the bilingual experiment overall. In a possible comparison of controlled (traditional) and experimental (bilingual) methods involving these students, the bilingual method might well fail to show the full extent of its potential benefits, not because it is linguistically unsound or intrinsically lacking, but because in small but crucial respects its pedagogical implementation was less than ideal.

Specific Lessons Involving Training Teachers to Teach Reading (e.g., Phonemic Awareness, Phonics Decoding, Vocabulary, Spelling and Comprehension) in California Schools, 1996–2006, and Helping to Develop AAVE Teacher Tips for a New Series of Elementary Readers (2007/2008)

The final category of experiences we wish to draw on derive from two sources: (a) Angela's experiences as a professor of Education at San Jose State University, in which she trained teachers to teach the elements of reading, including phonemic awareness and phonics (for decoding purposes), and vocabulary development and narrative/expository structure (for comprehension purposes) at the elementary and secondary levels, and observed their classroom lessons over the course of a decade (1996–2006); and (b) joint work we began to do in late 2007 to help a national elementary textbook publisher revise its kindergarten to sixth grade readers to meet the new California requirements that they provide "additional support to AAVE speakers in mastering phonological awareness and academic English."

Angela's Experiences with Effective and Ineffective Student Teachers

In visiting the classrooms of student teachers for more than a decade, Angela formulated six deep teaching principles that distinguish good or effective teachers from bad or ineffective ones. The six principles are discussed in detail in A. Rickford (2005), but they include:

Principle 1: Student Engagement
Principle 2: Learner Participation
Principle 3: Repetition and Reinforcement
Principle 4: High Expectations
Principle 5: Sound Teaching Pedagogy
Principle 6: Conceptual Understanding

Here we merely wish to highlight one example of an effective teacher, and one of an ineffective teacher, and hone in what distinguished the two cases.

Ms. Kong, one of the teachers Angela visited, scored high marks for her sound pedagogical techniques. For instance, in attempting to develop the phonemic awareness of her kindergarten students, she would say words like *mag, sag* and *tag* and systematically ask in relation to each word what its first, second and third sounds were. As the students gave the correct answer, she would write each letter on the board, until the whole word was formed. The fact that the words shared the /ag/ rime allowed students to focus in on the phonetic differences between the single varying segment, the onsets /m/, /s/, and /t/. And once those differences were well appreciated, she challenged them to stretch the words further by adding an /s/ at the end: *mags, sags,* and *tags.* She would explain the general principle ("Listen to each of the sounds then write the letter that corresponds to it"), write the words on the big classroom chalkboard, ask the students to write the words again on their small 12 × 6 inch chalkboards, and then challenge them to extend the words by one segment/letter. In short, her lesson plan was engaging, focused, concentrated, and carefully structured, with considerable repetition and reinforcement, and her students did well.

By contrast, another student teacher, Ms. Duncan, was less effective. She attempted to introduce her kindergarten students to nine letters and sounds of the alphabet at one sitting. She introduced each letter by name, then gave the corresponding sound, and then provided an example of a word that began with the sound being introduced, but also varied in their rimes and other respects, e.g., "P, p, *pig,*" and "S, s, *soap*" (as distinct from pairs like *pig* and *dig* in which the rimes were constant, and the only varying element was the consonantal onset). For *x,* she said "X, x, *x-ray*" and then gave examples of words like *box* in which the *x* occurred word-finally rather than initially. So many different elements were being taught at once, without focus, repetition, or reinforcement, that the children were quite confused. When she finally showed the children an alphabet card with the letter *y,* and asked them "What does this say?" there was no response.

Preparing "Teacher Tips" for a New Series of Elementary Readers

The final experience we wish to discuss is also our newest—helping to prepare and comment on teacher tips for a new California elementary reader series that provides additional support to AAVE speakers in mastering phonological awareness and academic English. We found the general goal commendable, and also liked the primary strategy for developing mastery of standard or academic English—Contrastive Analysis. The texts themselves include a Contrastive Analysis chart showing (virtually) all the differences between AAVE and Standard English, and numerous Teacher Tips to accompany specific stories and exercises, like this one that we helped to author for a grade 5 text:

> *Teacher Tip (AAVE), for page GS10, grade 5, Lines 1 and 2:*
> AAVE speakers may pronounce the negatives in lines 1 and 2 without a final *t*, as *didn'* or *couldn'*. If you're trying to develop their competence in switching to mainstream or standard English in <u>speaking</u> or <u>reading aloud</u>, you may offer practice in pronouncing these words with a final *t*. If pronunciation is not the <u>focus</u> of your lesson, you may ignore this vernacular pronunciation, since speakers of different dialects regularly vary in how they read or pronounce written text. In either case note that negative auxiliaries like *didn'* are systematic exceptions to the rule in AAVE and other Englishes in that you can only drop the second consonant in a syllable-final consonant cluster (a sequence of two or more consonants) if <u>both</u> consonants are voiced (*ha<u>nd</u>, han'*), with vocal folds vibrating, or voiceless (*pa<u>st</u>, pas'*), without such vibration. Since *nt* clusters are mixed (*n* is voiced, *t* voiceless), they normally don't lose their final *t* (e.g., *ant, pint*). Teachers may use non-negative words like *ant* when modeling the standard pronunciation of negatives like *didn't*.

Impressed as we are with the reading series, and happy though we are to have been involved in its development (as inside implementers), we harbor some anxiety that teachers using it might zero in on too many features, too relentlessly, forgetting the caution to ignore dialect differences unless they are relevant to the pedagogical focus of the lesson. Our goal, as adumbrated in Rickford and Rickford (2007), was to help teachers to develop linguistic versatility in their students. But might teachers using the new series—and others like it that the State Department of Education has mandated—become like the "Interrupting Teachers" Piestrup (1973) described, who harassed their AAVE-speaking students so much that they "withdrew from participation in reading, speaking softly and as seldom as possible" (pp. 131–2)? And might they actually produce lower reading scores than the "Black Artful Teachers" in Piestrup's study, who never interfered with their students' reading, but used rhythmic play and encouragement to involve and instruct them, and improve their reading scores? It will be some time before we know whether our anxieties about the implementation of these materials are justified, and some time beyond that before we understand how much of what we know about contrasts between a vernacular and standard variety to include or exclude from pedagogical texts. In this respect, as we venture from the role of outside agitators to inside implementers, we are venturing into relatively uncharted territory.

Conclusion

As we become inside implementers (consultants to textbook publishers, advisers to teachers and school districts), sociolinguists trying to raise the literacy levels of vernacular and Creole speakers and help them master academic or standard English as well will need to:

- Be the best linguists we can be, in terms of accurately describing vernacular/ standard contrasts, and spelling rules and decoding errors, to help teachers teach and students learn.
- But we WILL also have to step outside of our comfort zone and be willing to learn more about writing and writing pedagogy, reading and reading pedagogy, and the principles of effective and creative teaching more generally.
- We will also have to draw on examples from literature, music and other fields to provide specific examples and lesson plans. Here, we can productively learn from and collaborate with teachers and experts in other fields.
- And finally, we will have to recognize that we ARE in relatively uncharted territory and be prepared to learn from experience, and from the expertise of those who have previously served as consultants to school districts and text-book publishers.

In general, the need for sociolinguistic involvement in the challenges of improving the reading skills and levels of vernacular and/or Creole speakers remains great. But we still have much to learn about the best way to meld our expertise to the needs of the clienteles (students, teachers, administrators, text-book publishers) we hope to serve. The need for continued research and practice in this area is clear.

APPENDIX
A Lesson Plan for Teaching Possessive -s in Context from Sweetland (2004)—Day One of a Two-Day Plan

My Mother's Hair Is Like . . . A Reader Response Activity that Elicits Figurative Language and Possessive Constructions (by Julie Sweetland)

Overview

In the first phase of this two-day lesson, students (grades 4 and up) read the picture book *Hairs/Pelitos* by Sandra Cisneros and discuss the author's use of imagery and style to convey feelings about her family. Students then use Cisneros' text as a model to write a short piece that introduces their own family members through a physical characteristic or habit. The second day is dedicated to sharing and revision of student writing. Students are pushed to add or improve similes and sensory images, and the standard use of "apostrophe s" is reviewed in context.

Estimated Lesson Time

Two 60-minute sessions.

From Theory to Practice

Literary Background

Cisneros' writing style in this piece is deceptively simple—it imitates children's speech, yet is filled with wonderfully poetic images and language. The picture book is actually an excerpt from *The House on Mango Street*, a novel told in a series of vignettes rather than through a traditional plot structure. *Hairs/Pelitos* can therefore be used to model for children at least two characteristics of good writing: strong imagery and the power of a "snapshot" to create scene, mood, and character.

Linguistic Background

The linguistic purpose of this writing prompt is to elicit singular nominal possessive constructions (for example, "mother's hair") for discussion and study. Some languages and dialects allow possession to be indicated by simply juxtaposing two nouns; Arabic, Turkish, and Haitian Creole are just a few examples of such varieties. African American Vernacular English is another. Children who speak AAVE may therefore produce unmarked possessives such as "the boy coat" or "John house" in both speech and writing. A close analysis of children's linguistic patterns will reveal that AAVE speakers are more likely to omit the -'s before a consonant than before a vowel, in keeping with a general dispreference for consonant clusters characterizing the dialect as a whole. Children who speak other varieties may omit or misplace the apostrophe. While the review of the Standard English rules for marking possession should not overshadow the attention paid to the content and style of the children's pieces, this lesson provides a perfect opportunity for teaching a mechanics point in the context of children's writing.

Student Objectives

After completion of these lessons, students will be able to:

- Listen and respond to a story by participating in a class discussion.
- Demonstrate understanding of figurative language by identifying similes in the text and including at least one metaphor or simile in their own writing.

- Demonstrate understanding of sensory images by identifying examples from the text and including at least one sensory image in their own writing.
- Demonstrate understanding of the writing process by drafting, revising, and sharing an original descriptive narrative patterned after the literature modeled during prewriting.
- Identify possessive constructions, and apply the Standard English rule in their own writing.

Teaching the Lesson

Day One

Resources

- A copy of the picture book *Hairs/Pelitos* by Sandra Cisneros (also available as the chapter "Hairs" in *The House on Mango Street*)
- Overhead projector and supplies
- A copy of the text of *Hairs/Pelitos* on an overhead transparency to aid discussion
- Student handout with model texts and room for first draft

Preparation

- This lesson assumes that students have been previously introduced to the terms metaphor, simile, and sensory image. If not, you may wish to assign a brief exercise of some sort (a worksheet or two should be more than sufficient) prior to this lesson.
- Optional: Write a first draft of a short descriptive narrative that introduces each member of your family by means of a physical trait or habit and draws on figurative language. Copy the draft on to an overhead transparency to share with students as a model for their own writing.

Instruction and Activities

1. (3 minutes) Briefly preview the book by asking students to use the title to predict the content or theme of the book. You may wish to introduce the author—Sandra Cisneros is a poet and novelist who was born in Chicago to Mexican parents. Lots of her writing focuses on the experience of growing up in a bicultural setting. *Hairs/Pelitos* is "semiautobiographical fiction," which means that the story is based on the author's life, but she has changed some things for effect.
2. (1 minute) Before beginning to read, set a purpose for students' listening by asking them to listen for what they learn about each family member as their hair is described. Do we get hints about their personalities or family roles? Then, read the book aloud.
3. (5–7 minutes) Read book aloud.

4. (5 minutes) Ask the students to list all the facts they learned about the family. Lead students to realize that the form and style of the book packed a lot of information into a short, sweet story. You may wish to introduce the terms *vignette*, snapshot, or descriptive narrative.

5. (3–5 minutes) Discuss reasons Cisneros might have chosen to write about her family's hair (as opposed to something else). Accept and discuss all reasonable answers, but also guide students to realize that the author chose a theme that offered a great deal of contrast (everyone's hair was different) and also had some emotional or personal meaning (the smell of the mother's hair had lots of associations for her).

6. (5–7 minutes) Ask students to think about how they might approach writing a short book about their own families. If they were to introduce their parents and siblings, what would they say about their hair? Or—is there some other characteristic that would work better as a vehicle of introduction? Possibilities include other physical features (eyes, hands, laughs, voices); habits (such as different styles of eating, arguing, or using the remote control); or likes/dislikes (music preferences, vacation activities). You may wish to list these on the board or on chart paper. Allow several minutes for students to brainstorm possibilities aloud and to share impromptu descriptions of their family members with the class.

7. (3–5 minutes) Distribute handouts for students to use for their first drafts. Ask a volunteer to read the examples of previous students' personal versions of *Hairs*. Briefly discuss what makes the student versions both "good writing" and "like the author's." Students may point out that the versions are funny, realistic, and include interesting similes and vivid images. Encourage students to make their own versions just as good! (If you decided to write your own piece, now is a good time to share it as a model.)

8. (20 minutes/remaining time) Allow the rest of the class period for drafting. Tell students to finish their drafts for homework, and that there will be time to share at the beginning of tomorrow's class.

9. (1 minute) Ask for several volunteers to turn theirs in first thing in the morning, so that you may photocopy them on to overheads for the class to help revise.

Relevant English Language Arts Content Standards

[In Sweetland 2004, this follows the lesson plan for day two, which is not included here—JRR/AER]

This lesson addresses the following NCTE/IRA standards for the English Language Arts:

- Students read a wide range of print and non-print texts to build an understanding of texts, of themselves, and of the cultures of the United States and the world; to acquire new information; to respond to the needs and demands of society and the workplace; and for personal fulfillment. Among these texts are fiction and nonfiction, classic and contemporary works.

- Students apply a wide range of strategies to comprehend, interpret, evaluate, and appreciate texts. They draw on their prior experience, their interactions with other readers and writers, their knowledge of word meaning and of other texts, their word identification strategies, and their understanding of textual features (e.g., sound–letter correspondence, sentence structure, context, graphics).
- Students apply knowledge of language structure, language conventions (e.g., spelling and punctuation), media techniques, figurative language, and genre to create, critique, and discuss print and non-print texts.
- Students develop an understanding of and respect for diversity in language use, patterns, and dialects across cultures, ethnic groups, geographic regions, and social roles.
- Students use spoken, written, and visual language to accomplish their own purposes (e.g., for learning, enjoyment, persuasion, and the exchange of information).

Notes

1 We would like to express our gratitude to the following persons who helped us with this chapter, while absolving them of any responsibility for any weaknesses it may contain: Claude Reichard, Stanford Senior Lecturer in Writing, for helpful discussion of the UC Subject A materials; Hubert Devonish, Karen Carpenter and the staff of the Jamaican Language Unit at UWI, Mona, and the principal, teacher and students at the elementary school we visited in Jamaica; Patrick Callier, Stanford Linguistics undergraduate at the time, for technical assistance; William Labov and Tina Baker for permission to use Figure 3 from their work on the Individualized Reading Manual; and Julie Sweetland for permission to reproduce part of one of her lesson plans as an appendix. We also wish to thank the editors of this volume for helpful suggestions for improving this chapter.
2 For instance, National Assessment of Educational Progress (NAEP) data for 2007 show that the average score for White Americans in grade 4 was 231, and for African Americans 203 (28 points less); and the corresponding score for White Americans in grade 8 was 272, and for African Americans 245 (27 points less). Not all African American students are speakers of AAVE, but the Oakland Task Force's (1996) assertion that it was "the primary language of many African American students" (see Rickford and Rickford, 2000, p. 165) remains as true now as it was then. With respect to Creole speakers, Siegel (2005, p. 292) reported that according to NAEP results for 1999, "only 15 percent of eighth graders from the [primarily Creole-speaking] state [of Hawaii] scored at or above proficient compared with 24 percent nationally" [Bracketed comments are ours]. Siegel went on to note (p. 293) that "in the Commonwealth Caribbean, only a very small percentage of students reach the level needed to attend secondary school and even a smaller percentage of those pass the Caribbean Examinations Council examinations in English (Craig, 2001, p. 72)."
3 For instance, the California Department of Education recently developed new Reading/Language Arts criteria that reading texts should provide for the instructional needs of "English learners . . . and students who use African American English," and a number of linguists and educators (including William Labov and the co-authors of this chapter) were invited to address meetings at which the rationale for this policy change were explained to publishers. In the West Indies, experiments with bilingual education in Creole and English are taking place for the first time in Jamaica, under the direction of Professor Hubert Devonish and the Jamaica Language Unit at the University of the West Indies, Mona, Jamaica.

4 From the U.C. Office of the President, Student Affairs: http://www.ucop.edu/sas/awpe/index.html.

5 For information about the DWS, see http://www.ucop.edu/dws/dwshome.htm.

6 Even a few such incursions of AAVE features into an Academic English essay can, however, significantly affect teachers' holistic ratings of students' work (Smitherman, 2000, p. 174).

7 Here the measure is the proportion of words with orthographic triple consonant clusters read correctly. Labov also presented evidence of similar effectiveness as measured by national percentile scores of California students on the Woodcock-Johnson III Word-ID test, grades 2–4. See http://www.ling.upenn.edu/~wlabov/PowerPoints/Summit.ppt.

8 Julie Sweetland, whose 2006 dissertation was supervised by John R. Rickford, was an elementary school teacher before beginning graduate work at Stanford. She is currently Director of Research at the Center for Inspired Teaching in Washington, DC.

9 See also the work of Baugh (1999), Smitherman (2000) and Rickford & Rickford (2007) for helpful specific suggestions and examples, even though they don't constitute a comprehensive series of lesson plans. And see Rickford, Sweetland, & Rickford (2004) and Sweetland, Rickford, Rickford, & Grano (in preparation) for useful bibliographies on AAVE and Education.

References

Ball, A. (1992). Cultural preference and the expository writing of African American adolescents. *Written Communication* 9(4): 501–532.

Baugh, J. (1999). Reading, writing, and rap: Lyric shuffle and other motivational strategies to introduce and reinforce literacy. In J. Baugh, *Out of the mouths of slaves: African American language and educational malpractice* (pp. 31–40). Austin: University of Texas Press.

—— (2001). Applying linguistic knowledge of African American English to help students learn and teachers teach. In S. Lanehart (Ed.), *Sociocultural and historical contexts of African American vernacular English* (pp. 319–330) (Varieties of English around the World. General Series, 27). Amsterdam: John Benjamins.

Brown, D.W. (2009). *In other words: Lessons on grammar, code-switching, and academic writing*. Portsmouth, NH: Heinemann.

Calfee, R. & Chambliss, M.J. (1987). The structural design features of large texts. *Educational Psychologist* 22(3 & 4): 357–378.

Cassidy, F.G. (1961). *Jamaica talk: Three hundred years of the English language in Jamaica*. London: Macmillan.

Cassidy, F.G. & Le Page, R.B. 1967. *Dictionary of Jamaican English*. Cambridge: Cambridge University Press.

Craig, D.R. (2001). Language education revisited in the Commonwealth Caribbean. In P. Christie (Ed.), *Due respect: Papers on English and English-related creoles in the Caribbean in honour of Professor Robert Le Page* (pp. 61–76). Kingston: University of West Indies Press.

Crowell, S., Kolba, E., Stewart, W., & Johnson, K. (1974). *Talkacross: Bridging two dialects*. Chicago: Instructional Dynamics.

Devonish, H. & Carpenter, K. (2007). Towards full bilingualism in education: The Jamaican bilingual primary education project. *Social and Economic Studies* 56(1/2): 277–303.

Godley, A. (2004). African American students' production and correction of Academic Written English (AWE) conventions: Preliminary findings from a three year study. Paper presented at the American Association of Applied Linguistics Annual Conference, Portland, OR.

Labov, W. (1968). A study of the Non-Standard English of Negro and Puerto Rican speakers in New York City. Cooperative Research Project No. 3288. Philadelphia: U.S. Regional Survey.

Labov, W. & Baker, B. (2009). The reading road (A tutoring manual for struggling readers). Retrieved on July 14, 2009, from http://www.ling.upenn.edu/~wlabov/PRI/index.html.

Le Page, R.B. (1968). Problems to be faced in the use of English as medium of education in four West Indian territories. In J.A. Fishman, C.A. Ferguson, & J.D. Gupta (Eds.), *Language problems of developing countries* (pp. 431–43). New York: John Wiley.

Meier, T. (2008). *Black communications and learning to read: Building on children's linguistic and cultural strengths.* New York: Lawrence Erlbaum.

Piestrup, A.M. (1973). *Black dialect interference and accommodation of reading instruction in first grade.* Monographs of the Language-Behavior Research Laboratory, University of California, Berkeley, No. 4.

Rickford, A.E. (2005). Everything I needed to know about teaching I learned from my children: Six deep teaching principles for today's reading teachers. *Reading Improvement* 42(2): 112–28.

Rickford, A.E. & Rickford, J.R. (2007). Variation, versatility, and contrastive analysis in the classroom. In R. Bayley and C. Lucas (Eds.), *Sociolinguistic variation* (pp. 276–296). Cambridge: Cambridge University Press.

Rickford, J.R. (1999). Language diversity and academic achievement in the education of African American students—an overview of the issues. In C.T. Adger, D. Christian, & O. Taylor (Eds.), *Making the connection: Language and academic achievment among African American students* (pp. 1–20). McHenry, IL: Delta Systems, and Washington, DC: Center for Applied Linguistics.

—— (2002). Linguistics, education, and the Ebonics firestorm. In J.E. Alatis, H.E. Hamilton, & A.-H. Tan (Eds.), *Round Table on Languages and Linguistics, 2000: Linguistics, Language and the Professions* (pp. 25–45). Washington, DC: Georgetown University Press.

Rickford, J. & Rickford, R.J. (2000). *Spoken soul: The story of Black English.* New York: John Wiley.

Rickford, J.R., Sweetland, J., & Rickford, A.E. (2004). African American English and other vernaculars in education: A topic-coded bibliography. *Journal of English Linguistics* 32(3): 230–320.

Seymour, H., Roeper, T., de Villiers, J., & de Villiers, P. (2003). *Diagnostic evaluation of language variation.* San Antonio, TX: The Psychological Corporation.

Siegel, J. (2005). Applied Creolistics revisited. *Journal of Pidgin and Creole Languages* 20(2): 293–323.

Smitherman, G. (2000). *Black talk: Words and phrases from the Hood to the Amen Corner,* 2nd ed. Boston: Houghton Mifflin.

Sweetland, J. (2004). Sociolinguistic sensitivity in language arts instruction: A literature and writing curriculum for the intermediate grades. Teacher's Manual and Materials. Department of Linguistics, Stanford University.

—— (2006). *Teaching writing in the African American classroom: A sociolinguistic approach.* Ph.D. dissertation, Stanford University, Stanford, CA.

Sweetland, J., Rickford, J.R., Rickford, A.E, & Grano, T. (in preparation). *AAVE and education: An annotated bibliography.* Mahwah, NJ: Lawrence Erlbaum.

Wheeler, R.S. & Swords, R. (2006). *Codeswitching: Teaching standard English in urban classrooms. A grammar-based approach.* Urbana, IL: National Council for Teachers of English.

—— (Forthcoming, 2010). *Code-switching lessons: Editing strategies for teaching standard English in urban classrooms*. A First Hand curriculum resource. Portsmouth, NH: Heinemann.

Whiteman, M.F. (1981). Dialect influence in writing, in M.F. Whiteman (Ed.), *Variation in writing: Functional and linguistic-cultural differences*. Hillsdale, NJ: Erlbaum.

Afterword

Mariko Haneda

Taken together, the essays in this volume debunk persistent misconceptions about ethnolinguistic diversity in the United States, including the idea that African American English or Caribbean English are inferior to Standard English and that English-only instruction is the most effective way to teach minority children. The authors argue that we should regard the varied cultural-linguistic repertoires that students bring to classrooms as resources and build on them in academic instruction. Further, this volume poses fundamental questions about the reliance on standardized testing in English as the sole measure of language minority students' academic achievement, showing that it has a monolingual bias and does not capture the multilingual and/or multilectal resources students have at their disposal.

In this Afterword, I focus on where we go from here. In thinking about future directions, Alim and Baugh's and García's chapters are particularly useful. In Alim and Baugh's chapter, we learn that the secondary language-minority students with whom Alim worked, including speakers of AAE, are not bound to particular localities when it comes to their language practices. Instead, these young people engage in hybrid practices, incorporating regional phonological features exploited by popular rappers; they "fashion themselves as multiregional and multilectal Hip Hop Heads." Building on these cultural-linguistic realities of young people, Alim and Baugh propose Critical Hip Hop language pedagogies (CHHLPs), which aim for teachers and students to develop critical language awareness.

> CHHLPs create a Freireian critical pedagogy (Freire, 1970) of language that educates linguistically profiled and marginalized students about how language is used and, importantly, how language can be used against them.

Students engage in various sociolinguistic/ethnographic activities and projects, akin to Heath's work with African American youngsters reported in *Ways with Words*. For example, they conduct linguistic analyses of Alim's interviews with a popular rapper and also engage in language fieldwork, documenting and examining language use in popular media, their own language practices, and those around them. Through these processes, they first learn about how language is used among different people and across contexts and then interrogate how language can be used to discriminate against particular groups of people. CHHLP ultimately aims to empower these youths by helping them develop meta-linguistic awareness of language variation so that they can strategically use it to their advantage. In addition, Alim and Baugh point to the importance of teachers' developing a meta-ideological awareness to disrupt the dominant language ideology of Standard English and to create spaces where the cultural-linguistic resources of youths are not only validated but also mobilized to maximize their academic learning.

Focusing on U.S. Latinos, Ofelia García puts forth a dynamic model of bilingualism in place of the prevalent models: subtractive and additive bilingualism. She implies that the dominant models of bilingualism are premised on the ideology of standardization in which the notion of a discrete language is taken for granted. As García suggests, this neither reflects the realities of multilingual societies outside of the United States nor those of U.S. Latinos. In contrast, dynamic bilingualism is consonant with the new ways in which bilingualism is being constructed for a globalized world where *plurilingualism* thrives. A plurilingual person is viewed as "a social agent, has proficiency, of varying degrees, in several languages and experience of several cultures" (cited in García—Council of Europe 2000, *Common European framework of reference for languages*, p. 168). Bilingualism, conceptualized as plurilingualism, is not about adding a second language but about developing complex language practices that encompass several languages (including different varieties of the same language), multiple modalities, and various social contexts.

What García calls attention to in her chapter is the fact that U.S. Latinos have been practicing plurilingualism, transcending the traditional notion of *diglossia* (only one language being used in one domain). The language use by five New York Puerto Rican girls reported by Zentella (1997) is one such example. These girls grew up in bilingual homes where varieties of Spanish, popular and standard Puerto Rican Spanish, popular and standard English, and everything in between were used. However, as García points out, biliteracy education as practiced in the United States does not usually take account of this multilingual/multilectal reality and is premised on prevailing language ideologies (e.g., Spanish used to transition to English literacy, developing literacy skills in two languages separately). In order for instruction to build on the cultural-linguistic realities of U.S. Latino students, García proposes a flexible multiple model of biliteracy practices where teachers "encourage children to use all linguistic codes and modes as resources in order to engage in literacy practices in one or the other language:" what she calls *translanguaging* or *pluriliteracy*. By creating space for translanguaging, educators can disrupt dominant language ideologies.

While I find the proposals put forward by Alim and Baugh and Garcia exciting, their problematizations of location and boundaries raise additional questions. We need to remember that each ethnolinguistic group has its unique trajectories rooted in its cultural and historical experiences, resulting in differential cultural-linguistic realities in the present. Given that, it is inevitable that problems faced by different groups require different solutions. For example, as powerful as the idea of translanguaging is, it might take a different meaning in the situations faced by indigenous communities described by McCarty, Romero-Little, Warhol, and Zepeda, where language loss is at issue. Further, does the notion of translanguaging apply equally to U.S. Latinos living in urban areas in large Latino communities and those living in rural areas in small numbers? These are empirical questions that need to be answered through further research.

To conclude, the contributors to this volume portray the complex realities of ethnolinguistic diversity and its associated literacy practices and suggest concrete ways through which to change our current educational practices. While it takes time to transform official discourses of language and literacy education, I feel hopeful that much effort has been made by these contributors in mobilizing their academic expertise to level the educational playing field for the benefit of language minority students. As scholars, we need to be mindful of conducting research that addresses socially important problems faced by different ethnolinguistic groups. Research is not just for the consumption of other scholars. As Alim and Baugh eloquently argue, we should draw on a substantive body of research on "language, its structure, and its role in constructing identities and mediating inter-group relations" to create empowering pedagogy. Creating such pedagogies involves long-term collaboration with community members, students, and teachers. It requires us to step out of the comfort of the ivory tower and position ourselves as learners in particular communities. The contributors to this volume have already taken steps to achieve these goals. Many others need to follow in their footsteps to keep this momentum going.

References

Council of Europe (2000). *Common European framework of reference for languages: Learning, teaching, assessment*. Language Policy Division, Strasbourg. Retrieved July 17, 2007, from http://www.coe.int/t/dg4/linguistic/CADRE_EN.asp.

Heath, S.B. (1983). *Ways with words: Language, life and work in communities and classrooms*. Cambridge: Cambridge University Press.

Zentella, A.C. (1997). *Growing up bilingual: Puerto Rican children in New York*. Malden, MA: Blackwell.

Index

Made in the USA
Middletown, DE
10 March 2019